Payroll Records & Procedures

Payroll Records & Procedures

Fifth Edition

M. David Haddock, Jr.

Sherry Cohen

McGraw-Hill Irwin

Boston   Burr Ridge, IL   Dubuque, IA   Madison, WI   New York   San Francisco   St. Louis
Bangkok   Bogotá   Caracas   Kuala Lumpur   Lisbon   London   Madrid   Mexico City
Milan   Montreal   New Delhi   Santiago   Seoul   Singapore   Sydney   Taipei   Toronto

**McGraw-Hill
Irwin**

PAYROLL RECORDS & PROCEDURES

Published by McGraw-Hill/Irwin, a business unit of The McGraw-Hill Companies, Inc., 1221 Avenue of the Americas, New York, NY, 10020. Copyright © 2006, 2001, 1994, 1989, 1984 by The McGraw-Hill Companies, Inc. All rights reserved. No part of this publication may be reproduced or distributed in any form or by any means, or stored in a database or retrieval system, without the prior written consent of The McGraw-Hill Companies, Inc., including, but not limited to, in any network or other electronic storage or transmission, or broadcast for distance learning.

Some ancillaries, including electronic and print components, may not be available to customers outside the United States.

This book is printed on acid-free paper.

4 5 6 7 8 9 0 QPD/QPD 0 9 8 7

ISBN 978-0-07-298243-5
MHID 0-07-298243-8

Publisher: *Stewart Mattson*
Sponsoring editor: *Steve DeLancey*
Developmental editor: *Megan McFarlane*
Marketing manager: *Richard Kolasa*
Media producer: *Elizabeth Mavetz*
Project manager: *Bruce Gin*
Manager, New book production: *Heather D. Burbridge*
Lead designer: *Pam Verros*
Lead media project manager: *Cathy L. Tepper*
Supplement producer: *Gina F. DiMartino*
Developer, Media technology: *Brian Nacik*
Cover design: *Pam Verros*
Cover photograph: *Pam Verros*
Typeface: *10/12 Times Roman*
Compositor: *GTS–York, PA Campus*
Printer: *Quebecor World Dubuque Inc.*

Library of Congress Cataloging-in-Publication Data

Haddock, M. David.
 Payroll records & procedures / M. David Haddock, Jr., Sherry Cohen.—5th ed.
  p. cm.
 Rev. ed. of: Payroll records & procedures / Merle W. Wood, Sherry Cohen. ISBN 0-07-298243-8
 (alk. paper) 1. Payrolls—United States. 2. Payroll deductions—Law and legislation— United States. 3. Withholding tax—Law and legislation—United States. I. Title: Payroll records and procedures. II. Cohen, Sherry. III. Wood, Merle W. Payroll records & procedures. IV. Title.
HG4028.P5W66 2006
658.3′21—dc22   2005041483

This book is dedicated to the memory of Merle Wood, a distinguished business educator and author.

Preface

From the employees' point of view, there is no more important function of a business than making sure that each employee is paid every payroll period. Not only do they want to receive their pay on time, they want the amount of pay to be calculated correctly! Every business must rely on payroll employees who know how to do their job and how to do it accurately and on time. There are many career opportunities working in the payroll function. After all, every business must have a payroll office!

This text is written to help you understand the entire payroll function from all related areas—human resources, payroll clerk, payroll reporting officer, and the accountant responsible for general journal entries regarding payroll. Our goal in this text is to provide you with a complete framework of the payroll function so that you can successfully understand the purpose of payroll and carry out the related duties.

In addition to payroll, we have tried to introduce you to many business-related ideas and concepts through the margin notes and boxes like Point of Interest, Internet Connection, and A Case for Decision. We hope you will find this course accurate, interesting, and enlightening for you as you begin your business studies.

FEATURES AND ELEMENTS OF THIS TEXTBOOK

Organization

Each of the 11 chapters follows the same format, making it easy for you to track the development of your payroll knowledge. Each unit begins with learning objectives that state clearly what you are about to study. At appropriate points in the text, we refer you to Learning Through Practice Exercises, which are problems designed to reinforce key concepts discussed in the preceding section. The chapter concludes with a Summary stressing the main concepts in the unit, Study Questions, Review Exercises, Problems, and Learning Through Practice Exercises and Alternate Exercises.

Learning Objectives

Your authors have carefully worded each unit's learning objectives. These learning objectives should be kept in mind as you study each unit; they are the most important ideas that you should take away from each chapter.

Forms and Reports

Throughout the text you will find examples of forms and reports that are used in the payroll function. Sample company forms like a job application and a withholding memorandum are provided to demonstrate how a company documents actions taken in payroll. Federal and state forms are provided for you to learn how to actually fill out and file required reports.

A Case for Decision

Case studies focus on payroll functions and duties, many of them from a management point of view. The cases tie together many concepts illustrated in the chapters.

Summary

The end-of-unit summaries have been written so that you may quickly scan a list of the important concepts covered in the unit. This allows you to quickly assess if you have mastered the reading material before beginning to work on the homework. The end-of-unit summary reinforces the learning objectives stated at the beginning of each unit.

Study Questions

Each unit will pose questions that students need to think about and be able to answer. Payroll functions are covered by many state and federal laws and those laws directly affect how payroll works. The ability to speak and write is basic to success in today's business world. The study questions are designed to help you organize your thoughts and be able to express them in an oral or written presentation.

Review Exercises

Payroll requires accuracy. These exercises require you to perform the basic mathematical and procedural functions precisely so that the payroll department can issue checks to employees on time. The emphasis is on attention to detail; this is one of the most important characteristics of payroll. The procedural emphasis is on proper completion of forms. The local, state, and federal governments insist that payroll information on employees be reported meticulously and on time. We have included in your end-of-unit materials most of the required federal forms that the payroll department must file. Upon conclusion of this course, you should feel comfortable completing and filing these government documents.

Learning Through Practice

Additional student work is presented in these exercises. Alternate exercises have been prepared in this edition, supplying the instructor with additional work, which students may complete, or to supplement assignments during a year. Many of the exercises require written responses to situations and the completion of forms. These are an excellent source of training to reinforce the materials in the unit outside the classroom.

Glossary of Payroll Terms

At the end of the text a complete glossary is provided, offering students the definition of any new and unfamiliar terms in language that is easy to understand. New terms are indicated within the units in italicized print, making them a snap to identify.

Tax Tables

Current (as of the writing of the text) income tax withholding tables for the United States and California are provided at the end of the text. Frequent reference throughout the text is made to these tables, allowing you to become familiar with them quickly. As you will learn in this text, most states in the United States have an income tax on wages. California has been selected as the illustrated state in this text, but, although the rates in other states are most likely different, the fundamental procedures described for California would apply in all states with an income tax. We would encourage you to cover this unit in your course so students will learn state procedures.

The Fifth Edition at a Glance

We are proud to bring to you the fifth edition of **Payroll Records & Procedures.** Real-world applications are stressed in this practical text that will train students to perform many of the payroll functions for businesses in the United States.

In this edition

- New author—David Haddock, CPA, one of the coauthors of McGraw-Hill's highly successful *College Accounting,* teams with Sherry Cohen.
- New attractive design to grab students' attention.
- New organization of material (one unit was eliminated by taking its essential components and merging them in other units).
- Revised exercises and problems that require students to look up federal and state taxes.
- Learning Through Practice work papers moved from the back of the text to their related units.
- New federal forms used in illustrations.
- New illustrations showing deductions allowed pre–federal income tax (like 401-k and cafeteria plans).
- New discussions about IRAs, including the SIMPLE IRA.
- 2004 tax rates are used for federal and state calculations.

RETAINED STRENGTHS

In addition to a variety of new features, the fifth edition of **Payroll Records & Procedures** continues to utilize methods proven to be beneficial.

- The text's clear, straightforward style promotes understanding.
- Topics are logically organized for efficient learning. Related material is presented in a single unit, rather than being scattered through many units. For example, information about employee deductions is grouped into one unit, whether the deductions involve federal taxes, state taxes, local taxes, or voluntary deductions. Similarly, all information about the employer's federal payroll taxes, tax deposits, and tax returns appears in a single unit.
- Rather than being overwhelming, the text emphasizes the topics that students really need to know in order to begin performing payroll work successfully.
- The text presents techniques that will help students develop efficient working procedures. For example, the text properly explains the techniques for using tax tables. It also shows students how to prepare a tax calendar to keep track of the dates for filing tax reports.
- Interesting payroll-related and business-related facts are discussed in brief Point of Interest features that appear at various intervals in the text. These features alert students to new developments that affect payroll work and business practices.
- A number of payroll-related case problems are presented throughout the text. The student must determine how each problem, titled "A Case for Decision," should be resolved.

CAREER OPPORTUNITIES

Students are exposed in this text to the many opportunities for employment within the scope of the payroll function in a business. The role of the human resources department is shown as critical in the effective recruitment and employment of workers for all businesses. The importance of record keeping and accuracy is emphasized throughout the text, showing students that this is a valuable employment skill. The actual tasks that payroll clerks and payroll accountants perform are shown so students can explore potential employment areas. This stand-alone course could be the education needed for the business student's first job.

A PAYROLL PRACTICE SET

A comprehensive practice set requires students to perform payroll functions for a month in a small business, Ingram Heating and Cooling. This manual practice set will conclude with the end-of-quarter and end-of-year activities that all businesses must go through. The preparation of tax reporting forms and other tax documents will demonstrate to students how complex the payroll function is, even in a small business. This is a useful end-of-course comprehensive problem to assess the students' understanding of payroll.

Supplements to the Textbook

INSTRUCTOR'S RESOURCE CD-ROM (ISBN 0072982462)

Available only for instructor use, this CD employs all the teaching resources that support the textbook in one compact medium:

- *Instructor's Manual & Key:* Jointly created by text authors M. David Haddock, Jr., and Sherry Cohen, it provides tests for each unit in addition to the corresponding answer keys. These include the answer keys for the Study Questions, Discussion Questions, Learning Through Practice Exercises, and Alternate Learning Through Practice Exercises. The IM also provides an overview of the text's special features, other supplements, and teaching and grading suggestions.
- *Test Bank:* Supplies instructors with a series of unit tests, each of which utilizes a variety of questions, including true/false, multiple-choice, and short answer. Questions found here are comparable to the unit tests supplied in the *Instructor's Manual.*
- *Practice Set Instructor's Manual & Key:* Compiled by author Sherry Cohen, this supplement provides instructors with the answer key and tips to teaching *Ingram Heating and Cooling: A Payroll Practice Set,* an endeavor that leads students through the ins and outs of payroll preparation for a small business.
- *Microsoft PowerPoint Slides:* Designed for in-class usage, these presentations assist in highlighting the central themes found in each unit of the text.

ONLINE LEARNING CENTER (URL: www.mhhe.com/haddock5e)

- *Online Quizzes:* Prepared by Mabel Machin of Edmonds Community College, a combination of 10 to 12 multiple-choice and true/false questions are provided for each of the text's 11 units. Each quiz is graded by the Web site, and provides feedback answers to assist students in the learning process.
- *Microsoft PowerPoint Slides:* Can be downloaded to assist students in their study by highlighting the central themes found in each unit.
- *Tax Tables:* Updated annually so instructors can provide their students with the most current forms available.
- *Web Site Listings:* Provides instructors and students with easy access to company and organization Web sites mentioned in the text.

STUDENT SUPPLEMENT

- *Ingram Heating and Cooling: A Payroll Practice Set:* Developed by author Sherry Cohen as a course culminating activity. It places students in charge of the company's payroll records, requiring them to complete all the federal and state forms and reports. Students must also monitor the weekly payroll period in addition to the end-of-quarter and end-of-year activities.

About the Authors

David Haddock

Is a 30+-year veteran of higher education, serving in administrative and instructional roles at four different colleges. He currently is a full-time professor of accounting at Chattanooga State Technical Community College, a two-year institution located in Chattanooga, Tennessee. He also is a coauthor of *College Accounting,* 10th Edition Updated. In addition to these activities, he maintains a part-time CPA practice and serves on the board of directors of the Tennessee Society of CPAs. His wife Susie is a kindergarten teacher; they have four children.

Sherry Cohen

Currently works as a freelance educational and editorial consultant. Her areas of expertise include editing, writing, and rewriting computer science, financial, economy, and accounting books at both the college and professional levels. She was previously with the Gregg/McGraw-Hill Company for 22-years and held the position of executive editor for accounting.

Acknowledgments

Anna Alexander
Caldwell Community College

Juanita Clobes
Gateway Technical College

Joan Demko
Wor-Wic Community College

Janine Dillard
Lansdale School of Business

Cheryl Furbee
Cabrillo College

Lyle Hicks
Danville Area Community College

Lori Jacobson
North Idaho College

Cindy Killian
Wilkes Community College

Dorinda Lynn
Pensacola Junior College

Mabel Machin
Edmonds Community College

Marvin Mai
Empire College

Jim Meir
Cleveland State Community College

Lance Mertz
University of Alaska Southeast–Ketchikan Campus

Tim Nygaard
Madisonville Community College

Michelle Parker
Altamaha Technical College

Ruth Schaa
Black River Technical College

Tamika Stuckey
Lawson State Community College

Carolyn Strauch
Crowder College

Elaine Tuttle
Bellevue Community College

Charles Zaruba
Florida Metro University–Tampa

Brief Contents

Contents

Payroll Laws and Regulations

Objectives

Upon completion of this unit, you should be able to:

1. Explain how the social security tax and Medicare tax have evolved over the years.
2. Explain why the federal income tax is on a pay-as-you-go basis.
3. Define and explain the terms represented by these abbreviations: IRS, OASDI, FICA, FUTA, SUTA, ERISA.
4. List the types of payroll information that a business must maintain regarding each employee.
5. Explain the value of social security to employees and their families.
6. Explain why some states have a much higher state minimum wage than other states.
7. Explain the value to employees of the role the federal government has played in protecting workers.
8. Explain the main features of the Fair Labor Standards Act and its benefit to employees.
9. Explain the benefit of workers' compensation laws to employees and their families.

Government laws and regulations play an important role in payroll work, affecting virtually every stage of payroll operations. They determine how employees' earnings are computed, how deductions are made, how payroll records are kept, how taxes are reported and paid to the government, how accounting entries for the payroll are made, and so on.

In this unit, you will learn about the major laws and regulations that influence payroll work. There is no need for you to know every minor detail of these laws and regulations at this time, but you do need to have a basic understanding of them. In later units, you will see how business firms meet many of the legal requirements discussed here.

FEDERAL INCOME TAX LAWS

A constitutional amendment allowing Congress to impose a federal income tax on individuals and corporations went into effect in 1913. Since then, Congress has passed many laws dealing with the federal income tax. One law that has an important effect on payroll work is the Current Tax Payment Act of 1943. This law made it necessary for employers to withhold federal income tax from the earnings of their employees and to periodically send the amounts withheld to the government. This system is known as a "pay-as-you-go" basis and is the expressed preference of Congress.

Please notice that businesses are required to withhold payroll taxes from *employees'* earnings. A person may do work for a business as an independent contractor (also referred to as contract labor). An independent contractor is responsible for paying all employment taxes on those earnings. The Internal Revenue Service (IRS) has issued Publication 15-A, Employer's Supplemental Tax Guide that provides information to assist business owners in determining whether an individual providing services is an independent contractor or an employee. More information about contract labor will be covered in Unit 3.

This 1943 law caused employers to become an integral and one of the most important parts of the income tax collection system. With this law, most businesses became collectors of tax revenue for the government. This function is costly for a business, and it requires a complex system to implement and operate. It has steadily become more complex as laws and employee withholding items have become more numerous.

Among other things, the 1943 law also required employers to keep records of certain employee information. The law did not specify the exact system of records to be used for this information. However, over the years, such records have become standardized, and most businesses use much the same basic system. This is true whether a business uses a sophisticated computer system for payroll or a pencil-and-paper system. (The payroll records shown in this text-workbook are typical of the payroll forms that are now most widely used to gather the necessary income tax information in a usable form.)

All the federal laws governing payroll taxes are enforced by the Internal Revenue Service (IRS). The IRS is currently organized around four customer-focused divisions. The agency's hope is to work with taxpayers with common needs. The four divisions are:

- The Wage and Investment Operating Division
- The Small Business and Self-Employed Operating Division
- The Large and Mid-Size Business Operating Division
- The Tax-Exempt/Government Entities Operating Division

There are many job opportunities with the IRS for accounting majors. Please check the IRS Web site for current job openings (www.irs.gov).

The income tax amounts that firms withhold from their employees must be submitted at regular intervals to the IRS or to a bank authorized by the IRS to receive such funds. While the tax money is temporarily in the hands of the employer, it represents federal tax funds and, in accounting terms, a liability of the business. Businesses are required to file periodic reports with the IRS in order to indicate the amounts of federal payroll taxes withheld from their employees and the sums sent in.

STATE AND LOCAL INCOME TAX LAWS

Most states, and some local governments (cities and counties), impose an income tax on an individuals' wages. The laws relating to these taxes are usually quite similar to the major laws dealing with federal income tax. In most cases, employers are required to withhold state or local income tax from the earnings of their employees, to keep detailed records, to pay the tax withholdings to a state or local agency at regular intervals, and to file periodic tax reports with these agencies.

The same basic system of payroll records that is used to gather the information needed to satisfy federal income tax regulations normally can also be used to keep the information required by state and local income tax authorities.

SOCIAL SECURITY LAWS

In 1935, Congress passed the Social Security Act in order to provide financial security for workers and their families. Originally, the tax rate was 1 percent on wages up to $3,000 per year. This act has been amended a number of times and can be expected to undergo further changes. The federal social security program now consists of two main parts: (1) old-age, survivors, and disability insurance (OASDI), which is commonly known as social security;

Point of Interest

Payroll can be a very complicated operation. While most businesses in this country are small, there are some large companies with a quarter of a million employees or more. Some of these large businesses have employees in each of our 50 states as well as in a number of foreign countries. One can only imagine the skill and effort it takes to comply with the payroll laws in all of the 50 states as well as the foreign countries where their employees work. But it can be done. Indeed, it is being done.

Internet Connection

What employers need to know about the minimum wage and about other provisions of the Fair Labor Standards Act can be found at a Web site maintained by the Department of Labor, at http://www.dol.gov. The site covers topics such as tips, youth employment, and home-to-work travel.

and (2) health and hospital insurance, which is commonly known as Medicare. Medicare is designed to provide medical coverage for eligible persons, while social security provides retirement income as well as financial support for disabled workers. In addition, the survivors' portion of social security provides for the spouse and children of workers who die or are severely disabled.

To obtain funds for these social security programs, Congress passed two additional laws, the Federal Insurance Contributions Act (FICA) and Federal Unemployment Tax Act (FUTA). These laws and the unemployment compensation laws passed by the individual states (called SUTA) have had a major impact on payroll work.

The Federal Insurance Contributions Act (FICA) required most employees and employers to pay toward the cost of federal old-age, survivors, and disability insurance. (Some employees and employers, because of special circumstances, are exempt from FICA tax.) Business firms had to withhold a certain percentage from employees' earnings for the FICA tax and to match the total amount deducted as their own share of the tax.

The FICA tax has been adjusted upward many times. In the past 70 years, the percentage has risen from 1 percent of taxable earnings to a combined rate of 7.65 percent for social security and Medicare today. For many years, there was a single rate that covered both social security and Medicare. In 1990, both of these taxes were at a combined rate of 7.65 percent and were levied on wages up to $51,300. At that time, annual wages beyond $51,300 were not taxed under social security rules. However, in 1991 the system was changed. Social security was taxed at 6.2 percent, and Medicare was taxed separately at 1.45 percent.

Though the percentage rates have remained the same since 1991, the wage base on which social security tax is levied increases constantly. These continual increases, which cause larger and larger deductions, are imposed in order to cover the steady growth of social security and Medicare costs.

In 1991, when it became necessary to withhold social security and Medicare taxes separately from employee earnings, businesses were required to report these taxes separately. Prior to this time, the combined tax was commonly referred to as FICA. Now it is identified as two separate taxes—social security tax and Medicare tax. You can see the continual rate of increase in these two taxes over time as you review the chart on p. 4. Remember in looking at the chart that Medicare's wage base currently is unlimited.

In addition to the employees' contribution, the employer must pay an amount that matches the social security and Medicare taxes that are withheld from employees. At regular intervals, the money withheld for social security and Medicare taxes and the matching amount must be sent to the IRS or to a bank authorized to receive such tax payments. It is also necessary for the employer to file periodic reports with the IRS relating to the social security and Medicare taxes collected.

In years past, the social security tax was looked upon as an important, yet minor, tax upon earnings. Now these taxes are at the point where some workers (those workers with a number of allowances) actually pay more in social security tax than they do in income tax. Since the amounts withheld from employees is matched by employers, this tax has also become a significant cost for businesses.

REQUIRED PAYROLL RECORDS

Another requirement of the IRS concerns payroll records. Employers must keep detailed records with the following information.

1. The name, address, date of birth, and social security number of each employee.
2. Verification of work eligibility.
3. The amount and date of each wage payment and the period covered by the payment.
4. The amount of wages subject to social security and Medicare taxes.
5. The amount of social security and Medicare taxes withheld.
6. When and why an employee leaves the firm.

Most of this information can be kept in the same set of payroll records that is used to gather information about federal, state, and local income taxes. The many forms used in your payroll systems will be illustrated throughout the text.

	Wages Subject to Social Security/Medicare Taxes	
	Wages Subject to Social Security	Wages Subject to Medicare
2004	$87,900	All earnings
2003	$87,000	All earnings
2002	$84,900	All earnings
2001	$80,400	All earnings
2000	$76,200	All earnings
1999	$72,600	All earnings
1993	$57,600	$135,000
1992	$55,500	$130,200

FEDERAL UNEMPLOYMENT TAX ACT AND STATE UNEMPLOYMENT TAX ACTS

The Federal Unemployment Tax Act (FUTA) and all the unemployment compensation laws passed by the states (SUTA) are intended to finance the unemployment insurance portion of the social security program. These laws require that most employers pay a FUTA tax and a SUTA tax.

In order to speed up service and to cut costs, the Social Security Administration has directed that all recipients of social security benefits must designate the name of their bank so that the benefits can be sent by electronic funds transfer (EFT) rather than by the U.S. Postal Service. With this system, funds are deposited automatically in the recipient's bank account. Persons who would experience hardship with this system, such as those not having a bank account, continue to receive their checks by mail.

FUTA and SUTA laws specify that employers must make regular tax payments, file periodic tax reports, and keep certain categories of information in their payroll records. These forms are covered in Units 9 and 10.

The states calculate the unemployment tax rate based on the unemployment history of a business. If the business has a history of frequent layoffs with many people drawing unemployment because of the layoffs, that business will have a high SUTA tax rate. This system of rating employers is referred to as a *merit system* or *experience rating system*. A business with few or no unemployment claims against it will pay a relatively low rate of tax to the state. The amount of wages subject to the unemployment tax at the state level is independent from the amount subject to the FUTA. The current FUTA tax is paid on the first $7,000 earned by each employee. Each state sets a maximum amount of wages subject to the SUTA. A complete discussion of unemployment taxes will be covered in Unit 9.

THE FAIR LABOR STANDARDS ACT

In 1938, Congress passed the Fair Labor Standards Act (FLSA) commonly referred to as the federal wage and hour law. This law affects any firm involved in interstate commerce (any firm that does business in more than one state or produces goods or services used in more than one state). There are many provisions to the law, but the most important ones from the standpoint of payroll work deal with the minimum wage and with overtime compensation. This federal law is enforced by the Wage and Hour Division of the Employment Standards Administration (ESA) under the Department of Labor.

The Fair Labor Standards Act (FLSA) sets a *minimum* wage that employers must pay to their employees. There is no set maximum wage, and many employers pay workers more than the minimum wage. Some reasons for paying higher than minimum wage are a shortage of workers or the need to attract dependable workers. Congress has raised the minimum wage from time to time in order to keep pace with changes in economic conditions.

A second major function of the FLSA is to define exempt and nonexempt workers. Generally speaking, an exempt worker is a member of the management team and is not paid on an hourly basis. The word "exempt" means that that worker is exempt from the minimum wage and overtime provisions of the FLSA. A worker defined as "nonexempt" is covered by the FLSA and all minimum wage and overtime pay provisions apply to that worker.

The FLSA also requires that employers pay a special rate for overtime work to covered employees. (Certain types of employees, such as managers, are not covered by this provision of the law and are referred to as *exempt* employees.) The overtime earnings rate is set at 1 1/2 times an employee's regular hourly rate and is paid for any hours worked beyond 40 in a week. Notice that the law specifies that overtime must be paid for work done after *40 hours work per week*—not for work after an eight-hour day. Many firms pay time-and-a-half for any hours worked beyond eight hours in a day even though this is not required under the FLSA. In addition, some companies pay double time for work done on Sundays or holidays. Some companies even provide a bonus of several dollars per hour for workers on night shifts.

It is necessary for employers to keep detailed payroll information about all employees who are subject to the minimum wage and overtime pay provisions of the FLSA. Procedures for acquiring such information must be built into a firm's payroll system because the law requires that records be available for inspection by the U.S. Department of Labor.

A Point of Interest

Taxes always seem to be going higher and higher. There is usually a good reason for this. Consider social security and Medicare. In 1920, for example, the average length of life was estimated to be 54.1 years. In 2001, the average length of life was estimated to be 77.2 years. As our population grew older, there was a larger pool of people who retired on social security. Thus the cost of the program went up. And, as they have aged, there has also been an increase in medical bills for these people, much of which has been covered by Medicare. The tax on social security and Medicare has risen over the years because the cost of these benefits has increased steadily.

Internet Connection

Interested in job opportunities in payroll and other areas of accounting? The American Compensation Association offers a job line at http://www.acaonline.org. Another employment link page is at www.americanpayroll.org.

STATE MINIMUM WAGE LAWS

Some states have their own minimum wage laws and set their own minimum wage rates. These rates may be higher than the federal rate. If a state's minimum wage rate is higher than the federal rate, then employers must pay at the higher rate, the one established by the state. Normally, state minimum wage laws, like the federal law, require employers to keep certain types of payroll information, and these records are subject to inspection.

There are several states that do not have a state minimum wage law. These are Alabama, Arizona, Florida, Louisiana, Mississippi, South Carolina, and Tennessee. In those states with no minimum wage law and in other states where the minimum wage set by state law is lower than the federal minimum wage, the federal rate applies to employees who are covered by the FLSA.

The following 29 states use the federal minimum wage ($5.15 per hour), as of this writing, as their state minimum wage.

Arkansas	Michigan	New Mexico	Utah
Colorado	Minnesota	New York	Virginia
Georgia	Missouri	North Carolina	West Virginia
Idaho	Montana*	North Dakota	Wisconsin
Indiana	Nebraska	Oklahoma	Wyoming
Iowa	Nevada	Pennsylvania	
Kentucky	New Hampshire	South Dakota	
Maryland	New Jersey	Texas	

* $5.15 for large employers; $4 for small employers

Some states have their *own* minimum wage for employees who are *not* covered by the FLSA; in other words, for employees of companies not engaged in interstate commerce. As of January 1, 2004, these states and amounts were as follows.

Alaska	$7.15	Maine	$6.25
California	$6.75	Massachusetts	$6.75
Connecticut	$7.10	Oregon	$7.05
Delaware	$6.15	Rhode Island	$6.75
Hawaii	$6.25	Vermont	$6.75
Illinois (on 1/1/2005)	$6.50	Washington	$7.16

High—and going higher! When the FLSA was passed in 1938, the federal minimum wage was $0.25 an hour. Working one week at that rate amounted to $10 per week ($0.25 × 40 = $10)—an adequate rate for those days, many thought. Obviously, it would be impossible for workers to survive today with such a low wage. By the end of the century, the federal minimum wage was $5.15 per hour and there was talk of another increase. While many forces affect the level at which the minimum wage is set, the most important ones are the rate of inflation and the cost of living.

Two states, Ohio and Kansas, have a state minimum wage less than the federal rate. In Ohio the basic rate is $4.25 with provisions to lower the rate to $3.35 or $2.80 based on annual gross sales between $500,000 and $150,000. Kansas allows a minimum wage of $2.65.

As you review the various state minimum hourly rates listed above, you will notice that they differ widely. Economic conditions within the states, availability of labor, cost of living, and lack or abundance of industry are some of the reasons for the difference in minimum wages.

A Case for Decision 1-1

Don Haskins works as a stock clerk at a local store that is part of a large national chain of tire stores. James Matthews works for a small local tire shop that specializes in doing tire repair and recapping. Both men were hired just last week. Don is paid $5.15 per hour, while James is paid $4.85. Are these pay rates correct under FLSA? Why or why not?

Discussion of the Case

Don's store is engaged in interstate commerce, and by law he must be paid the federal minimum wage under the FLSA. James's tire store is engaged only in local business, so he does not have to be paid the federal minimum wage.

OTHER LAWS AFFECTING WAGES

There are a number of federal laws that affect the wages paid by firms holding contracts with agencies of the U.S. government. These laws are the Davis-Bacon Act of 1931, the Walsh-Healy Public Contracts Act of 1936, and the McNamara-O'Hara Service Contract Act of 1965. The Davis-Bacon Act applies to businesses that have contracts worth more than $2,000 with the federal government for the construction, repair, or alteration of public buildings. The Walsh-Healy Public Contracts Act covers firms holding contracts exceeding $10,000 with agencies of the federal government for the manufacture or supply of goods. The McNamara-O'Hara Service Contract Act applies to businesses that have contracts worth more than $2,500 to provide services to the federal government.

Businesses that are subject to such laws must pay a minimum wage established by the Secretary of Labor. These minimum wage rates are set on an industry-by-industry basis and normally are higher than the regular federal minimum wage.

WORKERS' COMPENSATION INSURANCE

Most states have laws that require employers to provide employees with *workers' compensation insurance,* which protects employees and their families from lost wages that occur because of job-related accidents, disability, or death. To obtain such insurance, employers will either contribute to a state workers' compensation fund or buy insurance coverage from a private insurance company. The amount paid to the fund or the insurance company is a percentage of the employer's total payroll. When an employee files a claim, the employer must supply the state or the insurance company with details about the claim and information about the employee's earnings. As claims are filed against the employer's coverage, the cost of the insurance typically increases.

STATE DISABILITY BENEFIT LAWS

California, Hawaii, New Jersey, New York, Rhode Island, and Puerto Rico have laws that are intended to provide disability insurance to employees who are absent from work because of illnesses or accidents that are *not* job-related. (Such illnesses or accidents are not covered by workers' compensation insurance.) The method used to finance disability benefits varies. Some states require only employees to pay for this protection; the employer deducts a certain amount from each employee's earnings and forwards it to a state fund or private insurance company. Other states specify that both the employer and the employees must contribute to pay for disability insurance.

FAIR EMPLOYMENT LAWS

There are federal, state, and local laws designed to enforce fair practices in employment. These *fair employment laws* are intended to prevent discrimination on the basis of race, color, religion, national origin, age, or sex. Such laws make it necessary for businesses to keep records that show they are following fair employment practices. The major federal laws that deal with job discrimination include:

- Title VII of the Civil Rights Act of 1964 (prohibits discrimination in employment based on one's race, color, religion, sex, or national origin).
- Equal Pay Act of 1963 (requires equal pay for men and women in equivalent jobs).
- Age Discrimination in Employment Act of 1967 (protects workers over 40 years of age, especially making it illegal, in most instances, to force one to retire because of age).
- Americans with Disabilities Act of 1990 and the Rehabilitation Act of 1973 (protects qualified workers with disabilities).
- Civil Rights Act of 1991 (provides for monetary damages to employees who have been intentionally discriminated against).

The Equal Employment Opportunity Commission (EEOC) is the federal agency responsible for enforcing these laws.

Another recent federal law affecting human resources departments is the Family and Medical Leave Act. The law requires employers of more than 50 employees to give up to 12 weeks of unpaid leave to eligible employees for the birth or adoption of a child or to take care of a parent, spouse, or child that has a serious illness. Under this law, the employee's position is protected, that is, he or she is assured of a job when reporting back to work.

A Case for Decision 1-2

John Mallard is 71 and in good health. He has been with his company for 32 years. He has an excellent attendance record and has received periodic increases in pay. He is currently a security guard at the plant's main gate. The company would like to replace him with a younger person. They suggest that he might want to retire. He declines because he likes his job. Then they offer him $10,000 as a bonus if he retires, $5,000 upon retirement and another $5,000 a year later. He gladly accepts. Is the company acting illegally?

Discussion of the Case

John Mallard cannot be forced to retire simply because of his age. He can, however, trade away his right to remain on the job. Buyouts such as this one are not uncommon in business.

PENSION SECURITY LAWS

Many businesses, especially large firms, have pension funds for their employees. The Employee Retirement Income Security Act (ERISA) was passed in 1974 to protect such funds. This federal law regulates pension fund operations and specifies the action that can be taken if a fund does not have enough money to pay the benefits that were promised to the employees.

Under ERISA, some employers and pension plan administrators must provide funds for an insurance program to protect employees' retirement funds. The Employee Benefits Security Administration (EBSA) is the federal agency responsible for enforcing the ERISA provisions.

EBSA also is the agency responsible for enforcing the reporting requirements of the Comprehensive Omnibus Budget Reconciliation Act of 1985 (also known as COBRA). The basic requirement of this act requires employers to allow continuation of health care benefits when a worker is dismissed, with the worker paying the cost of the health care premiums.

THE IMMIGRATION REFORM ACT

On June 1, 1985, the Immigration Reform Act went into effect. The act's provisions affect employers, employees, and job applicants.

Employers must now certify that newly hired employees have shown either proof of citizenship or papers that allow noncitizens to work in this country. For hiring an illegal immigrant, an employer faces fines from $250 to $2,000 per employee for the first offense, $2,000 to $3,000 for the second offense, and $3,000 to $10,000 for the third offense.

Employees and job applicants can help employers avoid these fines by offering valid proof that they are citizens or that they can work legally in the United States. Among the documents accepted as proof are certificates of U.S. citizenship or naturalization, valid foreign passports plus employment authorization forms, alien registration cards, photo IDs such as driver's licenses, and U.S. military cards together with social security cards and birth certificates.

A key form now required to be retained by the employer is the I-9, which will establish the right to work of the employee. This form is discussed in detail in Unit 2.

NEW HIRE REPORTING

Another federal law that affects employees is the Personal Responsibility and Work Opportunity Reconciliation Act of 1996, which is also know as the Welfare Reform Act. This law requires employers to file a New Hire Reporting Form with a special state registry within 20 days after a new employee starts work.

The state registry sends the names of new employees to the Federal Parent Locator Service for listing in a national directory. This directory allows officials in other states to find individuals who owe child support payments.

Learning Through Practice   Do Exercises 1.1 and 1.2 on page 13 of this text-workbook.

UNIT 1   REVIEW

Summary

After studying Unit 1 you should be able to:

- Explain the pay-as-you-go tax system of the federal government.
- Understand the purpose of the social security and Medicare systems.
- Know the levels of wages taxable under the social security and Medicare tax laws.
- List the types of information that a business must maintain on each employee.
- Understand the basic provisions of the Fair Labor Standards Act.
- Name and explain some of the major federal laws that affect employers and protect employees.

Study Questions

1. What was the first minimum hourly wage rate?
2. What happens to the income tax deducted from employee earnings by an employer?
3. List the two main parts of the social security program.
4. Why did Congress pass the Federal Insurance Contributions Act (FICA) and the Federal Unemployment Tax Act (FUTA)?
5. Who pays social security taxes? Who pays FUTA taxes?
6. What information related to payroll must an employer keep under the Federal Insurance Contributions Act?
7. How is the employee's share of the social security tax collected and paid to the IRS? How is the employer's share paid?
8. Explain how the Fair Labor Standards Act regulates the wages that employers pay to their employees.
9. What is the current federal minimum wage?
10. Name the laws that provide employee protection for the following:
    a. Accidents or illnesses that are job-related.
    b. Pension fund contributions.
11. List the methods used to finance the following:
    a. Workers' compensation benefits.
    b. Disability benefits.
12. What is the purpose of the Civil Rights Act of 1964?
13. Explain how the wage base and the tax rate are used to calculate the social security and Medicare taxes.
14. Explain when a business may ignore the minimum wage established under the Fair Labor Standards Act.
15. Which federal law gives a worker the right to return to a job after the birth or adoption of a child?
16. What is the current rate of tax for social security?
17. What is the current rate of tax for Medicare?
18. What is the maximum workers' pay subject to the Medicare tax?
19. What has been the trend over the past five years as to the amount of an employee's earnings that is subject to social security tax?
20. Which law prevents an employer from firing an employee who is over 40 solely because of age?

Discussion Questions

1. What are the major responsibilities of employers under the federal income tax laws?
2. Check the unemployment compensation law in your state, and answer the following questions:
   a. Can an unemployed worker in your state collect additional benefits if he or she has dependents? If so, how much is paid for each dependent?
   b. Can a woman in your state collect benefits during pregnancy?
3. In 1996, the minimum wage required by the Fair Labor Standards Act was $4.25 an hour. As of this writing, the rate is $5.15. Why does Congress raise the minimum wage from time to time?
4. Check the minimum wage situation in your state, and then answer the following questions:
   a. Does your state have a minimum wage?
   b. If so, what is the amount of the state minimum wage?
   c. Does the state minimum wage differ from the federal minimum wage?
5. What are some advantages and disadvantages of raising minimum wage rates?
6. What are the major responsibilities of employers under the Federal Insurance Contributions Act (FICA)?
7. Why were the federal income taxes owed by employees put on a pay-as-you-go basis starting in 1943?
8. How does SUTA affect employees and their employers when the employees lose their jobs as a result of a slowdown in business?
9. Which of the several state-level labor laws is designed specifically to benefit employees who are disabled as a result of a job-related accident?
10. Why do employers require new employees to show that they are citizens of the United States or have papers that allow them, as noncitizens, to work in this country?

Learning Through Practice

Unit 1 Exercises

EXERCISE 1.1

A number of laws that affect payroll work are described here. Read each description, and then match it with the name of the correct law. In the answer column, write the identifying letter of the law that has been described.

Name of Laws

A. Civil Rights Act
B. Current Tax Payment Act
C. Disability benefit laws
D. Employee Retirement Income Security Act
E. Fair Labor Standards Act
F. Federal Insurance Contributions Act

G. Federal Unemployment Tax Act
H. Immigration Reform Act
I. Social Security Act
J. Walsh-Healy Public Contracts Act
K. Worker's compensation laws

Description of Laws   **Answer**

1. A law that requires employers to withhold federal income tax from employee earnings.   1. _____

2. A law that requires employers to certify that newly hired employees have shown either proof of citizenship or papers that allow noncitizens to work in the United States.   2. _____

3. State laws that provide employees with insurance against job-related accidents and illnesses.   3. _____

4. A law that allows the Secretary of Labor to set special industry-by-industry minimum wage rates for firms that do business with the federal government.   4. _____

5. A law that imposes a tax on both employees and employers in order to finance the federal old-age, survivors, and disability insurance programs.   5. _____

6. A law that established the federal programs for old-age, survivors, and disability insurance and for unemployment insurance.   6. _____

7. A law that imposes a tax on employers to finance the federal program of benefits for jobless workers.   7. _____

8. A law that has provisions requiring employers to follow fair employment practices.   8. _____

9. A law that regulates pension fund operations.   9. _____

10. State laws that provide employees with insurance against accidents and illnesses that are not job-related.   10. _____

11. A law that requires firms involved in interstate commerce to pay a federal minimum wage and a special overtime rate.   11. _____

EXERCISE 1.2

Based on your study of payroll laws and regulations, decide whether each of the firms discussed here is acting in a legally acceptable way. If the firm is acting legally, write *Yes* in the answer column. If it is not, write *No* in the answer column.

Answer

1. Marilyn Blake, the owner of Web Page Designers, was late in sending employee income tax withholdings to the IRS because she had used the money to buy some new computer equipment that the firm needed and it took her a while to replace the funds.   1. _____

2. The Clothing Connection operates a chain of stores in shopping malls. The firm has a policy of paying the minimum wage to its inexperienced part-time workers but gives a higher wage to its experienced full-time employees.   2. _____

3. Strategic Network Systems has a large sales force that calls on businesses to market its computer equipment and software. Alan Davis, the firm's executive vice president, has a policy of not hiring women for sales jobs because he feels that the work is too tiring for them. He also does not hire men who are more than 40 years old for such jobs.

3. _____

4. The Houston Auto Parts Company is subject to both the federal minimum wage and a state minimum wage. The firm uses the minimum wage rate set by the state because it is higher than the federal rate.

4. _____

5. Pete Grays, a bricklayer at the Coney Construction Company, told the owner of the business that he would work overtime at his regular rate rather than time and a half if he received his overtime pay in cash without any deductions for income tax, social security, and Medicare. The owner agreed to this idea.

5. _____

6. In a job interview, Travis Carr, a manager at Standard Chemical, asked a potential employee questions about her religion and national origin. He feels that it is important to hire people with similar backgrounds so that everyone can work together comfortably.

6. _____

7. Alice Anderson, a telemarketing supervisor at the CVC Home Shopping Company, wanted to continue working when she reached the age of 65. She was in good health and had excellent performance ratings. However, the head of her department insisted that she retire so he could promote a younger employee into her job.

7. _____

8. Joanne Johnson, the owner of Frontier Fashions, a manufacturer of casual clothing, recently hired three new sewing machine operators who are not citizens. She did not ask them for proof that they are entitled to work in this country.

8. _____

9. The Sterling Hardware Company recently set up a retirement savings and profit-sharing plan for its employees. Because this plan will provide funds for retirement, some employees feel that they will not need old-age benefits from the social security system and have asked the firm to stop deducting social security tax from their earnings. Management has refused, and the firm is still deducting the tax.

9. _____

10. Lauren Hill, the owner of Delta Coffee and Snacks, does not bother to set up payroll records for new employees until she is sure that they will work out and stay with the job. She usually waits about three months before establishing such records.

10. _____

Alternate Learning Through Practice Exercises

Unit 1 Exercises

EXERCISE 1.1A

A number of laws that affect payroll work are described here. Read each description, and then match it with the name of the correct law. In the answer column, write the identifying letter of the law that has been described.

Names of Laws

A. Age Discrimination in Employment Act
B. Americans With Disabilities Act
C. Civil Rights Act of 1991
D. Current Tax Payment Act
E. Equal Pay Act
F. Fair Labor Standards Act
G. Federal Insurance Contributions Act
H. Federal Unemployment Tax Act
I. Immigration Reform Act
J. Title VII of the Civil Rights Act of 1964
K. Worker's compensation laws

Description of Laws   **Answer**

1. A law that requires firms involved in interstate commerce to pay a federal minimum wage and a special overtime rate.   1. _____

2. A law that prohibits discrimination in employment based on race, color, religion, sex, or national origin.   2. _____

3. A law that protects workers over 40 years of age from discrimination in hiring and makes it illegal, in most cases, to force qualified older workers to retire.   3. _____

4. A law that requires employers to withhold federal income tax from employee earnings.   4. _____

5. A law that provides monetary damages to employees who have been intentionally discriminated against.   5. _____

6. State laws that provide employees with insurance against job-related accidents and illnesses.   6. _____

7. A law that protects qualified disabled workers from discrimination in hiring, promotion, and dismissal.   7. _____

8. A law that imposes a tax on both employees and employers in order to finance the federal old-age, survivors, and disability insurance programs.   8. _____

9. A law that requires employers to pay the same wages to men and women who have equivalent jobs.   9. _____

10. A law that requires employers to certify that newly hired employees have shown either proof of citizenship or papers that allow noncitizens to work in the United States.   10. _____

11. A law that imposes a tax on employers to finance the federal program of benefits for jobless workers.   11. _____

EXERCISE 1.2A

Based on your study of payroll laws and regulations, decide whether each of the firms discussed here is acting in a legally acceptable way. If the firm is acting legally, write *Yes* in the answer column. If it is not, write *No* in the answer column.

Answer

1. Brian Bates, the owner of A-One Truck Repair, found several Web sites that claim that employers do not have to withhold income taxes from employee earnings. He therefore stopped deducting both federal and state income taxes.   1. _____

2. Kathy O'Donnell was a very successful travel agent at Holiday Tours. After an auto accident, her doctor cleared her to return to work, but the owner of the firm fired her. He felt that the sight of Kathy in the wheelchair that she now uses would be depressing to clients.   2. _____

3. Earl Brown was a sales representative at Alamo Products for many years. When he turned 68, the firm offered him a severance payment of $40,000 and an increased pension if he would retire. He accepted the offer.　3. _____

4. Ruth Dow, who owns a restaurant called the Candlelight Cafe, recently hired a new chef. When he started the job, he told her that he wanted to be paid "off the books" (in cash with no tax deductions). She refused.　4. _____

5. John Kelso is the manager of a furniture store. During the same week, he hired two sales associates. Both jobs are equivalent, and both new employees have similar education and experience. However, the manager decided to pay a weekly salary of $500 to the woman he hired and a weekly salary of $600 to the man he hired.　5. _____

6. Laci Clark recently started work as a cashier at a branch of Office Supplies Unlimited, a national chain. The manager explained that Laci would be expected to work overtime several hours a week. However, because his budget is tight, he would have to pay her the regular rate rather than time and a half for these hours.　6. _____

7. When Paul Gallo hired two new employees for his lawn care service, he asked them to provide evidence of citizenship or proof that they are entitled to work in this country if they are not citizens.　7. _____

8. Kim Lee operates Golden Harvest, a chain of three health food stores, within one state. The state has a minimum wage of $7.05 an hour, which she pays to the sales associates in two of the stores. In the third store, which is located in an area where labor is in short supply, she pays $8 an hour.　8. _____

9. When Don Hewitt went for a job interview at the South Coast Bank, the manager asked him about his religion and the national origin of his family. The manager told Don that he hires only people from certain groups because they are more reliable.　9. _____

10. After business slowed at the Stevens Company and it was necessary to cut the staff, one manager suggested that the firm simply lay off all employees over the age of 50.　10. _____

Unit Two

New Employee Records

Objectives

Upon completion of this unit, you should be able to:

1. Explain the use and value of the job application form.
2. List the kinds of information a job applicant should have on hand when preparing to complete a job application form.
3. Explain why job interviewers ask questions such as "What are your long-range job plans?" and "What special interests or hobbies do you have?"
4. Explain why businesses generally have personal interviews with job applicants.
5. List at least three items of information the job application form *cannot* request because of regulations under fair employment laws.
6. Complete a job application form using personal data.
7. List at least three documents that might be acceptable as proof of age and citizenship when applying for a social security card.
8. Complete an application (Form SS-5) for a social security card, using personal data.
9. Explain who can legally be claimed as a dependent under IRS regulations.
10. Complete an Employee's Withholding Allowance Certificate (Form W-4), using personal data.
11. Explain the possible penalty for giving false information on Form W-4, the employee withholding allowance certificate.
12. Set up an employee earnings record for yourself.
13. Explain why the information contained in payroll records must remain confidential.

INGRAM HEATING AND COOLING

As you work with this text, you will become familiar with the people and records of Ingram Heating and Cooling. This company is a small business located in San Jose, California. The company is named after its owner, William Ingram. The company provides heating and air-conditioning service in San Jose and a dozen other communities in the surrounding area. Ingram Heating and Cooling is one of 24 light industrial businesses operating out of an industrial park. Each business has offices in the front of the building, with extensive room at the back for storing inventory, doing fabrication, and performing other required work. At the rear of each building there is a loading dock and space for parking automobiles and light trucks on a paved parking lot.

This company has been in operation for 12 years, and the business is growing. The company installs six different capacity furnaces and four different capacity air conditioners. It also operates a full-service repair and maintenance department. The products that it installs are manufactured by Midwest Products, located in Ohio. This manufacturer has been in operation for 53 years and has a national reputation for quality heating and cooling equipment.

Ingram's business is very stable throughout the year. One of the primary problems faced by the company is locating and hiring competent installers and repair personnel for its growing business. Because of the shortage of installers and repair persons, the company frequently pays a good deal of overtime. The hourly wages paid to employees may seem inflated to some people. However, San Jose is located in Silicon Valley, the home of many high-tech companies that pay extremely high salaries. Moreover, housing in the area is scarce and very expensive. To stay in business, Ingram must offer competitive wages that compare with other businesses in the area.

The installation of furnaces and air conditioners is now handled by three 2-member teams. Each team is made up of a highly experienced installer and a skilled helper. Each team has its own van for transporting equipment and tools. In addition, there are three employees who do full-time maintenance and repair work, and each of them also has a light van for carrying equipment and tools. Each of the company trucks has a cellular telephone for communication with the company office.

There are two office employees. One is the secretary, receptionist, and repair coordinator. The other is the office manager and bookkeeper. The latter person also handles receipts, payments, contracts, banking, and payroll. The company owner, William Ingram, spends most of his time dealing with customers in preparing bids and negotiating contracts to install furnaces and air conditioners. He also handles the ordering of equipment and supplies that are used in installations and repairs. In addition, he handles all advertising and the hiring of employees. In emergencies, he assists in both repairing and installing furnace and air-conditioning equipment.

Since this is a small business with a limited number of employees, everyone works as a team member. There are good relations within the workforce, and morale is high. The owner of the company, Mr. Ingram, helps these relations along by sponsoring a company picnic during July, when all employees and their families join together in the Ingram's large backyard. He also sponsors a dinner for workers and their families at a popular local restaurant during the holiday season.

A NEW EMPLOYEE JOINS THE COMPANY

It is a common practice for businesses to have job seekers complete a job application form. There may even be tests of one sort or another—keyboarding skill, welding ability, forklift operation, or whatever the new employee is to specialize in. In addition to skill tests, many employers now require job applicants to submit to a drug-screening test. The application form asks for detailed information about the applicant's education, skills, and previous work experience. After a decision to hire is made, the new employee's application form becomes the starting point for a personnel file. Any records concerning this employee are placed in his or her file. For example, as an employee moves from one department to another, a copy of the transfer notice will be placed in the file. Commendations, pay increases, performance evaluations, and similar records can be found in the individual's personnel file.

In this unit, you will learn about the procedures that most businesses use to set up personnel files and payroll records for new employees. Small companies will have fewer formal records, but they should have a personnel file for each employee. Having an adequate system of payroll-related records is a legal requirement as well as a necessity for correct and efficient operation of the payroll system within the company.

Internet Connection

Network nationally at the American Payroll Association's listserv www.americanpayroll.org.

Today many businesses include in their job application form a statement indicating that either the company, or the employee, may terminate the job with or without cause, and with or without notice. When the employee signs the document, he or she is agreeing to these terms. In years past, job security was a major concern for a person joining a firm. Generally, many of today's workers have less of a feeling of job security than in the past.

Lucinda M. Renne has just completed a job application form for Ingram Heating and Cooling. She is a college business student and will work part-time for two hours per day, five days a week, as an office assistant.

Job application forms vary from business to business, but many are similar to the one shown in Figure 2.1 on pages 20 and 21, which is used by Ingram Heating and Cooling. Read through the application form. Notice the types of information that are requested and notice how Ms. Renne responded.

It is important for the applicant to be careful when filling out a job application form. The applicant should come prepared to give a good deal of specific information. This may include the dates that the person completed various steps in his or her education and the correct title, name, address, and telephone number of any references that the applicant might list. In addition, the applicant should be prepared to list exact dates, names, addresses, and telephone numbers of previous employers. Depending upon the job, the applicant may need to bring license numbers indicating special skills that are licensed by a state agency.

The applicant should use correct spelling and take care to print or write clearly. This is particularly important when listing numeric data such as telephone numbers and addresses. Never leave an item blank. If no response can be given, then write in "N/A."

Most businesses check the facts on the job application form carefully and gather additional information by contacting the schools, previous employers, and personal references that are listed. Then the manager involved in the hiring process judges the individual's strengths and weaknesses against the needs of the job. Of course, other factors, such as performance at a job interview and the results of any employment test, also play a role in management's decision.

It is quite common for an interviewer to ask a job applicant open-ended questions such as "Why would you like to work for this company?" or "What kind of work do you hope to be doing in five years?" or "What activities or hobbies do you like?" Answers to such questions often provide insight into the applicant's planning, logic, and general reasoning ability. In addition, it is possible to make a judgment about the applicant's communication skills, personality, and attitude.

A Case for Decision 2-1

Barney Powell was applying for a job as a stock clerk at a warehouse company. On the application form the company asked the question "Have you ever been arrested?" He had been arrested once for speeding and another time for running a red light when he was a high school senior four years ago. He was concerned that listing these arrests on the application form might mean he would not be considered for the job. So he didn't list them. He got the stock clerk job, but he always worried about the company finding out about his driving arrests. Was Barney wrong to leave out this information? What consequences could the omission have for him in the future?

Discussion of the Case

Should his company ever find out about these arrests, they will always look at Barney as a person who is not truthful, even if the auto arrests have no effect upon his work. Also, knowing about his driving arrests, his employers would probably never give him an advancement that involved any driving. There is also a chance that, if his company found out about this lack of honesty, they might immediately fire him from his job.

FIGURE 2.1   **A Sample Job Application Form**

Ingram Heating and Cooling
4466 Maritime Way San Jose, Ca. 95001

Please Read Before Signing Application

Ingram Heating and Cooling is an equal opportunity employer. All applicants and employees are considered for employment, development, advancement, and earnings based upon their skills, performance, and potential without regard to race, color, religion, sex, national origin, age, or handicap status.

I understand that the information I provide in this application must be complete and accurate to the best of my knowledge. I realize that falsification and/or incomplete information may jeopardize my employment now or in the future. Ingram Heating and Cooling or its agents may seek to verify this information and may make inquiries by securing consumer investigative reports concerning my character, criminal convictions, employment experience, education, and community standing. I further understand that if this information results in my dismissal, the nature and scope of these reports may be secured directly from the supplier of such information. I hereby authorize any previous employer to release to Ingram Heating and Cooling relevant information such as my work habits, performance, attendance, and reason for leaving.

I agree to conform to the rules and regulations of Ingram Heating and Cooling and understand that my employment can be terminated, with or without cause, and with or without notice, at any time, at the option of either Ingram Heating and Cooling or myself. I further understand that no manager, supervisor, or other representative of Ingram Heating and Cooling has any authority to enter into any agreement contrary to the foregoing.

Signature *Lucinda M. Renne*   Date *Nov. 27, 2005*

Personal Data

Name		Social Security Number	Home Phone
Lucinda M. Renne		442 | 69 | 5149	*(408)555-8871*

Address
3030 University Avenue, San Jose, Calif. 95166

Position Desired	Date Available	Willing to travel?	Relocate?
Office Assistant	*Immediately*	☐ Yes ☒ No	☐ Yes ☒ No

Are you a U.S. Citizen? ☒ Yes ☐ No	If No, Visa Type and Number
Have you been convicted of a crime? ☐ Yes ☒ No	If Yes, Please Detail–Offense and Disposition

Source

How were you referred?
☐ Classified Ad   ☐ Employment Agency   ☒ Other Source or Person
Please Identify–Name of Newspaper, Employment Agency, or Other Source or Person
My business teacher, Mrs. Green, Alhambra College

FIGURE 2.1 *(continued)*

U.S. Military Service

Branch	Final Rank	Date Entered	Date Discharged
N/A			

Service schools or special experience related to job for which you are applying?

Education

School Name	City, State	Dates From–To	Major Course of Study	Graduation Month/Year	Degree or Certificate
High School Emerson High School	San Jose, CA	2001 | 2005	Regular	6 | 2005	Regents Diploma
College(s) Alhambra College	San Jose, CA	2005 |	Business	|	
		|		|	
Graduate		|		|	
		|		|	
Other		|		|	
		|		|	

Employment

Firm Name	Address	Phone	Dates–From–To
Fashion Finds	66 Wayne St., San Jose	408/351-2842	6/17-8/24/2005
Position Held Sales associate	**Earnings–Beginning** $7.00 per hr.	**Ending**	**Supervisor–Name and Title** Anna Ramos, Manager
Reason for leaving This was a summer job.			
Firm Name Value Supermarket	**Address** 2763 Ross Ave., San Jose	**Phone** 408/769-8318	**Dates–From–To** 1/9-12/20/2004
Position Held Cashier	**Earnings–Beginning** $6.75 per hr.	**Ending**	**Supervisor–Name and Title** Frank Wells, Manager
Reason for leaving This was a part-time job after school and during vacations.			
Firm Name	**Address**	**Phone**	**Dates–From–To**
Position Held	**Earnings–Beginning**	**Ending**	**Supervisor–Name and Title**
Reason for leaving			
Firm Name	**Address**	**Phone**	**Dates–From–To**
Position Held	**Earnings–Beginning**	**Ending**	**Supervisor–Name and Title**
Reason for leaving			

Additional Experience

Please list any additional experiences you feel bear upon your skills or professional development.

Member of student government in high school, organized and helped to run a computer club for children at a local community center.

The job application form must conform to legal requirements under the fair employment laws. Job application forms must be free of bias. Questions relating to age, race, color, religion, national origin, marital status, or sex may not be asked by law.

Learning Through Practice   Do Exercise 2.1 on page 35 of this text-workbook.

THE PERSONNEL FILE

When a new employee is hired, it is necessary to start a *personnel file* for that person. A completed job application form, like the one on pages 20 and 21, would be placed in the file along with any other papers relating to the hiring process, such as the results of an employment test and evaluations made by staff members about the job interviews. Other pertinent data is added to the file during the employee's career with the firm. When the employee leaves the firm, a record of the reason and the date should be placed in the personnel file.

Large businesses usually have a human resources department that handles most of the procedures connected with hiring new employees. This department also keeps the personnel files. In a small business, the employee who does payroll work is often also in charge of the personnel files because much of the information required for setting up payroll records for a new employee is closely related to the information that appears in the employee's personnel file.

THE SOCIAL SECURITY NUMBER

By law, every employee must have a *social security number* (SSN), and an employer is required to obtain this number for its payroll records when a new employee begins work, or shortly thereafter.

If an employee does not have a social security number, the firm must ask the person to apply for one within seven days after starting the job. Until recently, applying for a social security number was a simple process. However, because many people were making illegal applications, additional requirements have been established.

An applicant must now complete a government form (Form SS-5) and present one primary and one secondary document to prove his or her age, citizenship, and identity. Assume that Lucinda Renne applied for her social security number recently. The completed form would appear as shown in Figure 2.2.

As proof of age and citizenship, the following documents are acceptable:

- Public record of birth established before age five. This is the preferred document and should be submitted if at all possible.
- Religious record of birth or baptism established before age three months.
- Hospital record of birth established before age five.

If none of the records listed above exists, one or more of the following documents listed below may be submitted:

- Driver's license
- Employee identification card
- Voter's registration card
- School record
- School identification card
- Marriage or divorce record
- Passport

FIGURE 2.2   **A Completed Application for a Social Security Card**

SOCIAL SECURITY ADMINISTRATION
Application for a Social Security Card

Form Approved
OMB No. 0960-0066

1	**NAME** ⟶ TO BE SHOWN ON CARD	First *Lucinda*	Full Middle Name *Mary*	Last *Renne*
	FULL NAME AT BIRTH IF OTHER THAN ABOVE	First	Full Middle Name	Last
	OTHER NAMES USED			

2 **MAILING ADDRESS** ⟶ Do Not Abbreviate

Street Address, Apt. No., PO Box, Rural Route No.
3030 University Avenue

City *San Jose*	State *California*	Zip Code *95166*

3 **CITIZENSHIP** ⟶ (Check One)

☒ U.S. Citizen　☐ Legal Alien Allowed To Work　☐ Legal Alien **Not** Allowed To Work (See Instructions On Page 1)　☐ Other (See Instructions On Page 1)

4 **SEX** ⟶　☐ Male　☒ Female

5 **RACE/ETHNIC DESCRIPTION** ⟶ (Check One Only - Voluntary)

☐ Asian, Asian-American or Pacific Islander　☐ Hispanic　☐ Black (Not Hispanic)　☐ North American Indian or Alaskan Native　☐ White (Not Hispanic)

6 **DATE OF BIRTH**　*4 / 22 /1985*　Month, Day, Year

7 **PLACE OF BIRTH** (Do Not Abbreviate)　*Sacramento*　City　*CA*　State or Foreign Country　FCI　Office Use Only

8
A. MOTHER'S MAIDEN NAME ⟶　First *Mary*　Full Middle Name *Louise*　Last Name At Her Birth *Madden*

B. MOTHER'S SOCIAL SECURITY NUMBER ⟶　☐☐☐—☐☐—☐☐☐☐

9
A. FATHER'S NAME ⟶　First *Joseph*　Full Middle Name *Foster*　Last *Renne*

B. FATHER'S SOCIAL SECURITY NUMBER ⟶　☐☐☐—☐☐—☐☐☐☐

10 Has the applicant or anyone acting on his/her behalf ever filed for or received a Social Security number card before?

☐ Yes (If "yes", answer questions 11-13.)　☒ No (If "no", go on to question 14.)　☐ Don't Know (If "don't know", go on to question 14.)

11 Enter the Social Security number previously assigned to the person listed in item 1. ⟶　☐☐☐—☐☐—☐☐☐☐

12 Enter the name shown on the most recent Social Security card issued for the person listed in item 1. ⟶　First　Middle Name　Last

13 Enter any different date of birth if used on an earlier application for a card. ⟶　_____ Month, Day, Year

14 **TODAY'S DATE**　*Sept. 5, 2005*　Month, Day, Year

15 **DAYTIME PHONE NUMBER**　(*408*) *555-8871*　Area Code　Number

I declare under penalty of perjury that I have examined all the information on this form, and on any accompanying statements or forms, and it is true and correct to the best of my knowledge.

16 **YOUR SIGNATURE**　▶ *Lucinda Mary Renne*

17 **YOUR RELATIONSHIP TO THE PERSON IN ITEM 1 IS:**
☒ Self　☐ Natural Or Adoptive Parent　☐ Legal Guardian　☐ Other (Specify)

DO NOT WRITE BELOW THIS LINE (FOR SSA USE ONLY)

NPN			DOC	NTI	CAN			ITV
PBC	EVI	EVA	EVC	PRA	NWR		DNR	UNIT

EVIDENCE SUBMITTED

SIGNATURE AND TITLE OF EMPLOYEE(S) REVIEWING EVIDENCE AND/OR CONDUCTING INTERVIEW

_____　DATE

_____
DCL　DATE

Form **SS-5** (10-2003)　EF (10-2003)　Destroy Prior Editions　Page 5

Point of Interest

For more than 60 years, taxpayers have needed to obtain social security numbers. These numbers were never intended to be used as a general identification number, but they have become just that. Since the Tax Reform Act of 1986, however, taxpayers have an additional responsibility. Parents must provide social security numbers for all persons claimed as exemptions on their income tax forms—even their children. This requires that the parents apply for such a number for each infant during the child's first year of life.

A few other documents are acceptable, such as adoption records, military discharge papers, and draft cards. It is essential, however, to have at least two documents that provide evidence of the applicant's identity, age, and U.S. citizenship or lawful alien status.

The completed application form plus the required documents can be sent to any social security office. Processing time can vary, but it generally takes about two weeks for the social security number to be issued. All documents will be returned to the sender. If there is a question about some of the background information that is supplied, an applicant may need to appear in person at an office of the Social Security Administration. If the applicant is over the age of 18 years when first applying for a social security card, he or she must apply in person.

Social security forms are available from field offices of the Social Security Administration (SSA), from some field offices of the IRS, from most post offices, and from the Social Security Web site, www.ssa.gov.

The social security number is important to both the employee and the employer. Not only does it identify the employee's social security account, but it also provides identification for the employee with the IRS and with state and local tax agencies. In addition, some large businesses use social security numbers as employee identification numbers because each social security number is unique and assigned to only one person.

A person keeps the same social security number for life, thus there is no need to apply for a new number when moving from one job to another. However, if a change of name occurs because of marriage or some other reason, it is necessary to report the change to the Social Security Administration and to get a replacement card showing the new name. Similarly, a lost social security card must be reported and a replacement obtained. Such replacement cards are supplied at no charge.

When a person retires, the social security number is essential. With it, the Social Security Administration can look up the employment record of the individual and, with this information, can determine just what the person's retirement benefits will be. If a worker becomes disabled, it will be necessary to provide the social security number before benefits can be determined. Securing those benefits begins with supplying the social security number.

Learning Through Practice Do Exercise 2.2 on page 35 of this text-workbook.

EMPLOYMENT ELIGIBILITY VERIFICATION

Since late 1986, all employees hired must complete Form I-9, Employment Eligibility Verification. This form requires the potential employee to certify that he or she is a citizen or national of the United States, or is a lawful permanent resident or an alien authorized to work until a certain date. Aliens must provide the appropriate alien number. Employers are required to examine the document(s) provided by the potential employee. Either one document from List A or one document from List B and one document from List C must be provided to the employer to verify that the applicant is eligible to be employed in the United State Form I-9 and the lists are shown in Figure 2.3 on pages 25–26.

FIGURE 2.3   Employment Eligibility Verification Form

U.S. Department of Justice
Immigration and Naturalization Service

OMB No. 1115-0136

Employment Eligibility Verification

Please read instructions carefully before completing this form. The instructions must be available during completion of this form. ANTI-DISCRIMINATION NOTICE: It is illegal to discriminate against work eligible individuals. Employers CANNOT specify which document(s) they will accept from an employee. The refusal to hire an individual because of a future expiration date may also constitute illegal discrimination.

Section 1. Employee Information and Verification. To be completed and signed by employee at the time employment begins.

Print Name: Last	First	Middle Initial	Maiden Name

Address *(Street Name and Number)*	Apt. #	Date of Birth *(month/day/year)*

City	State	Zip Code	Social Security #

I am aware that federal law provides for imprisonment and/or fines for false statements or use of false documents in connection with the completion of this form.	I attest, under penalty of perjury, that I am (check one of the following): ☐ A citizen or national of the United States ☐ A Lawful Permanent Resident (Alien # A_____) ☐ An alien authorized to work until ___/___/___ (Alien # or Admission #) _____

Employee's Signature	Date *(month/day/year)*

Preparer and/or Translator Certification.   *(To be completed and signed if Section 1 is prepared by a person other than the employee.) I attest, under penalty of perjury, that I have assisted in the completion of this form and that to the best of my knowledge the information is true and correct.*

Preparer's/Translator's Signature	Print Name

Address *(Street Name and Number, City, State, Zip Code)*	Date *(month/day/year)*

Section 2. Employer Review and Verification. To be completed and signed by employer. Examine one document from List A OR examine one document from List B and one from List C, as listed on the reverse of this form, and record the title, number and expiration date, if any, of the document(s)

List A	OR	List B	AND	List C
Document title: _____		_____		_____
Issuing authority: _____		_____		_____
Document #: _____		_____		_____
Expiration Date *(if any)*: ___/___/___		___/___/___		___/___/___
Document #: _____				
Expiration Date *(if any)*: ___/___/___				

CERTIFICATION - I attest, under penalty of perjury, that I have examined the document(s) presented by the above-named employee, that the above-listed document(s) appear to be genuine and to relate to the employee named, that the employee began employment on *(month/day/year)* ___/___/___ and that to the best of my knowledge the employee is eligible to work in the United States. (State employment agencies may omit the date the employee began employment.)

Signature of Employer or Authorized Representative	Print Name	Title

Business or Organization Name	Address *(Street Name and Number, City, State, Zip Code)*	Date *(month/day/year)*

Section 3. Updating and Reverification. To be completed and signed by employer.

A. New Name *(if applicable)*	B. Date of rehire *(month/day/year) (if applicable)*

C. If employee's previous grant of work authorization has expired, provide the information below for the document that establishes current employment eligibility.

Document Title:_____   Document #: _____   Expiration Date (if any): ___/___/___

I attest, under penalty of perjury, that to the best of my knowledge, this employee is eligible to work in the United States, and if the employee presented document(s), the document(s) I have examined appear to be genuine and to relate to the individual.

Signature of Employer or Authorized Representative	Date *(month/day/year)*

Form I-9 (Rev. 11-21-91)N Page 2

FIGURE 2.3 *(continued)*

LISTS OF ACCEPTABLE DOCUMENTS

LIST A		**LIST B**		**LIST C**
Documents that Establish Both Identity and Employment Eligibility	**OR**	Documents that Establish Identity	**AND**	Documents that Establish Employment Eligibility

LIST A

Documents that Establish Both Identity and Employment Eligibility

1. U.S. Passport (unexpired or expired)

2. Certificate of U.S. Citizenship *(INS Form N-560 or N-561)*

3. Certificate of Naturalization *(INS Form N-550 or N-570)*

4. Unexpired foreign passport, with *I-551 stamp or* attached *INS Form I-94* indicating unexpired employment authorization

5. Permanent Resident Card or Alien Registration Receipt Card with photograph *(INS Form I-151 or I-551)*

6. Unexpired Temporary Resident Card *(INS Form I-688)*

7. Unexpired Employment Authorization Card *(INS Form I-688A)*

8. Unexpired Reentry Permit *(INS Form I-327)*

9. Unexpired Refugee Travel Document *(INS Form I-571)*

10. Unexpired Employment Authorization Document issued by the INS which contains a photograph *(INS Form I-688B)*

OR

LIST B

Documents that Establish Identity

1. Driver's license or ID card issued by a state or outlying possession of the United States provided it contains a photograph or information such as name, date of birth, gender, height, eye color and address

2. ID card issued by federal, state or local government agencies or entities, provided it contains a photograph or information such as name, date of birth, gender, height, eye color and address

3. School ID card with a photograph

4. Voter's registration card

5. U.S. Military card or draft record

6. Military dependent's ID card

7. U.S. Coast Guard Merchant Mariner Card

8. Native American tribal document

9. Driver's license issued by a Canadian government authority

For persons under age 18 who are unable to present a document listed above:

10. School record or report card

11. Clinic, doctor or hospital record

12. Day-care or nursery school record

AND

LIST C

Documents that Establish Employment Eligibility

1. U.S. social security card issued by the Social Security Administration *(other than a card stating it is not valid for employment)*

2. Certification of Birth Abroad issued by the Department of State *(Form FS-545 or Form DS-1350)*

3. Original or certified copy of a birth certificate issued by a state, county, municipal authority or outlying possession of the United States bearing an official seal

4. Native American tribal document

5. U.S. Citizen ID Card *(INS Form I-197)*

6. ID Card for use of Resident Citizen in the United States *(INS Form I-179)*

7. Unexpired employment authorization document issued by the INS *(other than those listed under List A)*

Illustrations of many of these documents appear in Part 8 of the Handbook for Employers (M-274)

Form I-9 (Rev. 10/4/00)Y Page 3

Point of Interest

Plenty of social security numbers are still available. Over the past 60 years, there have been many millions of social security numbers issued. Every one of them has been different. One might wonder if the government will ever run out of numbers. We are assured that there are about 1 billion combinations of numbers still available. Only approximately one-third of the possible nine-digit social security number combinations have been issued up to this time. Part of the number indicates where in the country the card was issued.

Learning Through Practice Do Exercise 2.3 on page 35 of this text-workbook.

THE WITHHOLDING ALLOWANCE CERTIFICATE

Employers must also make sure that each new employee fills out a government form called an Employee's Withholding Allowance Certificate (Form W-4). This completed form shows how many withholding allowances the employee claims in connection with federal income tax. The complete two-page form, with instructions for determining the proper number of allowances, appears in Figure 2.4 on pages 28 and 29.

Notice in Figure 2.4 that when Lucinda Renne filled out her Form W-4, she wrote *0* for allowances (item 5 on the first page) because her father claims her on his Form W-4. She left blank the space where one might list any additional amount of federal income tax one wishes to have withheld from each paycheck (item 6 on the first page). The directions for this form are rather complex, but an employee with special allowance circumstances can determine the number of allowances to list, and any additional withholding required from each paycheck, by working through the form.

Notice, in Figure 2.4, instruction A. It states, "Enter '1' for yourself if no one else can claim you as a dependent." Now notice instruction B. The first line states, "You are single and have only one job. . . ." This means that a single person could claim *two* allowances. More allowances may be claimed as the person works through the complex instructions for completing Form W-4. But when this person files his or her income tax at the end of the year, only *one exemption* can be claimed. *Allowances* are different from *exemptions.*

Withholding allowances consist of personal allowances and special tax credits. Many taxpayers can claim two personal allowances for themselves and an additional personal allowance for each dependent, such as a spouse (husband or wife) or a child. (Generally, *dependents* are children or relatives who are receiving all or most of their financial support from the taxpayer.) Some workers are eligible for special tax credits that are intended to help the taxpayer with certain types of expense, such as the cost of caring for children or disabled dependents while the taxpayer is working.

Many workers do not claim all of the allowances they are entitled to when they complete a Form W-4. They may want to be certain that enough federal income tax is withheld so they do not owe additional tax at the end of the year. Or they may enjoy having a tax refund, which claiming fewer allowances will usually produce.

Internet Tax Addresses

An adequate file on each new employee has essential components to allow the company to work legally and efficiently. Check out the IRS Web site for comprehensive payroll tax information at www.irs.gov.

FIGURE 2.4 A Completed Form W-4

Form W-4 (2003)

Purpose. Complete Form W-4 so that your employer can withhold the correct Federal income tax from your pay. Because your tax situation may change, you may want to refigure your withholding each year.

Exemption from withholding. If you are exempt, complete only lines 1, 2, 3, 4, and 7 and sign the form to validate it. Your exemption for 2003 expires February 16, 2004. See **Pub. 505**, Tax Withholding and Estimated Tax.

Note: *You cannot claim exemption from withholding if: (a) your income exceeds $750 and includes more than $250 of unearned income (e.g., interest and dividends) and (b) another person can claim you as a dependent on their tax return.*

Basic instructions. If you are not exempt, complete the **Personal Allowances Worksheet** below. The worksheets on page 2 adjust your withholding allowances based on itemized deductions, certain credits, adjustments to income, or two-earner/two-job situations. Complete all worksheets that apply. **However, you may claim fewer (or zero) allowances.**

Head of household. Generally, you may claim head of household filing status on your tax return only if you are unmarried and pay more than 50% of the costs of keeping up a home for yourself and your dependent(s) or other qualifying individuals. See line **E** below.

Tax credits. You can take projected tax credits into account in figuring your allowable number of withholding allowances. Credits for child or dependent care expenses and the child tax credit may be claimed using the **Personal Allowances Worksheet** below. See **Pub. 919,** How Do I Adjust My Tax Withholding? for information on converting your other credits into withholding allowances.

Nonwage income. If you have a large amount of nonwage income, such as interest or dividends, consider making estimated tax payments using **Form 1040-ES,** Estimated Tax for Individuals. Otherwise, you may owe additional tax.

Two earners/two jobs. If you have a working spouse or more than one job, figure the total number of allowances you are entitled to claim on all jobs using worksheets from only one Form W-4. Your withholding usually will be most accurate when all allowances are claimed on the Form W-4 for the highest paying job and zero allowances are claimed on the others.

Nonresident alien. If you are a nonresident alien, see the **Instructions for Form 8233** before completing this Form W-4.

Check your withholding. After your Form W-4 takes effect, use Pub. 919 to see how the dollar amount you are having withheld compares to your projected total tax for 2003. See Pub. 919, especially if your earnings exceed $125,000 (Single) or $175,000 (Married).

Recent name change? If your name on line 1 differs from that shown on your social security card, call 1-800-772-1213 for a new social security card.

Personal Allowances Worksheet (Keep for your records.)

A Enter "1" for **yourself** if no one else can claim you as a dependent . . . . **A** _0_

B Enter "1" if: {
- You are single and have only one job; or
- You are married, have only one job, and your spouse does not work; or
- Your wages from a second job or your spouse's wages (or the total of both) are $1,000 or less. } . . **B** _____

C Enter "1" for your **spouse.** But, you may choose to enter "-0-" if you are married and have either a working spouse or more than one job. (Entering "-0-" may help you avoid having too little tax withheld.) . . . . **C** _____

D Enter number of **dependents** (other than your spouse or yourself) you will claim on your tax return . . . . **D** _____

E Enter "1" if you will file as **head of household** on your tax return (see conditions under **Head of household** above) . **E** _____

F Enter "1" if you have at least $1,500 of **child or dependent care expenses** for which you plan to claim a credit . . **F** _____

   (**Note:** *Do not include child support payments. See Pub. 503, Child and Dependent Care Expenses, for details.*)

G **Child Tax Credit** (including additional child tax credit):
- If your total income will be between $15,000 and $42,000 ($20,000 and $65,000 if married), enter "1" for each eligible child plus **1 additional** if you have three to five eligible children or **2 additional** if you have six or more eligible children.
- If your total income will be between $42,000 and $80,000 ($65,000 and $115,000 if married), enter "1" if you have one or two eligible children, "2" if you have three eligible children, "3" if you have four eligible children, or "4" if you have five or more eligible children. . **G** _____

H Add lines A through G and enter total here. **Note:** *This may be different from the number of exemptions you claim on your tax return.* ▶ **H** _____

For accuracy, complete all worksheets that apply.	• If you plan to **itemize or claim adjustments to income** and want to reduce your withholding, see the **Deductions and Adjustments Worksheet** on page 2.
	• If you have **more than one job** or are **married and you and your spouse both work** and the combined earnings from all jobs exceed $35,000, see the **Two-Earner/Two-Job Worksheet** on page 2 to avoid having too little tax withheld.
	• If **neither** of the above situations applies, **stop here** and enter the number from line H on line 5 of Form W-4 below.

-------------------- **Cut here and give Form W-4 to your employer. Keep the top part for your records.** --------------------

Form **W-4** Department of the Treasury Internal Revenue Service	**Employee's Withholding Allowance Certificate** ▶ **For Privacy Act and Paperwork Reduction Act Notice, see page 2.**	OMB No. 1545-0010 **2003**

1 Type or print your first name and middle initial *Lucinda M.*	Last name *Renne*	**2** Your social security number *442 69 5149*

Home address (number and street or rural route) *3030 University Avenue*	**3** ☒ Single ☐ Married ☐ Married, but withhold at higher Single rate. **Note:** *If married, but legally separated, or spouse is a nonresident alien, check the "Single" box.*
City or town, state, and ZIP code *San Jose, California 95166*	**4** If your last name differs from that shown on your social security card, check here. You must call 1-800-772-1213 for a new card. ▶ ☐

5	Total number of allowances you are claiming (from line **H** above **or** from the applicable worksheet on page 2)	**5**	_0_
6	Additional amount, if any, you want withheld from each paycheck	**6**	$
7	I claim exemption from withholding for 2003, and I certify that I meet **both** of the following conditions for exemption:		

- Last year I had a right to a refund of **all** Federal income tax withheld because I had **no** tax liability **and**
- This year I expect a refund of **all** Federal income tax withheld because I expect to have **no** tax liability.

If you meet both conditions, write "Exempt" here . . . . ▶ | **7** |

Under penalties of perjury, I certify that I am entitled to the number of withholding allowances claimed on this certificate, or I am entitled to claim exempt status.

Employee's signature (Form is not valid unless you sign it.) ▶ *Lucinda M. Renne*   Date ▶ *Nov. 27, 2005*

8 Employer's name and address (Employer: Complete lines 8 and 10 only if sending to the IRS.)	**9** Office code (optional)	**10** Employer identification number

Cat. No. 10220Q

FIGURE 2.4 *(continued)*

Form W-4 (2003)   Page **2**

Deductions and Adjustments Worksheet

Note:	*Use this worksheet **only** if you plan to itemize deductions, claim certain credits, or claim adjustments to income on your 2003 tax return.*	
1	Enter an estimate of your 2003 itemized deductions. These include qualifying home mortgage interest, charitable contributions, state and local taxes, medical expenses in excess of 7.5% of your income, and miscellaneous deductions. (For 2003, you may have to reduce your itemized deductions if your income is over $139,500 ($69,750 if married filing separately). See **Worksheet 3** in Pub. 919 for details.) . . .	**1** $
2	Enter: { $7,950 if married filing jointly or qualifying widow(er) / $7,000 if head of household / $4,750 if single / $3,975 if married filing separately }	**2** $
3	**Subtract** line 2 from line 1. If line 2 is greater than line 1, enter "-0-".	**3** $
4	Enter an estimate of your 2003 adjustments to income, including alimony, deductible IRA contributions, and student loan interest	**4** $
5	**Add** lines 3 and 4 and enter the total. Include any amount for credits from **Worksheet 7** in Pub. 919	**5** $
6	Enter an estimate of your 2003 nonwage income (such as dividends or interest)	**6** $
7	**Subtract** line 6 from line 5. Enter the result, but not less than "-0-"	**7** $
8	**Divide** the amount on line 7 by $3,000 and enter the result here. Drop any fraction	**8**
9	Enter the number from the **Personal Allowances Worksheet,** line H, page 1	**9**
10	**Add** lines 8 and 9 and enter the total here. If you plan to use the **Two-Earner/Two-Job Worksheet,** also enter this total on line 1 below. Otherwise, **stop here** and enter this total on Form W-4, line 5, page 1 .	**10**

Two-Earner/Two-Job Worksheet

Note:	*Use this worksheet **only** if the instructions under line H on page 1 direct you here.*	
1	Enter the number from line H, page 1 (or from line 10 above if you used the **Deductions and Adjustments Worksheet**)	**1**
2	Find the number in **Table 1** below that applies to the **lowest** paying job and enter it here	**2**
3	If line 1 is **more than or equal to** line 2, subtract line 2 from line 1. Enter the result here (if zero, enter "-0-") and on Form W-4, line 5, page 1. **Do not** use the rest of this worksheet	**3**
Note:	*If line 1 is **less than** line 2, enter "-0-" on Form W-4, line 5, page 1. Complete lines 4–9 below to calculate the additional withholding amount necessary to avoid a year-end tax bill.*	
4	Enter the number from line 2 of this worksheet **4**	
5	Enter the number from line 1 of this worksheet **5**	
6	**Subtract** line 5 from line 4	**6**
7	Find the amount in **Table 2** below that applies to the **highest** paying job and enter it here	**7** $
8	**Multiply** line 7 by line 6 and enter the result here. This is the additional annual withholding needed . .	**8** $
9	Divide line 8 by the number of pay periods remaining in 2003. For example, divide by 26 if you are paid every two weeks and you complete this form in December 2002. Enter the result here and on Form W-4, line 6, page 1. This is the additional amount to be withheld from each paycheck	**9** $

Table 1: Two-Earner/Two-Job Worksheet

Married Filing Jointly				All Others			
If wages from **LOWEST** paying job are—	Enter on line 2 above	If wages from **LOWEST** paying job are—	Enter on line 2 above	If wages from **LOWEST** paying job are—	Enter on line 2 above	If wages from **LOWEST** paying job are—	Enter on line 2 above
$0 - $4,000	0	44,001 - 50,000	8	$0 - $6,000	0	75,001 - 100,000	8
4,001 - 9,000	1	50,001 - 60,000	9	6,001 - 11,000	1	100,001 - 110,000	9
9,001 - 15,000	2	60,001 - 70,000	10	11,001 - 18,000	2	110,001 and over	10
15,001 - 20,000	3	70,001 - 90,000	11	18,001 - 25,000	3		
20,001 - 25,000	4	90,001 - 100,000	12	25,001 - 29,000	4		
25,001 - 33,000	5	100,001 - 115,000	13	29,001 - 40,000	5		
33,001 - 38,000	6	115,001 - 125,000	14	40,001 - 55,000	6		
38,001 - 44,000	7	125,001 and over	15	55,001 - 75,000	7		

Table 2: Two-Earner/Two-Job Worksheet

Married Filing Jointly		All Others	
If wages from **HIGHEST** paying job are—	Enter on line 7 above	If wages from **HIGHEST** paying job are—	Enter on line 7 above
$0 - $50,000	$450	$0 - $30,000	$450
50,001 - 100,000	800	30,001 - 70,000	800
100,001 - 150,000	900	70,001 - 140,000	900
150,001 - 270,000	1,050	140,001 - 300,000	1,050
270,001 and over	1,200	300,001 and over	1,200

A Case for Decision 2-2

James Thomas, who is 23 years old, is single, and lives alone, had to fill out Form W-4 for a new job. He knew listing an extra allowance would mean that less tax would be withheld from each of his paychecks so he would get more take-home pay. He also knew that to list a false allowance was illegal. Yet he listed an extra allowance to which he was not entitled. He has a 12-year-old sister living with an aunt in a distant city, and he sends her $20 each month for spending money. He claimed her as a dependent, knowing that his aunt provides for her food, clothing, and housing. He disregarded the notice near the bottom of the form that stated "Under penalties of perjury, I certify that I am entitled to the number of withholding allowances claimed on this certificate or entitled to claim exempt status." Is James going to find himself in trouble? What might happen to him?

Discussion of the Case

James has committed a felony by signing this untrue document. He may be fined, or he might be sent to jail. This is a very serious offense.

After completion of Form W-4, the employee signs the certificate portion of the form and gives it to his or her employer. By signing the form, the employee certifies that he or she is entitled to the number of allowances claimed on the certificate, under penalty of perjury. Often, perjury can result in a fine, a jail term, or both. The second page of Form W-4 contains worksheets that are designed to help employees determine the taxable income they will have so that a more exact amount of federal income tax can be withheld from their payroll checks by their employer. Many employees do not need to use the worksheets on page 2 of Form W-4.

Withholding allowances and special tax credits are important because they reduce the amount of income tax that must be withheld from payroll checks. From time to time, the laws and regulations about withholding allowances, special tax credits, and exemptions do change. For example, in the 1990s, a child tax credit was added for taxpayers who are at certain income levels. Employers can expect continued changes.

From time to time, employees have changes in their lives that bring about changes in the number of withholding allowances they can legally claim. For example, a worker gets married, a new child joins the family, an elderly relative becomes a dependent, or a child grows up and leaves home and becomes self-supporting. Whenever such a change takes place, the employee must notify his or her employer and fill out a new copy of Form W-4.

It is necessary for a business to keep a copy of the Form W-4 prepared by each employee in its payroll files because these papers provide legal support for the income tax deductions that the firm makes from employee earnings.

Learning Through Practice   Do Exercise 2.4 on page 35 in this text-workbook.

NEW HIRE REPORTING TO THE STATES

As noted in Unit 1, the Personal Responsibility and Work Opportunity Reconciliation Act of 1996 is a federal law that requires employers to report information about each newly hired employee to a state registry within 20 days after the employee starts work. The purpose of this procedure is to make it possible for government officials to find individuals who owe child support payments.

In California, where Ingram Heating and Cooling is located, employers must use Form DE 43, Report of New Employee(s). On this form, the employer lists the name, social security number, home address, and start or work date of each new employee. Form DE 43 is filed with the state, which places the information in its New Employee Registry.

Each state provides its own forms to employers for the reporting of newly hired employees. Check your own state's Web page for information about your state.

When you have money withheld for social security, you want it credited to *your* account. That is why there are social security numbers (SSN). These numbers are specific identifiers. Your social security number identifies you—just you. No other social security number is like it, and there is an important reason for this. There are more than 2 million people named Smith in this country. And, more specifically, there are more than 10,000 Joe Smiths. When your friend Joe Smith has money subtracted from his paycheck to go to his social security account, he wants to be certain it goes to *his* account, not to some other Joe Smith's account. His social security number gives him that assurance. But things could be worse. In China, for example, it is estimated that about *100 million* people have Chang as their family name!

THE EMPLOYEE EARNINGS RECORD

Employers must keep a separate yearly record of hours worked, earnings, deductions, and take-home pay for each employee. The top part of the employee earnings record usually contains basic payroll information such as the employee's name and address, social security number, marital status, number of withholding allowances, job title, starting date with the business, and rate of pay. This information is needed to meet the requirements of various laws and to help in preparing the payroll.

The record shown in Figure 2.5 is commonly known as an *employee earnings record*. This type of payroll record needs to be started when a new employee begins work. (In Unit 7, you will see exactly how the employee earnings record is used to keep track of payroll amounts throughout the year.)

FIGURE 2.5   **An Employee Earnings Record for Lucinda Renne**

EMPLOYEE EARNINGS RECORD FOR YEAR 20 __05__

Name ____ Lucinda M. Renne ____

Address ____ 3030 University Ave. ____

San Jose, CA 95166

Social Security No. __442-69-5149__

Job Title ____ Office Assistant ____

Date Employed __Nov. 27, 2005__

Date Terminated ____

Marital Status   M☐ S☒

No. of Withholding Allowances __0__

Regular Rate ____ $9.50 per hour ____

Voluntary Deductions:

IRA ____

U.S. Savings Bonds ____

PAYROLL PERIOD		HOURS		EARNINGS			DEDUCTIONS									NET PAY	YEAR-TO-DATE EARNINGS
Week	Ending Date	Reg.	O.T.	Regular	Overtime or Commission	Total Earnings	Federal Income Tax	Social Security Tax	Medicare Tax	State Income Tax	SDI Tax	IRA	Savings Bonds	Total deductions			
1st Quarter																	
1																	
2																	
3																	
4																	
5																	
6																	
7																	
8																	
9																	
10																	
11																	
12																	
13																	
14																	
1st Quarter Totals																	

Learning Through Practice   Do Exercise 2.5 on page 35 of this text-workbook.

A Case for Decision 2-3

Bob Hanson is one of six people in the payroll department at Tri-State Financial Services. Early one morning Bob passed his good friend Sally Ellis in the corridor and told her *very* confidentially that Lance Roberts, one of the sales executives in the firm, had just been directed by the court to pay $600 per month for child support. Sally, who was very surprised, couldn't wait to tell Wendy, her number one buddy in the sales department. The story spread quickly. The next day, Bob Hanson was called into the manager's office. The leak in confidentiality had been traced to Bob. After a brief discussion, Bob was fired. What should Bob have learned from this? What have you learned?

Discussion of the Case

Bob certainly should have learned from this incident that spreading rumors can turn out to be very costly. Serious gossip simply is not tolerated by most businesses. In addition, he should think about the things in his life that he would not want others to know. You, from this example, should have learned that passing on gossip to another is very unwise indeed.

CONFIDENTIALITY

It is essential that *all* personal information about employees that is kept by a firm be held in strict confidence. Generally, most of this information is found in the human resources department, but much is also located in the payroll department. While most of the information about employees is of a very general nature, some is not. Personnel records may contain information about arrests, criminal records, family problems, personal bankruptcy, divorce, garnishment of wages, illnesses, and other situations that would be embarrassing or damaging to an individual if the information became public.

For this reason, it is common for businesses to keep such records under lock and key. In addition, only a limited number of employees are authorized to use such records. Computerized personnel files, for example, should be available only to selected people—those who have been given the access code to the files. Outdated paper personnel files should not simply be thrown out; they should be shredded. No personnel information should ever be given to *anyone* on the telephone. It is of critical importance that all information about employees, even the most innocent information, be kept in *absolute confidence.*

Learning Through Practice   Do Exercise 2.6 on pages 42–43 in this text-workbook.

UNIT 2   REVIEW

Summary

In this unit you learned:

- What a job application is and how to fill one out.
- The types of information/documentation needed to complete a job application.
- That not all questions are appropriate to be asked of a potential employee.
- How to apply for a social security card.
- Who can be claimed as a dependent for tax withholding purposes.
- How to complete a W-4.
- How to complete an I-9.
- About records that must be kept for employees and about the confidentiality of those records.

Study Questions

1. How do businesses use job application forms?
2. What types of information are commonly requested on a job application form?
3. What information is usually included in a personnel file?
4. Why is it necessary for employers to keep personnel and payroll records?
5. By law, employees must each have a social security number. Why?
6. Under what circumstances may an employee need to obtain a new social security card?
7. Why do some employees write *0* for allowances when they fill out Form W-4?
8. Why does an employer require that a completed Form W-4 be on file for each employee?
9. Describe the general types of withholding allowances to which an employee may be entitled.
10. How does the payroll department use the W-4 form that is filed by each employee?
11. What information is recorded in an employee earnings record?

Discussion Questions

1. An essay-type question such as "Why do you want to work for this company?" is included in some job application interviews. What does the applicant's answer to this question help to tell the interviewer?
2. The following questions are asked on the job application form of the Drake Construction Company. Is it legal or illegal to ask each of these questions under current fair employment laws?
   a. Where were you born?
   b. What languages do you speak, read, or write fluently?
   c. Were you ever employed by Drake under another name?
   d. Are you a citizen of the United States?
3. What procedures might a business use to safeguard the confidentiality of its personnel files?
4. Jack Peterson lost his wallet which contained, among other things, his social security card. It was never returned. How can Jack get a replacement social security card?
5. What is the reason for requiring Form I-9 to be completed for new hires?

REVIEW EXERCISES

1. Determine how many withholding allowances may be claimed by each of the following employees. (Refer to Form W-4 on pages 28 and 29.)

   a. Kevin Daley is single and has one job. He heads a household that consists of himself, his widowed mother, who is a dependent, and his younger sister, who is self-supporting.

   b. Ruth Lenski has one job. Her dependent husband is disabled and cannot work. She spends $8,500 a year to have her husband cared for while she is at her job.

   c. Maria Ramirez is single and has one job. No one else can claim her as a dependent.

   d. Carol Van Patten is single and has two dependent children. She holds one job and expects to have a total income of $34,000 this year.

   e. Scott Hanson is married and has three dependent children. His wife, a former wage earner, is now a full-time mother and does not work outside the home. Mr. Hanson has a second job from which he earns $6,500 a year. He expects to have a total income of $48,000 this year.

2. Assume that you work in the payroll department of Sunnyvale Hospital. The following employees have asked your help in determining the number of withholding allowances they may claim. (Refer to Form W-4 on pages 28 and 29.)

   a. David Chu is single and has one job. He estimates that his total income this year will be $40,000 (all from his job) and that his itemized deductions will be $8,000. He expects to have no adjustments to his income. How many withholding allowances should he claim?

   b. Joyce DeVito is single and has two jobs. She estimates that her total income this year will be $45,000 (which includes $5,000 from her second job) and that her itemized deductions will be $12,000. She expects to have no adjustments to her income. How many withholding allowances should she claim?

   c. Nancy Abramson is married, has no children, and has one job. Her husband is attending medical school and currently has no earnings. They file a joint federal income tax return. Nancy estimates that her total income this year will be $50,000 (all from her job) and that her itemized deductions will be $10,000. She expects to have no adjustments to her income. How many withholding allowances should she claim?

Learning Through Practice

Unit 2 Exercises

EXERCISE 2.1

Becoming familiar with job application forms is important for both business and personal reasons. If you work in payroll or human resources in your business career, you may be handling such forms. If you become a supervisor or manager in any area of business operations, you will probably be using the information recorded on job application forms to evaluate potential new employees. Of course, whenever you are looking for a job, it is likely that you will be asked to fill out an application form. To gain experience with this type of form, complete the one on pages 36 and 37.

1. Assume that you are applying for the job of office assistant at Ingram Heating and Cooling when completing the job application form.
2. Use real information about yourself. If you do not have a social security number, use 442-69-5149 as your number.
3. Follow directions carefully. The best procedure is to look over all the directions on the form before starting to fill it out.
4. Write clearly, and spell words correctly. This will help you to make a good impression on your potential employer.
5. Provide complete and accurate information about your education, skills, and prior work experience. Most firms will check with your previous employers, and some will check with the schools you list. In addition, some firms will verify skills such as typing, business mathematics, and ability to use a computer by giving you a test.

EXERCISE 2.2

Even though you may have a social security number already, you should become familiar with the form used to apply for such a number (Form SS-5) because people who work in the area of payroll or human resources are sometimes asked by new employees for help in filling out this form. To gain experience with Form SS-5, complete the one on page 38. Use real information about yourself to prepare the form.

EXERCISE 2.3

As an applicant to Ingram Heating and Cooling, you will be required to fill in Section 1 of Form I-9, Employment Eligibility Verification. To gain experience with this form, complete the one on page 39 with your own information. Remember that Ingram will require you to furnish the appropriate paper documentation that will establish your eligibility for employment.

EXERCISE 2.4

If you work in the area of payroll or human resources, you will be dealing with the Employee's Withholding Allowance Certificate (Form W-4) whenever a new employee joins the firm or a current employee must make a change in his or her withholding allowances. Of course, you will fill out this form yourself whenever you start working for a new employer. To gain experience with Form W-4, complete the one on pages 40 and 41.

1. Read the instructions on Form W-4, and then determine the number of allowances that you can claim. Use the worksheet provided for this purpose in the upper part of the first page of the form. If necessary, also use the worksheets on the second page.
2. Enter the necessary information in the lower part of the first page of Form W-4. If you do not have a social security number, use 442-69-5149. Sign and date this part of the form. Use the current date.

EXERCISE 2.5

Assume that you have been hired by Ingram Heating and Cooling as an office assistant. This is the job you applied for in Exercise 2.1. Also assume that one of your duties will be to keep the firm's payroll records and that you must now set up an employee earnings record for yourself. Use the form on page 42.

Use real information about yourself. Assume that you start work today. Also assume that your regular rate of pay is $9.50 per hour. You have not signed up for either of the voluntary deductions. If you do not have a social security number, use 442-69-5149.

EXERCISE 2.1

Ingram Heating and Cooling
4466 Maritime Way • San Jose, Calif. 95001

Please Read Before Signing Application
Ingram Heating and Cooling is an equal opportunity employer. All applicants and employees are considered for employment, development, advancement, and earnings based upon their skills, performance, and potential without regard to race, color, religion, sex, national origin, age, or handicap status.

I understand that the information I provide in this application must be complete and accurate to the best of my knowledge. I realize that falsification and/or incomplete information may jeopardize my employment now or in the future. Ingram Heating and Cooling or its agents may seek to verify this information and may make inquiries by securing a consumer investigative report concerning my character, criminal convictions, employment experience, education, and community standing. I further understand that if this information results in my dismissal, the nature and scope of these reports may be secured directly from the supplier of such information. I hereby authorize any previous employer to release to Ingram Heating and Cooling relevant information such as my work habits, performance, attendance, and reason for leaving.

I agree to conform to the rules and regulations of Ingram Heating and Cooling and understand that my employment can be terminated, with or without cause, and with or without notice, at any time, at the option of either Ingram Heating and Cooling or myself. I further understand that no manager, supervisor, or other representative of Ingram Heating and Cooling has any authority to enter into any agreement contrary to the foregoing.

Signature   Date

Personal Data

Name		Social Security Number	Home Phone
Address			
Position Desired	Date Available	Willing to travel? ☐ Yes ☐ No	Relocate? ☐ Yes ☐ No
Are you a U.S. Citizen? ☐ Yes ☐ No	If No, Visa Type and Number		
Have you been convicted of a crime? ☐ Yes ☐ No	If Yes, Please Detail–Offense and Disposition		

Source

How were you referred?
☐ Classified Ad   ☐ Employment Agency   ☐ Other Source or Person
Please Identify–Name of Newspaper, Employment Agency, or Other Source or Person

EXERCISE 2.1 *(continued)*

U.S. Military Service

Branch	Final Rank	Date Entered	Date Discharged

Service schools or special experience related to job for which you are applying?

Education

School Name	City, State	Dates From–To	Major Course of Study	Graduation Month/Year	Degree or Certificate
High School					
College(s)					
Graduate					
Other					

Employment

Please list all employers beginning with your present employer

Firm Name	Address		Phone	Dates–From–To
Position Held	Earnings–Beginning	Ending	Supervisor–Name and Title	
Reason for leaving				
Firm Name	Address		Phone	Dates–From–To
Position Held	Earnings–Beginning	Ending	Supervisor–Name and Title	
Reason for leaving				
Firm Name	Address		Phone	Dates–From–To
Position Held	Earnings–Beginning	Ending	Supervisor–Name and Title	
Reason for leaving				
Firm Name	Address		Phone	Dates–From–To
Position Held	Earnings–Beginning	Ending	Supervisor–Name and Title	
Reason for leaving				

Additional Experience

Please list any additional experiences you feel bear upon your skills or professional development.

EXERCISE 2.2

SOCIAL SECURITY ADMINISTRATION
Application for a Social Security Card

Form Approved
OMB No. 0960-0066

1	**NAME** → TO BE SHOWN ON CARD	First	Full Middle Name	Last
	FULL NAME AT BIRTH IF OTHER THAN ABOVE	First	Full Middle Name	Last
	OTHER NAMES USED			

2 MAILING ADDRESS →
Do Not Abbreviate

Street Address, Apt. No., PO Box, Rural Route No.

City	State	Zip Code

3 CITIZENSHIP →
(Check One)

☐ U.S. Citizen   ☐ Legal Alien Allowed To Work   ☐ Legal Alien **Not** Allowed To Work (See Instructions On Page 1)   ☐ Other (See Instructions On Page 1)

4 SEX →   ☐ Male   ☐ Female

5 RACE/ETHNIC DESCRIPTION
(Check One Only - Voluntary)

☐ Asian, Asian-American or Pacific Islander   ☐ Hispanic   ☐ Black (Not Hispanic)   ☐ North American Indian or Alaskan Native   ☐ White (Not Hispanic)

6	**DATE OF BIRTH** ___ Month, Day, Year	7	**PLACE OF BIRTH** (Do Not Abbreviate) ___ City ___ State or Foreign Country FCI	Office Use Only

8	**A. MOTHER'S MAIDEN NAME** →	First	Full Middle Name	Last Name At Her Birth
	B. MOTHER'S SOCIAL SECURITY NUMBER →	☐☐☐ – ☐☐ – ☐☐☐☐		

9	**A. FATHER'S NAME** →	First	Full Middle Name	Last
	B. FATHER'S SOCIAL SECURITY NUMBER →	☐☐☐ – ☐☐ – ☐☐☐☐		

10 Has the applicant or anyone acting on his/her behalf ever filed for or received a Social Security number card before?

☐ Yes (If "yes", answer questions 11-13.)   ☐ No (If "no", go on to question 14.)   ☐ Don't Know (If "don't know", go on to question 14.)

11 Enter the Social Security number previously assigned to the person listed in item 1. →   ☐☐☐ – ☐☐ – ☐☐☐☐

12	Enter the name shown on the most recent Social Security card issued for the person listed in item 1. →	First	Middle Name	Last

13 Enter any different date of birth if used on an earlier application for a card. →   ___ Month, Day, Year

14	**TODAY'S DATE** ___ Month, Day, Year	15	**DAYTIME PHONE NUMBER** (___) ___ Area Code Number

I declare under penalty of perjury that I have examined all the information on this form, and on any accompanying statements or forms, and it is true and correct to the best of my knowledge.

16	**YOUR SIGNATURE** ▶	17	**YOUR RELATIONSHIP TO THE PERSON IN ITEM 1 IS:** ☐ Self ☐ Natural Or Adoptive Parent ☐ Legal Guardian ☐ Other (Specify)

DO NOT WRITE BELOW THIS LINE (FOR SSA USE ONLY)

NPN			DOC	NTI	CAN		ITV
PBC	EVI	EVA	EVC	PRA	NWR	DNR	UNIT

EVIDENCE SUBMITTED

SIGNATURE AND TITLE OF EMPLOYEE(S) REVIEWING EVIDENCE AND/OR CONDUCTING INTERVIEW

___ DATE

DCL ___ DATE

Form **SS-5** (10-2003) EF (10-2003)   Destroy Prior Editions   Page 5

EXERCISE 2.3

U.S. Department of Justice
Immigration and Naturalization Service

OMB No. 1115-0136
Employment Eligibility Verification

Please read instructions carefully before completing this form. The instructions must be available during completion of this form. **ANTI-DISCRIMINATION NOTICE:** It is illegal to discriminate against work eligible individuals. Employers **CANNOT** specify which document(s) they will accept from an employee. The refusal to hire an individual because of a future expiration date may also constitute illegal discrimination.

Section 1. Employee Information and Verification. To be completed and signed by employee at the time employment begins.

Print Name: Last	First	Middle Initial	Maiden Name

Address *(Street Name and Number)*	Apt. #	Date of Birth *(month/day/year)*

City	State	Zip Code	Social Security #

I am aware that federal law provides for imprisonment and/or fines for false statements or use of false documents in connection with the completion of this form.

I attest, under penalty of perjury, that I am (check one of the following):
☐ A citizen or national of the United States
☐ A Lawful Permanent Resident (Alien # A_____)
☐ An alien authorized to work until ___/___/___
(Alien # or Admission #) _____

Employee's Signature	Date *(month/day/year)*

Preparer and/or Translator Certification.   *(To be completed and signed if Section 1 is prepared by a person other than the employee.) I attest, under penalty of perjury, that I have assisted in the completion of this form and that to the best of my knowledge the information is true and correct.*

Preparer's/Translator's Signature	Print Name

Address *(Street Name and Number, City, State, Zip Code)*	Date *(month/day/year)*

Section 2. Employer Review and Verification. To be completed and signed by employer. Examine one document from List A OR examine one document from List B and one from List C, as listed on the reverse of this form, and record the title, number and expiration date, if any, of the document(s)

List A	OR	List B	AND	List C
Document title:_____		_____		_____
Issuing authority: _____		_____		_____
Document #: _____		_____		_____
Expiration Date *(if any):* ___/___/___		___/___/___		___/___/___
Document #: _____				
Expiration Date *(if any):* ___/___/___				

CERTIFICATION - I attest, under penalty of perjury, that I have examined the document(s) presented by the above-named employee, that the above-listed document(s) appear to be genuine and to relate to the employee named, that the employee began employment on *(month/day/year)* ___/___/___ **and that to the best of my knowledge the employee is eligible to work in the United States. (State employment agencies may omit the date the employee began employment.)**

Signature of Employer or Authorized Representative	Print Name	Title

Business or Organization Name	Address *(Street Name and Number, City, State, Zip Code)*	Date *(month/day/year)*

Section 3. Updating and Reverification. To be completed and signed by employer.

A. New Name *(if applicable)*	B. Date of rehire *(month/day/year)* *(if applicable)*

C. If employee's previous grant of work authorization has expired, provide the information below for the document that establishes current employment eligibility.

Document Title:_____   Document #:_____   Expiration Date (if any): ___/___/___

I attest, under penalty of perjury, that to the best of my knowledge, this employee is eligible to work in the United States, and if the employee presented document(s), the document(s) I have examined appear to be genuine and to relate to the individual.

Signature of Employer or Authorized Representative	Date *(month/day/year)*

Form I-9 (Rev. 11-21-91)N Page 2

EXERCISE 2.4

Form W-4 (2003)

Purpose. Complete Form W-4 so that your employer can withhold the correct Federal income tax from your pay. Because your tax situation may change, you may want to refigure your withholding each year.

Exemption from withholding. If you are exempt, complete only lines 1, 2, 3, 4, and 7 and sign the form to validate it. Your exemption for 2003 expires February 16, 2004. See **Pub. 505**, Tax Withholding and Estimated Tax.

Note: *You cannot claim exemption from withholding if: (a) your income exceeds $750 and includes more than $250 of unearned income (e.g., interest and dividends) and (b) another person can claim you as a dependent on their tax return.*

Basic instructions. If you are not exempt, complete the **Personal Allowances Worksheet** below. The worksheets on page 2 adjust your withholding allowances based on itemized deductions, certain credits, adjustments to income, or two-earner/two-job situations. Complete all worksheets that apply. **However, you may claim fewer (or zero) allowances.**

Head of household. Generally, you may claim head of household filing status on your tax return only if you are unmarried and pay more than 50% of the costs of keeping up a home for yourself and your dependent(s) or other qualifying individuals. See line **E** below.

Tax credits. You can take projected tax credits into account in figuring your allowable number of withholding allowances. Credits for child or dependent care expenses and the child tax credit may be claimed using the **Personal Allowances Worksheet** below. See **Pub. 919**, How Do I Adjust My Tax Withholding? for information on converting your other credits into withholding allowances.

Nonwage income. If you have a large amount of nonwage income, such as interest or dividends, consider making estimated tax payments using **Form 1040-ES**, Estimated Tax for Individuals. Otherwise, you may owe additional tax.

Two earners/two jobs. If you have a working spouse or more than one job, figure the total number of allowances you are entitled to claim on all jobs using worksheets from only one Form W-4. Your withholding usually will be most accurate when all allowances are claimed on the Form W-4 for the highest paying job and zero allowances are claimed on the others.

Nonresident alien. If you are a nonresident alien, see the **Instructions for Form 8233** before completing this Form W-4.

Check your withholding. After your Form W-4 takes effect, use Pub. 919 to see how the dollar amount you are having withheld compares to your projected total tax for 2003. See Pub. 919, especially if your earnings exceed $125,000 (Single) or $175,000 (Married).

Recent name change? If your name on line 1 differs from that shown on your social security card, call 1-800-772-1213 for a new social security card.

Personal Allowances Worksheet (Keep for your records.)

A Enter "1" for **yourself** if no one else can claim you as a dependent . . . . **A** _____

B Enter "1" if: {
- You are single and have only one job; or
- You are married, have only one job, and your spouse does not work; or
- Your wages from a second job or your spouse's wages (or the total of both) are $1,000 or less. } . . **B** _____

C Enter "1" for your **spouse.** But, you may choose to enter "-0-" if you are married and have either a working spouse or more than one job. (Entering "-0-" may help you avoid having too little tax withheld.) . . . . **C** _____

D Enter number of **dependents** (other than your spouse or yourself) you will claim on your tax return . . . . . . **D** _____

E Enter "1" if you will file as **head of household** on your tax return (see conditions under **Head of household** above) . **E** _____

F Enter "1" if you have at least $1,500 of **child or dependent care expenses** for which you plan to claim a credit . . **F** _____
(**Note:** *Do not include child support payments. See **Pub. 503**, Child and Dependent Care Expenses, for details.*)

G **Child Tax Credit** (including additional child tax credit):
- If your total income will be between $15,000 and $42,000 ($20,000 and $65,000 if married), enter "1" for each eligible child plus **1 additional** if you have three to five eligible children or **2 additional** if you have six or more eligible children.
- If your total income will be between $42,000 and $80,000 ($65,000 and $115,000 if married), enter "1" if you have one or two eligible children, "2" if you have three eligible children, "3" if you have four eligible children, or "4" if you have five or more eligible children. **G** _____

H Add lines A through G and enter total here. Note: *This may be different from the number of exemptions you claim on your tax return.* ▶ **H** _____

For accuracy, complete all worksheets that apply. {
- If you plan to **itemize or claim adjustments to income** and want to reduce your withholding, see the **Deductions and Adjustments Worksheet** on page 2.
- If you have **more than one job** or are **married and you and your spouse both work** and the combined earnings from all jobs exceed $35,000, see the **Two-Earner/Two-Job Worksheet** on page 2 to avoid having too little tax withheld.
- If **neither** of the above situations applies, **stop here** and enter the number from line H on line 5 of Form W-4 below.
}

- - - - - - - - - - - - - - - - - Cut here and give Form W-4 to your employer. Keep the top part for your records. - - - - - - - - - - - - - - - -

Form **W-4**
Department of the Treasury
Internal Revenue Service

Employee's Withholding Allowance Certificate

▶ **For Privacy Act and Paperwork Reduction Act Notice, see page 2.**

OMB No. 1545-0010

2003

1 Type or print your first name and middle initial	Last name	**2** Your social security number

Home address (number and street or rural route)	**3** ☐ Single ☐ Married ☐ Married, but withhold at higher Single rate.
	Note: *If married, but legally separated, or spouse is a nonresident alien, check the "Single" box.*

City or town, state, and ZIP code	**4** If your last name differs from that shown on your social security card, check here. You must call 1-800-772-1213 for a new card. ▶ ☐

5 Total number of allowances you are claiming (from line **H** above **or** from the applicable worksheet on page 2) **5** |_____

6 Additional amount, if any, you want withheld from each paycheck . . . . **6** $ |_____

7 I claim exemption from withholding for 2003, and I certify that I meet **both** of the following conditions for exemption:
- Last year I had a right to a refund of **all** Federal income tax withheld because I had **no** tax liability **and**
- This year I expect a refund of **all** Federal income tax withheld because I expect to have **no** tax liability.

If you meet both conditions, write "Exempt" here . . . . ▶ **7** |_____

Under penalties of perjury, I certify that I am entitled to the number of withholding allowances claimed on this certificate, or I am entitled to claim exempt status.

Employee's signature
(Form is not valid unless you sign it.) ▶ _____ Date ▶ _____

8 Employer's name and address (Employer: Complete lines 8 and 10 only if sending to the IRS.)	**9** Office code (optional)	**10** Employer identification number

Cat. No. 10220Q

EXERCISE 2.4 *(continued)*

Form W-4 (2003)   Page **2**

Deductions and Adjustments Worksheet

Note: *Use this worksheet **only** if you plan to itemize deductions, claim certain credits, or claim adjustments to income on your 2003 tax return.*

1 Enter an estimate of your 2003 itemized deductions. These include qualifying home mortgage interest, charitable contributions, state and local taxes, medical expenses in excess of 7.5% of your income, and miscellaneous deductions. (For 2003, you may have to reduce your itemized deductions if your income is over $139,500 ($69,750 if married filing separately). See **Worksheet 3** in Pub. 919 for details.) . . . **1** $ _____

2 Enter: { $7,950 if married filing jointly or qualifying widow(er) / $7,000 if head of household / $4,750 if single / $3,975 if married filing separately } . . . . **2** $ _____

3 **Subtract** line 2 from line 1. If line 2 is greater than line 1, enter "-0-" . . . . **3** $ _____

4 Enter an estimate of your 2003 adjustments to income, including alimony, deductible IRA contributions, and student loan interest **4** $ _____

5 **Add** lines 3 and 4 and enter the total. Include any amount for credits from **Worksheet 7** in Pub. 919 . **5** $ _____

6 Enter an estimate of your 2003 nonwage income (such as dividends or interest) . . . . **6** $ _____

7 **Subtract** line 6 from line 5. Enter the result, but not less than "-0-" . . . . **7** $ _____

8 **Divide** the amount on line 7 by $3,000 and enter the result here. Drop any fraction . . . . **8** _____

9 Enter the number from the **Personal Allowances Worksheet**, line H, page 1 . . . . **9** _____

10 **Add** lines 8 and 9 and enter the total here. If you plan to use the **Two-Earner/Two-Job Worksheet**, also enter this total on line 1 below. Otherwise, **stop here** and enter this total on Form W-4, line 5, page 1 . **10** _____

Two-Earner/Two-Job Worksheet

Note: *Use this worksheet **only** if the instructions under line H on page 1 direct you here.*

1 Enter the number from line H, page 1 (or from line 10 above if you used the **Deductions and Adjustments Worksheet**) **1** _____

2 Find the number in **Table 1** below that applies to the **lowest** paying job and enter it here . . . . . **2** _____

3 If line 1 is **more than or equal to** line 2, subtract line 2 from line 1. Enter the result here (if zero, enter "-0-") and on Form W-4, line 5, page 1. **Do not** use the rest of this worksheet . . . . **3** _____

Note: *If line 1 is **less than** line 2, enter "-0-" on Form W-4, line 5, page 1. Complete lines 4–9 below to calculate the additional withholding amount necessary to avoid a year-end tax bill.*

4 Enter the number from line 2 of this worksheet . . . . **4** _____

5 Enter the number from line 1 of this worksheet . . . . **5** _____

6 **Subtract** line 5 from line 4 . . . . **6** _____

7 Find the amount in **Table 2** below that applies to the **highest** paying job and enter it here . . . . . **7** $ _____

8 **Multiply** line 7 by line 6 and enter the result here. This is the additional annual withholding needed . . **8** $ _____

9 Divide line 8 by the number of pay periods remaining in 2003. For example, divide by 26 if you are paid every two weeks and you complete this form in December 2002. Enter the result here and on Form W-4, line 6, page 1. This is the additional amount to be withheld from each paycheck . . . . **9** $ _____

Table 1: Two-Earner/Two-Job Worksheet

Married Filing Jointly				All Others			
If wages from **LOWEST** paying job are—	Enter on line 2 above	If wages from **LOWEST** paying job are—	Enter on line 2 above	If wages from **LOWEST** paying job are—	Enter on line 2 above	If wages from **LOWEST** paying job are—	Enter on line 2 above
$0 - $4,000	0	44,001 - 50,000	8	$0 - $6,000	0	75,001 - 100,000	8
4,001 - 9,000	1	50,001 - 60,000	9	6,001 - 11,000	1	100,001 - 110,000	9
9,001 - 15,000	2	60,001 - 70,000	10	11,001 - 18,000	2	110,001 and over	10
15,001 - 20,000	3	70,001 - 90,000	11	18,001 - 25,000	3		
20,001 - 25,000	4	90,001 - 100,000	12	25,001 - 29,000	4		
25,001 - 33,000	5	100,001 - 115,000	13	29,001 - 40,000	5		
33,001 - 38,000	6	115,001 - 125,000	14	40,001 - 55,000	6		
38,001 - 44,000	7	125,001 and over	15	55,001 - 75,000	7		

Table 2: Two-Earner/Two-Job Worksheet

Married Filing Jointly		All Others	
If wages from **HIGHEST** paying job are—	Enter on line 7 above	If wages from **HIGHEST** paying job are—	Enter on line 7 above
$0 - $50,000	$450	$0 - $30,000	$450
50,001 - 100,000	800	30,001 - 70,000	800
100,001 - 150,000	900	70,001 - 140,000	900
150,001 - 270,000	1,050	140,001 - 300,000	1,050
270,001 and over	1,200	300,001 and over	1,200

EXERCISE 2.5

EMPLOYEE EARNINGS RECORD FOR YEAR 20 _____

Name _____

Address _____

_____

Social Security No. _____

Job Title _____

Date Employed _____

Date Terminated _____

Marital Status   M ☐   S ☐

No. of Withholding Allowances _____

Regular Rate _____

_____

Voluntary Deductions:

IRA _____

U.S. Savings Bonds _____

| PAYROLL PERIOD | | HOURS | | EARNINGS | | | DEDUCTIONS | | | | | | | | NET PAY | YEAR-TO-DATE EARNINGS |
Week	Ending Date	Reg.	O.T.	Regular	Overtime or Commission	Total Earnings	Federal Income Tax	Social Security Tax	Medicare Tax	State Income Tax	SDI Tax	IRA	Savings Bonds	Total deductions		
1st Quarter																
1																
2																
3																
4																
5																
6																
7																
8																
9																
10																
11																
12																
13																
14																
1st Quarter Totals																

EXERCISE 2.6

Some people have the mistaken idea that only business managers need to solve problems and make decisions. However, problem solving and decision making are a part of almost every worker's job. For example, consider the cases that follow. In both cases, a payroll clerk was faced with a difficult situation. Write a brief explanation of how you would handle each situation.

1. Teri Allison works in the payroll department of ABC Electronics, a large manufacturing company. Her best friend, Kim Shaw, works in the marketing department. One day, Kim told Teri that she was due to receive a salary increase in about two months but that her supervisor had not told her the amount. Kim was eager to have this information, and she asked her friend to tip her off as soon as the payroll department was notified about the increase. Kim said that there was nothing wrong with this because she was asking for information about her own salary, not the salary of someone else.

_____

_____

_____

_____

_____

_____

_____

_____

_____

_____

_____
_____
_____
_____
_____

2. Jeff Morgan is in the habit of leaving payroll records open on his desk when he goes to lunch or visits the file room down the hall. Several times recently, when he returned to his office, he thought he saw a fellow employee looking over the records on his desk. However, he could not be sure because this employee always had a reasonable excuse for being near Jeff's desk.

_____
_____
_____
_____
_____
_____
_____
_____
_____
_____
_____
_____
_____
_____
_____
_____

Alternate Learning Through Practice Exercises

Unit 2 Exercises

EXERCISE 2.1A

Becoming familiar with job application forms is important for both business and personal reasons. If you work in payroll or human resources in your business career, you may be handling such forms. If you become a supervisor or manager in any area of business operations, you will probably be using the information recorded on job application forms to evaluate potential new employees. Of course, whenever you are looking for a job, it is likely that you will be asked to fill out an application form. To gain experience with this type of form, complete the one on pages 46 and 47.

Assume that you are the office assistant at Ingram Heating and Cooling. Robert Lesko, an old friend who recently graduated from a technical college, wants to apply for a job at Ingram. He asks for your help in preparing the job application form. The information that you will need is provided below.

1. In preparing the job application form, follow directions carefully, write clearly, and spell words correctly. Look over all directions before you start to write.

2. Assume that Robert Lesko has signed the job application form and dated it June 24, 2004. (Of course, in actual practice, job seekers must prepare and sign their own application forms.)

Information About the Job Applicant
- His full name is Robert Allen Lesko. His social security number is 442-69-5149. His address is 779 Davis Avenue, San Jose, CA 95163. His telephone number is (408)237-4851.
- He is applying for the job of installer's helper and is available immediately. He is willing to travel or relocate.
- He is a U.S. citizen and has not been convicted of a crime.
- He saw an advertisement for the job on a Web site called www.techjobs.com.
- He served in the U.S. Army from July 1998 to July 2002. His final rank was Corporal, and he was a member of a transportation unit that serviced trucks and other army vehicles.
- He attended Emerson High School in San Jose from 1994 to 1998. He followed the regular course of study and received a Regents Diploma in June 1998. From 2002 to 2004, he attended Lawson Technical College in San Jose. He received an Associate's Degree in June 2004. His major was Heating and Air Conditioning Technology.
- From January 6, 2004 to May 8, 2004, he worked at Apex Heating and Cooling as a part-time installer's helper. This job paid $9 an hour and was an internship arranged by the college. His supervisor was Dennis O'Hara, the manager. This firm is located at 817 Evans Street in San Jose. Its telephone number is (408) 642-3311.
- From September 10, 1996 through April 30, 1998, he worked at Bay Auto Repair and Tires on a part-time basis after school and during summers. He installed new tires and repaired dents and scratches. The job paid $6.75 an hour. His supervisor was John Tonelli, the manager. This firm is located at 1869 Pine Avenue in San Jose. Its telephone number is (408) 527-6973.

EXERCISE 2.2A

Even though you may have a social security number already, you should become familiar with the form used to apply for such a number (Form SS-5) because people who work in the area of payroll or human resources are sometimes asked by new employees for help in filling out this form. To gain experience with Form SS-5, complete the one on page 48. Use the following information.

- The applicant's name is Lisa Marie Watkins. She lives at 2709 Mission Road, San Bruno, CA 94096.
- She is a U.S. citizen, who was born on April 11, 1986, in San Jose, California.
- Her mother's maiden name was Deborah Ann McNally (social security number is 416-09-2738). Her father's name is Thomas Henry Watkins (social security number is 249-15-7622).

Exercise continues on page 49.

EXERCISE 2.1A

Ingram Heating and Cooling
4466 Maritime Way • San Jose, Calif. 95001

Please Read Before Signing Application

Ingram Heating and Cooling is an equal opportunity employer. All applicants and employees are considered for employment, development, advancement, and earnings based upon their skills, performance, and potential without regard to race, color, religion, sex, national origin, age, or handicap status.

I understand that the information I provide in this application must be complete and accurate to the best of my knowledge. I realize that falsification and/or incomplete information may jeopardize my employment now or in the future. Ingram Heating and Cooling or its agents may seek to verify this information and may make inquiries by securing a consumer investigative report concerning my character, criminal convictions, employment experience, education, and community standing. I further understand that if this information results in my dismissal, the nature and scope of these reports may be secured directly from the supplier of such information. I hereby authorize any previous employer to release to Ingram Heating and Cooling relevant information such as my work habits, performance, attendance, and reason for leaving.

I agree to conform to the rules and regulations of Ingram Heating and Cooling and understand that my employment can be terminated, with or without cause, and with or without notice, at any time, at the option of either Ingram Heating and Cooling or myself. I further understand that no manager, supervisor, or other representative of Ingram Heating and Cooling has any authority to enter into any agreement contrary to the foregoing.

Signature _____   Date _____

Personal Data

Name	Social Security Number	Home Phone
Address		

Position Desired	Date Available	Willing to travel? ☐ Yes ☐ No	Relocate? ☐ Yes ☐ No

Are you a U.S. Citizen? ☐ Yes ☐ No	If No, Visa Type and Number
Have you been convicted of a crime? ☐ Yes ☐ No	If Yes, Please Detail–Offense and Disposition

Source

How were you referred? ☐ Classified Ad   ☐ Employment Agency   ☐ Other Source or Person
Please Identify–Name of Newspaper, Employment Agency, or Other Source or Person

EXERCISE 2.1A *(continued)*

U.S. Military Service

Branch	Final Rank	Date Entered	Date Discharged

Service schools or special experience related to job for which you are applying?

Education

School Name	City, State	Dates From–To	Major Course of Study	Graduation Month/Year	Degree or Certificate
High School					
College(s)					
Graduate					
Other					

Employment

Please list all employers beginning with your present employer

Firm Name	Address		Phone	Dates–From–To
Position Held	Earnings–Beginning	Ending	Supervisor–Name and Title	
Reason for leaving				
Firm Name	Address		Phone	Dates–From–To
Position Held	Earnings–Beginning	Ending	Supervisor–Name and Title	
Reason for leaving				
Firm Name	Address		Phone	Dates–From–To
Position Held	Earnings–Beginning	Ending	Supervisor–Name and Title	
Reason for leaving				
Firm Name	Address		Phone	Dates–From–To
Position Held	Earnings–Beginning	Ending	Supervisor–Name and Title	
Reason for leaving				

Additional Experience

Please list any additional experiences you feel bear upon your skills or professional development.

SOCIAL SECURITY ADMINISTRATION
Application for a Social Security Card

Form Approved
OMB No. 0960-0066

	NAME ⟶ TO BE SHOWN ON CARD	First	Full Middle Name	Last
1	FULL NAME AT BIRTH IF OTHER THAN ABOVE	First	Full Middle Name	Last
	OTHER NAMES USED			

2 MAILING ADDRESS ⟶ Do Not Abbreviate

Street Address, Apt. No., PO Box, Rural Route No.

City	State	Zip Code

3 CITIZENSHIP ⟶ (Check One)

☐ U.S. Citizen   ☐ Legal Alien Allowed To Work   ☐ Legal Alien **Not** Allowed To Work (See Instructions On Page 1)   ☐ Other (See Instructions On Page 1)

4 SEX ⟶   ☐ Male   ☐ Female

5 RACE/ETHNIC DESCRIPTION (Check One Only - Voluntary)

☐ Asian, Asian-American or Pacific Islander   ☐ Hispanic   ☐ Black (Not Hispanic)   ☐ North American Indian or Alaskan Native   ☐ White (Not Hispanic)

6 DATE OF BIRTH _____ Month, Day, Year

7 PLACE OF BIRTH (Do Not Abbreviate) _____ City   State or Foreign Country   FCI

Office Use Only

8
A. MOTHER'S MAIDEN NAME ⟶ First   Full Middle Name   Last Name At Her Birth

B. MOTHER'S SOCIAL SECURITY NUMBER ⟶ ☐☐☐—☐☐—☐☐☐☐

9
A. FATHER'S NAME ⟶ First   Full Middle Name   Last

B. FATHER'S SOCIAL SECURITY NUMBER ⟶ ☐☐☐—☐☐—☐☐☐☐

10 Has the applicant or anyone acting on his/her behalf ever filed for or received a Social Security number card before?

☐ Yes (If "yes", answer questions 11-13.)   ☐ No (If "no", go on to question 14.)   ☐ Don't Know (If "don't know", go on to question 14.)

11 Enter the Social Security number previously assigned to the person listed in item 1. ⟶ ☐☐☐—☐☐—☐☐☐☐

12 Enter the name shown on the most recent Social Security card issued for the person listed in item 1. ⟶ First   Middle Name   Last

13 Enter any different date of birth if used on an earlier application for a card. ⟶ _____ Month, Day, Year

14 TODAY'S DATE _____ Month, Day, Year

15 DAYTIME PHONE NUMBER ( ) _____ Area Code   Number

I declare under penalty of perjury that I have examined all the information on this form, and on any accompanying statements or forms, and it is true and correct to the best of my knowledge.

16 YOUR SIGNATURE ▶

17 YOUR RELATIONSHIP TO THE PERSON IN ITEM 1 IS:
☐ Self   ☐ Natural Or Adoptive Parent   ☐ Legal Guardian   ☐ Other (Specify)

DO NOT WRITE BELOW THIS LINE (FOR SSA USE ONLY)						
NPN		DOC	NTI	CAN		ITV
PBC	EVI	EVA	EVC	PRA	NWR	DNR	UNIT

EVIDENCE SUBMITTED

SIGNATURE AND TITLE OF EMPLOYEE(S) REVIEWING EVIDENCE AND/OR CONDUCTING INTERVIEW

_____ DATE _____

DCL _____ DATE _____

- She has never had a social security number.
- Enter June 6, 2004, as today's date and (408) 317-4296 as the daytime phone number.
- Assume that Lisa Watkins has signed the form and checked "Self" as the preparer of the form.

EXERCISE 2.3A

As an applicant to Ingram Heating and Cooling, Robert Lesko will be required to fill in Section 1 of Form I-9, Employment Eligibility Verification. Prepare this section of the form on page 50 for Lesko. Use information from Exercise 2.1A. Lesko's date of birth is March 7, 1980. Assume that Lesko has signed Section 1 and dated it August 1, 2004. (Of course, in actual practice, only the job applicant can legally sign this form.)

EXERCISE 2.4A

If you work in the area of payroll or human resources, you will be dealing with the Employee's Withholding Allowance Certificate (Form W-4) whenever a new employee joins the firm or a current employee must make a change in his or her withholding allowances. Of course, you will fill out this form yourself whenever you start working for a new employer. To gain experience with Form W-4, complete the one on pages 51 and 52 for Robert Lesko.

Obtain Lesko's address and social security number from Exercise 2.1A. He is married, and his wife works at a full-time job. Therefore, he plans to claim one withholding allowance for himself. Assume that Lesko has signed Form W-4 and dated it August 1, 2004.

EXERCISE 2.5A

Assume that Robert Lesko has been hired by Ingram Heating and Cooling as an installer's helper. This is the job he applied for in Exercise 2.1A. Set up an employee earnings record for him. Use the form given on page 53.

Obtain Lesko's address and social security number from Exercise 2.1A. His date of employment is August 1, 2004. His marital status and number of withholding allowances are shown on the Form W-4 prepared in Exercise 2.4A. His regular rate of pay is $15 an hour. He has signed up for a deduction of $30 a week for savings bonds.

EXERCISE 2.6A

Some people have the mistaken idea that only business managers need to solve problems and make decisions. However, problem solving and decision making are a part of almost every worker's job. For example, consider the cases that follow. In both cases, a payroll employee was faced with a difficult decision. Write a brief explanation of how you would handle each situation. Case #2 can be found on page 53.

1. Ryan Beck is a payroll clerk at the Walden Furniture Company. Today, an old friend of his, Gary Phillips, joined the firm. Gary came to the payroll department to prepare and sign the Employee's Withholding Allowance Certificate (Form W-4). When Ryan looked at the form, he saw that Gary was claiming more withholding allowances than he is entitled to claim.

_____

_____

_____

_____

_____

_____

_____

_____

_____

_____

_____

_____

_____

_____

_____

_____

EXERCISE 2.3A

U.S. Department of Justice
Immigration and Naturalization Service

OMB No. 1115-0136

Employment Eligibility Verification

Please read instructions carefully before completing this form. The instructions must be available during completion of this form. **ANTI-DISCRIMINATION NOTICE:** It is illegal to discriminate against work eligible individuals. Employers CANNOT specify which document(s) they will accept from an employee. The refusal to hire an individual because of a future expiration date may also constitute illegal discrimination.

Section 1. Employee Information and Verification. To be completed and signed by employee at the time employment begins.

Print Name: Last	First	Middle Initial	Maiden Name
Address *(Street Name and Number)*		Apt. #	Date of Birth *(month/day/year)*
City	State	Zip Code	Social Security #

I am aware that federal law provides for imprisonment and/or fines for false statements or use of false documents in connection with the completion of this form.

I attest, under penalty of perjury, that I am (check one of the following):
☐ A citizen or national of the United States
☐ A Lawful Permanent Resident (Alien # A_____)
☐ An alien authorized to work until ___/___/___
(Alien # or Admission #) _____

Employee's Signature	Date *(month/day/year)*

Preparer and/or Translator Certification.   *(To be completed and signed if Section 1 is prepared by a person other than the employee.) I attest, under penalty of perjury, that I have assisted in the completion of this form and that to the best of my knowledge the information is true and correct.*

Preparer's/Translator's Signature	Print Name
Address *(Street Name and Number, City, State, Zip Code)*	Date *(month/day/year)*

Section 2. Employer Review and Verification. To be completed and signed by employer. Examine one document from List A OR examine one document from List B and one from List C, as listed on the reverse of this form, and record the title, number and expiration date, if any, of the document(s)

List A	OR	List B	AND	List C
Document title: _____		_____		_____
Issuing authority: _____		_____		_____
Document #: _____		_____		_____
Expiration Date *(if any):* ___/___/___		___/___/___		___/___/___
Document #: _____				
Expiration Date *(if any):* ___/___/___				

CERTIFICATION - I attest, under penalty of perjury, that I have examined the document(s) presented by the above-named employee, that the above-listed document(s) appear to be genuine and to relate to the employee named, that the employee began employment on *(month/day/year)* ___/___/___ **and that to the best of my knowledge the employee is eligible to work in the United States. (State employment agencies may omit the date the employee began employment.)**

Signature of Employer or Authorized Representative	Print Name	Title
Business or Organization Name	Address *(Street Name and Number, City, State, Zip Code)*	Date *(month/day/year)*

Section 3. Updating and Reverification. To be completed and signed by employer.

A. New Name *(if applicable)*	B. Date of rehire *(month/day/year) (if applicable)*

C. If employee's previous grant of work authorization has expired, provide the information below for the document that establishes current employment eligibility.

Document Title:_____   Document #: _____   Expiration Date (if any): ___/___/___

I attest, under penalty of perjury, that to the best of my knowledge, this employee is eligible to work in the United States, and if the employee presented document(s), the document(s) I have examined appear to be genuine and to relate to the individual.

Signature of Employer or Authorized Representative	Date *(month/day/year)*

EXERCISE 2.4A

Form W-4 (2003)

Purpose. Complete Form W-4 so that your employer can withhold the correct Federal income tax from your pay. Because your tax situation may change, you may want to refigure your withholding each year.

Exemption from withholding. If you are exempt, complete only lines 1, 2, 3, 4, and 7 and sign the form to validate it. Your exemption for 2003 expires February 16, 2004. See **Pub. 505,** Tax Withholding and Estimated Tax.

Note: *You cannot claim exemption from withholding if: (a) your income exceeds $750 and includes more than $250 of unearned income (e.g., interest and dividends) and (b) another person can claim you as a dependent on their tax return.*

Basic instructions. If you are not exempt, complete the **Personal Allowances Worksheet** below. The worksheets on page 2 adjust your withholding allowances based on itemized deductions, certain credits, adjustments to income, or two-earner/two-job situations. Complete all worksheets that apply. **However, you may claim fewer (or zero) allowances.**

Head of household. Generally, you may claim head of household filing status on your tax return only if you are unmarried and pay more than 50% of the costs of keeping up a home for yourself and your dependent(s) or other qualifying individuals. See line **E** below.

Tax credits. You can take projected tax credits into account in figuring your allowable number of withholding allowances. Credits for child or dependent care expenses and the child tax credit may be claimed using the **Personal Allowances Worksheet** below. See **Pub. 919,** How Do I Adjust My Tax Withholding? for information on converting your other credits into withholding allowances.

Nonwage income. If you have a large amount of nonwage income, such as interest or dividends, consider making estimated tax payments using Form 1040-ES, Estimated Tax for Individuals. Otherwise, you may owe additional tax.

Two earners/two jobs. If you have a working spouse or more than one job, figure the total number of allowances you are entitled to claim on all jobs using worksheets from only one Form W-4. Your withholding usually will be most accurate when all allowances are claimed on the Form W-4 for the highest paying job and zero allowances are claimed on the others.

Nonresident alien. If you are a nonresident alien, see the **Instructions for Form 8233** before completing this Form W-4.

Check your withholding. After your Form W 4 takes effect, use Pub. 919 to see how the dollar amount you are having withheld compares to your projected total tax for 2003. See Pub. 919, especially if your earnings exceed $125,000 (Single) or $175,000 (Married).

Recent name change? If your name on line 1 differs from that shown on your social security card, call 1-800-772-1213 for a new social security card.

Personal Allowances Worksheet (Keep for your records.)

A Enter "1" for **yourself** if no one else can claim you as a dependent . . . . **A** _____

B Enter "1" if:
- You are single and have only one job; or
- You are married, have only one job, and your spouse does not work; or
- Your wages from a second job or your spouse's wages (or the total of both) are $1,000 or less.

. . **B** _____

C Enter "1" for your **spouse.** But, you may choose to enter "-0-" if you are married and have either a working spouse or more than one job. (Entering "-0-" may help you avoid having too little tax withheld.) . . . . **C** _____

D Enter number of **dependents** (other than your spouse or yourself) you will claim on your tax return . . . . . . **D** _____

E Enter "1" if you will file as **head of household** on your tax return (see conditions under **Head of household** above) . **E** _____

F Enter "1" if you have at least $1,500 of **child or dependent care expenses** for which you plan to claim a credit . . **F** _____

    (**Note:** *Do not include child support payments. See Pub. 503, Child and Dependent Care Expenses, for details.*)

G **Child Tax Credit** (including additional child tax credit):
- If your total income will be between $15,000 and $42,000 ($20,000 and $65,000 if married), enter "1" for each eligible child plus **1 additional** if you have three to five eligible children or **2 additional** if you have six or more eligible children.
- If your total income will be between $42,000 and $80,000 ($65,000 and $115,000 if married), enter "1" if you have one or two eligible children, "2" if you have three eligible children, "3" if you have four eligible children, or "4" if you have five or more eligible children. . **G** _____

H Add lines A through G and enter total here. **Note:** *This may be different from the number of exemptions you claim on your tax return.* ▶ **H** _____

For accuracy, complete all worksheets that apply.
- If you plan to **itemize or claim adjustments to income** and want to reduce your withholding, see the **Deductions and Adjustments Worksheet** on page 2.
- If you have **more than one job** or are **married and you and your spouse both work** and the combined earnings from all jobs exceed $35,000, see the **Two-Earner/Two-Job Worksheet** on page 2 to avoid having too little tax withheld.
- If **neither** of the above situations applies, **stop here** and enter the number from line H on line 5 of Form W-4 below.

- - - - - - - - - - - - - - - Cut here and give Form W-4 to your employer. Keep the top part for your records. - - - - - - - - - - - - - - -

Form **W-4** Department of the Treasury Internal Revenue Service	**Employee's Withholding Allowance Certificate** ▶ **For Privacy Act and Paperwork Reduction Act Notice, see page 2.**	OMB No. 1545-0010 2003

1 Type or print your first name and middle initial	Last name	**2** Your social security number

Home address (number and street or rural route)	**3** ☐ Single ☐ Married ☐ Married, but withhold at higher Single rate. **Note:** *If married, but legally separated, or spouse is a nonresident alien, check the "Single" box.*

City or town, state, and ZIP code	**4** If your last name differs from that shown on your social security card, check here. You must call 1-800-772-1213 for a new card. ▶ ☐

5 Total number of allowances you are claiming (from line **H** above **or** from the applicable worksheet on page 2) . . . **5** _____

6 Additional amount, if any, you want withheld from each paycheck . . . . **6** $ _____

7 I claim exemption from withholding for 2003, and I certify that I meet **both** of the following conditions for exemption:
- Last year I had a right to a refund of **all** Federal income tax withheld because I had **no** tax liability **and**
- This year I expect a refund of **all** Federal income tax withheld because I expect to have **no** tax liability.

If you meet both conditions, write "Exempt" here . . . . ▶ | **7** |

Under penalties of perjury, I certify that I am entitled to the number of withholding allowances claimed on this certificate, or I am entitled to claim exempt status.

Employee's signature
(Form is not valid
unless you sign it.) ▶ _____   Date ▶ _____

8 Employer's name and address (Employer: Complete lines 8 and 10 only if sending to the IRS.)	**9** Office code (optional)	**10** Employer identification number

Cat. No. 10220Q

EXERCISE 2.4A *(continued)*

Form W-4 (2003)   Page **2**

Deductions and Adjustments Worksheet

Note: *Use this worksheet **only** if you plan to itemize deductions, claim certain credits, or claim adjustments to income on your 2003 tax return.*

1 Enter an estimate of your 2003 itemized deductions. These include qualifying home mortgage interest, charitable contributions, state and local taxes, medical expenses in excess of 7.5% of your income, and miscellaneous deductions. (For 2003, you may have to reduce your itemized deductions if your income is over $139,500 ($69,750 if married filing separately). See **Worksheet 3** in Pub. 919 for details.) . . .   **1** $ _____

2 Enter: { $7,950 if married filing jointly or qualifying widow(er) / $7,000 if head of household / $4,750 if single / $3,975 if married filing separately } . . . .   **2** $ _____

3 **Subtract** line 2 from line 1. If line 2 is greater than line 1, enter "-0-" . . . .   **3** $ _____

4 Enter an estimate of your 2003 adjustments to income, including alimony, deductible IRA contributions, and student loan interest   **4** $ _____

5 **Add** lines 3 and 4 and enter the total. Include any amount for credits from **Worksheet 7** in Pub. 919   **5** $ _____

6 Enter an estimate of your 2003 nonwage income (such as dividends or interest) . . . .   **6** $ _____

7 **Subtract** line 6 from line 5. Enter the result, but not less than "-0-" . . . .   **7** $ _____

8 **Divide** the amount on line 7 by $3,000 and enter the result here. Drop any fraction . . . .   **8** _____

9 Enter the number from the **Personal Allowances Worksheet,** line H, page 1 . . . .   **9** _____

10 **Add** lines 8 and 9 and enter the total here. If you plan to use the **Two-Earner/Two-Job Worksheet,** also enter this total on line 1 below. Otherwise, **stop here** and enter this total on Form W-4, line 5, page 1 . **10** _____

Two-Earner/Two-Job Worksheet

Note: *Use this worksheet **only** if the instructions under line H on page 1 direct you here.*

1 Enter the number from line H, page 1 (or from line 10 above if you used the **Deductions and Adjustments Worksheet**)   **1** _____

2 Find the number in **Table 1** below that applies to the **lowest** paying job and enter it here . . . . .   **2** _____

3 If line 1 Is **more than or equal to** line 2, subtract line 2 from line 1. Enter the result here (if zero, enter "-0-") and on Form W-4, line 5, page 1. **Do not** use the rest of this worksheet . . . .   **3** _____

Note: *If line 1 is **less than** line 2, enter "-0-" on Form W-4, line 5, page 1. Complete lines 4–9 below to calculate the additional withholding amount necessary to avoid a year-end tax bill.*

4 Enter the number from line 2 of this worksheet . . . .   **4** _____

5 Enter the number from line 1 of this worksheet . . . .   **5** _____

6 **Subtract** line 5 from line 4 . . . .   **6** _____

7 Find the amount in **Table 2** below that applies to the **highest** paying job and enter it here . . . . .   **7** $ _____

8 **Multiply** line 7 by line 6 and enter the result here. This is the additional annual withholding needed . .   **8** $ _____

9 Divide line 8 by the number of pay periods remaining in 2003. For example, divide by 26 if you are paid every two weeks and you complete this form in December 2002. Enter the result here and on Form W-4, line 6, page 1. This is the additional amount to be withheld from each paycheck . . . .   **9** $ _____

Table 1: Two-Earner/Two-Job Worksheet

Married Filing Jointly				All Others			
If wages from **LOWEST** paying job are—	Enter on line 2 above	If wages from **LOWEST** paying job are—	Enter on line 2 above	If wages from **LOWEST** paying job are—	Enter on line 2 above	If wages from **LOWEST** paying job are—	Enter on line 2 above
$0 - $4,000	0	44,001 - 50,000	8	$0 - $6,000	0	75,001 - 100,000	8
4,001 - 9,000	1	50,001 - 60,000	9	6,001 - 11,000	1	100,001 - 110,000	9
9,001 - 15,000	2	60,001 - 70,000	10	11,001 - 18,000	2	110,001 and over	10
15,001 - 20,000	3	70,001 - 90,000	11	18,001 - 25,000	3		
20,001 - 25,000	4	90,001 - 100,000	12	25,001 - 29,000	4		
25,001 - 33,000	5	100,001 - 115,000	13	29,001 - 40,000	5		
33,001 - 38,000	6	115,001 - 125,000	14	40,001 - 55,000	6		
38,001 - 44,000	7	125,001 and over	15	55,001 - 75,000	7		

Table 2: Two-Earner/Two-Job Worksheet

Married Filing Jointly		All Others	
If wages from **HIGHEST** paying job are—	Enter on line 7 above	If wages from **HIGHEST** paying job are—	Enter on line 7 above
$0 - $50,000	$450	$0 - $30,000	$450
50,001 - 100,000	800	30,001 - 70,000	800
100,001 - 150,000	900	70,001 - 140,000	900
150,001 - 270,000	1,050	140,001 - 300,000	1,050
270,001 and over	1,200	300,001 and over	1,200

EXERCISE 2.5A

EMPLOYEE EARNINGS RECORD FOR YEAR 20 ____

Name _____

Address _____

_____

Social Security No. _____

Job Title _____

Date Employed _____

Date Terminated _____

Marital Status   M ☐   S ☐

No. of Withholding Allowances _____

Regular Rate _____

_____

Voluntary Deductions:

IRA _____

U.S. Savings Bonds _____

PAYROLL PERIOD		HOURS		EARNINGS			DEDUCTIONS								NET PAY	YEAR-TO-DATE EARNINGS
Week	Ending Date	Reg.	O.T.	Regular	Overtime or Commission	Total Earnings	Federal Income Tax	Social Security Tax	Medicare Tax	State Income Tax	SDI Tax	IRA	Savings Bonds	Total deductions		
1st Quarter																
1																
2																
3																
4																
5																
6																
7																
8																
9																
10																
11																
12																
13																
14																
1st Quarter Totals																

(Continued from Exercise 2.6A on page 49.)

2. Brenda Hall is a payroll supervisor at K & M Department Stores. Recently, several women who are merchandise managers asked her for a list of the salaries of all merchandise managers at the firm. These women believe that they are being paid much less than men who hold the same job. They would like to file a class-action lawsuit against the firm.

_____

_____

_____

Unit **Three**

Time and Work Records

Objectives

Upon completion of this unit, you should be able to:

1. Define and explain the common payroll periods: weekly, biweekly, semimonthly, and monthly.
2. Explain why time records are kept by businesses.
3. Explain the use and value of time cards and time clocks.
4. Explain how time sheets are used in recording hours worked.
5. Explain, in general terms, how electronic time-recording systems work.
6. Explain how the quarter-hour system works.
7. Explain what flextime is and how it is used.
8. Explain, in general terms, the advantages workers have when they work full-time at home.
9. Name the federal law that requires businesses to keep, for three years, records of dates of work, rates of pay, and earnings of all employees.
10. Explain the piece-work system used by some firms to pay their employees.
11. Explain how the commission basis is used in paying some employees.
12. Explain how payment of salary plus commission works.
13. Explain what labor distribution is and how it is used.
14. Explain how temporary workers are paid.
15. Explain how contract workers are paid.
16. Explain the difference between temporary and contract workers.
17. Know how Forms 1099 and 1096 are used.

Businesses are required to keep a record of the time worked by their employees. This procedure is necessary to meet the requirements of the Fair Labor Standards Act and to provide the information needed for computing the payroll. Depending on the kinds of jobs that employees hold, it may also be necessary for a business to keep a record of how much work each employee produces.

In this unit, you will learn about time and work records. But before studying these records, you need to become familiar with the different types of payroll periods that businesses use. Time and work records are designed to gather information for each payroll period.

PAYROLL PERIODS

Every business selects a payroll period that serves its needs. Generally, the payroll period is weekly, biweekly, semimonthly, or monthly. These payroll periods are shown in Figure 3.1.

Point of Interest

Where does the money go? While these are only general figures, a family of four, on average, distributes its income as follows: 30 percent on housing; 20 percent on food; 10 to 15 percent on transportation; 10 percent on utilities; 20 percent on clothing, health care, and insurance; and 5 percent on savings. These figures will differ widely across the country. But the point is, besides focusing on *earning* money, we also really need to focus on how we *spend* it.

FIGURE 3.1

Weekly, Biweekly, Semimonthly, and Monthly Payroll Periods

Weekly Payroll Period
Ends once every week on a specific day, such as every Friday.

November						
S	M	T	W	T	F	S
		1	2	3	4	5
6	7	8	9	10	11	12
13	14	15	16	17	18	19
20	21	22	23	24	25	26
27	28	29	30			

December						
S	M	T	W	T	F	S
				1	2	3
4	5	6	7	8	9	10
11	12	13	14	15	16	17
18	19	20	21	22	23	24
25	26	27	28	29	30	31

Biweekly Payroll Period
Ends every other week on a specific day, such as every other Friday.

November						
S	M	T	W	T	F	S
		1	2	3	4	5
6	7	8	9	10	11	12
13	14	15	16	17	18	19
20	21	22	23	24	25	26
27	28	29	30			

December						
S	M	T	W	T	F	S
				1	2	3
4	5	6	7	8	9	10
11	12	13	14	15	16	17
18	19	20	21	22	23	24
25	26	27	28	29	30	31

Semimonthly Payroll Period
Ends twice every month on specific dates, such as the first and the fifteenth.

November						
S	M	T	W	T	F	S
		1	2	3	4	5
6	7	8	9	10	11	12
13	14	15	16	17	18	19
20	21	22	23	24	25	26
27	28	29	30			

December						
S	M	T	W	T	F	S
				1	2	3
4	5	6	7	8	9	10
11	12	13	14	15	16	17
18	19	20	21	22	23	24
25	26	27	28	29	30	31

Monthly Payroll Period
Ends each month on a specific date, such as the last.

November						
S	M	T	W	T	F	S
		1	2	3	4	5
6	7	8	9	10	11	12
13	14	15	16	17	18	19
20	21	22	23	24	25	26
27	28	29	30			

December						
S	M	T	W	T	F	S
				1	2	3
4	5	6	7	8	9	10
11	12	13	14	15	16	17
18	19	20	21	22	23	24
25	26	27	28	29	30	31

Many businesses use different payroll periods for different types of employees. For example, a business may pay its factory workers on a weekly basis and its supervisors and managers on a monthly basis.

Because it takes time to compute employee earnings and prepare payroll records, there is generally an interval between the end of a payroll period and the date when employees are paid. This delay may be only a day or two or as long as a week or more. The difference depends on how quickly payroll data can be gathered and how quickly it can be processed.

The firm shown in Figure 3.2, for example, has a weekly payroll period that ends on Saturday, and it hands out paychecks on the following Wednesday. Thus, for the payroll period ending November 12, the employees will receive their checks on November 16. Similarly, for the payroll period ending November 19, the checks will be given out on November 23. For a larger business with many employees, it may take a week or more to prepare the payroll.

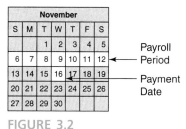

Payroll Period

Payment Date

FIGURE 3.2

Payroll Period and Payment Date

THE NEED FOR TIME RECORDS

If a firm is covered by the Fair Labor Standards Act, time records must be kept for all employees except those who are exempt from the overtime pay requirements of the law. Exempt employees usually hold professional, managerial, or supervisory jobs; however, employees who sell goods or services for a commission are also exempt in some cases. (You will learn more about sales commissions in Unit 4.)

Internet Addresses

Have questions about time and work records? Joining an association in the payroll field will reward you with tips of the trade. There's the American Payroll Association, www.americanpayroll.org. In Canada, www.payroll.ca. For the United Kingdom, www.payrollcheck.co.uk.

According to the Fair Labor Standards Act, time records must show the day and the time when an employee's workweek starts, the number of hours worked each day, and the total hours worked during the week. The various kinds of time records illustrated in this unit meet these requirements.

TIMEKEEPING DEVICES AND SYSTEMS

An accurate and complete set of time records is a necessary part of an efficient payroll system. A business must therefore have an orderly method of recording the hours that each employee works during each payroll period. One concern, as you can imagine, is that the hours worked be recorded accurately and honestly. It is never appropriate for an employee to "sign in" or "sign out" for another employee.

One of the major purposes of time records is to determine employee earnings. The hours worked multiplied by the employee's hourly rate of pay equals the earnings for the period (40 hours for the week × $10.20 hourly rate = $408 gross pay for the week). You can see how essential it is to have an accurate record of the number of hours worked. Several methods are used to keep track of hours worked.

Time Clocks and Time Cards

Time clocks and time cards have been in use for more than 70 years. Many businesses still use them even though there now are superior systems available. A time clock keeps track of the hours worked by each employee. The *time clock,* as shown in Figure 3.3, is a mechanical or electronic device that prints on the card the time at which a card is inserted into the clock.

A time clock and its accompanying racks of time cards are often referred to as a *clock station.* In a large firm, there may be a number of clock stations in different locations within the firm. These clock stations are usually placed near building entrances but as close to employee work areas as possible.

The time-clock/time-card system operates in a very simple manner. At the beginning of each workweek, a *time card,* like the one shown in Figure 3.4, is prepared for each employee. Each card is intended for use by a specific employee, and his or her name and identification number as well as the ending date of the workweek are printed on the card. These time cards are arranged in numbered slots in a rack that is attached to one side of the time clock; usually the side closest to the building entrance. Another rack is attached to the other side of the time clock. When an employee arrives for work each morning, he or she takes the proper time card from the rack and inserts it into the time clock, which stamps the time of arrival in the proper column and on the proper line. The employee then places the card in the numbered slot in the rack on the *other side* of the time clock.

If the employees leave their work area for lunch, they select their cards from the rack and insert them into the time clock. The time of leaving is stamped on the card. The employees then place their cards in the numbered slots in the first rack. This process of clocking in and out is repeated when employees return from lunch and when they leave work at the end of the day.

FIGURE 3.3
A Time Clock

Point of Interest

Several electronic time-recording machines are now available for use. One system uses palm prints to identify the worker. The employee places his or her hand on a glass plate, and the machine automatically identifies the worker and records the time in or the time out. It also automatically sends the data to a computer, where work hours are added, overtime is calculated, and reports on tardy workers, as well as hours of regular and overtime worked by each employee, are printed out.

Another system uses a card much like a credit card in appearance. This system also calculates hours worked and overtime and creates other reports.

FIGURE 3.4
A Sample Time Card

Name   Philip O'Hara   Employee No. 29

Week Ending   November 12, 2005

Days	Regular				Other		Hours
	In	Out	In	Out	In	Out	
Sun.							
Mon.	7⁵⁵	12⁰¹	12⁵⁴	5⁰⁵			
Tues	7⁵⁷	11⁵⁹	1⁰¹	5⁰³			
Wed.	8⁰⁵	12⁰²	12⁵⁶	5⁰⁷	6⁰¹	8⁵⁹	
Thurs.	8⁰¹	12⁰⁵	1⁰⁴	5⁰¹			
Fri.	7⁵⁹	11⁵⁸	12⁵⁹	5⁰²			
Sat.							

Extra Hours Approved		Hours	Rate	Earnings
	Regular		$9.00	
	Overtime		$13.50	
Supervisor	Total Hours		Gross Earnings	

At the end of each week, time cards are collected from the racks in order to determine how many hours each employee worked during the pay period. In a large firm, this task may be done by a special clerk called a *timekeeper* who takes care of time records, or it may be done by some other member of the payroll department. In a smaller firm, the bookkeeper, office clerk, or other employee who handles payroll work for the business would collect the time cards and do the required computations. The section for regular and overtime earnings at the bottom of each time card is completed by the payroll department at the end of the week. (In Unit 4, you will see how earnings are determined and how they are entered on the time card.)

COMPUTING TIME WORKED

Many businesses expect employees to clock in and to be at their work stations when the workday begins. In general, this means that if you are to be at work at 8:00 a.m., you need to clock in early enough to give yourself time to get to your work station by 8:00. Some

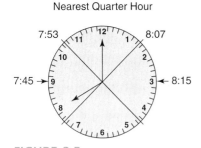

Nearest Quarter Hour

FIGURE 3.5

Time Clock Showing Quarter-Hour System

businesses, however, use the *quarter-hour system* to compute the time worked by their employees. With the quarter-hour system, time is figured to the nearest quarter hour, not to the exact minute. To see how this system operates, study the clock face in Figure 3.5.

Notice that for employees who check in any time between 7:53 and 8:07, the firm considers their starting time to be 8:00. However, for employees who check in any time between 8:08 and 8:22, the firm considers their starting time to be 8:15. The quarter-hour time system makes it easier for a business to calculate time worked and earnings.

The disadvantage to the system is that it can cost the company money because of lost work. Every time an employee checks in at 8:06, the company is paying this worker for a tenth of an hour (6 minutes) for time *not* working. The question is, Is this system, which makes payroll easier to compute, worth what it is costing the company? Most employers would agree that it is not worth the cost. Indeed, this system is currently used in a limited number of businesses.

A Case for Discussion 3-1

There are rules about checking in and checking out. Dan Kline worked in the crowded stockroom of Miller's Auto Repair and Supply. His boss, Mickey, was about his age and was fast becoming a good personal friend. Mickey parked his car at the rear of the auto shop, close to the outside door of the stockroom. Mickey always worked his full day, but he occasionally asked Dan to "clock him out" at the end of the day. The time clock was located far away at the front of the business. Dan knew the company policy against clocking another employee out. Though he didn't like to do this, Dan was frequently clocking his friend out. This permitted Mickey to quickly step out of the rear door, get into his car, and be on his way. One day Mr. Miller, the owner, saw Dan clocking Mickey out. The next day Mr. Miller called Mickey and Dan into his office. They were not fired, but they were told to stop what they had been doing. How would you have handled this if you were Dan? If you were Mickey? If you were the owner? How might other employees look upon this practice?

Discussion of the Case

Dan should have told his friend that he would not clock him out. Employees must follow the rules. If other employees saw this happening, they might do the same thing. Some might even leave early. Time records have to be accurate and *true* if the payroll department is to do its job.

Learning Through Practice

Do Exercise 3.1 on page 71 of this text-workbook.

Time Sheets

Time clocks and time cards are widely used, especially in large businesses that have many employees with varying work schedules. Factories, hotels, large offices, and department stores are examples of such businesses. Small firms having a manageable number of employees often use *time sheets* to record hours worked. One simple but very useful time sheet is shown in Figure 3.6.

This sheet is used by Ingram Heating and Cooling to keep a record of the time worked by all of its employees: office employees and installation and repair crews. Notice that the sheet covers a weekly period and has space for the employees to enter the time when they arrive for work and the time they leave their jobs at the end of each day. At the end of the week, the time sheet is totaled by the office assistant to determine the hours worked by each employee during the period. Notice that one employee, Pamela Cook, was 10 minutes late on Wednesday. This company pays for full-time even when an employee is late. The firm keeps a record of such lateness, and after several occurrences, not surprisingly, such an employee is scheduled for a conference with the owner.

At Ingram, the time sheet is kept near the office manager's desk and the employees sign in and out for themselves. However, in some firms, a supervisor makes all entries on the time sheet in order to ensure accuracy. At Ingram, when the installation and repair crews pick up their trucks in the morning, they sign in on the time sheet. They return to the business at the close of the day to drop off their trucks, at which time they sign out. These workers also take a half-hour off for lunch.

A Case for Discussion 3-2

Karen Tipton is a recent high school graduate. She loved her sales job at Yardley Fashions. The company used the quarter-hour system for employee timekeeping. Except for the first few days when she arrived at a few minutes before 8:00, she had arrived at 8:05 or 8:06 every day for the past two weeks. She also arrived back from lunch at 1:05 or 1:06. She was just barely missing the time when she would be docked for being late. She felt that it was her right to just squeeze by on the time to go to work, and she was devastated when the owner called her in and told her that her lateness would have to stop. Can you understand why Karen did this? Would you have done this? What might happen with other employees if they saw Karen getting away with this practice day after day?

Discussion of the Case

Karen should have known that she was heading for trouble. If she was confused about the time system (which is doubtful), she could have asked the manager. In any case, someone should have talked to her and explained the problem. Otherwise, it wouldn't be long until other workers might take advantage of the time system. That could cause a lot of problems at the store.

FIGURE 3.6   **Time Sheet Used at Ingram Heating and Cooling**

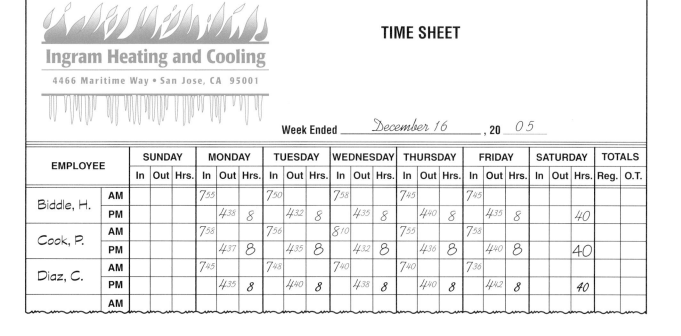

EMPLOYEE		SUNDAY			MONDAY			TUESDAY			WEDNESDAY			THURSDAY			FRIDAY			SATURDAY			TOTALS	
		In	Out	Hrs.	In	Out	Hrs.	In	Out	Hrs.	In	Out	Hrs.	In	Out	Hrs.	In	Out	Hrs.	In	Out	Hrs.	Reg.	O.T.
Biddle, H.	AM				7⁵⁵			7⁵⁰			7⁵⁸			7⁴⁵			7⁴⁵							
	PM					4³⁸	8		4³²	8		4³⁵	8		4⁴⁰	8		4³⁵	8			40		
Cook, P.	AM				7⁵⁸			7⁵⁶			8¹⁰			7⁵⁵			7⁵⁸							
	PM					4³⁷	8		4³⁵	8		4³²	8		4³⁶	8		4⁴⁰	8			40		
Diaz, C.	AM				7⁴⁵			7⁴⁸			7⁴⁰			7⁴⁰			7³⁶							
	PM					4³⁵	8		4⁴⁰	8		4³⁸	8		4⁴⁰	8		4⁴²	8			40		
	AM																							

FIGURE 3.7 **An Individual Time Sheet Is Filled In by Each Employee and Then Turned In to the Supervisor**

TIME SHEET

Days	Time				Hours Worked	Reason for Absence
	In	Out	In	Out		
Sun.						
Mon.	8:30	12:05	1:00	5:30	8	
Tues.	8:25	11:55	1:00	7:00	$9\frac{1}{2}$	
Wed.	8:30	12:00	1:05	6:30	9	
Thurs.	8:30	12:30	1:25	5:30	8	
Fri.	8:35	12:00	1:00	5:35	8	
Sat.						
Weekly Total					$42\frac{1}{2}$	

Employee No. __106__

Employee Name __Marie Santos__

Department __Accounting__

Week Ending __December 16, 2005__

Employee Signature *Marie Santos*

Supervisor's Approval *Joyce McNally*

A larger firm than Ingram probably would have a separate time sheet for each department. Some firms use an individual time sheet for each employee as shown in Figure 3.7. Time sheets of this type are filled out by the employee and given to a supervisor for review and approval.

Learning Through Practice Do Exercise 3.2 on page 71 of this text-workbook.

FILING TIME RECORDS

It is common practice to safely store time records after they are used in preparing the payroll. Businesses covered by the Fair Labor Standards Act are required to keep such records for up to three years. However, even if a firm is not subject to this law, it is helpful to have time records on file for several years in case a question arises about how many hours an employee worked or how much he or she was paid.

DEALING WITH LATENESS TO WORK

In metropolitan areas such as Dallas, Los Angeles, Chicago, and New York, there is a steady and growing problem with commuting. Many workers, through no fault of their own, are significantly late to work, not as a result of their own actions but because of frequent commuting problems. Even leaving home at an earlier hour may not work because of the growing problem with crowded highways.

Internet Connection

Looking for solutions to time and labor management?   See sample systems at Kronos www.kronos.com.

Point of Interest

How would you like to do all of your work at home? The workplace is changing, no doubt about it. Many people still work in offices and shops, but a growing number now work at home. It is the people working at home who are making the biggest changes in today's workforce. In a Bureau of Labor Statistics survey, the U.S. government estimated that 25 million workers engaged in work at home to some degree in May 2001. This number continues to grow steadily, mostly because of the use of computers and supporting communications systems.

Finding a Solution

One solution for some workers is to join the growing number of people who use rapid transit—trains, buses, subways, ferries, or van pools. Some localities have special lanes, so-called diamond lanes, that are restricted during rush hours to the use of vehicles with three or more passengers. Other devices speed up the commute. In San Francisco, as an example, vehicles with three or more passengers can use a special toll entrance to the Oakland Bay Bridge and they pay no toll. This speeds their crossing significantly. Other vehicles are in a massive traffic jam and pay a $2 toll. This system encourages people to carpool, and such ride sharing reduces highway congestion.

There is never a perfect way for a company to deal with employees being late for work. One system is simply to dock (not pay) such workers for being tardy, often in 10-minute increments. Another is to let the employee work at the end of the day to make up for the time lost by lateness. In some cases, depending on the job, the employee may wish to move to a night shift, where the commute is less of a problem. One thing is certain. When an employee is habitually late to work and this affects the amount of work getting done, the employer may simply be forced to replace the worker with one who reports to work on time each day.

Work-at-Home Arrangements

Today, depending upon the nature of the job, many workers are actually working part or all of the day at home on a personal computer that is connected to an office network. A person in the office can switch on a screen and see exactly what the worker is keyboarding at any moment. It has been found that, in most cases, employees actually put in more than the required eight hours per day when they work from a home computer.

Many workers who work at home with computers like the arrangement. If they must attend an afternoon school meeting or take a child to the doctor, they log off the system and take care of such special needs. They keep track of their hours on-line and make up any missed time. Some people do their best work in the evening, so they may work from early afternoon into the evening to log the required time at their home workstation. Such flexibility is generally very popular with employees.

Flextime Systems

A growing number of companies are setting up flextime systems, which permit workers to have flexible work hours. One popular system has employees work 9-hour days Monday through Thursday and 8 hours on Friday (44 hours). They then have their regular weekend off. The second week they work four 9-hour days Monday through Thursday (36 hours). This gives them 80 hours of work for the two-week period (44 + 36 = 80). The workers *average* 40 hours of work per week for the two-week period. With 80 hours of work for the two-week period, they then take a three-day weekend at the end of the second week.

It is not uncommon for some workers to arrive at 7:00 a.m., while the rest of the company begins at 8:00 a.m. Such early birds find the morning drive to work easier at that hour, when there are fewer drivers on the road. This system works particularly well for utility and construction workers. Early birds like having a three-day weekend every other week.

Other companies offer different flextime arrangements. For example, going to work each day at 9:00 in the morning and working until 5:30 with a half-hour off for lunch. This work schedule can also help to avoid the worst of the morning highway traffic. Some employees work flexible hours by job-sharing. Employees who wish to work only part-time may work a four-hour shift from 9:00 until 1:00 p.m. each workday. A second worker doing that same work begins at 1:00 p.m. and works a four-hour shift, until 5:00 p.m. There are many variations of flexible work schedules, and these are usually determined by the particular kind of business involved.

WORK RECORDS

In some manufacturing facilities, employees are paid according to the piece-rate system—how much work they produce during each payroll period. For example, employees in a clothing factory may be paid according to how many garments they sew.

Another example, Tom Tracy assembles one section of a small table in a furniture factory where he works. He is paid $1.65 for each assembly. In an eight-hour shift, he assembled 57 table sections and earned $94.05 (57 units $\times$ $1.65 each = $94.05).

Production Records

When the piece-rate system is used, the employer must keep very accurate records of what each employee produces. Different businesses have different methods of recording employee production. Some firms have special time cards that include both the time worked each day and the number of items produced. The time is recorded on these cards by a time clock, and the number of items is entered by hand. Other firms have special forms that employees complete to show their daily production. An example of such a production record is shown in Figure 3.8.

This form was prepared by an employee of Cyclone Electronics, who is paid according to how many units of each product he assembles each day. A separate time card is kept for this piece-rate employee. The Fair Labor Standards Act requires that employers maintain both time and production records for such employees.

Sales Records

Some salespeople receive a commission for each item they sell. The commission is usually a percentage of the sales price of the item. When salespeople are paid in this way, the employer must keep records of the amounts they sell during each payroll period. Like production records, sales records vary from business to business, with each firm developing a system that serves its own needs. Some businesses may pay a salesperson strictly on the dollar amount of sales generated. In other cases, the salesperson receives a salary as well as a commission. In some sales jobs, a person must first reach a set sales quota before the commission begins. Notice in Figure 3.9 that S. Martin must make $2,000 in sales before his 9 percent commission goes into effect.

In a small business, an office employee usually has responsibility for analyzing sales orders, totaling the amounts sold by various salespeople, and preparing a sales report. In a large business, most of this work would be done with the help of a computer. In many cases, it is not legally necessary for a firm to keep time records for employees who are paid on the basis of the sales they make. However, sales records must be kept in order to accurately determine the earnings of these employees.

Labor Distribution

In some businesses, particularly manufacturing, the cost of labor is often charged against specific jobs or projects. The employee or the supervisor may mark the time card to indicate which job is to be charged. For example, in an aircraft factory, each of a dozen planes

FIGURE 3.8
An Example of a Production Record

Production Record

Week Ended _____ *December 3* _____ , 20 *05*

Days	Machines Assembled			Hours
	Model 101	Model 102	Model 103	
Sun.				
Mon.	9	5	6	8
Tues.	8	6	5	8
Wed.	5	6	1	8
Thurs.	7	10	6	8
Fri.	11	6	2	8
Sat.				
Weekly Total	40	33	20	40

Employee's Signature _____ *Norman Schwartz* _____

Supervisor's Signature _____ *Peter McConnell* _____

FIGURE 3.9   Sales and Commission Report

Sales and Commission Report

Month Ending _____ November 30, 2005 _____

Salesperson	Amount of Sales	Quota	Commission Rate	Amount of Commission
Anderson, A.	$ 8,200	–0–	9%	
Koehler, M.	$ 8,450	–0–	9%	
Lloyd, R.	$ 5,800	–0–	4%	
Martin, S.	$ 7,500	$2,000	9%	
Yamashiro, J	$ 6,600	–0–	4%	
Totals	$ 36,550			

under construction will take many months to build. Each hour of labor devoted to each plane is carefully recorded.

The costs of materials and overhead (general costs such as those for the supplies and utilities involved in running a manufacturing operation) are also recorded. Thus management will be able to calculate the cost of each aircraft. An employee might work on several different projects or jobs for a portion of the workday. The amount of time spent on each project will be noted on the employee's time card so that each project can be charged with the correct labor cost.

OTHER KINDS OF WORKERS

While we tend to think of all workers as laboring for eight hours per day, five days a week, at some set rate of pay, that is not always the case. Businesses have differing needs and various kinds of employees now meet those needs.

Temporary Workers

When a business needs a replacement for a worker who is going on medical leave or vacation, it frequently fills that job with a temporary worker, hired from one of the many temporary job services that now exist. The number of temps, as they are called, skyrocketed from 184,000 in 1970 to 2.3 million in 2003. Such employees usually receive their pay from the temp agency, not the company for which they work. And while these people are called "temps," some of them stay on for two or more years. The company that hires such employees pays the temp agency the workers' salaries plus a fee to cover the service of the agency.

FIGURE 3.10 **Form 1099, Miscellaneous Income**

9595 ☐ VOID ☐ CORRECTED

PAYER'S name, street address, city, state, ZIP code, and telephone no. Capitol Publishing Company 555 Gateway Plaza Sacramento, CA 94280 (916) 374-6908	1 Rents $	OMB No. 1545-0115 **2003** Form **1099-MISC**		**Miscellaneous Income**
	2 Royalties $			
	3 Other income $	4 Federal income tax withheld $		**Copy A** **For Internal Revenue Service Center** **File with Form 1096.**
PAYER'S Federal identification number: 08-4625116 — RECIPIENT'S identification number: 154-38-7689	5 Fishing boat proceeds $	6 Medical and health care payments $		
RECIPIENT'S name Taylor Sims	7 Nonemployee compensation $ 892.00	8 Substitute payments in lieu of dividends or interest $		For Privacy Act and Paperwork Reduction Act Notice, see the **2003 General Instructions for Forms 1099, 1098, 5498, and W-2G.**
Street address (including apt. no.) 42 Rose Court-Apt. 9	9 Payer made direct sales of $5,000 or more of consumer products to a buyer (recipient) for resale ► ☐	10 Crop insurance proceeds $		
City, state, and ZIP code Sacramento, CA 95834	11	12		
Account number (optional) — 2nd TIN not. ☐	13 Excess golden parachute payments $	14 Gross proceeds paid to an attorney $		
15	16 State tax withheld $ $	17 State/Payer's state no.	18 State income $ $	

Form **1099-MISC** Cat. No. 14425J Department of the Treasury - Internal Revenue Service

Do Not Cut or Separate Forms on This Page — Do Not Cut or Separate Forms on This Page

Contract Workers

Increasingly, businesses are hiring people who work under a contract arrangement. Their job is very carefully described and outlined in a written agreement, which includes dates when progress reports are due and a completion date. Otherwise, the contract worker is independent. He or she may even schedule travel to secure the information needed to complete the assigned work. A typical assignment might be to do an extensive study of some segment of the company. It might involve making recommendations. There is no time clock to punch, and there are no specific work hours. The goal is to complete the assigned work in a specified amount of time. The contract worker is paid an agreed-upon fee, usually on a monthly basis or upon completion of the task.

Note that a contract worker is not an employee, and no taxes are deducted from his or her earnings. This worker must pay his or her own payroll taxes.

Each contract worker who receives more than $600 in a year should receive a Form 1099, Miscellaneous Income. The business must issue this form no later than January 31 for the preceding year. The business will send, by February 28 to the Internal Revenue Service (IRS), a copy of all Form 1099s that it issues. The totals of the Form 1099s are reported on a cover Form 1096, Annual Summary and Transmittal of U.S. Information Returns, which accompanies the copies to the IRS. Forms 1099 and 1096 are shown in Figures 3.10 and 3.11.

FIGURE 3.11   **Form 1096, Annual Summary and Transmittal of U.S. Information Returns**

Do Not Staple   6969

Form **1096** Department of the Treasury Internal Revenue Service	**Annual Summary and Transmittal of U.S. Information Returns**	OMB No. 1545-0108 20**03**

FILER'S name

Capitol Publishing Company
555 Gateway Plaza
Sacramento, CA 94280

City, state, and ZIP code

Name of person to contact *Ann Vesio*	Telephone number (*916*) *374-6908*	**For Official Use Only**
E-mail address *avesio@cappub.com*	Fax number (*916*) *374-6945*	

1 Employer identification number *03-4625116*	2 Social security number	3 Total number of forms *48*	4 Federal income tax withheld $	5 Total amount reported with this Form 1096 $ *57600.00*

Enter an "X" in only one box below to indicate the type of form being filed.   If this is your **final return**, enter an "X" here . . . ▶ ☐

W-2G 32	1098 81	1098-E 84	1098-T 83	1099-A 80	1099-B 79	1099-C 85	1099-CAP 73	1099-DIV 91	1099-G 86	1099-H 71	1099-INT 92	1099-LTC 93	1099-MISC 95
☐	☐	☐	☐	☐	☐	☐	☐	☐	☐	☐	☐	☐	☒

1099-MSA 94	1099-OID 96	1099-PATR 97	1099-Q 31	1099-R 98	1099-S 75	5498 28	5498-ESA 72	5498-MSA 27					
☐	☐	☐	☐	☐	☐	☐	☐	☐					

Return this entire page to the Internal Revenue Service. Photocopies are not acceptable.

Under penalties of perjury, I declare that I have examined this return and accompanying documents, and, to the best of my knowledge and belief, they are true, correct, and complete.

Signature ▶ *Ann Vesio*   **Title** ▶ *Controller*   **Date** ▶ *2/10/04*

UNIT 3   REVIEW

Summary

Unit 3 was intended to introduce you to the commonly used methods for keeping records of time worked and production of employees. You should now be able to:

- Explain the four commonly used time periods for paying workers.
- Discuss why employers need to maintain employee time and work records.
- Give a general description of electronic and paper timekeeping systems.
- Define and discuss flexible work assignments and flextime practices.
- Know how to utilize several production- and sales-based incentive pay plans.
- Apply the quarter-hour system to calculate time worked for hourly workers.
- Discuss the use of temporary and contract workers, how they are paid, and how those payments are reported to the IRS.
- Understand how payments for wages are assigned to projects and activities to help a business analyze its labor costs.
- Understand when to use a Form 1099 and Form 1096, and be able to complete those forms.

Learning Through Practice

Do Exercises 3.3 and 3.4 on pages 71, 73, and 74 of this text-workbook.

Study Questions

1. Define each of the following payroll periods:
   a. Weekly   c. Biweekly
   b. Monthly   d. Semimonthly
2. Howard worked from 8:00 in the morning until 3:00 in the afternoon with ½ hour for lunch. How many hours did he work that day?
3. A firm covered by the Fair Labor Standards Act (FLSA) does not have to keep time records for employees who are exempt from the overtime pay requirements. Indicate the status (exempt or nonexempt) of each of the following kinds of employees:
   a. Company president   d. File clerk
   b. Accountant   e. Vice president—sales
   c. Sewing machine operator   f. Plant superintendent
4. What information about time worked must an employer keep under the FLSA?
5. Describe the use of the quarter-hour system to compute time worked.
6. For how many years does FLSA require that the time records of workers be saved?
7. What types of employees are paid on the basis of units produced?
8. Explain what is meant by a salesperson's meeting a quota before he or she begins to earn a commission on sales.
9. What is the purpose of charging labor costs to a specific project or job?
10. Who should receive a Form 1099?

REVIEW EXERCISES

1. Happy Home is a retail home furnishings store. Salespeople at the store are paid on the basis of their total sales. The sales made by three such employees during a single day in October are given here.

Salesperson	Amount of Sales
Craig Hodges	$715.00
Linda Chavez	397.00
Craig Hodges	495.00
Michael Kaminski	567.00
Linda Chavez	579.00
Michael Kaminski	531.50
Craig Hodges	625.00
Linda Chavez	660.00
Michael Kaminski	419.50
Craig Hodges	450.00
Linda Chavez	519.00

   a. Compute the total sales for each salesperson for the day.
   b. Determine each salesperson's gross earnings (earnings before deductions). Use a commission rate of 7 percent of total sales.

2. Heather Ross is a sales associate at the Computer Warehouse, a retail store. She made the following sales during the week of August 16.

Category	Sales	Sales Returns
Computers	$3,775	$275
Software	2,400	200
Supplies (cables, disks, etc.)	700	40
Books	80	0

   a. The firm pays a commission on all net sales (sales minus sales returns). Compute the net sales that Heather Ross had for the week of August 16.
   b. Heather Ross receives a commission of 6 percent of her net sales. Determine her gross earnings for the week of August 16.

3. During the week of August 23, Heather Ross's net sales of computers and software increased 20 percent over the previous week. Her net sales of supplies and books remained the same. (Obtain the data for the previous week from Review Exercise 2.)

   a. Compute her net sales for the week of August 23.
   b. Determine her gross earnings for the week of August 23. Her commission is 6 percent of net sales.

4. During the week of January 12, three factory employees at the Handy Appliance Company worked as follows.

	Peter Nagel		Julie Adams		Greg Gomez	
Day	Hours	Pieces	Hours	Pieces	Hours	Pieces
Monday	8	210	8	195	8	240
Tuesday	8	200	8	215	9	260
Wednesday	8	220	8	205	7½	225
Thursday	9	190	8	200	8	215
Friday	0	0	8	195	10	300

   a. Compute the total pieces produced by each employee.
   b. Compute the regular and overtime hours for each employee. (Consider all hours over 40 as overtime.)

5. For the week of January 19, Peter Nagel increased his production by 25 percent. Compute the total number of pieces that he produced. (Obtain the data for the previous week from Review Exercise 4.)

6. Sight-and-Sound assembles customized multimedia entertainment systems. A job cost card used by the firm to record the time spent on one project shows the following data for six employees.

Employee	Start	End
Paul McManus	7:00 a.m.	8:15 a.m.
Cheryl Gray	8:15 a.m.	8:45 a.m.
Lisa Myers	9:15 a.m.	10:45 a.m.
Joseph Pacelli	10:45 a.m.	12:00 p.m.
Dale Moore	1:00 p.m.	3:45 p.m.
David Roth	3:45 p.m.	4:45 p.m.

Determine the time spent on the project by each employee and the total time spent by all employees.

7. Determine the number of payroll periods in a year for each of the following situations.
   a. Weekly payroll period
   b. Biweekly payroll period
   c. Semimonthly payroll period
   d. Monthly payroll period

8. On Monday of one week, Brian O'Neil worked from 8:25 to 12:05 in the morning and from 12:59 to 5:03 in the afternoon. His firm uses the quarter-hour time system. How many hours of work will the firm record for Brian that day?

9. Refer to Review Exercise 8 for the hours that Brian O'Neil worked on Monday. During the same week, he also worked 7 hours on Tuesday, 10 hours on Wednesday, and 8 hours each on Thursday and Friday.
   a. How many hours did Brian work during the entire week?
   b. Brian belongs to a union. Under the contract between his employer and the union, overtime is paid for all hours worked beyond 35 in a week. How many hours of overtime did Brian work during the week described here?

10. The Far Horizons Travel Agency has a biweekly payroll period and does not pay employees when they take time off for personal reasons. During the first week of one payroll period, Camille DeCosta worked from 8:00 to 12:00 and from 1:00 to 5:00, Monday through Friday. During the second week, she worked from 8:00 to 12:00 and 1:00 to 5:00, Monday through Wednesday. On Thursday, she worked from 8:00 to 11:00. With the permission of her employer, Camille took the rest of the week off to help with preparations for her sister's wedding, which was scheduled for Saturday. Compute Camille's total hours for the two-week period.

11. The Valley Exercise Studio pays its employees on a weekly basis and uses the quarter-hour system to compute time spent on the job. Information from the weekly time card of one employee, Beverly Roberts, is as follows.

Day	a.m.	p.m.
Monday	8:00–12:00	1:01–5:02
Tuesday	7:55–12:02	12:59–5:30
Wednesday	7:58–12:00	1:00–5:47
Thursday	7:59–11:59	1:01–5:03
Friday	7:45–12:03	12:59–6:05

Compute the total hours that Beverly worked during the week. How many of these hours were overtime hours? (Consider any hours worked beyond 40 in the week as overtime.)

12. The Harborside Hotel uses regular clock time rather than the quarter-hour system in preparing its payroll. During the week of April 21, the following two employees clocked in and out at the times shown. The normal schedule for these employees is from 8:00 to 12:00 in the morning and from 1:00 to 5:00 in the afternoon, Monday through Friday.

Day	Harry O'Brien	Ruth Jones
Monday	8:05–12:05	7:57–12:03
	1:00–5:02	1:01–5:06
Tuesday	8:25–12:00	8:02–12:00
	1:06–5:05	1:00–5:04
Wednesday	8:30–12:04	8:10–12:04
	1:10–5:03	1:01–5:06
Thursday	7:57–11:59	8:28–12:00
	12:56–5:06	1:00–5:00
Friday	8:00–11:58	7:55–12:00
		1:30–5:04

How many hours of work will the hotel record for Harry O'Brien and for Ruth Jones? (Count the exact number of hours and minutes that each of these employees spent on the job during the week.)

Learning Through Practice

Unit 3 Exercises

EXERCISE 3.1

Time cards for two employees of Pacific Express Airlines are shown on page 72.

1. Calculate the number of hours that each employee worked each day. Enter this information in the Hours column on the right side of the time card. The employer uses the quarter-hour system.
2. Calculate the number of regular hours, the number of overtime hours, and the total hours for the week. Enter this information at the bottom of the time card. All time beyond 40 hours should be treated as overtime.

Note: Save the time cards for use in Exercise 4.1.

EXERCISE 3.2

A time sheet used by the Donald Advertising Agency is shown on page 72. Instructions for completing the time sheet are also given.

1. Calculate the number of hours worked by each employee in the morning (a.m.) and afternoon (p.m.) of each day. Enter this information in the Hrs. (hours) column of the time sheet. The agency uses the quarter-hour system.
2. Calculate the number of regular hours and the number of overtime hours that each employee worked during the week. Enter this information in the Totals section of the time sheet. All time beyond 40 hours should be treated as overtime.

EXERCISE 3.3

The *Dallas Daily Banner*, a local newspaper, pays Juan Matos $100 for each picture he takes that they use in the paper. During 2005, the paper printed 16 of Juan's pictures. Using this data and the following information, complete a Form 1099 for Juan (see page 73). The *Dallas Daily Banner* is located at 112 Main Street, Dallas, TX 75208. Its employer identification number is 04-0215490 and its telephone number is (214) 763-9821.

Juan's social security number is 123-45-6789 and his address is 645 East Main Street, Dallas, TX 75208. Enter the total of his payments in box 7—Nonemployee compensation.

EXERCISE 3.4

Read the cases below and on page 74, and then write a brief evaluation of how you would handle each situation. Put yourself in the place of the people involved.

1. Cathy Craig and David Sanders are both payroll clerks at the Western Printing Company. One of David's duties is totaling the time cards at the end of each payroll period. Then he gives the cards to Cathy, who uses the information on them to compute employee earnings. David is very reliable when it comes to meeting schedules. In fact, he often has the time cards ready for Cathy ahead of schedule. However, since Cathy joined the firm two months ago, she has had a big problem with the accuracy of his work. She finds many mistakes in the figures that he enters on the time cards, so she has to check all his computations and make corrections. Naturally, this slows down Cathy's own work. Recently, her supervisor praised the quality of Cathy's work but told her that she must speed up. Cathy did not say anything about her problem with David because she did not like the idea of complaining about him to the supervisor.

_____

_____

_____

_____

_____

_____

_____

EXERCISE 3.1

Kaitlin Smith — Employee No. 51

Name __Kaitlin Smith__ Employee No. __51__

Week Ending __June 21, 2005__

Days	Regular				Other		Hours
	In	Out	In	Out	In	Out	
Sun.							
Mon.	8^{02}	11^{59}	12^{59}	5^{01}			
Tues	7^{55}	12^{03}	1^{00}	5^{05}			
Wed.	7^{56}	12^{01}	12^{56}	5^{04}			
Thurs.	7^{57}	12^{04}	12^{58}	4^{59}	5^{31}	7^{30}	
Fri.	7^{56}	12^{05}	1^{02}	5^{03}	5^{59}	8^{01}	
Sat.							

Extra Hours Approved		Hours	Rate	Earnings
	Regular		$12.80	
	Overtime		$19.20	
Supervisor	Total Hours		Gross Earnings	

Peter Fong — Employee No. 52

Name __Peter Fong__ Employee No. __52__

Week Ending __June 21, 2005__

Days	Regular				Other		Hours
	In	Out	In	Out	In	Out	
Sun.	8^{00}	12^{01}	12^{58}	5^{02}			
Mon.	8^{03}	11^{57}	12^{59}	5^{00}	5^{32}	7^{29}	
Tues	7^{55}	12^{00}	1^{05}	5^{01}			
Wed.	8^{01}	12^{04}	1^{00}	4^{59}			
Thurs.	7^{58}	11^{59}	1^{01}	5^{05}			
Fri.	7^{55}	12^{01}					
Sat.							

Extra Hours Approved		Hours	Rate	Earnings
	Regular		$12.20	
	Overtime		$18.30	
Supervisor	Total Hours		Gross Earnings	

EXERCISE 3.2

DONALD ADVERTISING
TIME SHEET

Week Ended __July 19__ , 20 __05__

EMPLOYEE		SUNDAY			MONDAY			TUESDAY			WEDNESDAY			THURSDAY			FRIDAY			SATURDAY			TOTALS	
		In	Out	Hrs.	In	Out	Hrs.	In	Out	Hrs.	In	Out	Hrs.	In	Out	Hrs.	In	Out	Hrs.	In	Out	Hrs.	Reg.	O.T.
Arnold, Henry	AM				9^{00}	12^{00}		8^{55}	12^{00}		9^{05}	1^{00}		9^{00}	12^{05}		9^{00}	12^{00}						
	PM				1^{05}	6^{00}		1^{00}	6^{00}					1^{00}	5^{55}		1^{05}	7^{00}						
Bennett, Susan	AM				9^{10}	12^{10}		9^{00}	12^{00}		8^{55}	12^{00}		9^{00}	12^{00}		9^{00}	11^{55}						
	PM				1^{00}	6^{05}		1^{05}	6^{00}		1^{30}	6^{30}		12^{55}	7^{30}		12^{30}	6^{30}						
Mueller, Carl	AM				9^{30}	1^{00}		9^{00}	1^{05}		9^{00}	12^{55}		8^{30}	1^{00}		9^{00}	1^{00}						
	PM				1^{30}	6^{00}		2^{00}	6^{55}		2^{00}	7^{35}		2^{05}	6^{30}		2^{00}	5^{55}						
Van Zant, Lois	AM				8^{55}	12^{00}		8^{30}	12^{00}		9^{00}	11^{55}		8^{00}	12^{00}		9^{00}	12^{00}						
	PM				1^{00}	7^{00}		12^{30}	3^{00}		1^{00}	6^{00}		1^{05}	6^{00}		12^{35}	6^{30}						
	AM																							

EXERCISE 3.3

9595 ☐ VOID ☐ CORRECTED			
PAYER'S name, street address, city, state, ZIP code, and telephone no.	**1** Rents $	OMB No. 1545-0115 2003 Form **1099-MISC**	**Miscellaneous Income**
	2 Royalties $		
	3 Other income $	**4** Federal income tax withheld $	**Copy A** **For** **Internal Revenue Service Center**
PAYER'S Federal identification number RECIPIENT'S identification number	**5** Fishing boat proceeds $	**6** Medical and health care payments $	**File with Form 1096.**
RECIPIENT'S name	**7** Nonemployee compensation $	**8** Substitute payments in lieu of dividends or interest $	For Privacy Act and Paperwork Reduction Act Notice, see the **2003 General Instructions for Forms 1099, 1098, 5498, and W-2G.**
Street address (including apt. no.)	**9** Payer made direct sales of $5,000 or more of consumer products to a buyer (recipient) for resale ▶ ☐	**10** Crop insurance proceeds $	
City, state, and ZIP code	**11**	**12**	
Account number (optional) 2nd TIN not. ☐	**13** Excess golden parachute payments $	**14** Gross proceeds paid to an attorney $	
15	**16** State tax withheld $ $	**17** State/Payer's state no.	**18** State income $ $

Form **1099-MISC**   Cat. No. 14425J   Department of the Treasury - Internal Revenue Service

Do Not Cut or Separate Forms on This Page — Do Not Cut or Separate Forms on This Page

(Continued from Exercise 3.4 on page 71.)

_____

_____

_____

_____

_____

_____

_____

_____

_____

_____

2. Sue Stevens and Jill Reed are good friends. Both are employed by HGH Electronics. Sue works in the payroll section of the accounting department, and Jill is a programmer trainee in the systems software department. One Monday morning, Jill was 30 minutes late for work. At lunch, she told Sue that her car was at the garage for major repairs and that she would be late every morning during the week. She explained that she was getting a ride from her father. Unfortunately, her father was not able to drop her off until 9:30. Jill was upset about having some of her pay deducted for lateness, especially since she would need the money for the repairs. She then asked Sue to sign in for her on the office time sheet during the rest of the week. In that way, her manager would think that she was arriving at 9:00 and she would receive her full pay for the rest of the week.

_____

_____

_____

_____

_____

_____

_____

_____

_____

_____

_____

_____

_____

_____

_____

_____

_____

_____

Alternate Learning Through Practice Exercises

Unit 3 Exercises

EXERCISE 3.1A   Time cards for two employees of the Grandview Hotel are shown below.

1. Calculate the number of hours that each employee worked each day. Enter this information in the Hours column on the right side of the time card. The employer uses the quarter-hour system.

2. Calculate the number of regular hours, the number of overtime hours, and the total hours for the week. Enter this information at the bottom of the time card. All time beyond 40 hours should be treated as overtime.

Note: Save the time cards for use in Exercise 4.1A.

EXERCISE 3.1A

Name	Charles Delgado		Employee No.	26

Week Ending   April 14, 2005

Days	Regular				Other		Hours
	In	Out	In	Out	In	Out	
Sun.							
Mon.	8^{01}	12^{00}	1^{03}	3^{05}			
Tues	7^{59}	11^{58}	12^{57}	5^{02}			
Wed.	8^{03}	12^{04}	12^{59}	5^{01}			
Thurs.	7^{57}	11^{56}	1^{02}	5^{05}	6^{01}	8^{35}	
Fri.	7^{55}	12^{02}	1^{05}	4^{59}	5^{56}	8^{01}	
Sat.	8^{02}	12^{03}					

Extra Hours Approved		Hours	Rate	Earnings
	Regular		$10.60	
	Overtime		$15.90	
Supervisor	Total Hours		Gross Earnings	

Name	Jennifer Abbati		Employee No.	27

Week Ending   April 14, 2005

Days	Regular				Other		Hours
	In	Out	In	Out	In	Out	
Sun.							
Mon.	7^{55}	12^{31}	1^{04}	5^{06}			
Tues	7^{58}	12^{02}	1^{00}	5^{03}			
Wed.	8^{00}	11^{58}	12^{56}	6^{01}			
Thurs.	7^{59}	12^{01}	1^{04}	6^{32}			
Fri.	8^{01}	11^{59}	1^{01}	4^{58}	5^{31}	7^{33}	
Sat.							

Extra Hours Approved		Hours	Rate	Earnings
	Regular		$10.80	
	Overtime		$16.20	
Supervisor	Total Hours		Gross Earnings	

EXERCISE 3.2A   A time sheet used by Career Builders, an employment agency, is shown on page 76. Instructions for completing the time sheet are given below.

1. Calculate the number of hours worked by each employee in the morning (a.m.) and afternoon (p.m.) of each day. Enter this information in the Hrs. (hours) column of the time sheet. The agency uses the quarter-hour system.

2. Calculate the number of regular hours and the number of overtime hours that each employee worked during the week. Enter this information in the Totals section of the time sheet. All time beyond 40 hours should be treated as overtime.

EXERCISE 3.2A

CAREER BUILDERS
TIME SHEET

Week Ended ___January 7___ , 20 _05_

EMPLOYEE		SUNDAY			MONDAY			TUESDAY			WEDNESDAY			THURSDAY			FRIDAY			SATURDAY			TOTALS	
		In	Out	Hrs.	In	Out	Hrs.	In	Out	Hrs.	In	Out	Hrs.	In	Out	Hrs.	In	Out	Hrs.	In	Out	Hrs.	Reg.	O.T.
Acosta, Eric	AM				9⁰⁵	1⁰²		8⁵⁵	1⁰⁰		9⁰⁰	1³⁰		9⁰⁰	1⁰⁰		8⁰⁵	1⁰⁰						
	PM				2⁰⁰	6³⁵		2⁰⁵	6⁰⁰		2³⁰	6⁰⁰		2⁰⁵	7⁰⁰		2⁰⁰	6⁰⁵						
Bryan, Nancy	AM				9⁰⁰	12⁰⁰		9¹⁵	12¹⁵		9⁰⁰	1⁰⁰		9⁰⁵	12⁰⁰		8⁵⁵	12⁰⁰						
	PM				12⁵⁵	6⁰⁰		1⁰⁰	6⁰⁰					1⁰⁰	6⁰⁰		12³⁰	7²⁵						
Long, Darren	AM				10⁰⁰	1⁰⁵		9⁰⁰	1⁰⁰		8⁵⁵	1⁰⁰		9⁰⁰	1⁰⁰		9⁰⁰	12⁵⁵						
	PM				1³⁰	6²⁵		2⁰⁰	6⁰⁵		2⁰⁵	7⁰⁰		2⁰⁰	6⁰⁵		2⁰⁰	7⁰⁰						
Patel, Nina	AM				8⁵⁵	12⁰⁰		9⁰⁰	12⁰⁰		9⁰⁵	11⁵⁵		9⁰⁵	12⁰⁰		8²⁵	12³⁰						
	PM				1⁰⁵	6⁰⁰		12⁵⁵	6⁰⁰		1⁰⁰	7³⁰		1⁰⁰	6⁰⁰		1⁰⁰	5⁰⁰						
	AM																							

EXERCISE 3.3A

The Prime Advertising Agency uses several freelance artists to assist its design staff. During 2005, the firm paid the following amounts to Donna Franz for her design work: March 8, $420; June 26, $750; August 5, $540; and October 18, $610. Using this data and the following information, complete a Form 1099 for Donna (see page 77).

The Prime Advertising Agency is located at 2641 Delta Drive, Sacramento, CA 95834. Its employer identification number is 08-5736127. Its telephone number is (916) 644-8169. Donna's social security number is 345-56-8790, and her address is 211 Brook Avenue, Sacramento, CA 95834. Enter the total of her payments in box 7—Nonemployee compensation.

EXERCISE 3.4A

Read the cases below and on page 77, and then write a brief explanation of how you would handle each situation. Put yourself in the place of Bill Chung and Lori Palmer.

1. Bill Chung recently went to work at the Toy Bazaar as manager of the games department. He soon noticed that several of the sales associates in the department make a habit of arriving 15 or 20 minutes late in the morning or after the lunch break. Their colleagues cover for them by punching their time cards. When Bill mentioned the situation to another manager at the store, the other manager gave him the following advice: "Just close your eyes to these small violations of the rules. You have a very good staff, and it isn't a smart idea to get them upset."

_____
_____
_____
_____
_____
_____
_____
_____
_____
_____
_____
_____
_____

EXERCISE 3.3A

9595   ☐ VOID   ☐ CORRECTED

PAYER'S name, street address, city, state, ZIP code, and telephone no.		**1** Rents $	OMB No. 1545-0115	
		2 Royalties $	**2003** Form **1099-MISC**	**Miscellaneous Income**
		3 Other income $	**4** Federal income tax withheld $	**Copy A** **For Internal Revenue Service Center**
PAYER'S Federal identification number	RECIPIENT'S identification number	**5** Fishing boat proceeds $	**6** Medical and health care payments $	File with Form 1096.
RECIPIENT'S name		**7** Nonemployee compensation $	**8** Substitute payments in lieu of dividends or interest $	For Privacy Act and Paperwork Reduction Act Notice, see the **2003 General Instructions for Forms 1099, 1098, 5498, and W-2G.**
Street address (including apt. no.)		**9** Payer made direct sales of $5,000 or more of consumer products to a buyer (recipient) for resale ▶ ☐	**10** Crop insurance proceeds $	
City, state, and ZIP code		**11**	**12**	
Account number (optional)	2nd TIN not. ☐	**13** Excess golden parachute payments $	**14** Gross proceeds paid to an attorney $	
15		**16** State tax withheld $ $	**17** State/Payer's state no.	**18** State income $ $

Form **1099-MISC**   Cat. No. 14425J   Department of the Treasury - Internal Revenue Service

Do Not Cut or Separate Forms on This Page   —   Do Not Cut or Separate Forms on This Page

(Continued from Exercise 3.4A on page 76.)

2. Lori Palmer owns and manages a small insurance agency. Last week, Paul King, one of the sales agents, asked Lori if he could come in at 9:30 a.m. rather than 9:00 a.m. from now on because he must take his son to day care. He offered to make up the time by working an additional 30 minutes at the end of the day. Paul has been with the firm for five years and has done a good job.

_____
_____
_____
_____
_____
_____
_____
_____
_____
_____
_____
_____
_____
_____
_____
_____
_____
_____

Determining Gross Earnings

Upon completion of this unit, you should be able to:

1. Define and explain the following terms commonly used in connection with employee pay: *overtime, regular time, gross earnings, hourly rate, salary, piece rate, commission, salary-commission, bonus,* and *profit sharing.*
2. Compute gross earnings based on regular hours worked and overtime hours worked.
3. Compute earnings on fractions of hours worked.
4. Compute hourly pay for employees paid at weekly, biweekly, semimonthly, and monthly rates.
5. Calculate earnings of employees who are paid on a piece-rate plan.
6. Calculate earnings of employees who receive a night-rate bonus or meal-break payments.
7. Calculate the overtime rate of employees who are paid on the piece-rate plan and who work overtime hours.
8. Calculate gross earnings for employees who are paid a base salary plus a commission.
9. Calculate gross earnings for an employee who is paid a monthly salary but missed several hours of work.

At the end of each payroll period, it is necessary for a business to determine how much money its employees have earned. The amounts owed to the employees before any deductions are made are generally referred to as *wages* or *salaries.* However, people who do payroll work often use the term *gross earnings* to describe these amounts.

There are a number of different methods for computing gross earnings. The method used for each employee depends on the type of pay plan under which the employee works. In this unit, you will learn about the various kinds of pay plans and see how gross earnings are determined according to each plan.

As you study these plans, notice that the hourly rate plan and the salary plan are based on the amount of time an employee spends on the job. However, the piece-rate plan and the commission plan are based on the amount of work an employee produces. The salary-plus-commission plan involves a combination of time on the job and work produced.

COMPUTING GROSS EARNINGS

Payroll involves many computations. Today, people use calculators or computers for this work. However, it is important for you to understand the mathematical operations involved in determining payroll amounts.

Internet Connection

What do kids have to do with payroll? View the basics about child-support enforcement systems at   http://www.acf.dhhs.gov/programs/cse.

THE HOURLY RATE PLAN

Employees who are paid according to the *hourly rate plan* receive a fixed amount for each hour they work. Under this plan, gross earnings are found by multiplying an employee's hourly rate by the number of hours worked during the payroll period.

Example

Samio Martinez installs furnaces and air-conditioning equipment for Ingram Heating and Cooling. His regular hourly rate is $28.60 per hour. In a week when he works 40 hours, his gross earnings are $1,144.

Here is how the gross earnings of this employee were computed.

$28.60   hourly rate
$\times$ 40   number of hours worked
$1,144   gross earnings

To many, $1,144 will seem like an extremely high wage for one week of work. It is. But one must remember that Mr. Martinez works in the San Jose, California, area. This is currently one of the highest cost-of-living areas in the country. Where living costs are high, it follows that wages and salaries are high. In addition, this employee must be skilled in electrical work, electronics, plumbing, welding, and sheet metal work, and also must know and understand the various codes, or laws, relative to the installation of heating and air-conditioning equipment. He is a master craftsman.

Frequently, an employee works for a fraction of an hour at his or her regular rate of pay. For example, on one day an employee might work 7 hours and 12 minutes. In such cases, most firms figure the time to the nearest higher quarter-hour and pay the employee on that basis. In this case, the time worked would be figured at 7 1/4 hours.

Example

During one week, Mr. Martinez worked only 37 1/2 hours because he had to take time off for a medical examination. The 37 1/2 hours he worked were at his regular rate of pay. His gross earnings for this week were $1,072.50. He received $1,058.20 for 37 full hours of work ($28.60 $\times$ 37 = $1,058.20) and $14.30 for one half-hour of work (1/2, or .50, $\times$ his hourly rate of $28.60 = $14.30).

When multiplying by simple fractions, first convert them to decimal amounts: 1/4 = .25; 1/2 = .50; 3/4 = .75.

If Mr. Martinez had worked for a quarter of an hour, he would have received $7.15 for that quarter-hour of work ($28.60 $\times$ .25). Similarly, if Mr. Martinez had worked for three-quarters of an hour, he would have received $21.45 ($28.60 $\times$ .75) for the work done during that time.

HANDLING OVERTIME PAYMENTS

Keep in mind that many businesses are subject to the Fair Labor Standards Act. One section of this law requires that employees be paid a special overtime rate for all time worked beyond the regular hours (40 hours) in any week. The overtime rate must be at least 1 1/2 times the regular hourly rate. Businesses do not have to pay overtime if an employee works more than 8 hours in a day. Many business, however, *do* pay overtime for work beyond 8 hours in one day, even though not required to do so under FLSA rules. The overtime rate for Samio Martinez is $42.90 per hour (28.60 $\times$ 1.5 = 42.90). Multiply the hourly rate by 1.5 to get the overtime rate.

Example

During one week, Mr. Martinez worked 43 hours and his gross earnings were $1,272.70. (**Note:** His company is covered under FLSA rules.)

Step 1

$28.60	regular hourly rate
× 40	regular hours worked
$1,144	regular earnings

Step 2

$42.90	overtime hourly rate
× 3	overtime hours worked
$128.70	overtime earnings

Step 3

$1,144.00	regular gross earnings
+ 128.70	overtime gross earnings
$1,272.70	gross earnings

When an employee has both regular and overtime earnings, the two amounts are added to determine the employee's gross earnings.

Example

Ven Nguyen, a repair and maintenance worker at Ingram Heating and Cooling, was asked to work 5 hours on a Saturday and 4 hours on the following Sunday in addition to his usual 40 hours. The company seldom has employees work on weekends, but some emergency repairs were requested by a customer. His regular hourly rate is $19.75 per hour. His overtime rate is $29.63 ($19.75 × 1.5). His gross earnings for the 45 hours he worked that week would be calculated as follows:

Step 1

$19.75	regular hourly rate
× 40	regular hours worked
$790	regular earnings

Step 2

$29.63	overtime hourly rate
× 5	overtime hours worked
$148.15	overtime earnings

Step 3

$790.00	regular earnings
+ 148.15	overtime earnings
$938.15	gross earnings

During a week in which he worked 45 hours, Mr. Nguyen had gross earnings of $938.15. His regular earnings were $790 ($19.75 × 40 hours = $790) and his overtime earnings were ($29.63 × 5 hours = $148.15).

The hourly rate plan is especially suited for employees whose work schedules often vary from one payroll period to another. This plan is widely used for production employees in factories, for construction workers, and for service employees in retail stores, restaurants, and hotels.

FIGURE 4.1

A Time Card Shows Hours Worked and Rate of Pay

Name	Philip O'Hara				Employee No.		29
Week Ending	November 12, 2005						

Days	Regular				Other		Hours
	In	Out	In	Out	In	Out	
Sun.							
Mon.	7⁵⁵	12⁰¹	12⁵⁴	5⁰⁵			8
Tues	7⁵⁷	11⁵⁹	1⁰¹	5⁰³			8
Wed.	8⁰⁵	12⁰²	12⁵⁶	5⁰⁷	6⁰¹	8⁵⁹	11
Thurs.	8⁰¹	12⁰⁵	1⁰⁴	5⁰¹			8
Fri.	7⁵⁹	11⁵⁸	12⁵⁹	5⁰²			8
Sat.							

Extra Hours Approved		Hours	Rate	Earnings
	Regular	40	$9.00	$360.00
M. Rossi	Overtime	3	$13.50	$40.50
Supervisor	Total Hours	43	Gross Earnings	$400.50

When employees of larger businesses are paid according to the hourly rate plan, the hours they work are usually recorded on time cards. At the end of each payroll period, the total hours are determined as you saw in Unit 3. The time cards contain the information about hours worked. This information, along with the rate of pay, is needed to calculate employee earnings for the period. In a manual system, the person who does payroll work for the firm enters the earnings on the time cards, as shown in Figure 4.1.

In a computerized system, the total hours worked are entered by the payroll clerk for all employees. The payroll program then calculates the gross earnings, deductions, and net pay for each employee.

NIGHT BONUS

Some firms pay a bonus to employees who work on the night shift. For example, a firm might pay a bonus of $3 per hour for hours worked between 8:00 p.m. and 8:00 a.m. This bonus is in addition to the overtime pay.

Example

Donald Terry is a helper on a two-man window installation team making $10 per hour. While on a complex job, Donald completed his regular day at 5:30 p.m. and continued working until 10:30 p.m. On that day, he earned his regular pay for 8 hours work and 5 hours overtime pay (from 5:30 p.m. to 10:30 p.m.). He also earned 2 1/2 hours (8:00 p.m. to 10:30 p.m.) of the bonus night rate. The company pays $3 per hour as a night bonus for work done between 8:00 p.m. and 8:00 a.m.

$80.00	8 hours at $10 per hour (regular earnings)
75.00	5 hours at $15 per hour (overtime earnings)
7.50	2 1/2 hours at $3 per hour (night bonus)
$162.50	gross earnings

Big business or small, you still get a paycheck. But what kinds of businesses do the hiring and issuing of those paychecks? How big—or small—are they? It is estimated that 20 percent of all employees work for firms with over 5,000 employees and 35 percent work for firms with from 100 to 5,000 employees. The largest group, 45 percent, work for firms that have fewer than 100 employees.

Medium- and small-sized businesses employ 80 percent of the approximately 110 million job holders in the country. One can only imagine all of the work that is involved in preparing the payroll checks for all of these employees. And this work goes on week after week, month after month, and year after year.

When an employee works overtime during a time period when a night bonus is in effect, overtime is paid for all overtime hours worked. The night bonus is still paid, but it is added onto the regular earnings plus the overtime earnings.

MEAL BREAK

Many companies have a policy whereby employees who work 10 or more hours in a single day get paid for a half-hour or even a one-hour dinner break. This amount is paid at the overtime rate. The workers remain on the payroll during that dinner period. Some companies will also reimburse the employees for the cost of the meal. The reimbursement check for the meal is not a part of the payroll check. Instead, it is a separate payment.

Learning Through Practice

Do Exercises 4.1 and 4.2 on page 93 of this text-workbook.

THE SALARY PLAN

When the *salary plan* is used, employees are paid a fixed amount for each payroll period. This period may be weekly, biweekly, semimonthly, or monthly, depending on the business involved.

For example, Alan McDermit, the manager of the branch of the Bank of Commerce, where Ingram Heating and Cooling does its banking, has a salary of $1,325 per week. He is paid $2,650 biweekly for two weeks of work. When an employee on the salary plan works the required amount of time during a payroll period, no computations are needed to find the gross earnings.

Adjusting the Pay of Salaried Employees

If an employee on the salary plan works less than the required number of hours during a payroll period, the employer may deduct for the time lost. For example, one day Mr. McDermit had to take off 3 hours for personal business. According to company policy, he was not paid for those three hours.

To compute the gross earnings of a salaried employee in this type of situation, it is necessary to first determine the employee's regular hourly rate, even though he is on a weekly salary. Then the regular hourly rate is multiplied by the total number of hours worked during the period.

Example

Mr. McDermit is paid $1,325 for a regular 40-hour workweek. His hourly pay is one-fortieth of this amount ($1,325 ÷ 40 = $33.125 or $33.13). His salary for the week where he took 3 hours of time off would be for 37 hours of work at $33.13 per hour ($33.13 × 37 = $1,225.81). Since he is paid biweekly, his check will be for one full week of work and the partial week of work ($1,325 + $1,225.81 = $2,550.81). **Note:** Generally, when you work with dollar amounts, fractions of less than 5 are dropped. Therefore $33.125 is rounded up and recorded as $33.13 while $33.124 is rounded down to $33.12.

Some salaried employees are exempt from the overtime pay requirement of the Fair Labor Standards Act because they have professional, managerial, or supervisory jobs. However, many salaried employees are subject to the overtime pay requirement. These are usually salaried employees who work in clerical or service jobs. They must receive at least 1 1/2 times the regular hourly rate for all work beyond 40 hours in any week. To compute the gross earnings of a salaried employee who is entitled to overtime, it is necessary to find the employee's regular hourly rate first. As shown previously, this is done by dividing the weekly salary by the number of hours in the regular workweek.

Example

Helen Tillery is a supervisor of new accounts at Central County Bank. Her salary is $660 for a 40-hour week. She is a minor supervisor, and the company is required to pay her overtime for work done beyond 40 hours per week. Generally, she works overtime only one time per month: the day that a report is required listing details about all new accounts set up during the month. On one such week she worked 44 hours. Her salary that week was $759.00.

Her regular, overtime, and gross earnings were determined as follows:

Step 1

$660 ÷ 40 hours = $16.50/hour

Step 2

$16.50	regular hourly rate
× 1.5	
$24.75	overtime hourly rate

Step 3

$24.75	overtime hourly rate
× 4	overtime hours worked
$99.00	overtime earnings

Step 4

$660.00	regular weekly salary
+ 99.00	overtime earnings
$759.00	gross earnings

Biweekly, Semimonthly, and Monthly Salaries

It is a bit complicated to find the overtime rate for salaried employees who are paid on a biweekly, semimonthly, or monthly basis. In these cases, it is necessary to first find the weekly salary. Then the hourly rate and the overtime rate can be determined easily.

Example

Rita Lopez has a regular workweek of 40 hours and receives overtime pay for all hours beyond 40 in any week. Her regular salary is $1,950 per month. During one month, she worked 5 hours overtime and had gross earnings of $2,034.40.

Here is how the regular hourly rate, overtime earnings, and gross earnings of this employee were computed.

Step 1

$1,950	regular monthly salary
× 12	months in a year
$23,400	regular yearly salary

Step 2

$23,400 ÷ 52 weeks = $450 weekly salary

Step 3

$450 ÷ 40 hours = $11.25 per hour rate

Step 4

$11.25   regular hourly rate

$\underline{\times\ 1.5}$

$16.875   overtime hourly rate

Step 5

$16.88   overtime hourly rate (rounded)

$\underline{\times\ 5}$ overtime hours worked

$84.40   overtime earnings

Step 6

$1,950.00   regular monthly salary

$\underline{+\ 84.40}$ overtime earnings

$2,034.40   gross earnings

Notice that this employee's regularly monthly salary is multiplied by 12 to find her yearly salary. If an employee is paid on a biweekly basis, it is necessary to multiply the amount of the biweekly salary by 26 to determine the yearly salary. Such an employee, paid on a biweekly basis, has 26 paydays in a year. For an employee paid on a semimonthly basis, it is necessary to multiply the amount of the semimonthly salary by 24 to find the yearly salary. Such an employee is paid 24 times per year.

The salary plan is widely used for employees who hold professional, managerial, supervisory, administrative, and clerical jobs. The hours worked by such employees usually are recorded on time sheets, which are totaled at the end of each payroll period. Time sheets are often used to record the hours worked by salaried employees who are subject to the overtime pay requirements of the Fair Labor Standards Act. Employers are required to keep records of the time worked by such employees.

Instead of receiving pay for overtime, some businesses allow the employee to take time off equal to the overtime hours. This practice is called compensatory time off.

Learning Through Practice

Do Exercise 4.3 on page 93 of this text-workbook.

THE PIECE-RATE PLAN

Employees who are paid according to the *piece-rate plan* receive a certain amount for each item they produce. To determine gross earnings under this plan, it is necessary to multiply the rate per item by the number of items completed during the payroll period.

Example

Marjorie Lawson works in a factory where she assembles parts for electronic games. Her piece rate is 29 cents. During one week, she completed 2,100 items and had gross earnings of $609 ($.29 × 2,100 items = $609).

The computation of gross earnings for a piece-rate employee is more complex if the employee is paid different rates for different levels of production or for different types of items.

Example

John Potter receives a piece rate of 16 cents per item for all items up to 2,000 that he completes in any week. For items beyond that number, he receives a rate of 21 cents per item. Such special rates are designed to encourage high production. During one week, Mr. Potter completed 2,840 items. His earnings at the 16-cent rate were $320 ($.16 × 2,000 items = $320), and his earnings at the 21-cent rate were $176.40 ($.21 × 840 = $176.40). His gross earnings for the week were $496.40 ($320 + $176.40 = $496.40).

Point of Interest

Example

Marsha Ong, an employee at Murphy Electronics, is paid on a piece-rate basis. She assembles three different subparts that are used in cellular telephones. Her rate of pay and number of units produced during one 40-hour week are:

Subassembly 167J	$2.88	85 items
Subassembly 4730	1.25	106 items
Subassembly A39	.46	185 items

Her pay is determined by first computing the amount earned for each of these subassemblies. Then those earnings are added together to find her gross earnings for the week.

Step 1

Subassembly 167J

$2.88	rate of pay
× 85	items produced
$244.80	gross earnings

Step 2

Subassembly 4730

$1.25	rate of pay
× 106	items produced
$132.50	gross earnings

Step 3

Subassembly A39

$.46	rate of pay
× 185	items produced
$85.10	gross earnings

Step 4

Gross Earnings

Subassembly 167J	$244.80
Subassembly 4730	132.50
Subassembly A39	85.10
Total	$462.40

MEETING FLSA MINIMUM WAGE REQUIREMENTS

If a firm is covered by the Fair Labor Standards Act, it must ensure that the weekly earnings of its piece-rate employees are at least equal to the federal minimum wage. To check this, the person who handles payroll work must determine the regular hourly rate of each piece-rate employee for the week. As you learned before, an employee's hourly rate is found by dividing the gross earnings by the number of hours worked. In the case of Marsha Ong,

Internet Tax Addresses

Developing as a professional in the payroll field is a goal achieved by learning from others. One journal of interest is the *World at Work Journal* available online at http://www.acaonline.org/journal. Other useful materials can be found through http://www.americanpayroll.org/pubs1.html (and /pubs2.html), which include *ePayXpress, PaytecH,* and also *Pay State Update.*

her gross earnings of $462.40 were divided by 40 to find her hourly pay rate is $11.56, well above the required minimum wage.

Businesses that are subject to the Fair Labor Standards Act must also give overtime pay to piece-rate employees who work beyond 40 hours in any week. The overtime rate for such an employee may change every week, based on the employee's earnings. There are two methods for computing the overtime earnings of piece-rate employees. With one method, the piece-rate employees receive one-half of their regular hourly rate for each overtime hour. The other method involves the use of a special, agreed-upon piece rate for all items produced during overtime hours. This rate must be at least 1 1/2 times the regular piece rate.

Example

In one week, Marsha Ong worked 43 hours and had gross earnings of $480 based on her piece rate. Her hourly rate of pay was $11.16 ($480 ÷ 43 = $11.16). Her overtime rate of pay is one-half of her hourly rate of pay, or $5.58 ($11.16 ÷ 2 = $5.58). Her overtime earnings for 3 hours are $16.74 ($5.58 × 3 = $16.74). This amount is added to her piece-rate earnings to arrive at her gross earnings ($480 + $16.74 = $496.74).

Example

Lois Magnum works in a furniture factory, where she cuts wooden parts for furniture. Her regular piece rate is 42 cents, and her established overtime piece rate is 63 cents. This rate was agreed upon by management and labor in the factory. During one week, she completed 820 items in the first 40 hours and 54 items in 3 overtime hours. She had regular earnings of $344.40 ($.42 × 820 items = $344.40). She had overtime earnings of $34.02 ($.63 × 54 items = $34.02). Her gross earnings for the week were $378.42 ($344.40 + $34.02 = $378.42).

The second method of computing overtime pay for piece-rate employees can only be used when the employer and the employee have agreed on it before the overtime work is done.

The piece-rate plan is an incentive plan. Since wages are based on how much work an employee does, the employee can earn more by producing more. This type of pay plan is commonly used in factories and for certain kinds of service jobs where production is measurable.

As you saw in Unit 3, a firm must keep production records that show the work completed by its piece-rate employees. At the end of each payroll period, the items produced are totaled, and the necessary information is sent to the person who does the payroll work.

Learning Through Practice

Do Exercise 4.4 on page 94 of this text-workbook.

THE COMMISSION PLAN

The *commission plan* is an incentive plan that many firms use for their salespeople. With this pay plan, the amount of earnings depends on the amount of goods sold during a payroll period. Each salesperson receives a certain percentage of his or her sales for the period. This percentage is called the *commission rate.* To find gross earnings under the commission plan, it is necessary to multiply the amount of sales by the commission rate.

Example   Joyce Grant works as a salesperson for a firm that produces computer software for medical and dental offices. She receives a commission of 9 percent on all her sales. Last week, her sales totaled $12,650. Her gross earnings were $1,138.50 ($12,650 × .09 = $1,138.50).

Many salespeople who work on the commission plan spend the majority of their time outside the premises of their employer. Their work requires that they constantly visit customers and potential customers. As a result, their hours of work can vary a great deal from day to day and week to week. Salespeople of this type are exempt from the overtime pay provisions of the Fair Labor Standards Act.

Other salespeople who are on the commission plan work in their employer's store or office and have a normal 40-hour workweek. These salespeople may be subject to the overtime pay provisions of the Fair Labor Standards Act. They may also be covered by the federal minimum wage requirement of the FLSA. It is the responsibility of the employer to check that such workers are receiving at least the federal minimum wage for each payroll period.

Example   Alan Westfall is a salesperson at a furniture store. His commission rate is 8 percent. One week he spent 40 hours on the job and had sales of $7,000. His gross earnings were $560. His regular hourly rate that week was $14 ($560 ÷ 40 hours = $14.00). This is well beyond the federal minimum wage of $5.15 in effect at the time of this writing.

When the commission plan is used, it is necessary for a firm to keep detailed sales records. At the end of each payroll period, information from these records is needed to compute the commissions that are due the salespeople.

Learning Through Practice   Do Exercise 4.5 on page 94 of this text-workbook.

THE SALARY-PLUS-COMMISSION PLAN

The commission plan encourages a high level of sales. However, the earnings of salespersons on this plan often fluctuate greatly from one payroll period to another. During periods of low sales, such employees may find it difficult to take care of their basic living expenses and meet their other financial obligations. For this reason, many firms pay both a salary and a commission to their salespeople. The *salary-commission plan* (or salary-plus-commission plan) provides a certain amount of security for these employees while also giving an incentive for strong selling efforts.

In some cases, there is another reason for using the salary-plus-commission plan. An employee's job may combine selling activities with other types of activities, such as setting up merchandise displays for customers. The payment of the salary and a commission provides fair compensation for both the nonselling and selling parts of the job.

The computation of gross earnings under the salary-plus-commission plan involves the use of procedures with which you are already familiar.

Example   Shaun Martin is a sales manager at the Sierra Lumber Company. His job consists of both selling and administrative duties. Because of this mix of work, he receives a salary of $405 a week and a sales commission of 9 percent. However, he also has a sales quota of $2,000. This means that he must make $2,000 (his quota) in sales each week before he can draw any commission. During one week, Shaun Martin sold goods totaling $7,500. He had gross earnings of $900 for the period.

Here is how the gross earnings of this employee were determined.

Step 1

$7,500	total sales for week
− 2,000	weekly sales quota
$5,500	sales on which commission is due

Step 2

$5,500	sales on which commission is due
× .09	commission rate
$495.00	commission earnings

Step 3

$405.00	salary
+ 495.00	commission earnings
$900.00	gross earnings

This employee is exempt from the overtime pay requirement of the Fair Labor Standards Act because he holds a managerial job. However, some employees on the salary-plus-commission plan *are* subject to this requirement. Salary-plus-commission employees in businesses covered by the Fair Labor Standards Act are also subject to the minimum wage requirement.

Learning Through Practice

Do Exercise 4.6 on page 95 of this text-workbook.

BONUSES AND PROFIT-SHARING PAYMENTS

Some firms pay their employees other amounts besides regular wages or salaries. These amounts are usually in the form of bonuses or profit-sharing payments. The government laws covering such amounts are complex. Some types of bonuses and profit-sharing payments must be added to regular wages or salaries and used in computing the regular hourly rates and overtime rates of the employees, but other types are not subject to this requirement. To ensure correct payroll treatment of bonuses and profit-sharing payments, it is wise for a business to check with the U.S. Department of Labor before giving such payments to its employees.

Bonuses

A *bonus* is a reward for extra effort on the job. There are a number of different types of bonuses. One common type is a gift that is given to the employees of a firm after a successful period of operations. A bonus of this nature is often paid at the end of the year. Another common type of bonus is one paid to salespeople for selling certain kinds of goods, usually slow-moving items or new products that require greater sales effort. Still another common type of bonus is one paid to the managers of a firm if yearly sales and profits rise above a certain level. This type of bonus is usually part of a working agreement or contract that each manager has with the firm.

Profit-Sharing Payments

Some businesses provide *profit-sharing* plans for their employees. Such plans give the employees a part of the profits that the firm earns each year. Profit-sharing payments can take several forms. The employees may receive cash or stock in the business, or the profit-sharing payments may be placed in an account that employees can draw on when they retire.

No matter how the details of profit-sharing plans vary, they are all intended to encourage hard work and loyalty from the employees. Bonuses also help to achieve these goals.

TIPS

While it is not possible to prove, some claim that the word "tip" is an abbreviation for the expression "*to i*nsure *p*romptness." In certain types of work, it is common for employees to receive tips in addition to the wages paid by their employers. Waiters, waitresses, bartenders, hairstylists, bellhops, and taxi drivers are some examples of employees who often fall into this category.

A *tip* is a gift from a customer for service that he or she obtained. Any person who normally receives tips amounting to more than $20 a month while performing a job is considered a *tipped employee.* By law, such employees may be paid a rate that is below the minimum wage because their tips can be used in computing this wage. Up to 50 percent of the minimum wage can come from tips received during the payroll period.

Example

Bruce Howard, a food server, works 40 hours a week and receives a salary of $185 from his employer plus tips from customers. As of this writing, the minimum wage for a 40-hour week is $206 ($5.15 × 40 = $206). This means that Mr. Howard's salary is $21 less than the required amount ($206 − $185 = $21). However, the law provides that the employer can take a credit of up to 50 percent of an employee's tips to apply toward meeting the minimum wage requirement. Since Mr. Howard normally receives about $215 per week in tips, his employer can take a credit of up to $107.50 of his tips ($215 × .50 = $107.50). This amount can be applied toward the minimum wage requirement. Together, the salary of $185 and the credit of $107.50 for tips exceed the minimum wage of $206 for a 40-hour week.

The employer must keep track of tips in order to properly record and report the individual worker's earnings. The amount of tips is reported on Form W-2 (to be covered in Unit 9). Many businesses maintain a "tip sheet" that each employee fills in at the end of a shift recording the amount of tips received during that shift. This system helps the business meet the record-keeping requirements of the U.S. Department of Labor.

ACCURACY IN PAYROLL WORK

Payroll work involves many computations, and these computations must be done with total accuracy. Imagine how disastrous it would be if a firm paid its employees the wrong amounts because their earnings had been incorrectly calculated. When payroll is prepared manually, one method of ensuring accuracy is to require the payroll clerk to include the calculator tape with the completed payroll records. The tape can then be checked against payroll records by another employee.

Today, firms use accounting software to record their business transactions. Most accounting software packages include a payroll module that simplifies record keeping. Once the initial data about an employee is entered, the payroll clerk enters each employee's work for the current payroll period and the computer calculates the gross earnings, required deductions, and net pay. Smaller businesses may utilize a spreadsheet software program that will calculate the same figures (gross earnings, required deductions, and net pay). Whatever method is used to calculate payroll amounts, the business should maintain a printout or written documentation of the calculations for each employee in each pay period.

UNIT 4 .REVIEW

Summary

Unit 4 challenged you to learn about calculating an employee's earnings. You should now be able to:

- Define commonly used payroll terms like *hourly rate, salary, piece rate, commission, salary plus commission, bonus,* and *profit sharing.*
- Compute the gross earnings of an employee who has worked regular hours and overtime hours.
- Compute an employee's gross earnings using a fraction of an hour technique.
- Compute the gross earnings of employees paid on a weekly, biweekly, semimonthly, or monthly basis.
- Compute gross earnings and overtime pay for employees paid on a piece-rate basis.
- Compute earnings for employees paid on a salary-plus-commission basis.

Study Questions

1. Match the pay plans in Column A with the description given in Column B.

Column A	Column B
——— **a.** Commission plan	**1.** An incentive plan that pays salespeople on the basis of sales made.
——— **b.** Bonus	
——— **c.** Piece-rate plan	**2.** A plan that provides a fixed amount for each hour worked.
——— **d.** Hourly rate plan	
——— **e.** Salary-plus-commission plan	**3.** A combination plan that pays salespeople for time on the job and the amount of sales made.
——— **f.** Salary plan	**4.** A plan in which a company distributes part of its earnings to employees in the form of cash or stock.
——— **g.** Profit-sharing plan	
	5. A reward for extra effort on the job.
	6. An incentive plan that pays factory workers for items produced.
	7. A plan that provides a fixed amount for each pay period.

2. Define *gross earnings.*
3. Are salaried employees always exempt from the overtime pay provisions of the Fair Labor Standards Act (FLSA)? Explain.
4. What method is used to determine the hourly rate for employees who are paid a monthly salary?
5. Under the FLSA, what is the minimum pay for each hour of overtime worked by an employee whose regular hourly rate is $12?
6. Are salespeople who are paid on the commission plan or salary-commission plan entitled to receive the minimum wage? Explain.
7. Piece-rate employees are subject to the minimum wage provision of the FLSA. What records are needed to ensure compliance?
8. Explain the method of computing earnings under the piece-rate plan.
9. Describe the two methods that may be used to calculate overtime earnings for piece-rate employees.
10. Why must a business track the amount of tips that its employees receive?

REVIEW EXERCISES

When calculating the regular hourly rate and the overtime hourly rate in these exercises, carry the amounts to three decimal places and then round them to two decimal places.

1. Wendy Martin works in a film processing laboratory. She is paid $12.50 an hour for a 40-hour week and twice her regular hourly rate (double time) for all hours over 40. One week, she worked 44 hours. What were her regular earnings, overtime earnings, and total earnings for the week?

2. Patrick Nolan is a bank teller. He receives a weekly salary of $630 for a 35-hour week. What is his regular hourly rate?

3. Theresa Montero works as a medical technician at Valley Hospital. She receives a monthly salary of $2,500. Her overtime rate is 1 1/2 times her regular hourly rate, and she is paid this rate for work beyond 40 hours in any week. For a week in which she worked 44 hours, compute her regular hourly rate, her regular earnings, her overtime earnings, and her total earnings.

4. Derek Anderson is a chef in a restaurant. He receives $18 an hour and regularly works 8 hours a day, Monday through Friday. For work on Saturday, he receives time and a half; and for work on Sunday, he is paid double time. One week in July, he worked full-time Monday through Friday plus 4 hours on Saturday and 4 hours on Sunday. Compute his regular earnings, overtime earnings, and total earnings for the week.

5. Marti Ellis works 40 hours a week in a clothing factory. She is paid 95 cents for each acceptable unit produced. During the week of June 7, she produced 605 units, but 25 units were rejected because they were defective. How much did she earn that week?

6. Refer to Review Exercise 5. During the week of June 14, Marti Ellis produced 722 acceptable units in 44 hours. Besides her piece-rate earnings, she is paid one-half of her regular hourly rate for each hour over 40 hours that she works in a week. Compute her gross earnings for the week.

7. Vincent DeCarlo sells real estate. The agency where he works collects a commission of 6 percent on all sales and pays 3 percent (or one-half the total commission earned) to its salespeople. During March, Vincent made the following sales: a condominium apartment for $60,000, a house for $225,000, and a building lot for $40,000. What were his commission earnings for March?

8. Nora Van Kirk is the sales manager for Business Solutions Software. She receives a salary of $800 a week and commission of 1 1/2 percent of the firm's annual sales over $2 million. Last year, the firm's sales were $5.6 million. Compute her gross earnings for the year.

9. Jason Peters sells farm machinery. He is paid a salary of $1,600 a month and has a monthly sales quota of $5,000. He receives a commission of 10 percent on all sales above his monthly quota of $5,000 and an additional 2 percent on all sales above $10,000 in a month. Last month, his sales were $18,500. What were his gross earnings?

10. Mary Conrad sells dental equipment and supplies on a commission basis. During one week, her sales were $8,650. She receives 8 percent for the first $3,000 of sales, 10 percent for the next $3,000 of sales, and 12 percent for all sales over $6,000. What were her gross earnings for the week?

Problems

1. The On-Line Shoppers Market is an Internet shopping service. Employees in its technical department work 40 hours a week and are paid time and a half for all overtime hours. The information that follows includes the hours and wage rates of four employees during the week of May 15. Compute the regular earnings, overtime rate, overtime earnings, and gross earnings for each employee.

Employee	Hours Worked	Regular Hourly Rate
Laura Chase	44 1/2	$15.60
Edward Klein	45	13.50
Frank Nunez	42	17.00
Sandra Stewart	45	14.50

2. Power Electronics, a maker of computer games, pays its production workers according to the piece-rate plan. These workers receive $4 per 100 units for the first 1,000 units they produce, $5.50 per 100 units for the next 500 units, and $6 per 100 units for all units over 1,500. The units produced by five employees in 8 hours one day are listed here. Compute the piece-rate earnings and hourly rate for each employee. (**Hint:** Since the employees' piece rates are for batches of 100 units, determine the number of batches of 100 units produced by each employee before making the earnings calculations.)

Employee	Units Produced
Ryan Davis	2,200
Jan Ericson	2,800
John Ostrowski	3,600
Sheila Scott	3,400
Russell Thayer	2,400

3. During one week, Paul Fitzgerald, a factory employee, worked 44 hours and produced 1,050 items. Of this total, 150 items were produced in overtime hours. His regular rate is 65 cents an item. He and his employer have an agreement that he will receive an additional 35 cents a unit for items produced during overtime hours.

   a. Compute his total piece-rate earnings for the week.

   b. Assume that instead of a bonus rate for items produced in overtime hours, this employee receives his regular rate of 65 cents an item for all items produced and one-half of his regular hourly rate for all hours worked beyond 40 in a week. Compute his regular hourly rate and his overtime hourly rate for the week. Also compute his total earnings for the week.

4. Employees at the Shelby Science Museum normally work 40 hours a week. They are paid 1 1/2 times their regular hourly rate for any hours over 40 worked in a week. Information for seven employees during the week of October 7 is listed here.

Employee	Rate of Pay	Hours Worked
Carlton Ames	$13.50 an hour	45
Mark Bodine	$14.10 an hour	42
Patricia Connolly	$750 a week	44
Ann Hoffman	$3,500 a month	40
George Janovic	$700 a week	41 1/2
Stacey King	$3,120 a month	43
Roy McDonald	$48,000 a year	42

   Compute the regular hourly rate, overtime hourly rate, regular earnings, overtime earnings, and gross earnings for each employee. Set up a table with this data.

5. The Office Depot sells office supplies and equipment at a discount. It pays its salespeople on a weekly basis. Some of these employees receive a salary plus a commission on sales; others are paid only a commission on sales. However, all of the firm's salespeople are subject to the minimum wage provision of the Fair Labor Standards Act. The following information concerns four salespeople during the week ended June 21.

Employee	Hours	Weekly Salary	Sales	Commission Rate
Casey Donahue	40	0	$18,250	4%
Sarah Martin	35	$350	6,500	2
Joseph Rossi	30	0	14,700	4
Joyce Winters	40	300	7,000	2

   Compute the commission, gross earnings, and hourly rate for each salesperson. Set up a table showing the weekly salary and the amounts that you computed for each salesperson.

Learning Through Practice

Unit 4 Exercises

EXERCISE 4.1 Complete the time cards that you totaled in Exercise 3.1 on page 72. Determine the regular, overtime, and gross earnings of the two employees of Pacific Express Airlines. Enter the amounts that you compute at the bottom of the time cards.

EXERCISE 4.2 The following employees of Southern Pactel are paid according to the hourly rate plan. Find their gross earnings.

1. Nathan Parks is a cable installer. His regular hourly rate is $15.20. Last week, he worked 36 1/2 hours.

   Gross earnings $ _____

2. Maureen Kelly is a service coordinator. Her regular hourly rate is $17.40. Last week, she worked 42 hours, Monday through Friday. She receives time and a half for any hours beyond 40 in her normal workweek.

   Overtime rate $ _____   Regular earnings $ _____

   Overtime earnings $ _____

   Gross earnings $ _____

3. Paul Lazlo is an equipment installer. His regular hourly rate is $14.60. Last week, he worked 42 hours, Monday through Friday, and 6 hours on Saturday. He receives time and a half for any hours beyond 40 in his normal workweek and double time for any hours worked on weekends and holidays.

   Overtime rate (time and a half) $ _____

   Overtime rate (double time) $ _____

   Regular earnings $ _____

   Overtime earnings (time and a half) $ _____

   Overtime earnings (double time) $ _____

   Gross earnings $ _____

EXERCISE 4.3 The following employees work at the law firm of Douglas & Goldman. They are paid according to the salary plan. Compute their gross earnings.

1. Kari Nelson is a legal secretary. She has a regular weekly salary of $600 and a regular workweek of 40 hours. Last week, she worked 44 hours. Her overtime rate for all hours beyond 40 is 1 1/2 times her regular hourly rate.

   Regular hourly rate $ _____   Weekly salary $ _____

   Overtime rate $ _____   Overtime earnings $ _____

                                                   Gross earnings $ _____

2. George Ramos is a paralegal. He has a regular weekly salary of $670 and a regular workweek of 40 hours. Last week, he spent only 36 hours on the job because he had to take some time off for personal business. He will not be paid for that time.

   Regular hourly rate $ _____   Gross earnings $ _____

3. Susan Marshak is the office manager at Douglas & Goldman. She has a regular monthly salary of $3,500 and a regular workweek of 40 hours. Last month, she had 6 hours of overtime. She is paid 1 1/2 times her regular hourly rate for any overtime work.

Yearly salary	$ _____	Monthly salary	$ _____
Weekly salary	$ _____	Overtime earnings	$ _____
Regular hourly rate	$ _____	Gross earnings	$ _____
Overtime rate	$ _____		

EXERCISE 4.4

The following employees of Kid's Stuff, a toy company, are paid according to the piece-rate plan. Find their gross earnings.

1. Gary Conners is paid 48 cents for each item that he produces. Last week, he completed 1,100 items.

   Gross earnings $ _____

2. Stephanie Boaz receives a piece rate of 34 cents for all items up to 1,500 that she completes in any week. For items beyond that number, she receives a rate of 52 cents per item. Last week, she completed 1,725 items.

   Gross earnings $ _____

3. Todd Wilson is paid 38 cents for each item that he produces. His regular workweek is 40 hours, and he receives half of his regular hourly rate for each overtime hour. Last week, he worked 45 hours and completed 1,850 items.

Regularly hourly rate	$ _____	Piece-rate earnings	$ _____
Overtime rate	$ _____	Overtime earnings	$ _____
		Gross earnings	$ _____

EXERCISE 4.5

Find the gross earnings of the following employees, who are paid according to the commission plan.

1. Vicki Chan sells medical equipment to hospitals. She has a commission rate of 4 percent. Last week, her sales totaled $46,750.

   Gross earnings $ _____

2. Peter Rinaldi sells sporting goods in a large discount store. He has a commission rate of 6 percent. Last week, his sales totaled $7,820.

   Gross earnings $ _____

   Compute the regular hourly rate of this employee for the week to be sure that it meets or exceeds the current minimum wage rate. Peter Rinaldi has a regular workweek of 40 hours.

   Regular hourly rate $ _____

3. Nancy Newman sells paintings and drawings in an art gallery. She receives a commission rate of 3 percent on paintings and 1 1/2 percent on drawings. Last week, her sales of paintings totaled $31,450 and her sales of drawings totaled $8,700.

Commission on paintings	$ _____
Commission on drawings	$ _____
Gross earnings	$ _____

EXERCISE 4.6

Find the gross earnings of the following employees, who are paid according to the salary-plus-commission plan.

1. Roger DeVere sells carpeting in a home improvement center. He receives a weekly salary of $300 and a commission rate of 3 percent on all sales. Last week, his sales totaled $16,500.

   Weekly salary $ _____

   Commission $ _____

   Gross earnings $ _____

2. Wayne Preston sells auto parts to service stations and discount stores. He receives a monthly salary of $1,600 and a commission rate of 4 percent on any sales above his monthly quota of $30,000. Last month, his sales totaled $118,000.

   Sales above quota $ _____   Monthly salary $ _____

                                                  Commission $ _____

                                                  Gross earnings $ _____

3. Ann-Marie Olson is a regional sales manager for a firm that produces accounting software. She receives a monthly salary of $3,120 and a commission rate of 5 percent on all sales that she makes. She also receives a commission of 1/2 of 1 percent on the sales made by the salespeople who work under her supervision. Last month, her sales totaled $18,500 and the sales of the other salespeople in her region totaled $124,000.

   Monthly salary $ _____

   Commission on personal sales $ _____

   Commission on sales of other salespeople $ _____

   Gross earnings $ _____

Name _____ Date _____

Unit 4 Exercises

EXERCISE 4.1A Complete the time cards that you totaled in Exercise 3.1A on page 75. Determine the regular, overtime, and gross earnings of the two employees of the Grandview Hotel. Enter the amounts that you compute at the bottom of the time cards.

EXERCISE 4.2A The following employees of Empire TV Production are paid according to the hourly rate plan. Find their gross earnings.

1. Bruce Stern is a lighting technician. His regular hourly rate is $18.60. Last week, he worked 35 1/2 hours.

   Gross earnings $ _____

2. Irene Brody is a casting assistant. Her regular hourly rate is $15.80. Last week, she worked 46 hours, Monday through Friday. She receives time and a half for any hours beyond 40 in her normal workweek.

   Overtime rate $ _____   Regular earnings $ _____

                                                   Overtime earnings $ _____

                                                   Gross earnings $ _____

3. John McHale is a camera operator. His regular hourly rate is $24.20. Last week, he worked 43 hours, Monday through Friday, and 4 hours on Saturday. He receives time and a half for any hours beyond 40 in his normal workweek and double time for any hours worked on weekends and holidays.

   Overtime rate (time and a half) $ _____

   Overtime rate (double time) $ _____

   Regular earnings $ _____

   Overtime earnings (time and a half) $ _____

   Overtime earnings (double time) $ _____

   Gross earnings $ _____

EXERCISE 4.3A The following employees work at the Mesa Medical Group. They are paid according to the salary plan. Compute their gross earnings.

1. Denise DeLuca is the receptionist. She has a regular weekly salary of $560 and a regular workweek of 40 hours. Last week, she worked 45 hours. Her overtime rate for all hours beyond 40 is 1 1/2 times her regular hourly rate.

   Regular hourly rate $ _____   Weekly salary $ _____

   Overtime rate $ _____   Overtime earnings $ _____

                                                        Gross earnings $ _____

2. Terry Miles is a laboratory technician. He has a weekly salary of $730 and a regular workweek of 40 hours. Last week, he spent only 32 hours on the job because he had to take a day off for personal business. He will not be paid for that time.

   Regular hourly rate $ _____   Gross earnings $ _____

3. Keesha Blake is the office manager and bookkeeper. She has a regular monthly salary of $3,640 and a regular workweek of 40 hours. Last month, she had 4 hours of overtime. She is paid 1 1/2 times her regular hourly rate for any overtime work.

Yearly salary	$ _____	Monthly salary	$ _____
Weekly salary	$ _____	Overtime earnings	$ _____
Regular hourly rate	$ _____	Gross earnings	$ _____
Overtime rate	$ _____		

EXERCISE 4.4A   The following employees of Precision Electronics are paid according to the piece-rate plan. Find their gross earnings.

1. Joseph Alessi is paid 86 cents for each item that he produces. Last week, he completed 650 items.

    Gross earnings $ _____

2. Sarah Young receives a piece rate of 48 cents for all items up to 1,200 that she completes in any week. For items beyond that number, she receives a rate of 65 cents per item. Last week, she completed 1,272 items.

    Gross earnings $ _____

3. Cameron Cox is paid 54 cents for each item that he produces. His regular workweek is 40 hours, and he receives half of his regular hourly rate for each overtime hour. Last week, he worked 47 hours and completed 920 items.

Regular hourly rate	$ _____	Piece-rate earnings	$ _____
Overtime rate	$ _____	Overtime earnings	$ _____
		Gross earnings	$ _____

EXERCISE 4.5A   Find the gross earnings of the following employees, who are paid according to the commission plan.

1. Harry Kreeger sells kitchen equipment to restaurants. He has a commission rate of 2 percent. Last week, his sales totaled $54,360.

    Gross earnings $ _____

2. Joan Melendez sells clothing at a luxury boutique. She has a commission rate of 3 percent. Last week, her sales totaled $32,600.

    Gross earnings $ _____

    Compute the regular hourly rate of this employee for the week to be sure that it meets the current minimum wage. Joan Melendez has a regular workweek of 40 hours.

    Regular hourly rate $ _____

3. Don Slater sells security systems for homes and businesses. He receives a commission rate of 2 1/2 percent on the home systems and 4 percent on the business systems. Last week, his sales of home systems totaled $22,400 and his sales of business systems totaled $16,850.

    Commission on home systems $ _____

    Commission on business systems $ _____

    Gross earnings $ _____

EXERCISE 4.6A   Find the gross earnings of the following employees, who are paid according to the salary-plus-commission plan.

1. Brady Quinn sells furniture at a department store. He receives a weekly salary of $350 and a commission rate of 2 percent on all sales. Last week, his sales totaled $27,345.

   Weekly salary $ _____

   Commission $ _____

   Gross earnings $ _____

2. Ellen Pasternak sells fitness equipment to health clubs. She receives a monthly salary of $1,780 and a commission rate of 5 percent on any sales above her monthly quota of $50,000. Last month, her sales totaled $122,000.

   Sales above quota $ _____   Monthly salary $ _____

                                                  Commission $ _____

                                                  Gross earnings $ _____

3. Laura Gibbs is the sales manager for a company that produces educational toys. She receives a monthly salary of $3,600 and a commission rate of 4 percent on all sales that she makes. She also receives a commission of 1/2 of 1 percent on the sales made by the salespeople who work under her supervision. Last month, her sales totaled $12,200 and the sales of the other salespeople totaled $410,000.

   Monthly salary $ _____

   Commission on personal sales $ _____

   Commission on sales of other salespeople $ _____

   Gross earnings $ _____

Unit **Five**

Determining Payroll Deductions

Objectives

Upon completion of this unit, you should be able to:

1. List the four factors that are used in determining deductions from the federal income tax wage-bracket tables.
2. Name several common "pretax" items that lessen the amount of income tax for employees.
3. Use federal and state wage-bracket tables to determine income taxes due on employee earnings.
4. Calculate social security and Medicare taxes on employee earnings.
5. Compute the earnings from tips of an employee, and explain how taxes on these earnings are recorded.
6. Subtract total deductions from gross earnings to determine net pay.
7. Explain why it is important to use the correct wage-bracket tax tables to determine both federal and state income tax on employee earnings.
8. State the current rates on employee earnings for social security tax and Medicare tax.
9. Explain what state disability and state unemployment taxes are, including who pays these taxes and who benefits from them.
10. Define each of these terms as they relate to deductions from employee earnings: *voluntary deductions, garnishment of wages, union checkoff, retirement accounts, pension plans, savings plans,* and *charitable contributions.*

The amount of money an employee receives as take-home pay today is usually less than the amount the employee earns. The difference between these two figures is the result of *deductions* made from the employee's gross earnings.

Some deductions, such as federal income tax, social security tax, and Medicare tax are required by law. Other deductions are *voluntary*. Voluntary deductions cover items that employees want and that employers make available, such as health insurance, life insurance, savings bonds, and retirement accounts. If employees belong to a union, there may also be deductions for union dues and assessments.

There are other deductions available for employees that are referred to as *pretax deductions*. These deductions are called pretax because the deduction is subtracted from gross earnings prior to computing the federal income tax. Probably, the most common pretax deduction is the 401-K contribution by an employee to a retirement plan. This deduction allows the employee to defer paying federal income tax on this contribution amount at the time of the contribution. Tax will be paid when the employee draws the money out at retirement. Another common group of pretax deductions fall under the IRS Section 125 cafeteria plan provisions that allow deductions prior to the calculation of federal income tax. It is called a cafeteria plan because the employee may elect to have amounts withheld from gross

Point of Interest

earnings that can be used to reimburse the employee for child care expenses and out-of-pocket health care amounts not reimbursed by insurance. A final provision of Section 125 allows the employee's portion of a group health insurance plan to be deducted prior to the calculation of federal income tax.

Employers are responsible for making the correct deductions from the earnings of their employees, keeping accurate records of these deductions, and sending the money withheld to the proper agencies. They are also responsible for providing detailed information to the employee regarding earnings, deductions, and net pay. In this unit, you will learn about the various types of deductions and the methods used to determine them. You will also see how take-home pay is computed. In later units, you will learn the procedures for recording deductions and paying the amounts that are withheld to the appropriate agencies.

Most employees are subject to federal income tax and social security and Medicare taxes. Other required deductions vary from state to state and city to city. Such deductions may include state and local income taxes, state disability tax, state unemployment tax, and other special taxes on earnings. In addition, courts may require deductions from the wages of an employee who has overdue debts.

DETERMINING FEDERAL INCOME TAX

As you learned in Unit 1, employers are required by federal law to withhold federal income tax from employee earnings at the end of each payroll period and send those amounts to the federal government at regular intervals. This payroll function, which is performed by private businesses, is a critical and valuable function assisting our government in the collection of income taxes in a prompt and efficient manner.

The Wage-Bracket Method

There are several different methods for determining federal income tax deductions. The simplest method, the *wage-bracket method,* involves the use of wage-bracket tables provided by the IRS (Internal Revenue Service). The federal tables are contained in an IRS publication, the *Employer's Tax Guide.* This guide, also identified as Publication 15 and Circular E, is revised each year. When there are changes in the law during the year, additional revisions are released. Four factors are used in the design of these tax tables:

- The length of the payroll period
- The employee's gross earnings for the period
- The employee's marital status
- The number of withholding allowances claimed by the employee

There are separate tables for married and single persons and for daily, weekly, biweekly, semimonthly, monthly, and miscellaneous payroll periods.

Notice how the table in Figure 5.1 on page 102 is used to find the federal income tax withheld for Ms. Renne. Lucinda Renne is single and has zero withholding allowances because her father claims her as an exemption. During one week when she worked 10 hours, she earned $95 and her federal income tax was $5.

Her number of withholding allowances and marital status are found by looking at the top section of her employee earnings record for the year. See Figure 2.4 on pages 28 and 29. Here are the steps involved in determining the correct amount of federal income tax for Lucinda Renne.

Point of Interest

Who heads today's families? The U.S. Bureau of Census found in 2002 that families with children under 18 had the following heads of households:

Single father	5%
Single mother	23
Married couples	69
Neither parent present	4

FIGURE 5.1   Federal Income Tax Table for Single Persons Paid Weekly

SINGLE Persons—WEEKLY Payroll Period
(For Wages Paid Through December 2004)

If the wages are—		And the number of withholding allowances claimed is—										
At least	But less than	0	1	2	3	4	5	6	7	8	9	10
		The amount of income tax to be withheld is—										
$0	$55	$0	$0	$0	$0	$0	$0	$0	$0	$0	$0	$0
55	60	1	0	0	0	0	0	0	0	0	0	0
60	65	1	0	0	0	0	0	0	0	0	0	0
65	70	2	0	0	0	0	0	0	0	0	0	0
70	75	2	0	0	0	0	0	0	0	0	0	0
75	80	3	0	0	0	0	0	0	0	0	0	0
80	85	3	0	0	0	0	0	0	0	0	0	0
85	90	4	0	0	0	0	0	0	0	0	0	0
90	95	4	0	0	0	0	0	0	0	0	0	0
95	100	5	0	0	0	0	0	0	0	0	0	0
100	105	5	0	0	0	0	0	0	0	0	0	0
105	110	6	0	0	0	0	0	0	0	0	0	0
110	115	6	0	0	0	0	0	0	0	0	0	0
510	520	63	54	45	36	27	18	11	5	0	0	0
520	530	64	55	46	38	29	20	12	6	0	0	0
530	540	66	57	48	39	30	21	13	7	1	0	0
540	550	67	58	49	41	32	23	14	8	2	0	0
550	560	69	60	51	42	33	24	15	9	3	0	0
560	570	70	61	52	44	35	26	17	10	4	0	0
570	580	72	63	54	45	36	27	18	11	5	0	0
580	590	73	64	55	47	38	29	20	12	6	0	0
590	600	75	66	57	48	39	30	21	13	7	1	0

1. Use the federal income tax wage-bracket tables.

2. Locate the tax withholding table "SINGLE Persons—WEEKLY Payroll Period."

3. Look down the first two left-hand columns of the table to find the double-column wage bracket that covers the gross earnings of this employee. In the case of Ms. Renne, the proper wage bracket reads "At least $95 . . . but less than $100."

4. Look at the top of the table to find the column for the number of withholding allowances the employee claims. Because Ms. Renne claims zero allowances, the column labeled "0" is the proper column to use to determine her tax.

5. Follow the line for the employee's wage bracket across the table until you reach the column that shows the number of withholding allowances the employee claims. The figure that appears at this point in the table is the amount of federal income tax to be withheld. In the case of Ms. Renne, the correct amount is $5.

The person who does payroll work for a business must be sure to use the correct income tax withholding table for each employee. The table chosen must match the payroll period and the marital status of the employee. The information about an employee's marital status, withholding allowances, and other important payroll data is found on Form W-4, the Employee's Withholding Allowance Certificate. Refer to Figure 2.1 on pages 20 and 21 and

Figure 2.3 on pages 25 and 26 to review this form. Remember that when a new employee joins a firm, the employer must have the employee complete and sign a Form W-4. When an existing employee wants to change his or her marital status or number of withholding allowances, a new W-4 should be prepared by the employee.

Other Systems for Determining Withholding Tax

Besides the wage-bracket tables, the *Employer's Tax Guide* also provides information about several other methods that can be used for determining federal income tax withholding. These methods are generally used by firms that have computerized their payroll process. One of these methods is the *percentage method of withholding.* The percentage method of withholding utilizes the same basic approach as the wage-bracket method. Circular E contains tables for the various frequencies of pay periods broken into single and married sections. Each table further breaks down wages into intervals with a different percentage of tax for each interval (see Figure 5.2).

As you examine Table 1, you will notice that as the employee makes more money, the tax rate increases. If we used the percentage method to calculate Ms. Renne's federal income tax, we would follow these steps.

1. Use Table 1—Weekly Payroll Period.
2. Use the (a) Single side of the table.
3. Look down the left column to find where her wages of $95 will fall. Her wages of $95 are over $51 but not over $187, so the amount of income tax to withhold is 10 percent of the excess over $51.
4. The excess over $51 is calculated as follows: $95 − $51 = $44.
5. The amount of tax will be 10 percent × $44, or $4.40.

Because this employee claims no withholding allowances, the computation of her federal income tax deduction using the percentage method is quite simple. Circular E provides detailed instructions and examples for employees who claim withholding allowances under this method.

While some small businesses still do their payroll using the wage-bracket tables, many others use any one of a variety of computerized payroll systems developed for small businesses. These software packages are simple to operate and reasonably priced. Not only do they compute the payroll and print the payroll checks, they also are able to generate the reports that are required by federal and state tax agencies.

READING THE WAGE-BRACKET TABLES PROPERLY

State and local tax authorities also issue wage-bracket tables to employers for determining income tax deductions. These tables work in the same way as the federal tables.

All wage-bracket tables are divided into rows that cover the various wage brackets and columns that cover the different numbers of withholding allowances. Care must be taken to select the correct row and the correct column for each employee.

The Zero Allowance Column

Look at the partial federal income tax table in Figure 5.1. Notice that the first withholding allowance column is labeled "0." This column is used only for employees who do not claim any withholding allowances. (Some employees select zero allowances, even though they are entitled to at least one withholding allowance.)

It is easy to become confused and think the first column is the 1 allowance column. Some payroll clerks use a red pencil and draw a wavy vertical line through the white space in the 0 column on all of the wage-bracket tables as a reminder. Of course, they are careful not to block out the figures in the 0 column. The presence of the red wavy line in the first column is a constant remainder that this column is for zero allowances and not for one allowance.

FIGURE 5.2 Circular E. Tables for Percentage Method of Withholding

Tables for Percentage Method of Withholding
(For Wages Paid Through December 2004)

TABLE 1—WEEKLY Payroll Period

(a) SINGLE person (including head of household)—

If the amount of wages (after subtracting withholding allowances) is:		The amount of income tax to withhold is:	
Not over $51		$0	
Over—	**But not over—**		**of excess over—**
$51	—$187 . .	10%	—$51
$187	—$592 . .	$13.60 plus 15%	—$187
$592	—$1,317 . .	$74.35 plus 25%	—$592
$1,317	—$2,860 . .	$255.60 plus 28%	—$1,317
$2,860	—$6,177 . .	$687.64 plus 33%	—$2,860
$6,177	. . . . . .	$1,782.25 plus 35%	—$6,177

(b) MARRIED person—

If the amount of wages (after subtracting withholding allowances) is:		The amount of income tax to withhold is:	
Not over $154		$0	
Over—	**But not over—**		**of excess over—**
$154	—$429 . .	10%	—$154
$429	—$1,245 . .	$27.50 plus 15%	—$429
$1,245	—$2,270 . .	$149.90 plus 25%	—$1,245
$2,270	—$3,568 . .	$406.15 plus 28%	—$2,270
$3,568	—$6,271 . .	$769.59 plus 33%	—$3,568
$6,271	. . . . . .	$1,661.58 plus 35%	—$6,271

TABLE 2—BIWEEKLY Payroll Period

(a) SINGLE person (including head of household)—

If the amount of wages (after subtracting withholding allowances) is:		The amount of income tax to withhold is:	
Not over $102		$0	
Over—	**But not over—**		**of excess over—**
$102	—$373 . .	10%	—$102
$373	—$1,185 . .	$27.10 plus 15%	—$373
$1,185	—$2,635 . .	$148.90 plus 25%	—$1,185
$2,635	—$5,719 . .	$511.40 plus 28%	—$2,635
$5,719	—$12,354 . .	$1,374.92 plus 33%	—$5,719
$12,354	. . . . . .	$3,564.47 plus 35%	—$12,354

(b) MARRIED person—

If the amount of wages (after subtracting withholding allowances) is:		The amount of income tax to withhold is:	
Not over $308		$0	
Over—	**But not over—**		**of excess over—**
$308	—$858 . .	10%	—$308
$858	—$2,490 . .	$55.00 plus 15%	—$858
$2,490	—$4,540 . .	$299.80 plus 25%	—$2,490
$4,540	—$7,137 . .	$812.30 plus 28%	—$4,540
$7,137	—$12,542 . .	$1,539.46 plus 33%	—$7,137
$12,542	. . . . . .	$3,323.11 plus 35%	—$12,542

TABLE 3—SEMIMONTHLY Payroll Period

(a) SINGLE person (including head of household)—

If the amount of wages (after subtracting withholding allowances) is:		The amount of income tax to withhold is:	
Not over $110		$0	
Over—	**But not over—**		**of excess over—**
$110	—$404 . .	10%	—$110
$404	—$1,283 . .	$29.40 plus 15%	—$404
$1,283	—$2,854 . .	$161.25 plus 25%	—$1,283
$2,854	—$6,196 . .	$554.00 plus 28%	—$2,854
$6,196	—$13,383 . .	$1,489.76 plus 33%	—$6,196
$13,383	. . . . . .	$3,861.47 plus 35%	—$13,383

(b) MARRIED person—

If the amount of wages (after subtracting withholding allowances) is:		The amount of income tax to withhold is:	
Not over $333		$0	
Over—	**But not over—**		**of excess over—**
$333	—$929 . .	10%	—$333
$929	—$2,698 . .	$59.60 plus 15%	—$929
$2,698	—$4,919 . .	$324.95 plus 25%	—$2,698
$4,919	—$7,731 . .	$880.20 plus 28%	—$4,919
$7,731	—$13,588 . .	$1,667.56 plus 33%	—$7,731
$13,588	. . . . . .	$3,600.37 plus 35%	—$13,588

TABLE 4—MONTHLY Payroll Period

(a) SINGLE person (including head of household)—

If the amount of wages (after subtracting withholding allowances) is:		The amount of income tax to withhold is:	
Not over $221		$0	
Over—	**But not over—**		**of excess over—**
$221	—$808 . .	10%	—$221
$808	—$2,567 . .	$58.70 plus 15%	—$808
$2,567	—$5,708 . .	$322.55 plus 25%	—$2,567
$5,708	—$12,392 . .	$1,107.80 plus 28%	—$5,708
$12,392	—$26,767 . .	$2,979.32 plus 33%	—$12,392
$26,767	. . . . . .	$7,723.07 plus 35%	—$26,767

(b) MARRIED person—

If the amount of wages (after subtracting withholding allowances) is:		The amount of income tax to withhold is:	
Not over $667		$0	
Over—	**But not over—**		**of excess over—**
$667	—$1,858 . .	10%	—$667
$1,858	—$5,396 . .	$119.10 plus 15%	—$1,858
$5,396	—$9,838 . .	$649.80 plus 25%	—$5,396
$9,838	—$15,463 . .	$1,760.30 plus 28%	—$9,838
$15,463	—$27,175 . .	$3,335.30 plus 33%	—$15,463
$27,175	. . . . . .	$7,200.26 plus 35%	—$27,175

The Wage-Bracket Lines

It is easy to select the wrong wage-bracket line for an employee if you do not pay careful attention to the headings in the wages section of the tax table. For example, refer to the federal income tax table shown in Figure 5.1. The employee had weekly earnings of $95. Therefore, the proper wage bracket for the employee is "At least $95 but less than $100." Note that the wage bracket immediately above this line also includes $95, but it is not the correct wage bracket because it reads "At least $90 but less than $95."

Using a Guide to Read the Wage-Bracket Lines

When an income tax table is being used, errors can occur because the payroll clerk's eyes do not move across the wage-bracket lines correctly. Instead, they stray to the line above or the line below. A simple way to avoid this problem is to place a ruler or other straight-edge device under the wage-bracket line to be read. Some payroll clerks find it even more efficient to use a guide, such as the one shown in Figure 5.3, to locate tax amounts on a table.

The guide looks like the letter L reversed. The horizontal edge makes it easy to read the wage-bracket line properly, and the vertical edge makes it easier to find the correct withholding allowance column. Notice how the guide was useful when looking up the federal income tax to be withheld for Ven Nguyen, a repair and maintenance employee for Ingram Heating and Cooling. He earned $600 that week, and he has four allowances.

The guide was placed just below the line that reads, "At least $600 . . . But less than $610," and just to the right of the 4 allowances column. The correct withholding amount

FIGURE 5.3 **Federal Income tax Table for Married Persons Paid Weekly.** A guide is being shown with this table.

MARRIED Persons—WEEKLY Payroll Period

(For Wages Paid Through December 2004)

If the wages are—		And the number of withholding allowances claimed is—										
At least	But less than	0	1	2	3	4	5	6	7	8	9	10
		The amount of income tax to be withheld is—										
$0	$125	$0	$0	$0	$0	$0	$0	$0	$0	$0	$0	$0
125	130	0	0	0	0	0	0	0	0	0	0	0
130	135	0	0	0	0	0	0	0	0	0	0	0
135	140	0	0	0	0	0	0	0	0	0	0	0
140	145	0	0	0	0	0	0	0	0	0	0	0
145	150	0	0	0	0	0	0	0	0	0	0	0
150	155	0	0	0	0	0	0	0	0	0	0	0
155	160	0	0	0	0	0	0	0	0	0	0	0
160	165	1	0	0	0	0	0	0	0	0	0	0
165	170	1	0	0	0	0	0	0	0	0	0	0
540	550	45	36	27	21	15	9	3	0	0	0	0
550	560	46	37	29	22	16	10	4	0	0	0	0
560	570	48	39	30	23	17	11	5	0	0	0	0
570	580	49	40	32	24	18	12	6	0	0	0	0
580	590	51	42	33	25	19	13	7	1	0	0	0
590	600	52	43	35	26	20	14	8	2	0	0	0
600	610	54	45	36	27	21	15	9	3	0	0	0
610	620	55	46	38	29	22	16	10	4	0	0	0
620	630	57	48	39	30	23	17	11	5	0	0	0
630	640	58	49	41	32	24	18	12	6	0	0	0
640	650	60	51	42	33	25	19	13	7	1	0	0
650	660	61	52	44	35	26	20	14	8	2	0	0
660	670	63	54	45	36	27	21	15	9	3	0	0
670	680	64	55	47	38	29	22	16	10	4	0	0
680	690	66	57	48	39	30	23	17	11	5	0	0
690	700	67	58	50	41	32	24	18	12	6	0	0
700	710	69	60	51	42	33	25	19	13	7	1	0
710	720	70	61	53	44	35	26	20	14	8	2	0
720	730	72	63	54	45	36	27	21	15	9	3	0
730	740	73	64	56	47	38	29	22	16	10	4	0

According to a recent study by the U.S. Bureau of Labor Statistics, women's earnings are approximately 77 percent of men's earnings. This earnings gap between men and women has narrowed over the years, but is still a challenge facing many companies.

for federal income tax is shown where the vertical and horizontal bars meet. The tax withholding amount is $21.

Learning Through Practice

Do Exercise 5.1 on page 123 of this text-workbook.

DETERMINING SOCIAL SECURITY TAX

The Federal Insurance Contributions Act (FICA) requires most employers and employees to pay a tax to support the federal social security system. This system provides old-age, disability, and Medicare benefits to retired and disabled persons. In some cases, the program also provides benefits to survivors of deceased workers. Originally, employers and employees each paid a single tax amount, which was known as *social security tax* or *FICA tax,* to cover all portions of the system. However, since 1991, the federal government has required payment of a separate social security tax and a separate Medicare tax.

The current social security tax supports old-age, disability, and survivor's programs. The current Medicare tax supports health care for the elderly. Each of these taxes is calculated and reported separately for payroll reporting.

At the time of this writing the social security tax is at the rate of 6.2 percent on the first $87,900 earned by an employee during the calendar year (January 1 through December 31). The wage base has been adjusted upward over the past several years while the tax rate, 6.2 percent, has remained constant. Medicare tax is at the rate of 1.45 percent on *all* earnings. This tax rate has also remained constant for a number of years. There is no wage base on Medicare, so the tax is payable on all wages. For both social security and Medicare, the amounts paid by employees must be matched by the employer. Thus, the employer must pay an amount that is equal to the total social security and Medicare taxes that are withheld from the earnings of its employees. For example, suppose that a business has five employees and withholds $1,200 from their earnings for social security and Medicare taxes. The business must pay the federal government $1,200 to match the amount of social security and Medicare taxes withheld.

Although the tax rates for social security and Medicare have not increased in recent years, you can easily see that as wages increase the deduction from employee earnings for social security and Medicare will increase. The matching portion on social security and Medicare paid by employers will also increase. Please note that the matching requirement applies only to social security and Medicare taxes. Obviously, the employers are not required to match the amount of federal income tax withheld from its employees!

Keep in mind that both the social security and Medicare tax rates and the base amount of taxable wages may increase in the future. Federal legislation passed in 1983 specified that the amount of taxable wages for social security will be adjusted each year according to changes in average earnings throughout the United States.

Computing Social Security Tax

Social security tax is computed by multiplying an employee's earnings subject to the social security tax by the current tax rate. In 2004, the social security tax rate was 6.2 percent and the maximum earnings taxed for social security was $87,900.

Examples

One week Donald Zanka had gross earnings of $415. His social security tax was $25.73 ($415 × .062 = $25.73). Since the tax rate is 6.2 percent, in order to multiply, the percentage is changed to its decimal equivalent of .062.

Point of Interest

Where does the income of the federal government in the United States come from, and just as important, how is it spent? In 1996 the greater part of income was from individual income tax, a total of $656 billion. Corporations paid $175 billion in taxes. Social security and other retirement contributions totaled $509 billion. Social security, Medicare, and other retirement payments cost $597 billion. Review this table to see the percentages of federal income and outlays.

Income

Personal income taxes	42%
Social security, Medicare, and other retirement taxes	33
Corporate income taxes	11
Excise, estate, gift, and other miscellaneous taxes	7
Borrowing to cover deficit	7

Outlays

Social security, Medicare, and other retirement programs	37%
National defense, veterans, and foreign affairs	20
Social programs	18
Net interest on debt	15
Physical, human, and community development	8
Law enforcement	2

Doris Kosta's social security tax on earnings of $659.65 would be $40.90.

$659.65   gross earnings
$\times$ .062   social security tax rate
_____
1.31930
39.5790
_____
$40.89830   = $40.90 social security tax

Maximum Social Security Tax

There is a maximum amount of earnings subject to social security tax during each calendar year. This maximum tends to increase from year to year. The person who does payroll work for a firm must be sure to avoid making social security deductions from an employee whose wages from that firm have passed the maximum taxable amount for the year. The employee earnings records kept for each employee shows his or her year-to-date wages. These records should be checked before preparing the payroll to find out whether any employees are close to the limit for social security tax.

For example, William Ingram, the president and general manager of Ingram Heating and Cooling, has a weekly salary of $3,280. The wage base for social security tax at the time of this writing is $87,900. Mr. Ingram's annual gross earnings at his rate of pay will be $170,560 ($3,280 $\times$ 52 weeks = $170,560). Thus the payroll clerk must be careful as Mr. Ingram approaches the social security tax base of $87,900 and stop taking social security tax from his paychecks when he reaches that point.

DETERMINING MEDICARE TAX

The tax for Medicare is 1.45 percent on all earnings for the year, no matter how much an employee may make. There is no cutoff point, as there is for social security.

Herman Dostler earned $393 one week. The Medicare tax on this amount of earnings is $5.70. The way to determine the Medicare tax is to do a simple calculation. Multiply the employee's earnings, $393, by the tax rate of 1.45 percent. The rate, 1.45 percent, must be converted to its decimal equivalent, .0145. The amount of tax owed is $5.70 ($393 × .0145 = $5.6985, or $5.70 when the amount is rounded).

EARNINGS NOT SUBJECT TO SOCIAL SECURITY AND MEDICARE TAXES

As mentioned in the introduction to this unit, there are some earnings that are not taxed for social security and Medicare purposes. IRS Publications 15 and 15B contain lists and descriptions of those items. One of the more common benefits offered employees is to participate in a cafeteria plan benefit covered under Section 125 of the Internal Revenue Code. Under this plan, the employee may elect to have the employer (or agent of the employer) retain a certain amount of dollars to be used to pay for child care, medical expenses, or health insurance premiums. Under this plan, the amounts withheld are not subject to the social security or Medicare tax. The employer (or agent) will reimburse the employee on the basis of submission of paid bills. The employee will forfeit any amounts that are not claimed under these provisions at the end of each year.

Because the employee pays no social security or Medicare tax on these deductions, the business does not have to match the amounts, thus saving the business money. The rules for determining the tax liability for social security and Medicare on Section 125 plans are very complex and the payroll clerk should always seek assistance from the company's certified public accountant (CPA) or the local IRS office.

Learning Through Practice

Do Exercise 5.2 on page 123 of this text-workbook.

STATE AND LOCAL INCOME TAXES

Many states impose income taxes on individuals and require businesses to withhold such taxes from employee earnings. As of this writing, personal income taxes have been established in 42 states, the District of Columbia, and Puerto Rico. The states without such taxes on wages and salaries are Alaska, Connecticut, Florida, Nevada, New Hampshire, South Dakota, Tennessee, Texas, Washington, and Wyoming. (Several of these states levy personal income tax on interest and dividends but not on wages and salaries.)

Keep in mind that there may be items not subject to federal or state income tax. The amounts of these items must be deducted from gross earnings to determine the amount of gross earnings subject to income tax. Dependent care, accident and medical insurance, Section 401 retirement plan contributions, and contributions to a SIMPLE retirement account are all examples of items not subject to income taxes.

Computing State Withholding Tax

The tax rates and procedures for payment vary from state to state; however, like the federal government, most states require employers to deduct withholding tax from employee earnings at the end of each payroll period. The methods used to determine the withholding amounts for state income tax often are quite similar to those used for federal income tax. For example, Ingram Heating and Cooling, which is located in California, makes use of wage-bracket tables. The California income tax tables for single and married taxpayers are located in the Appendix. Such tax tables are provided to employers by the state tax agency. You will find that they are designed much like the federal wage-bracket tables. They are functional and easy to use.

In California, there are separate tables for single persons, married persons, and unmarried persons who are heads of household. (The last category generally covers single persons who have their own household and one or more dependents living with them.) The

California income tax tables cover weekly, biweekly, semimonthly, monthly, and miscellaneous payroll periods.

Notice how the weekly pay period tax table for married persons is used to determine the amount of state income tax owed by Samio Martinez for the week when he earned $975. He is married and claims five withholding allowances. Turn to the Appendix and follow this process.

His state income tax on earnings of $975 is $13.00. The wage bracket used to determine the tax states, "At least $960 . . . But less than $980." Notice that, like the federal tax tables, the first allowance column is for employees who claim no allowances. Mr. Martinez's tax is determined by reading across to the column for a person with five allowances.

The California income tax table for married persons stops at $2,200 of weekly earnings. For persons who earn more than $2,200 per week, the income tax is the table amount *plus* 9.3 percent of the amount over $2,180.

Pamela Cook is a single worker who claims one allowance. She earned $600 during one week. Her state income tax on that amount is $16.31. To find this tax amount, use the tax table for single persons paid weekly shown in the Appendix. Follow down the left-hand columns. She earned "At least $600 . . . But less than $620." Follow across the table to the 1 allowance column. Her tax is $16.31.

In some cities and counties, individuals must pay a local income tax as well as a state income tax. Although the laws covering such taxes vary, employers usually are required to withhold local income taxes in the same way that they withhold federal and state income taxes.

In addition to providing wage-bracket tables, most state and local income tax authorities allow employers to use percentage methods to compute tax deductions for their employees. Among firms that have computerized payroll systems, the annualizing method is a common way to determine the amount to be withheld for state and local income taxes.

Learning Through Practice

Do Exercise 5.3 on page 123 of this text-workbook.

State Disability Insurance Tax

California, Hawaii, New Jersey, New York, and Rhode Island have disability insurance programs. These programs provide benefits to employees who are unable to work because of illness or injuries that are *not* job-related. (Employees who have job-related illnesses or injuries receive benefits from workers' compensation insurance.) The details of the various disability insurance programs differ. Some programs are completely financed by deductions from employee earnings. Other programs require contributions by both employers and employees.

In California, where Ingram Heating and Cooling is located, only the employees pay state disability insurance (SDI) tax. This tax is withheld from their earnings at a rate specified by the state. The tax rate and the wage base on which the tax is payable are usually adjusted each year. As of 2004, the rate in California is 1.18 percent and is payable on the first $68,829 earned by an employee during a calendar year. The maximum that can be withheld for SDI tax during a year is $812.18.

Example

In one week Doris Kosta earned $560. She will have $6.61 deducted from her earnings for state disability insurance tax ($560 × .0118 = $6.61) up to the maximum taxable amount. Notice that the rate of 1.18 percent is changed to the decimal .0118 in order to do the computation.

$$\begin{array}{ll} \$560 & \text{gross earnings} \\ \underline{\times\ .0118} & \text{SDI rate} \\ \$6.61 & \text{SDI tax} \end{array}$$

Just as with social security tax, the person who does payroll work for a firm must be careful not to make any SDI deductions from employees whose wages have reached the maximum taxable amount for the year. The employee earnings records must be checked periodically to assure that no employee is close to reaching the maximum earnings on which SDI should be withheld.

Learning Through Practice   Do Exercise 5.4 on page 123 of this text-workbook.

State Unemployment Compensation Tax

State unemployment compensation systems provide income for employees who lose their jobs through no fault of their own and cannot find other jobs right away. In most states, the system is supported by employer contributions. However, Alaska and New Jersey also require that employees contribute to state unemployment compensation tax through a payroll deduction. In California the state unemployment insurance (SUI) program is financed entirely by employers through a payroll tax based on the first $7,000 in wages paid to each employee each year.

Garnishments

Sometimes a court orders an employer to make deductions from the wages of an employee who has overdue debts, including child support. This process is known as *garnishment.* The amounts withheld are sent directly to the creditor or are given to the court, which turns the money over to the creditor. The garnishment procedure continues during each payroll period until the employee's debt is paid.

TREATMENT OF TIPS FOR FEDERAL WITHHOLDING TAXES

Tips are subject to federal income tax, social security tax, and Medicare tax. Employees who receive $20 or more per month in tips must report the figure to their employer by the tenth of the next month. These employees must also report their total tips for the year on their annual federal income tax returns.

Diana Wills is a waitress at a small restaurant. She keeps track of her tips in a special IRS booklet (Publication 1244). The booklet contains daily record sheets (Form 4070A) and a monthly report form (Form 4070).

A completed Form 4070A for a one-month period is shown in Figure 5.4. At the end of the month, Ms. Wills prepared Form 4070, shown in Figure 5.5 on page 111, using the totals from Form 4070A. Her completed Form 4070A for the month of November appears in Figure 5.4 on page 111.

Employees keep track of tips on a daily basis on Form 4070A. At the end of the month, all the tips are totaled. The figures are then entered on Form 4070, and this form is given to the employer. The IRS booklet contains a year's supply of Form 4070.

The employer must collect federal income tax, social security tax, and Medicare tax on tips, either by withholding the amounts from wages or by using other funds that the employee makes available. Thus, at the end of each month, when Diana Wills reports her tips on Form 4070, her employer will either withhold enough from her wages to pay these taxes or ask Diana Wills for the amount that is due.

Learning Through Practice   Do Exercise 5.5 on page 123 of this text-workbook.

DEDUCTIONS REQUIRED BY UNION CONTRACTS

In some firms, employees belong to a union and are covered by a contract requiring that union deductions be made from their earnings. The contract, which is signed by both the employer and the union, specifies that the employer will withhold union initiation fees, dues, and assessments. These deductions are often made on a monthly basis, and the amount withheld

FIGURE 5.4   **Form 4070A**

Form **4070A** (Rev. June 1999) Department of the Treasury Internal Revenue Service	**Employee's Daily Record of Tips** This is a voluntary form provided for your convenience. See instructions for records you must keep.	OMB No. 1545-0065
Employee's name and address *Diana Wills* *4060 Carol Street* *San Jose, CA 95144*	Employer's name *Josephine Mackey* Establishment name (if different) *The Red Skillet*	Month and year *Nov. 2004*

Date tips rec'd.	Date of entry	a. Tips received directly from customers and other employees	b. Credit card tips received	c. Tips paid out to other employees	d. Names of employees to whom you paid tips
1	1	38.20	16.50		
2	2	29.40	15.30		
3	3	42.95	21.00		
4	4	37.60	19.20		
5	5	41.25	13.70		
Subtotals		189.40	85.70		
15	15	47.20	19.80		
Subtotals		241.90	110.30		
23	23	38.30	14.40		
24	24	41.70	19.80		
25	25	49.20	25.30		
Subtotals		327.00	151.40		
30	30	37.25	16.40		
Subtotals from pages 1, 2, and 3		189.40 241.90 327.00	85.70 110.30 151.40		
Totals		873.10	399.20		

Left-margin "Date tips rec'd." columns list: 6, 7, 8, 9, 10, 11, 12, 13, 14, 15, 16, 17, 18, 19, 20, 21, 22, 26, 27, 28, 29, 30, 31

1. Report total cash tips (col. **a**) on Form 4070, line **1**.
2. Report total credit card tips (col. **b**) on Form 4070, line **2**.
3. Report total tips paid out (col. **c**) on Form 4070, line **3**.

is then turned over to the union. The withholding of union amounts from employee earnings is known as a *checkoff.*

Despite the fact that the union deductions are generally specified by a contract with the union, the employer must have a written authorization from each employee before making these deductions. However, under the terms of the contract, new employees usually are obliged to sign such an authorization in order to work at the firm.

FIGURE 5.5

Form 4070 Employee's Report of Tips to Employer

Form **4070** (Rev. June 1999) Department of the Treasury Internal Revenue Service	**Employee's Report of Tips to Employer** ► For Paperwork Reduction Act Notice, see back of form.	OMB No. 1545-0065
Employee's name and address *Diana L. Wills* *4060 Carol Street* *San Jose, CA 95144*		Social security number *282 : 90 : 3071*
Employer's name and address (include establishment name, if different) *Josephine Mackey* *The Red Skillet* *4490 Maritime Way* *San Jose, CA 95001*		1 Cash tips received *873.10*
		2 Credit card tips received *399.20*
		3 Tips paid out
Month or shorter period in which tips were received from *Nov. 1, 2004*, to *Nov. 30, 2004*		4 Net tips (lines **1** + **2** - **3**) *1272.30*
Signature *Diana L. Wills*		Date *Nov. 30, 2004*

VOLUNTARY DEDUCTIONS

In addition to deductions required by law and those required by union contract, many employees have voluntary deductions. These deductions cover such items as health insurance, life insurance, membership in a company pension plan, purchases of saving bonds, purchases of company stock, and contributions to charity.

A large firm may have many different voluntary deductions available for employees to choose from; however, small firms usually offer only a few such deductions or none at all. For example, at Ingram Heating and Cooling, there are just two types of voluntary deductions available—deductions for a Roth Individual Retirement Account (IRA) or for United States savings bonds. Note that contributions to a Roth IRA are treated as taxable earnings (not as a pretax deduction) because when the funds in a Roth IRA are drawn out at retirement, the amounts withdrawn are tax free!

No matter what the size of the firm, it must obtain written authorization from employees for *any* voluntary deductions they wish to have. The exact contents of this form will differ from company to company. The form used by Ingram Heating and Cooling is shown in Figure 5.6. This is the form that Moses Forbisher filled out and signed in June for the withholding of $20 a week as an investment in a Roth IRA. This amount will be deducted from his gross earnings at the end of each weekly payroll period.

As a convenience for its employees, Ingram Heating and Cooling withholds the Roth IRA amounts and forwards those amounts to its bank, the Bank of Commerce. Of course, individuals may open IRA accounts at any financial institution of their choice. Ingram offers this voluntary deduction simply to help its employees save for retirement.

The authorization form that employees complete and sign must be kept in the company's payroll files to provide legal backing for the voluntary deductions that are made from employee earnings.

Information about the voluntary deductions selected by employees appears on each employee earnings record, as shown on Figure 2.5 on page 31. This makes the information easily available to the payroll clerk as weekly deductions are made.

FIGURE 5.6
Authorization for Voluntary Deductions

Ingram Heating and Cooling
4466 Maritime Way   San Jose, CA 95001

AUTHORIZATION FOR VOLUNTARY DEDUCTIONS

I hereby authorize Ingram Heating and Cooling to make deductions from my weekly earnings for the following items:

☑ Roth IRA *$20 per week*

☐ U.S. Savings Bond

I understand that this authorization is to remain in effect until two weeks after I have revoked it in writing.

Employee Signature *Moses R. Forbisher* Date *6/14/2005*

Internet Tax Addresses

Which fringe benefits are excluded from taxable income? Demystify this issue, which many people find hard to understand, by learning about it at www. payroll-taxes.com.

Insurance

Many firms offer their employees the opportunity to buy health insurance from a group plan. The details of these plans vary from business to business. Some plans provide hospital, eye care, medical, and dental benefits, but other plans include just one or two types of benefits. The cost of the health insurance is covered by regular deductions from the earnings of all employees who have joined the plan. These deductions are usually made at the end of each payroll period but may be made less often; once a month, for example. The employer uses the amounts withheld to pay premiums to the insurance company. As mentioned earlier in this unit, the amounts withheld from employees for health insurance premium payments under a cafeteria plan may not be subject to social security and Medicare taxes.

In some cases, the employees pay a part of the cost of health insurance and the employer contributes the rest. However, even if the employees pay the full cost of the policy, group health insurance is generally less expensive than health insurance purchased by an individual.

In addition to group health insurance, some firms also make it possible for the employees to obtain group life insurance. Again, the employer makes regular deductions from the earnings of all participating employees and uses the funds to pay the insurance company.

Pension Plans

Some businesses, especially large ones, operate *pension plans* for employees. These plans provide retirement benefits and are intended to supplement the retirement income supplied by the social security system. Many pension plans require contributions from both the employer and the employee, while other pension plans are financed completely by the employer. When employees contribute, the employer usually deducts the necessary amounts from their earnings at the end of each payroll period. These deductions are generally made until the employee retires or leaves the company. The sums withheld for a pension plan are almost always a percentage of the wages of participating employees. The most widely used retirement plan currently is the 401-K plan. Amounts withheld from employee earnings that go into these plans are not subject to income tax and must be tracked and reported very carefully.

Savings Plans

In some firms, employees are able to obtain savings bonds or even purchase company stock through payroll deductions. Every participating employee decides how much he or she wants withheld for such purposes. The firm deducts the specified amount from the employee's earnings at the end of each payroll period and uses the funds to buy savings bonds or shares of stock for the employee. If there is not enough money to make the required purchase, the employer holds the money until a sufficient sum is available. The bonds or stock certificates are turned over to the employee at regular intervals. Savings plans of this type are popular because they provide a convenient way to save.

Charitable Contributions

In many areas, groups of charitable organizations raise money through a United Way campaign. The United Way encourages businesses to contribute funds and to allow their employees to contribute through payroll deductions. Employees of participating firms who want to make contributions decide on the amount they wish to give. The employer withholds the money from their earnings at the end of each payroll period and sends it to the United Way or other selected organizations.

COMPUTING NET PAY

Example

After the deductions have been figured, it is necessary to compute the amount of the *net pay* (take-home pay) for each employee. The first step in the process of determining net pay is to add the various deductions. The next step is to subtract the total of the deductions from the employee's gross earnings.

One week Mina Hook, an employee of Ingram Heating and Cooling, had gross earnings of $1,000. Her total deductions were $244.02, and her net pay was $755.98.

Deductions		Earnings	
Federal income tax	$114.00	Gross earnings	$1,000.00
Social security tax	62.00	Total deductions	244.02
Medicare tax	14.50	Net pay	$755.98
State income tax	26.72		
State disability tax	11.80		
Roth IRA	15.00		
Total deductions	$244.02		

A Case for Decision 5-1

One Friday at 4:50, Jane Thompson, the payroll clerk at King Furniture, was clearing her desk when Alex Sanders, the manager of the warehouse, came to talk to her. She was thinking about a personal problem that had been bothering her, so she did not concentrate on what he was saying. In fact, as he finished, she realized that she had not really caught everything he told her. She felt foolish about asking him to repeat the information. In any case, she was reasonably sure that she understood the situation—he now had one less withholding allowance.

She made a note about the change before she left the office that afternoon. When she arrived at work on Monday, she updated Mr. Sanders's earnings record to show that he now had three withholding allowances rather than four.

At the end of the next payroll period, Jane got an unpleasant surprise when Mr. Sanders visited her again. He was visibly upset as he tossed his paycheck in front of her. He explained that he should be receiving more take-home pay because he now had an *additional* withholding allowance—not one less. Jane took his earnings record from her file to check the number of allowances. She saw that she had removed one allowance, rather than adding one as he had requested.

Jane then changed the earnings record to show five allowances, took back his paycheck, computed his deductions and net pay again, and issued a new paycheck. It was a great deal of extra work, and she felt that Mr. Sanders was really to blame. He had spoken in a very rapid, disorganized way, and she did not know how anyone could have understood his instructions.

Discussion of the Case

Payroll work involves more than just computing amounts and preparing records. It also requires an ability to communicate properly with other people—to listen carefully, speak clearly, and write clearly. Receiving and giving accurate information are vital skills for payroll clerks. Unfortunately, Jane let her personal concerns interfere with her job.

Although Alex Sanders may not have communicated well, Jane failed to listen to him with full attention. She made the situation worse by not asking questions to make sure that she had the correct information. Jane let her fear of looking foolish prevent her from getting the facts straight. Finally, she made the mistake of not obtaining written confirmation for the change in his withholding allowances. She violated a required payroll procedure by not having him fill out a new copy of the Employee's Withholding Allowance Certificate, Form W-4.

Learning Through Practice

Do Exercise 5.6 on page 124 of this text-workbook.

UNIT 5 REVIEW

Summary

Unit 5 described the most common deductions from employee earnings. You should now be able to:

- Determine the appropriate tax table to use in each employee's situation.
- Discuss the Section 125 cafeteria plan options and Section 401-K retirement plan options available to employees to lessen the income tax.
- Look up from the appropriate tax table the amount of income tax to be withheld.
- Compute the amount of social security and Medicare taxes to be withheld.
- Compute the earnings from tips an employee receives and determine taxes on those tips.
- Determine an employee's net pay by subtracting all deductions from gross earnings.
- Discuss the importance of using the correct tax wage-bracket tables to determine the amounts of federal and state income tax on employee earnings.
- State the current federal rates for social security tax and Medicare tax and the maximum amount of earnings subject to those two taxes.
- Discuss state disability tax and state unemployment taxes, including who pays the taxes and who benefits from the taxes.
- Define the following terms: *voluntary deductions*, *garnishment of wages*, *union checkoff*, *retirement accounts*, *pension plans*, *savings plans*, and *charitable contributions*.

Study Questions

1. An employer may be required to make a number of different deductions from an employee's earnings. List five such required deductions.
2. What factors determine the amount of federal income tax withheld from an employee's earnings?
3. List the steps for using wage-bracket tables to determine the amount of withholding for federal income tax.
4. What publication contains wage-bracket tables for federal income tax? Who issues this publication?
5. What is the name of the payroll record that provides information about an employee's marital status and withholding allowances?
6. Explain the procedures to be followed when computing the social security tax on an employee's earnings.
7. Describe the state taxes that an employer may be required to withhold from employee earnings and the methods used to determine these taxes.
8. Explain how an employee who receives tips keeps track of these earnings and how tips are reported to the employer.
9. List and explain three common nontax deductions that an employee may have withheld from his or her earnings.
10. What payroll record provides information about voluntary deductions to be withheld from an employee's earnings?
11. Outline the steps for computing net pay.
12. Explain the purpose of state disability insurance.
13. Which federal form must be completed when an employee wishes to change the number of withholding allowances claimed?
14. Explain why a signed request form is required when an employee wishes to have a new voluntary deduction taken from his or her gross earnings.

REVIEW EXERCISES

Use these general instructions for each of the ten review exercises. To determine federal income tax, use the wage-bracket tables in the Appendix at the back of the book. To compute the social security and Medicare taxes, use the percentage method. Assume that the social security rate is 6.2 percent (on the first $87,900 of earnings in each calendar year) and the Medicare rate is 1.45 percent (on all earnings). When a deduction is required for state income tax, the rate is given. Multiply the earnings of each employee by the given rate. In all computations, carry amounts to at least three decimal places and round them to two decimal places.

1. Information about five employees of the Image Biotech Company is given here. For each of these employees, determine the amount of federal income tax, social security tax, and Medicare tax that the employer must withhold.

Employee	Marital Status	Withholding Allowances	Weekly Gross Earnings
Janet Cole	S	1	$695.00
Lisa Fernandez	M	2	890.00
Duane Hadley	M	3	745.00
Amy Jennings	S	0	625.00
Michael Zorin	M	5	980.00

2. David Yasuda is a sound engineer in a recording studio. He earns $1,100 a week. Compute the social security tax and Medicare tax to be withheld from his weekly earnings.

3. Marianne DeWitt is a nurse at Shaw Medical Center. Last week, she earned $770. She is married and claims three withholding allowances. Determine the amount of federal income tax to be deducted from her earnings.

4. Web Consultants is a firm that sets up sites on the Internet for clients. This firm must withhold state income tax from the earnings of its employees. The state charges a flat rate of 4 percent. Based on the information that follows, compute the amount of state income tax to be withheld from the earnings of each employee for the week ended March 7.

Employee	Gross Earnings
John Califano	$1,620
Keesha Graham	960
Randall Rhodes	775
Jeffrey Stein	850
Mary Beth Travis	1,240

5. Dennis Murphy does construction work in California. Last week, he earned $980. He is single and claims one withholding allowance. His payroll deductions for the week include $49.07 for state income tax, $11.56 for state disability insurance tax, $30 for savings bonds, and $20 for the United Way. Determine his deduction for federal income tax, and compute his deductions for social security tax and Medicare tax. Then compute his total payroll deductions and his net pay for the week.

6. California has a state disability insurance (SDI) tax. As of this writing, the rate for the tax is 1.18 percent of the first $68,829 earned by each employee in a calendar year. Employers must withhold the amount of the disability tax from employee earnings. For the week ended November 7, five employees of a San Francisco insurance company had the year-to-date and weekly gross earnings shown below. Compute the amount of SDI tax to be deducted from the earnings of these employees for the week ended November 7.

Employee	Year-to-Date Gross Earnings as of Oct. 31	Gross Earnings for Week Ended Nov. 7
Robert Ayala	$28,125	$625
Dawn Ferris	68,000	1,700
Stanley Hall	59,800	1,500
Mark Wilenski	31,275	695
Ruth Young	29,385	653

7. Reed Patterson is a college student who works part-time at a bookstore in Rochester, New York. Assume that the withholding for state disability insurance tax in New York is 0.6 percent of weekly earnings up to but not over 60 cents per week.
   a. Compute the amount of disability insurance tax withheld during a week when Reed earned $79.
   b. Compute the amount of disability insurance tax withheld during a week when Reed earned $105.

8. A few states require employees to contribute to the state unemployment compensation fund. The current unemployment tax rate paid by employees in one state is 0.5 percent of the first $7,000 earned in a calendar year. For the week ended January 7, Kathleen O'Hara, a secretary, had a salary of $580.
   a. Compute the amount of state unemployment tax to be withheld from Kathleen's earnings for the week ended January 7. Also compute the total amount of this tax that Kathleen will pay during the calendar year.
   b. Assume that Kathleen's earnings are the same each week throughout the year. How many of her paychecks will include a deduction for this tax before the payroll department stops withholding the tax?

9. Sunrise Graphics prepares computer animations for television commercials. For the month ended December 31, the year-to-date and monthly gross earnings of three employees are shown below. Compute the amount of social security tax and Medicare tax to be withheld from the earnings of these employees for the month ended December 31.

Employee	Year-to-Date Gross Earnings as of Nov. 30	Gross Earnings for Month Ended Dec. 31
Richard Aoki	$57,750	$5,250
Rebecca Mills	82,100	5,800
Laura Savino	82,000	6,300

10. Fashion Finds is a retail store that sells clothing. The earnings of its employees are subject to a state income tax of 3 percent and a city income tax of 1.5 percent. Compute the amount of state income tax and the amount of city income tax to be withheld from the weekly earnings of the following employees.

Employee	Gross Earnings
Anthony Bruno	$652
Diane Dempsey	710
Martin McGill	495
Sarah Yates	548

Problems

In the following problems, use a rate of 6.2 percent of the first $87,900 of earnings in a calendar year to compute the social security tax and use a rate of 1.45 percent of all earnings to compute the Medicare tax. Use the wage-bracket tables in the Appendix to determine federal income tax and state income tax. Use a rate of 1.18 percent of the first $68,829 of earnings in a calendar year to compute the state disability insurance tax levied by California. In your computations, carry amounts to at least three decimal places and round them to two decimal places.

1. Words and Images is a small advertising agency in Los Angeles. Payroll information for the week ended January 7 is given below.

Employee	Marital Status	Withholding Allowances	Weekly Gross Earnings
Beverly Chung	S	1	$660
Vernon Hayes	M	4	1,050
Sylvia Marcus	M	1	985
Tyler Thompson	M	2	740

a. Determine the federal income tax and the state income tax to be withheld from the earnings of each employee.

b. Compute the amount of social security tax and the amount of Medicare tax to be withheld from the earnings of each employee.

c. Compute the amount of state disability insurance tax to be withheld from the earnings of each employee.

Set up a table with your answers to this problem.

2. Alvarez and Logan is a firm of architects and interior designers. It pays its salaried employees on a monthly basis. The following information concerns four salaried employees during the month ended December 31.

Employee	Year-to-Date Gross Earnings as of Nov. 30	Gross Earnings for Month Ended Dec. 31
Troy Adams	$47,960	$4,360
Donna Mason	65,450	5,950
Vincent Torre	87,210	6,110
Eileen Walsh	81,480	5,420

a. Compute the amount of social security tax to be withheld from the earnings of each employee.

b. Compute the amount of Medicare tax to be withheld from the earnings of each employee.

3. Career Builders is an employment agency in San Diego. Its payroll information for the week ended March 21 is as follows.

Employee	Marital Status	Withholding Allowances	Weekly Gross Earnings
Ellen Ashley	M	2	$1,120
George Beck	S	0	680
Joan Jacobs	M	1	895
Carl Sadowski	M	4	1,250
Marion Taylor	S	1	590
Walter Wang	M	3	965

a. Determine the federal income tax and the state income tax to be withheld from the earnings of each employee.

b. Compute the amount of social security tax and the amount of Medicare tax to be withheld from the earnings of each employee.

c. Compute the amount of state disability insurance tax to be withheld from the earnings of each employee.

Set up a table with your answers to this problem.

4. Paul Kagan works as a waiter at the Express Coffee Shop. The four pages of Form 4070A that he completed in May are shown in Figure 5.7 on page 120. Add the columns to find the subtotals for each page. Then add the subtotals to determine the totals of all tips collected during the month. Enter the totals on page 4 of Form 4070A. Enter the overall total for the month on Form 4070, which is shown in Figure 5.7 on page 121.

FIGURE 5.7

Forms 4070A and 4070

Form **4070A** (Rev. June 1999) Department of the Treasury Internal Revenue Service	**Employee's Daily Record of Tips** This is a voluntary form provided for your convenience. See instructions for records you must keep.	OMB No. 1545-0065

Employee's name and address Paul C. Kagan 343 Niles St. Charlotte, NC 28273	Employer's name Christine Kelly	Month and year May 2005
	Establishment name (if different) Express Coffee Shop	

Date tips rec'd.	Date of entry	**a.** Tips received directly from customers and other employees	**b.** Credit card tips received	**c.** Tips paid out to other employees	**d.** Names of employees to whom you paid tips
1	5/1	11.60	14.00		
2	5/2	12.10	11.50		
3	–		–		
4	–	–	–		
5	5/5	8.00	16.50		
Subtotals					

For Paperwork Reduction Act Notice, see Instructions on the back of Form 4070.   Page 1

Date tips rec'd.	Date of entry	**a.** Tips received directly from customers and other employees	**b.** Credit card tips received	**c.** Tips paid out to other employees	**d.** Names of employees to whom you paid tips
6	5/6	10.90	4.00		
7	5/7	12.30	31.40		
8	5/8	14.10	16.60		
9	5/9	8.40	14.20		
10	–		–		
11	–	–	–		
12	5/12	10.20	12.80		
13	5/13	14.10	22.00		
14	5/14	4.50	11.60		
15	5/15	12.00	15.00		
Subtotals					

Date tips rec'd.	Date of entry	**a.** Tips received directly from customers and other employees	**b.** Credit card tips received	**c.** Tips paid out to other employees	**d.** Names of employees to whom you paid tips
16	5/16	8.20	15.00		
17	–		–		
18	–		–		
19	5/19	12.30	10.00		
20	5/20	5.00	8.30		
21	5/21	16.00	14.50		
22	5/22	14.10	22.00		
23	5/23	21.20	16.30		
24	–	–	–		
25	–	–	–		
Subtotals					

Date tips rec'd.	Date of entry	**a.** Tips received directly from customers and other employees	**b.** Credit card tips received	**c.** Tips paid out to other employees	**d.** Names of employees to whom you paid tips
26	5/26	8.10	12.00		
27	5/27	4.30	8.30		
28	5/28	6.00	10.60		
29	5/29	9.80	32.00		
30	5/30	7.70	14.60		
31	–		–	–	
Subtotals from pages 1, 2, and 3					
Totals					

1. Report total cash tips (col. **a**) on Form 4070, line **1**.

2. Report total credit card tips (col. **b**) on Form 4070, line **2**.

3. Report total tips paid out (col. **c**) on Form 4070, line **3**.

FIGURE 5.7
(*continued*)

Form **4070** (Rev. June 1999) Department of the Treasury Internal Revenue Service	**Employee's Report of Tips to Employer** ▶ **For Paperwork Reduction Act Notice, see back of form.**	OMB No. 1545-0065

Employee's name and address Paul C. Kagan 343 Niles St. Charlotte, NC 28273	**Social security number** 408 ⋮ 69 ⋮ 3161

Employer's name and address (include establishment name, if different) Christine Kelly Express Coffee Shop 6621 Fairfax Ave. Charlotte, NC 28273	**1** Cash tips received
	2 Credit card tips received
	3 Tips paid out

Month or shorter period in which tips were received from May 1 , 2005 , to May 31 , 2005	**4** Net tips (lines **1 + 2 - 3**)

Signature Paul C. Kagan	Date May 31, 2005

Learning Through Practice

Unit 5 Exercises

EXERCISE 5.1

Trail Blazer Products is a manufacturer of casual shoes and boots. A payroll summary for the purchasing department of this firm appears below. The gross earnings shown are for the week ended March 7. Use this information and the information in the table that lists marital status and withholding allowances to determine the amount of federal income tax to be withheld for each employee. Enter the federal income tax deductions in the payroll summary. The necessary tax tables are given in the Appendix. (Save the payroll summary for use in Exercises 5.2 through 5.5.)

Employee No.	Employee	Marital Status	Withholding Allowances
1	Wade Collins	M	5
2	Robert Dvorak	S	1
3	Jane Koslow	M	3
4	Barry O'Brien	M	2
5	Marilyn Reiss	M	1
6	Nancy Sorenson	S	0

Trail Blazer Products—Payroll Summary for Purchasing Department

Empl. No.	Gross Earnings	Federal Income Tax	Social Security Tax	Medicare Tax	State Income Tax	State Disability Tax	Total Deductions	Net Pay
1	$1,192	$_____	$_____	$_____	$_____	$_____	$_____	$_____
2	664	_____	_____	_____	_____	_____	_____	_____
3	1,056	_____	_____	_____	_____	_____	_____	_____
4	920	_____	_____	_____	_____	_____	_____	_____
5	715	_____	_____	_____	_____	_____	_____	_____
6	608	_____	_____	_____	_____	_____	_____	_____

EXERCISE 5.2

Refer to the payroll information for Trail Blazer Products in Exercise 5.1. Compute the amount of social security tax and the amount of Medicare tax to be withheld from the earnings of each employee. Use 6.2 percent as the rate for social security tax and 1.45 percent as the rate for Medicare tax. Carry amounts to at least three decimal places, and round them to two decimal places. Enter the deductions for social security tax and Medicare tax in the payroll summary.

EXERCISE 5.3

Trail Blazer Products is located in California, which has a state income tax. Determine the amount of this tax to be withheld from the earnings of each employee. Refer to the payroll information in Exercise 5.1. The necessary tax tables appear in the Appendix. Enter the deductions for state income tax in the payroll summary.

EXERCISE 5.4

The employees of Trail Blazer Products are subject to the state disability insurance tax levied by California. Compute the amount of this tax to be withheld from the earnings of each employee. Refer to the payroll information in Exercise 5.1. Use 1.18 percent as the tax rate. Enter the deductions for state disability insurance tax in the payroll summary.

EXERCISE 5.5

Complete the payroll summary in Exercise 5.1 by computing the total deductions and net pay for each employee. Enter these amounts in the payroll summary.

EXERCISE 5.6

On Monday morning, Bill King, a payroll clerk at the Woodland Furniture Company, had the following telephone conversation with Lyle Scott, the sales manager.

Scott: I'd like to join the payroll savings plan right away. Please deduct $50 each week from my salary for savings bonds.

King: Okay, but you'll need to come down to my office to sign an authorization form.

Scott: I'm too busy to come to your office now. Just begin the deduction, and I'll come by soon.

King: I've already told you that I can't do things that way. Rules are rules. You need to come in to sign the form.

Scott: Don't you realize that we're in the middle of the busiest selling season? I can't be bothered with a lot of red tape now. I've made a simple request. Why won't you take care of it?

King: I'm busy too, and I can't spend my time on the telephone with you. I've told you what the rules are. If you don't want to follow them, that's your problem.

Scott: You are uncooperative and rude. You can be sure that I'll discuss this with your supervisor!

King: Go ahead. I'm only going by the rules that my supervisor laid down. I'm just doing my job.

1. Do you think that Bill King handled the conversation with Lyle Scott properly? Explain.

_____
_____
_____
_____
_____
_____
_____
_____
_____
_____

2. If you had been in Bill King's place, how would you have handled this call from Lyle Scott?

_____
_____
_____
_____
_____
_____
_____
_____
_____
_____

Alternate Learning Through Practice Exercises

Unit 5 Alternate Exercises

EXERCISE 5.1A

Nortek Cameras is a manufacturer of high-quality digital cameras for professional photographers. A payroll summary for the marketing department of the firm appears below. The gross earnings shown are for the week ended July 7. Use this information and the information in the table that lists marital status and withholding allowances to determine the amount of federal income tax to be withheld for each employee. Enter the federal income tax deductions in the payroll summary. The necessary tax tables are given in the Appendix. (Save the payroll summary for use in Exercises 5.2A through 5.5A.)

Employee No.	Employee	Marital Status	Withholding Allowances
1	David Abboud	S	1
2	Lisa Backett	M	3
3	Clay Fisher	M	6
4	Kelly McCord	M	4
5	Anna Perez	S	0
6	Alison Shaw	M	1

Nortek Cameras—Payroll Summary for Marketing Department

Empl. No.	Gross Earnings	Federal Income Tax	Social Security Tax	Medicare Tax	State Income Tax	State Disability Tax	Total Deductions	Net Pay
1	$785	_____	_____	_____	_____	_____	_____	_____
2	1,250	_____	_____	_____	_____	_____	_____	_____
3	1,390	_____	_____	_____	_____	_____	_____	_____
4	1,172	_____	_____	_____	_____	_____	_____	_____
5	810	_____	_____	_____	_____	_____	_____	_____
6	724	_____	_____	_____	_____	_____	_____	_____

EXERCISE 5.2A

Refer to the payroll information for Nortek Cameras in Exercise 5.1A. Compute the amount of social security tax and the amount of Medicare tax to be withheld from the earnings of each employee. Use 6.2 percent as the rate for social security tax and 1.45 percent as the rate for Medicare tax. Carry amounts to at least three decimal places, and round them to two decimal places. Enter the deductions for social security tax and Medicare tax in the payroll summary.

EXERCISE 5.3A

Nortek Cameras is located in California, which has a state income tax. Determine the amount of this tax to be withheld from the earnings of each employee. Refer to the payroll information in Exercise 5.1A. The necessary tax tables appear in the Appendix. Enter the deductions for state income tax in the payroll summary.

EXERCISE 5.4A

The employees of Nortek Cameras are subject to the state disability insurance tax levied by California. Compute the amount of this tax to be withheld from the earnings of each employee. Use 1.18 percent as the tax rate. Enter the deductions for state disability insurance tax in the payroll summary.

EXERCISE 5.5A

Complete the payroll summary in Exercise 5.1A by computing the total deductions and net pay for each employee. Enter the amounts in the payroll summary.

EXERCISE 5.6A

Craig Wilson is a payroll supervisor at Cole Financial Services. When the firm made some changes in its retirement plan, Craig was asked by the manager of the payroll department to explain the changes to employees in other departments.

Craig is nervous about speaking in public, so he very carefully wrote out a presentation and prepared charts to illustrate his key points. During his session with the sales department, several employees interrupted his presentation with questions. Craig became rattled and angry and said to the group: "If you'll just shut up and let me finish, you might learn something. I've never heard so many dumb questions."

After Craig's manager learned what had happened, she told him that he had acted in a very unprofessional manner. She decided to handle the rest of the sessions herself.

1. Do you think that Craig Wilson's manager was justified in her criticism of his behavior? Explain.

_____

_____

_____

_____

_____

_____

_____

_____

_____

_____

2. If you had been in Craig Wilson's place, how would you have handled the interruptions during his presentation?

_____

_____

_____

_____

_____

_____

_____

_____

_____

_____

The Payroll Register

Objectives

Upon completion of this unit, you should be able to:

1. Explain the function of the payroll register.
2. Transfer payroll data from time cards or time sheets to a payroll register.
3. Locate and correct errors that may occur in the payroll register.
4. Total and prove a payroll register.
5. Prepare a proof of the payroll register.
6. Use the payroll register to answer detailed questions about employees' pay rates, hours worked, amounts of various deductions, net pay, and the totals of various columns.
7. Explain why it is essential that payroll records be both accurate and legible.
8. Identify and explain the use of each column of a standard payroll register.
9. Explain what is meant by the term *transposition of numbers.*
10. Compute federal income tax using the percentage method.
11. Compute, for one state (California), income tax for employees whose earnings exceed the earnings covered by the wage-bracket tables.

No matter what its size, every business must keep a detailed set of payroll records. Whether these records exist in a digital format or on sheets of paper in a filing cabinet, these records are essential to the operation of a business. Payroll records contain information needed to satisfy the requirements of federal and state laws and to prepare tax reports. Just as important, these records provide information that helps management control operations. Employee wages are a major expense in most businesses. In fact, for many companies, wages constitute the single largest operating expense. Thus it is essential for management to watch payroll figures closely, and this can be done only when there is an accurate, well-organized system of payroll records.

Two basic types of records are widely used to keep payroll information—the payroll register and the employee earnings record. In this unit, you will learn about the preparation and use of the payroll register. Employee earnings records are discussed in Unit 7.

USING THE PERCENTAGE METHOD WITH THE WAGE-BRACKET TABLES

In Unit 5 you learned how to determine income taxes from both federal and state wage-bracket tables. However, suppose that during one week, three of the employees of Ingram Heating and Cooling had weekly salaries that are *not shown on the wage-bracket tables.* In such cases, it is necessary to compute the income taxes owed by using the percentage method. Figure 6.1 shows the bottom of the federal wage-bracket tables for both single and married workers paid on a weekly basis.

Example

Henry Biddle, as an example, is married and claims two withholding allowances. In one week his earnings were $1,410.40. If you look at the IRS wage-bracket table for a married worker paid weekly, you will find that the table cuts off before this wage is reached. Figure 6.2 on page 128 shows a federal table for the percentage method specifying the amount to be

Point of Interest

Money, money, money! It is estimated that there is about 7 *billion* dollars in change (almost $70 per household) out of circulation. It is being stashed in people's homes—in piggy banks, fruit jars, and cigar boxes. The U.S. Mint produces about $52 million worth of coins *per day* to keep up with the demand for coins.

FIGURE 6.1

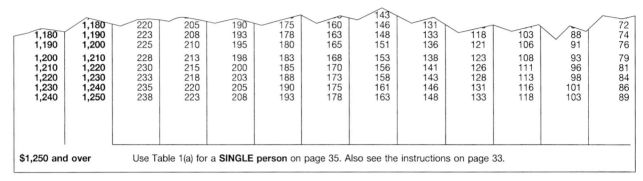

1,180	1,190	220	205	190	175	160	146	131	118	103	88	72
1,180	1,190	223	208	193	178	163	148	133	118	103	88	74
1,190	1,200	225	210	195	180	165	151	136	121	106	91	76
1,200	1,210	228	213	198	183	168	153	138	123	108	93	79
1,210	1,220	230	215	200	185	170	156	141	126	111	96	81
1,220	1,230	233	218	203	188	173	158	143	128	113	98	84
1,230	1,240	235	220	205	190	175	161	146	131	116	101	86
1,240	1,250	238	223	208	193	178	163	148	133	118	103	89

$1,250 and over   Use Table 1(a) for a **SINGLE person** on page 35. Also see the instructions on page 33.

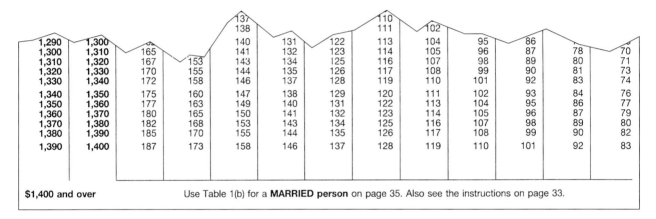

1,290	1,300			140	131	122	113	104	95	86		70
1,300	1,310	165		141	132	123	114	105	96	87	78	70
1,310	1,320	167	153	143	134	125	116	107	98	89	80	71
1,320	1,330	170	155	144	135	126	117	108	99	90	81	73
1,330	1,340	172	158	146	137	128	119	110	101	92	83	74
1,340	1,350	175	160	147	138	129	120	111	102	93	84	76
1,350	1,360	177	163	149	140	131	122	113	104	95	86	77
1,360	1,370	180	165	150	141	132	123	114	105	96	87	79
1,370	1,380	182	168	153	143	134	125	116	107	98	89	80
1,380	1,390	185	170	155	144	135	126	117	108	99	90	82
1,390	1,400	187	173	158	146	137	128	119	110	101	92	83

$1,400 and over   Use Table 1(b) for a **MARRIED person** on page 35. Also see the instructions on page 33.

FIGURE 6.2

Source: IRS Publication 15, Circular E, p. 33

Table 5. **Percentage Method—2004 Amount for One Withholding Allowance**

Payroll Period	One Withholding Allowance
Weekly	$ 59.62
Biweekly	119.23
Semimonthly	129.17
Monthly.	258.33
Quarterly	775.00
Semiannually.	1,550.00
Annually	3,100.00
Daily or miscellaneous (each day of the payroll period)	11.92

Internet Connection

A super newsletter for learning about payroll, especially state issues, is *Payroll Perspectives.* As a guest, you can stroll through a sample issue or archived issues at www.taxcast.com.

deducted for one withholding allowance. (This is Table 5 in IRS Publication 15, Circular E.) Notice that the table lists payroll periods from weekly through annually.

Since Biddle's earnings of $1,410.40 in one week put him off the wage-bracket table, the payroll clerk is directed to use the percentage method for computing the amount of federal income tax to withhold. Here is how the weekly federal income tax withholding for Henry Biddle is computed.

Step 1

$59.62	amount for one withholding allowance
× 2	number of allowances claimed
$119.24	total allowances

Step 2

$1,410.40	gross earnings
− 119.24	total allowances
$1,291.16	taxable earnings

Once Biddle's taxable earnings of $1,291.16 are determined, the amount of federal income tax is found by using Table 1 in Circular E. The portion of this table for a weekly payroll period is shown in Figure 6.3.

Look at the right side of table—the one for married persons. Read down the left-hand column to find the bracket in which Mr. Biddle's weekly taxable earnings fall. This range is the third line down: "$1,245 − $2,270." The tax amount is "$149.90 plus 25% of excess over $1,245."

FIGURE 6.3

Tables for Percentage Method of Withholding
(For Wages Paid Through December 2004)

TABLE 1—WEEKLY Payroll Period

(a) SINGLE person (including head of household)—

If the amount of wages (after subtracting withholding allowances) is: / The amount of income tax to withhold is:

Not over $51 . . . . . $0

Over—	But not over—		of excess over—
$51	—$187	10%	—$51
$187	—$592	$13.60 plus 15%	—$187
$592	—$1,317	$74.35 plus 25%	—$592
$1,317	—$2,860	$255.60 plus 28%	—$1,317
$2,860	—$6,177	$687.64 plus 33%	—$2,860
$6,177	. . . . . .	$1,782.25 plus 35%	—$6,177

(b) MARRIED person—

If the amount of wages (after subtracting withholding allowances) is: / The amount of income tax to withhold is:

Not over $154 . . . . . $0

Over—	But not over—		of excess over—
$154	—$429	10%	—$154
$429	—$1,245	$27.50 plus 15%	—$429
$1,245	—$2,270	$149.90 plus 25%	—$1,245
$2,270	—$3,568	$406.15 plus 28%	—$2,270
$3,568	—$6,271	$769.59 plus 33%	—$3,568
$6,271	. . . . . .	$1,661.58 plus 35%	—$6,271

TABLE 2—BIWEEKLY Payroll Period

(a) SINGLE person (including head of household)—

If the amount (after sub

(b) MARRIED person—

If the amou

Step 1

The amount of income tax
to withhold is: $149.90   plus

Step 2

25% of excess over $1,245

$1,291.16
− 1,245.00
—————
$46.16   Excess

Step 3

$46.16
× .25
—————
$11.54   +11.54
—————
Total federal income tax $161.44

While the percentage method for computing federal income tax withholding may seem complex at first, if one follows the step-by-step directions found in Circular E, it is relatively easy to use.

COMPUTING CALIFORNIA INCOME TAX WHEN EARNINGS EXCEED THE WAGE BRACKETS

Like the IRS, California has a system for computing state income tax for employees whose earnings level exceeds the amounts covered by the wage-bracket tables. The California system is much simpler to use than that provided by the IRS. Figure 6.4 shows the bottom sections of the California wage-bracket tables for single and married workers who are paid weekly.

Single taxpayers who have earnings above $1,100 in a week are taxed the amount as shown on the wage-bracket table for $1,100 *plus* 9.3 percent of the amount *over* $1,080.

The same system is used for married employees who have weekly earnings of over $2,200. They are taxed the amount as shown on the wage-bracket table for earnings of $2,200 *plus* 9.3 percent of the amount *over* $2,180.

FORMAT OF THE PAYROLL REGISTER

The payroll register provides a summary of the hours worked, earnings, deductions, and net pay of all employees for a payroll period. The format of this record varies from business to business, but most payroll registers are similar to the one shown in Figure 6.5 on pages 132 and 133, which is used by Ingram Heating and Cooling.

Notice that the beginning and ending dates for the payroll period are entered at the top of the payroll register sheet. The rest of the sheet contains columns that make it possible to record the necessary data for the payroll period in an efficient way. The information for each employee is placed on a separate line, and the totals for the period are entered below the amounts for the last employee.

Payroll register sheets may be kept in a bound book or a binder. Some firms use a separate sheet for each department. However, in a small business such as Ingram Heating and Cooling, complete information for all employees usually appears on a single payroll register sheet.

Making Entries in the Payroll Register

The first section of the payroll register shows the name, marital status, number of withholding allowances, and regular pay rate for each employee. This information is taken from the employee earnings record. In a small company with few changes in personnel, this information is often just copied from the previous week's payroll register.

Point of Interest

Is some of this money yours? Since 1989, there have been some $1 billion in federal employee pension checks that have not been cashed. But that's just the beginning. It is estimated that the federal government holds some $10 billion in other unclaimed funds. For example, there are $63 million worth of uncashed federal income tax refunds from just one year, 1996! As for the states, it is estimated that they have over $13 billion of unclaimed funds. Corporations, it is estimated, have billions more!

FIGURE 6.4   California Tax Tables

Single Tax Payer California

						9.55					
580		13.91	12.35	10.75	9.17	7.59	6.01		2.85	1.27	
	600	16.69	15.11	13.53	11.95	10.37	8.79	7.21	5.63	4.05	2.47	0.89
600	620	17.89	16.31	14.73	13.15	11.57	9.99	8.41	6.83	5.25	3.67	2.09
620	660	19.69	18.11	16.53	14.95	13.37	11.79	10.21	8.63	7.05	5.47	3.89
660	700	22.61	21.03	19.45	17.87	16.29	14.71	13.13	11.55	9.97	8.39	6.81
700	740	25.81	24.23	22.65	21.07	19.49	17.91	16.33	14.75	13.17	11.59	10.01
740	780	29.01	27.43	25.85	24.27	22.69	21.11	19.53	17.95	16.37	14.79	13.21
780	820	32.21	30.63	29.05	27.47	25.89	24.31	22.73	21.15	19.57	17.99	16.41
820	860	35.77	34.19	32.61	31.03	29.45	27.87	26.29	24.71	23.13	21.55	19.97
860	900	39.49	37.91	36.33	34.75	33.17	31.59	30.01	28.43	26.85	25.27	23.69
900	940	43.21	41.63	40.05	38.47	36.89	35.31	33.73	32.15	30.57	28.99	27.41
940	980	46.93	45.35	43.77	42.19	40.61	39.03	37.45	35.87	34.29	32.71	31.13
980	1020	50.65	49.07	47.49	45.91	44.33	42.75	41.17	39.59	38.01	36.43	34.85
1020	1060	54.37	52.79	51.21	49.63	48.05	46.47	44.89	43.31	41.73	40.15	38.57
1060	1100	58.09	56.51	54.93	53.35	51.77	50.19	48.61	47.03	45.45	43.87	42.29

1100 and over   (Table Amount PLUS 9.3 Percent of the Amount Over 1080)

Married Tax Payer California

								51.75			
1640		69.87				59.69	58.11	56.53	54.95	53.37	51.79	50.21
1680		73.59				63.36	61.78	60.20	58.62	57.04	55.46	53.88
1720		77.31			68.66	67.08	65.50	63.92	62.34	60.76	59.18	57.60
		2.61	81.03	73.96	72.38	70.80	69.22	67.64	66.06	64.48	62.90	61.32
1760	1800	86.33	84.75	77.68	76.10	74.52	72.94	71.36	69.78	68.20	66.62	65.04
1800	1840	90.05	88.47	81.40	79.82	78.24	76.66	75.08	73.50	71.92	70.34	68.76
1840	1880	93.77	92.19	85.12	83.54	81.96	80.38	78.80	77.22	75.64	74.06	72.48
1880	1920	97.49	95.91	88.84	87.26	85.68	84.10	82.52	80.94	79.36	77.78	76.20
1920	1960	101.21	99.63	92.56	90.98	89.40	87.82	86.24	84.66	83.08	81.50	79.92
1960	2000	104.93	103.35	96.28	94.70	93.12	91.54	89.96	88.38	86.80	85.22	83.64
2000	2040	108.65	107.07	100.00	98.42	96.84	95.26	93.68	92.10	90.52	88.94	87.36
2040	2080	112.37	110.79	103.72	102.14	100.56	98.98	97.40	95.82	94.24	92.66	91.08
2080	2120	116.09	114.51	107.44	105.86	104.28	102.70	101.12	99.54	97.96	96.38	94.80
2120	2160	119.81	118.23	111.16	109.58	108.00	106.42	104.84	103.26	101.68	100.10	98.52
2160	2200	123.53	121.95	114.88	113.30	111.72	110.14	108.56	106.98	105.40	103.82	102.24

2200 and over   (Table Amount PLUS 9.3 Percent of the Amount Over 2180)

It is common practice to record the names of the employees in alphabetical order. However, some firms, especially large ones, assign an identification number to each employee and enter the employees in numeric order. In these businesses, both employee numbers and names appear in the payroll register.

Recording Hours Worked

The process of recording figures for the payroll period starts with the hours worked by the employees. This information is transferred to the Hours section of the payroll register from time cards or time sheets. There is a column for regular hours and overtime hours.

FIGURE 6.5　**Payroll Register**

For the Period Beginning _January 11_ , **2005**　　and Ending _January 17_ , **2005**

	EMPLOYEE DATA				HOURS		EARNINGS					
	Name	Marital Status	No. of With. Allow.	Regular Rate	Regular	Overtime	Regular		Overtime		Total Earnings	
1	Biddle, Henry	M	2	$32.80 per hr.	40	2	1,312	00	98	40	1,410	40
2	Cook, Pamela	S	1	$872 per wk.	40		872	00			872	00
3	Diaz, Carmen	S	1	$18.20 per hr.	40	3	728	00	81	90	809	90
4	Dostler, Herman	M	2	$15.30 per hr.	36		550	80			550	80
5	Forbisher, Moses	M	4	$16.80 per hr.	40	2	672	00	50	40	722	40
6	Hook, Mina	M	0	$1,000 + comm.			1,000	00			1,000	00
7	Ingram, William	M	4	$3,280 per wk.			3,280	00			3,280	00
8	Kosta, Doris	M	1	$18.60 per hr.	40	8	744	00	223	20	967	20
9	Martinez, Samio	M	5	$28.60 per hr.	40	6	1,144	00	257	40	1,401	40
10	Moraga, Rose	M	2	$16.45 per hr.	40	1	658	00	24	68	682	68
11	Nguyen, Ven	M	4	$19.75 per hr.	40	3	790	00	88	89	878	89
12	Potter, Robert	M	3	$29.60 per hr.	40	$1\frac{1}{2}$	1,184	00	66	60	1,250	60
13	Zanka, Donald	M	3	$18.20 per hr.	40	2	728	00	54	60	782	60
14	Totals						13,662	80	946	07	14,608	87
15												
16												
17												
18												
19												
20												
21												

FIGURE 6.6

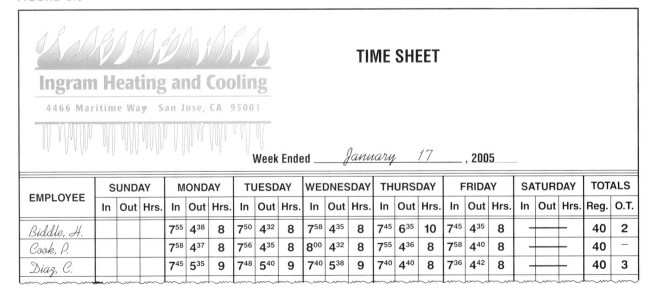

Ingram Heating and Cooling
4466 Maritime Way　San Jose, CA　95001

TIME SHEET

Week Ended _January 17_ , 2005

EMPLOYEE	SUNDAY			MONDAY			TUESDAY			WEDNESDAY			THURSDAY			FRIDAY			SATURDAY			TOTALS	
	In	Out	Hrs.	In	Out	Hrs.	In	Out	Hrs.	In	Out	Hrs.	In	Out	Hrs.	In	Out	Hrs.	In	Out	Hrs.	Reg.	O.T.
Biddle, H.				7^{55}	4^{38}	8	7^{50}	4^{32}	8	7^{58}	4^{35}	8	7^{45}	6^{35}	10	7^{45}	4^{35}	8				40	2
Cook, P.				7^{58}	4^{37}	8	7^{56}	4^{35}	8	8^{00}	4^{32}	8	7^{55}	4^{36}	8	7^{58}	4^{40}	8				40	—
Diaz, C.				7^{45}	5^{35}	9	7^{48}	5^{40}	9	7^{40}	5^{38}	9	7^{40}	4^{40}	8	7^{36}	4^{42}	8				40	3

FIGURE 6.5 *(continued)*
REGISTER

Date Paid _____, 2005

| EMPLOYEE DATA | | | | | | | | HOURS | EARNINGS | | |
Federal Income Tax	Social Security Tax	Medicare Tax	State Income Tax	SDI Tax	IRA	Savings Bonds		Total Deductions	Amount	Check No.
249 14	87 44	20 45	46 85	16 64	10 00			430 52	979 88	
130 00	54 06	12 64	37 91	10 29	15 00	10 00		269 90	602 10	
113 00	50 21	11 74	30 63	9 56				215 14	594 76	
29 00	34 15	7 99	3 18	6 50	15 00			95 82	454 98	
36 00	44 79	10 47	4 98	8 52	20 00			124 76	597 64	
114 00	62 00	14 50	26 72	11 80	15 00			244 02	755 98	
622 18	203 36	47 56	214 02	38 70	35 00	50 00		1,210 82	2,069 18	
99 00	59 97	14 02	22 74	11 41	35 00	20 00		262 14	705 06	
128 65	86 89	20 32	42 11	16 54	25 00			319 51	1,081 89	
48 00	42 33	9 90	6 54	8 06				114 83	567 85	
59 00	54 49	12 74	10 58	10 37	15 00			162 18	716 71	
125 00	77 54	18 13	33 44	14 76	20 00	10 00		298 87	951 16	
54 00	48 52	11 35	8 96	9 23	10 00			142 06	640 54	
1,806 97	905 75	211 81	488 66	172 38	215 00	90 00		3,890 57	10,718 73	

At Ingram Heating and Cooling, the weekly time sheets list all hourly employees on a single sheet. Regular hours and overtime hours are shown. For example, notice how the totals for Carmen Diaz on the time sheet in Figure 6.6 on page 132 were recorded in the payroll register.

All employees of Ingram Heating and Cooling are paid on an hourly basis except for William Ingram and Mina Hook. These employees hold managerial jobs that are exempt from the overtime pay provisions of the Fair Labor Standards Act. As a result, no record is kept of the hours they work and no hours are entered for them in the payroll register.

Entering Employee Earnings

Once the information about hours worked has been recorded, the next step is to enter the employee earnings for the period. If a firm uses time cards, these amounts are transferred from the time cards to the Earnings section of the payroll register. At Ingram Heating and Cooling, employee earnings are computed on a printing electronic calculator, and the entries in the payroll register are made directly from the calculator tape. The calculator tape shown in Figure 6.7 lists the regular, overtime, and gross earnings of Henry Biddle. Notice how these figures were recorded in the payroll register.

Dealing With Different Payroll Needs

Payroll records, while basically the same, may differ somewhat from company to company. For example, if Ingram Heating and Cooling had many employees who received a night-rate bonus, the company would probably want to have a column for this bonus in the payroll register and the employee earnings records.

FIGURE 6.7

```
   $32.80*
    x 40
$1,312.00*

   $32.80*
    x 1.5
   $49.20

   $49.20*
    x 2
   $98.40*

$1,312.00*
  + 98.40
$1,410.40
```

Point of Interest

The minimum wage: just how big (or small) is it? Lennie Pugh is single and is a recent Tennessee high school graduate. He now works full-time (40 hours per week) at the job he held part-time during his senior year. He is paid $5.15 per hour, the present minimum wage, and he claims one withholding allowance. Here are his weekly earnings, deductions, and net pay using current deduction rates. Tennessee does not have a state income tax.

Earnings ($5.15 per hour)		$206.00
Deductions:		
Federal income tax	$9.00	
Social security tax	12.77	
Medicare tax	2.99	
Total deductions		$24.76
Net weekly pay		$181.24

His net pay per year would be ($181.24 × 52 weeks = $9,424.48). Minimum wage, while it does provide some security for workers, is just that—*minimum* wage.

FIGURE 6.8

```
    $249.14*
      87.44
      20.45
      46.85
      16.64
      10.00
    ─────────
    $430.52*


  $1,410.40*
  –  430.52
    ─────────
    $979.88*
```

Some small companies have a number of special types of employee pay or employee deductions. Rather than buying a payroll record system with printed column headings, they buy blank, columnar paper. This is available with different numbers of columns at most stationery stores. The users then print the headings in by hand, and the result is that the payroll register is tailor-made to exactly fit their needs. They may also prepare their own version of the individual employee earnings record sheets this same way.

Notice that the payroll register used by Ingram Heating and Cooling is designed for the recording of federal income tax, social security tax, Medicare tax, state income tax, state disability insurance (SDI) tax, and two voluntary deductions: the Roth IRA and government savings bonds.

Payroll Deductions

After the Earnings section of the payroll register is completed, it is necessary to enter the various employee deductions. As you saw in Unit 5, the amounts of the various tax deductions are determined from tax tables or are computed. The amounts of the voluntary deductions are obtained from the employee earnings records. Refer to the payroll register in Figure 6.5 on pages 132 and 133 to see how the deductions for Henry Biddle were entered. These same deductions were discussed in Unit 5. They are totaled on the calculator tape shown in Figure 6.8.

FIGURE 6.9 **Payroll Register**

PAYROLL

For the Period Beginning _January 11_ , 2005   **and Ending** _January 17_ , 2005

	EMPLOYEE DATA				HOURS		EARNINGS		
	Name	Marital Status	No. of With. Allow.	Regular Rate	Regular	Overtime	Regular	Overtime	Total Earnings
1	Biddle, Henry	M	2	$32.80 per hr.	40	2	1,312 00	98 40	1,410 40
2	Cook, Pamela	S	1	$872 per wk.	40		872 00		872 00
12	Potter, Robert	M	3	$29.60 per hr.	40	1½	1,184 00	66 60	1250 60
13	Zanka, Donald	M	3	$18.20 per hr.	40	2	728 00	54 60	782 60
14	Totals						13,662 80	946 07	14,608 87
15									
16							**1**	**2**	**3**
17									

Now you can charge your income tax payment! In 1998 the IRS ruled that taxpayers may use their credit cards to pay their income tax. There is, however, a small "convenience fee" charged, based on the size of the tax bill. All major U.S. credit card companies but one have signed up to provide this service. Many state and local authorities now permit residents to pay their personal and property taxes with credit cards.

Computing and Recording Net Pay

The final step in completing the payroll register is to enter the amount of net pay for each employee. The net pay is found by subtracting the employee's total deductions from his or her total (gross) earnings. Refer to the payroll register in Figure 6.5 on pages 132 and 133 to see how the net pay for Mr. Biddle was entered. The calculator tape shown in Figure 6.8 on page 134 provided the necessary amount.

The Date Paid line and the Check No. column are left blank until the paychecks are prepared and issued.

Learning Through Practice

Do Exercise 6.1 on page 147 of this text-workbook.

Totaling and Proving the Payroll Register

After the information for all employees has been entered in the payroll register, it is necessary to total and prove this record. The required procedures are as follows and are shown in the payroll register in Figure 6.5, which is on pages 132 and 133. After all individual entries are made, a single line is drawn across the money columns in the Earnings, Deductions, and Net Pay sections. This line appears directly under the figures for the last employee. Then the amounts in each column are added to find the totals. At Ingram Heating and Cooling, and many other businesses, an electronic calculator is used for these computations.

Next, the totals are checked for accuracy. If they are correct, the figures are entered in the payroll register and a double line is drawn under them. The double line indicates that the columns are in balance. If the totals are not correct, the error or errors must be located and corrected.

Proving the Payroll Register

The steps that should be followed to prove the payroll register are outlined here. Refer to the payroll register shown in Figure 6.9 after you read each step. Numbers 1 through 12 have been placed below the column totals to help you follow the process.

FIGURE 6.9 *(continued)*

REGISTER

Date Paid _____ , 20 _____

				DEDUCTIONS							NET PAY	
Federal Income Tax		Social Security Tax		Medicare Tax		State Income Tax		SDI Tax		IRA		Savings Bonds		Total Deductions		Amount		Check No.
249	14	87	44	20	45	46	85	16	64	10	00			430	52	979	88	
130	00	54	06	12	64	37	91	10	29	15	00	10	00	269	90	602	10	
125	00	77	54	18	13	33	44	14	76	20	00	10	00	298	87	951	16	
54	00	48	52	11	35	8	96	9	23	10	00			142	06	640	54	
1,806	97	905	75	211	81	488	66	172	38	215	00	90	00	3,890	57	10,718	73	
4		**5**		**6**		**7**		**8**		**9**		**10**		**11**		**12**		

Point of Interest

1. Add the totals of the columns for the two types of earnings: regular and overtime. The sum of these two figures should be the same as the total of the Total Earnings column (Columns 1 + 2 = Column 3).
2. Add the totals of the columns for the various types of deductions. The sum of these figures should be the same as the total of the Total Deductions column (Columns 4 + 5 + 6 + 7 + 8 + 9 + 10 = Column 11).
3. Subtract the total of the Total Deductions column from the total of the Total Earnings column. The result of this computation should be the same as the total of the Amount column in the Net Pay section (Column 3 − Column 11 = Column 12).

This method of proving the payroll register is known as *cross-footing*. Should you find that the column totals do not prove out, the next step is to verify the column totals by adding them a second time.

In your work to prove the payroll register, you will probably have some hint of where any errors might lie. For example, if Column 1 plus Column 2 does not equal Column 3, an error exists within one of those three columns. If Columns 4 through 10 do not equal Column 11 when added, it is logical that the error lies somewhere in one of the deduction columns. In this case, it may be necessary to check the deduction figures for each employee and to recalculate the figures until the error is located. Any column totals that are affected must be corrected, and the payroll register must be cross-footed again as a final proof. Then the double line should be drawn below the column totals to show that the payroll register is proved and in balance.

Some businesses require that a formal proof of the payroll register is prepared prior to issuing any paychecks. This is generally given to the business owner or manager for review. The proof of payroll register is prepared directly from the column totals on the payroll register. An example of such a statement is shown in Figure 6.10.

FIGURE 6.10

PROOF OF PAYROLL REGISTER
For Week Ending January 17, 2005

Earnings

Regular	$13,662.80	
Overtime	946.07	
Total Earnings		$14,608.87

Deductions

Federal income tax	$1,806.97	
Social security tax	905.75	
Medicare tax	211.81	
State income tax	488.66	
SDI tax	172.38	
IRA	215.00	
Savings bonds	90.00	
Total Deductions		$ 3,890.57
Net Pay		$10,718.30

In a recent corporate survey of five countries (United States, United Kingdom, Germany, France, and Canada), the regular use of the Internet for communications is increasing by rates of 13 to 25 percent from the previous year. These communications are both with internal workers and external customers. In the United States, 84 percent reported using the Internet every day or several times a day for communications. E-mail and other text messaging programs now dominate the business communication world. The common challenge of e-mail providers is how to filter "spam" from important messages.

Learning Through Practice

Do Exercise 6.2 on page 147 of this text-workbook.

Checking Payroll Computations for Accuracy

Proving the totals of the payroll register is a good way of verifying the accuracy of figures that have been recorded. However, the process of locating and correcting errors at this stage can be very time-consuming. It is therefore important to make *sure* that the computations for each employee are accurate before the amounts are entered in the payroll register. It is also essential that these amounts be written carefully and accurately. For example, sometimes numbers are turned around: *$45.68* is written as *$45.86* or *$54.68.* This is called *transposition* of numbers. Transposition errors are easy to make, and generally they are quite difficult to locate. Writing the numbers carefully is also important. The number *6* is sometimes mistaken for a *0.* A 7 can be mistaken for a *1.* There are several other numbers that can be confused if they are written carelessly. The point is, care in writing numbers is essential in payroll work.

As you have learned already, electronic calculators are widely used to make payroll computations in small businesses. They increase the speed of payroll work and provide a high level of accuracy if they are operated properly.

Despite the use of electronic calculators in so many businesses, there are still situations in which it is necessary to do payroll computations by hand. For example, the calculator may not be working, or it may be in use by another member of the staff. Thus everyone who performs payroll activities should know how to make the required computations manually and how to check these computations. There are two simple methods for verifying amounts that are added and subtracted by hand.

- After you add a series of figures, check the accuracy of the total by adding the figures again in the opposite direction. If you add the numbers from top to bottom at first, verify your work by adding up the number column the second time. Adding a second time in the same direction presents the same combinations of figures, and you may repeat an error. Changing direction changes the combinations of figures.

- After you subtract one figure from another, check the accuracy of your work by adding the difference to the amount that was subtracted. The total of these two figures should equal the amount from which the subtraction was made.

When adding and subtracting payroll figures by hand, use these techniques for verification. The time you devote to such procedures will help you avoid spending much more time later trying to locate and correct errors in the payroll records you prepare.

Learning Through Practice

Do Exercise 6.3 on page 147 of this text-workbook.

READING THE PAYROLL REGISTER

The reason for keeping accounting records such as payroll registers is to read them at a later time to secure needed information. The payroll register is easy to read and to use. For example, look at the completed payroll register in Figure 6.5 on pages 132 and 133. Here are several questions that might be asked. "What is the hourly pay rate for Doris Kosta?" To answer this, one needs to find this person's name and read across to the Regular Rate column. The answer is $18.60. "How much did all the employees earn during the week of January 17?" To answer this, one would find the total of the Total Earnings column, $14,608.87. One might want to know the number of withholding allowances one of the workers claims. That question could be answered quickly. How about finding the names of all employees who have deductions for savings bonds during this particular week? Again, the answer is available in the payroll register and it is easy to find. If an employee loses his or her check before cashing it, it would be easy to find the check number in the payroll register so that a stop payment order can be issued.

USING THE PAYROLL REGISTER

After the payroll register is completed, it is used in a number of other ways. For example, it provides information that is needed for the following tasks:

- Making entries in the employee earnings records kept by the firm.
- Preparing paychecks or pay envelopes for the employees.
- Making payroll entries in the firm's accounting records.
- Preparing payroll reports for government agencies.
- Preparing payroll reports for management.

The many uses of the payroll register make it clear why accuracy is so important in computing the amounts that appear in this record.

Learning Through Practice

Do Exercise 6.4 on page 147 of this text-workbook.

A Case for Decision 6-1

Bob Benson was very happy about his progress at Pacific Video. Although he had been with Pacific Video only six weeks, he had already received a lot of praise from his supervisor, Joanne James. In fact, Mrs. James told Bob that she had never seen a payroll clerk handle the job so well in such a short time.

Until the week of August 7, Bob worked mostly with time and production records. However, during that week, one of the experienced payroll clerks was away on vacation, and Mrs. James asked him to prepare the payroll register. To impress her even more, Bob decided that he would do all the payroll computations and complete the payroll register in half the time the experienced clerk usually took. This was a hard goal to meet, but Bob did it. He worked at top speed and did not stop for any of the usual coffee breaks.

The day after Bob finished the payroll register, Mrs. James asked him to come to her office. He expected to receive a compliment for finishing the payroll assignment so quickly. Instead, she said, "Bob, this payroll register is a mess. Pamela tried to use it in preparing the paychecks, but she couldn't make out many of the figures because they are unreadable. The same thing happened when she wanted to use the payroll register to make entries in the employee earnings records. You'll have to prepare a new payroll register right away. And please, do it properly this time."

Naturally, Bob felt bad about the situation as he listened to Mrs. James's comments. But he felt even worse later on, when he found that even *he* could not read some of the figures he had written! He spent almost an entire afternoon recalculating payroll amounts and totals as he prepared the new payroll register.

Discussion of the Case

Payroll records, as is true with all business records, are useless if they are not written accurately and clearly. If they cannot be read, and trusted, they have no value. In a firm like Pacific Video, several people work with the information in payroll records, and so the records must be correct and easy to read. Otherwise, the entire payroll process can break down, as it did when Bob prepared the unreadable payroll register.

Even if only one person performs all pay activities for a business, it is still essential that the records be written clearly. Poor or careless handwriting leads to errors, confusion, and delays for the person who prepares the records as well as for others who need to make reference to payroll documents. Notice that Bob had trouble reading his own entries when he looked at the payroll register he had first prepared. As a result, he had to spend time recalculating figures. Another point to keep in mind about the need for clear writing is that payroll records must be available for inspection by representatives of government agencies, auditors, and company managers. Speed is important in office work, but not at the expense of accurate, readable records.

UNIT 6   REVIEW

Summary

After completion of this unit, you should now understand the use and design of a payroll register. You should also be able to:

- Transfer payroll data from time cards and time sheets to the payroll register.
- Determine the various deductions from employee earnings and record them in the payroll register.
- Total and prove the payroll register.
- Recognize common types of errors, such as transposition errors, that may occur when payroll records are prepared.
- Understand the importance of accurately recording information in the payroll register.
- Use the percentage method for calculating federal income tax.
- Use the California withholding tables and rates to determine the California withholding taxes.
- Understand how to use the California procedures for calculating state income tax when employee earnings exceed the wage brackets shown on the withholding tables.

Study Questions

1. Why is it necessary for a business to keep detailed payroll records?
2. Businesses use different formats for their payroll registers. Why?
3. What information is commonly shown in a payroll register for each employee?
4. When the payroll register is prepared, what information is obtained from the employee earnings records?
5. What payroll records provide information for completing the Hours and Earnings sections of the payroll register?
6. List the major steps when preparing the payroll register.
7. Describe the procedures for locating errors in the payroll register.
8. Outline the procedures for totaling the payroll register.
9. Name two basic skills all payroll employees must have if they are to complete payroll tasks efficiently and accurately.
10. List three uses of the information contained in the payroll register.
11. How can the tapes from a calculator used in preparing the payroll register be of value?
12. How is the payroll register used in the preparation of payroll checks?
13. When verifying the total to a column of dollar amounts, why is it wise to add *up* the column the second time, rather than adding down the column again?
14. Three dates are shown across the top of the payroll register. What does each date signify?
15. What does the double line under the payroll register totals indicate?

REVIEW EXERCISES

In these exercises, use the tax tables in the Appendix whenever you must determine federal or state income tax. Compute social security tax at a rate of 6.2 percent and Medicare tax at a rate of 1.45 percent. For California businesses use a rate of 1.18 percent to compute the state disability insurance tax levied by California. In your calculations, carry amounts to three decimal places and round them to two decimal places.

1. The Scenic Landscaping Service designs, plants, and maintains gardens and lawns. Its payroll register for the week ended May 7 shows the following information about four employees.

Employee	Marital Status	Withholding Allowances	Regular Hourly Rate	Hours Worked
Julie Arnez	M	3	$17.40	44
Spiro Costas	S	1	16.80	42
Drew Vincent	M	2	19.50	41
Ellen Wagner	S	0	15.60	43

a. Compute the regular, overtime, and total earnings for each employee. All hours beyond 40 in a week are considered overtime hours and are paid at a rate of 1 1/2 times the regular hourly rate.

b. Determine the deductions for federal income tax, social security tax, and Medicare tax for each employee.

c. Compute the total deductions and net pay for each employee.

Set up a table with your answers.

2. Guardian Home Security sells alarm systems to homeowners and operates a monitoring service for the alarm systems. The information given below is from the firm's payroll register for the week ended January 14.

Employee	Marital Status	Withholding Allowances	Regular Pay Rate	Hours Worked
Michael Corsi	M	2	$640 per week	46
Vanessa Hall	S	1	$580 per week	44
Megan McCarthy	M	1	$710 per week	37
Scott Porter	M	0	$672 per week	45

a. Compute the regular, overtime, and total earnings for each employee. All hours worked beyond 40 in a week by these employees are treated as overtime hours and are paid at a rate of 1 1/2 times the regular hourly rate.

b. Determine the deductions for federal income tax, social security tax, and Medicare tax for each employee.

c. Compute the total deductions and net pay for each employee.

Set up a table with your answers.

3. Nina Morrison is a costume designer at a movie studio in California. She earns a salary of $1,380 a week. She is married and claims four withholding allowances. Her required deductions include federal income tax, state income tax, social security tax, Medicare tax, and state disability insurance tax. She also has a voluntary deduction of $100 a week for a retirement savings plan.

Determine the amount of each tax deduction from Nina's earnings, her total deductions, and her net pay.

4. Henry Ling is a physical therapist at Coastal Health Care, a health maintenance organization in California. He earns a salary of $1,250 a week. He is married and claims three withholding allowances. His required deductions include federal income tax, state income tax, social security tax, Medicare tax, and state disability insurance tax. His voluntary deductions consist of $20 for group life insurance, 6 percent of his weekly salary for the firm's retirement savings plan, and $10 for the United Way.

Determine the amount of each tax deduction from Henry's earnings, his total deductions, and his net pay.

5. The Mountainside Ski Lodge pays its employees weekly. Its payroll register for the week ended October 21 shows the following information about four employees.

Employee	Marital Status	Withholding Allowances	Regular Pay Rate	Hours Worked
David Hollis	S	0	$18.30 per hour	42
Karen Saunders	M	1	$16.40 per hour	45
Carl Schmidt	M	2	$806 per week	38
Andrea Vargas	S	1	$824 per week	41

a. Compute the regular, overtime, and total earnings for each employee. These employees receive time and a half for all hours worked beyond 40 in a week.

b. Determine the deductions for federal income tax, social security tax, and Medicare tax for each employee.

c. Compute the total deductions and net pay for each employee.

Set up a table with your answers.

6. Gail Henderson works in an electronics factory in California. She is single and claims one withholding allowance. She has a regular hourly rate of $17.25. Last week, she worked 46 hours. Her 6 overtime hours were worked on a holiday, for which her employer pays double time (twice her regular hourly rate).

a. Compute Gail's regular, overtime, and total earnings.

b. Determine Gail's deductions for federal income tax, state income tax, social security tax, Medicare tax, and state disability insurance tax.

c. Compute Gail's total deductions and net pay.

Problems

To determine federal and state income tax in these problems, use the tax tables in the Appendix. Use a rate of 6.2 percent to compute social security tax, a rate of 1.45 percent to compute Medicare tax, and a rate of 1.18 percent to compute the state disability insurance tax levied by California. Treat all hours worked beyond 40 in a week as overtime, and use an overtime rate of 1 1/2 times the regular hourly rate. In your calculations, carry amounts to three decimal places and round them to two decimal places.

1. High-Tech Market Trends is a firm that does market research for clients in the computer industry. It is located in San Jose, California. Because the firm recently started operations, it has only three employees. Payroll information about these employees for the week beginning January 15 and ending January 21 is given below.

Employee	Marital Status	Withholding Allowances	Regular Pay Rate	Hours Worked
Kelly Carter	S	1	$596 per week	45
James Cirmak	M	3	$828 per week	42
Paula Reed	M	1	$1,042 per week	40

To complete this problem, use the payroll register in Figure 6.11.

a. Compute the earnings, deductions, and net pay of each employee. Record these amounts in the payroll register. The required deductions are federal income tax, social security tax, Medicare tax, state income tax, and state disability insurance tax. There are no voluntary deductions.

b. Total, prove, and rule the payroll register.

FIGURE 6.11

PAYROLL

For the Period Beginning _____ , 20 _____ and Ending _____ , 20 _____

	EMPLOYEE DATA				HOURS		EARNINGS		
	Name	Marital Status	No.of With. Allow.	Regular Rate	Regular	Overtime	Regular	Overtime	Total Earnings
1									
2									
3									
4									
5									
6									
7									
8									

2. The Frosty Air-Conditioning Company installs and services central air-conditioning units. It is located in Sacramento, California. The following payroll information is for the firm's employees during the week of March 8 through March 14.

Employee	Marital Status	Withholding Allowances	Regular Pay Rate	Hours Worked	Savings Bonds
Alison Moore	M	1	$624 per week	42	$25
George Rivera	M	2	$21.25 per hour	40	50
Keith Sims	M	0	$19.20 per hour	44	0
Gary Webb	S	1	$22.50 per hour	41	100

To complete this problem, use the payroll register in Figure 6.12.

a. Compute the earnings, deductions, and net pay of each employee. Record these amounts in the payroll register. The required deductions are federal income tax, social security tax, Medicare tax, state income tax, and state disability insurance tax. Some of the employees have a voluntary deduction for savings bonds.

b. Total, prove, and rule the payroll register.

FIGURE 6.12

PAYROLL

For the Period Beginning _____ , 20 _____ and Ending _____ , 20 _____

	EMPLOYEE DATA				HOURS		EARNINGS		
	Name	Marital Status	No.of With. Allow.	Regular Rate	Regular	Overtime	Regular	Overtime	Total Earnings
1									
2									
3									
4									
5									
6									
7									
8									

FIGURE 6.11 *(continued)*

REGISTER

Date Paid _____ , 20 _____

Federal Income Tax		Social Security Tax		Medicare Tax		State Income Tax		SDI Tax		IRA		Savings Bonds		Total Deductions		Amount		Check No.
DEDUCTIONS																NET PAY		

3. The following employees are executives who work in the home office of California Style, a chain of furniture stores located throughout the state. These executives are paid on a weekly basis. Information for the week beginning April 10 and ending April 16 is shown.

Employee	Marital Status	Withholding Allowances	Weekly Salary	SIMPLE IRA
Pamela Austen	M	4	$1,350	$30
Roger Dupont	S	1	965	0
Mary Elias	M	2	1,120	25
Aaron Jacobs	M	3	1,275	25
Nora O'Shea	S	1	1,080	30

To complete this problem, use the payroll register in Figure 6.13.

a. Compute the deductions and net pay of each employee. Record these amounts as well as the earnings of each employee in the payroll register. The required deductions are federal income tax, social security tax, Medicare tax, state income tax, and state

FIGURE 6.12 *(continued)*

REGISTER

Date Paid _____ , 20 _____

Federal Income Tax		Social Security Tax		Medicare Tax		State Income Tax		SDI Tax		IRA		Savings Bonds		Total Deductions		Amount		Check No.
DEDUCTIONS																NET PAY		

FIGURE 6.13

PAYROLL

For the Period Beginning _____ **, 20** _____   **and Ending** _____ **, 20** _____

	EMPLOYEE DATA				HOURS		EARNINGS		
	Name	Marital Status	No.of With. Allow.	Regular Rate	Regular	Overtime	Regular	Overtime	Total Earnings
1									
2									
3									
4									
5									
6									
7									
8									

disability insurance tax. Some of the employees have a voluntary deduction for IRA contributions.

b. Total, prove, and rule the payroll register.

4. The Computer Solutions Company is located in a state with no income tax on wages. The company employs four people and pays them on a weekly basis. It has begun offering a SIMPLE IRA retirement plan for its employees. (Recall from Unit 5 that employee contributions to this plan are not taxed for income tax purposes). Information for the week of February 5–12 is shown on the next page:

FIGURE 6.14

PAYROLL

For the Period Beginning _____ **, 20** _____   **and Ending** _____ **, 20** _____

	EMPLOYEE DATA				HOURS		EARNINGS		
	Name	Marital Status	No.of With. Allow.	Regular Rate	Regular	Overtime	Regular	Overtime	Total Earnings
1									
2									
3									
4									
5									
6									
7									
8									

FIGURE 6.13 *(continued)*

REGISTER

Date Paid _____ , 20 _____

| DEDUCTIONS | | | | | | | | NET PAY | |
Federal Income Tax	Social Security Tax	Medicare Tax	State Income Tax	SDI Tax	IRA	Savings Bonds	Total Deductions	Amount	Check No.

Employee	Marital Status	Withholding Allowances	Weekly Salary	SIMPLE IRA
Betty Bossman	M	2	1,300	75
Charles Chang	S	0	750	45
Harry Doggonite	M	0	1,000	0
Susan Swift	M	3	$850	$50

Use the payroll register in Figure 6.14 to complete this problem.

a. Compute the deductions and net pay for each employee. Record these amounts in the payroll register. The required deductions are federal income tax, social security tax, Medicare tax, and the employees' Simple IRA contributions.

b. Total, prove, and rule the payroll register.

FIGURE 6.14 *(continued)*

REGISTER

Date Paid _____ , 20 _____

| DEDUCTIONS | | | | | | | | NET PAY | |
Federal Income Tax	Social Security Tax	Medicare Tax	State Income Tax	SDI Tax	IRA	Savings Bonds	Total Deductions	Amount	Check No.

Learning Through Practice

Unit 6 Exercises

EXERCISE 6.1

Plato.Com is a firm that sells books at a discount over the Internet. It is located in San Francisco, California. Payroll information for the staff of the firm's shipping department is shown below. This information covers the week beginning March 8 and ending March 14.

Employee	Marital Status	Withholding Allowances	Regular Hourly Rate	Hours Worked	IRA
Paul Alioto	M	3	$18.20	42	$50
Shannon Curtis	M	1	16.90	41	30
Wade Jenkins	S	0	13.80	46	0
Leslie Keller	M	2	14.50	40	0
Joan Van Zant	S	1	13.40	44	30
Michael Yong	M	2	17.60	40	25

Prepare a payroll register for the shipping department. Use the form for Exercise 6.1 given on pages 148 and 149.

a. Compute the earnings, deductions, and net pay for each employee.

b. Consider all hours worked beyond 40 in the week as overtime. The overtime rate paid by the firm is 1 1/2 times the regular hourly rate.

c. Use the tax tables in the Appendix to determine federal income tax and state income tax. Use a rate of 6.2 percent for social security tax, a rate of 1.45 percent for Medicare tax, and a rate of 1.18 percent for the state disability insurance tax levied by California. Carry amounts to three decimal places, and round them to two decimal places.

d. Some employees have a voluntary deduction for IRA contributions.

Note: Save your payroll register for use in Exercise 6.2.

EXERCISE 6.2

Total, prove, and rule the payroll register that you prepared in Exercise 6.1.

EXERCISE 6.3

A payroll register for the purchasing department of Plato.Com is given on pages 148 and 149. The Employee Data and Earnings sections have been completed. Determine the deductions and net pay of each employee. Use the tax tables in the Appendix to find federal income tax and state income tax. Use a rate of 6.2 percent for social security tax, a rate of 1.45 percent for Medicare tax, and a rate of 1.18 percent for state disability insurance tax. Record the amounts in the payroll register. Then total, prove, and rule the payroll register.

EXERCISE 6.4

Column totals from a payroll register are given below. Use the answer space on page 150 to prepare a formal proof of the payroll register.

Earnings:		Deductions:	
Regular	$7,468.20	Federal income tax	$1,200.00
Overtime	3,781.38	Social security tax	697.47
		Medicare tax	163.12
		State income tax	220.00
		SDI tax	132.75
Net pay:	$8,410.71	IRA	210.00

EXERCISE 6.1

PAYROLL

For the Period Beginning _____ **, 20** _____ **and Ending** _____ **, 20** _____

	EMPLOYEE DATA				HOURS		EARNINGS		
	Name	Marital Status	No.of With. Allow.	Regular Rate	Regular	Overtime	Regular	Overtime	Total Earnings
1									
2									
3									
4									
5									
6									
7									
8									

EXERCISE 6.3

PAYROLL

For the Period Beginning *March 8* **, 2005** **and Ending** *March 14* **, 2005**

	EMPLOYEE DATA				HOURS		EARNINGS		
	Name	Marital Status	No.of With. Allow.	Regular Rate	Regular	Overtime	Regular	Overtime	Total Earnings
1	Alvarez, Raymond	M	1	$815/wk.	40		815 00		815 00
2	Case, Charlene	S	1	$692/wk.	40		692 00		692 00
3	Lomas, John	M	4	$1,126/wk.	40		1,126 00		1,126 00
4	Mikulski, Sarah	M	2	$944/wk.	40		944 00		944 00
5	Taylor, Dwight	S	0	$757/wk.	40		757 00		757 00
6	Totals						4,334 00		4,334 00
7									
8									

EXERCISE 6.1 *(continued)*

REGISTER

Date Paid _____ , 20 _____

| | | DEDUCTIONS | | | | | | NET PAY | |
Federal Income Tax	Social Security Tax	Medicare Tax	State Income Tax	SDI Tax	IRA	Savings Bonds	Total Deductions	Amount	Check No.

EXERCISE 6.3 *(continued)*

REGISTER

Date Paid _____ , 20 _____

| | | DEDUCTIONS | | | | | | NET PAY | |
Federal Income Tax	Social Security Tax	Medicare Tax	State Income Tax	SDI Tax	IRA	Savings Bonds	Total Deductions	Amount	Check No.
					50 00				
					25 00				
					50 00				
					50 00				
					30 00				

Unit 6 Exercises

EXERCISE 6.1A

E-Music sells songs over the Internet. It is located in Los Angeles, California. Payroll information for the staff of its technical operations department is shown below. This information covers the week beginning April 7 and ending April 13.

Employee	Marital Status	Withholding Allowances	Regular Hourly Rate	Hours Worked	IRA
Susan Bailey	M	3	$21.50	40	$30
William Brice	S	0	17.60	45	50
Ahmad Hassan	S	1	18.40	42	25
John Olivo	M	4	22.10	44	25
Sharon Sanders	M	2	23.50	40	30
Jane Segretti	S	1	18.80	43	0

Prepare a payroll register for the technical operations department. Use the form for Exercise 6.1A given on pages 152 and 153.

a. Compute the earnings, deductions, and net pay for each employee.

b. Consider all hours worked beyond 40 in the week as overtime. The overtime rate to be paid by the firm is 1 1/2 times the regular hourly rate.

c. Use the tax tables in the Appendix to determine federal income tax and state income tax. Use a rate of 6.2 percent for social security tax, a rate of 1.45 percent for Medicare tax, and a rate of 1.18 percent for the state disability tax levied by California. Carry amounts to three decimal places, and round them to two decimal places.

d. Some employees have a voluntary deduction for IRA contributions.

Note: Save your payroll register for use in Exercise 6.2A.

EXERCISE 6.2A

Total, prove, and rule the payroll register that you prepared in Exercise 6.1A.

EXERCISE 6.3A

A payroll register for the marketing department of E-Music is given on pages 152 and 153. The Employee Data and Earnings sections have been completed. Determine the deductions and net pay of each employee. Use the tax tables in the Appendix to find federal income tax and state income tax. Use a rate of 6.2 percent for social security tax, a rate of 1.45 percent for Medicare tax, and a rate of 1.18 percent for state disability insurance tax. Record the amounts in the payroll register. Then total, prove, and rule the payroll register.

EXERCISE 6.4A

Column totals from a payroll register are given below. Use the answer space on page 154 to prepare a formal proof of the payroll register.

Earnings:		Deductions:	
Regular	$13,235.60	Federal income tax	$2,101.00
Overtime	2,682.30	Social security tax	986.91
		Medicare tax	230.81
		State income tax	318.52
		SDI tax	187.83
Net pay:	$11,797.83	IRA	295.00

EXERCISE 6.1A

PAYROLL

For the Period Beginning _____ , 20 _____ and Ending _____ , 20 _____

	EMPLOYEE DATA				HOURS		EARNINGS		
	Name	Marital Status	No. of With. Allow.	Regular Rate	Regular	Overtime	Regular	Overtime	Total Earnings
1									
2									
3									
4									
5									
6									
7									
8									

EXERCISE 6.3A

PAYROLL

For the Period Beginning _April 7_ , 2005 and Ending _April 13_ , 2005

	EMPLOYEE DATA				HOURS		EARNINGS		
	Name	Marital Status	No. of With. Allow.	Regular Rate	Regular	Overtime	Regular	Overtime	Total Earnings
1	Dixon, Carter	S	1	$697/wk.	40		697 00		697 00
2	Kumar, Janet	S	0	$825/wk.	40		825 00		825 00
3	O'Malley, Brian	M	2	$948/wk.	40		948 00		948 00
4	Roski, Daniel	M	3	$1,220/wk.	40		1,220 00		1,220 00
5	Tate, Joanne	S	1	$783/wk.	40		783 00		783 00
6	Totals						4,473 00		4,473 00
7									
8									

EXERCISE 6.1A *(continued)*

REGISTER

Date Paid ______________________, 20 ____

DEDUCTIONS								NET PAY	
Federal Income Tax	Social Security Tax	Medicare Tax	State Income Tax	SDI Tax	IRA	Savings Bonds	Total Deductions	Amount	Check No.

EXERCISE 6.3A *(continued)*

REGISTER

Date Paid ______________________, 20 ____

DEDUCTIONS								NET PAY	
Federal Income Tax	Social Security Tax	Medicare Tax	State Income Tax	SDI Tax	IRA	Savings Bonds	Total Deductions	Amount	Check No.
					25 00				
					50 00				
					30 00				
					60 00				
					25 00				

Unit Seven

Employee Earnings Records

Objectives

Upon completion of this unit, you should be able to:

1. Explain the value and use of the employee earnings record.
2. Complete the top portion of an employee earnings record.
3. Post data to an employee earnings record.
4. Total and balance employee earnings records at the end of the quarter and at the end of the year.
5. Compute the new year-to-date earnings figure in an employee earnings record.
6. Make required, authorized corrections to personal data on employee earnings records.
7. Answer questions based on information contained in an employee earnings record.
8. Explain the relationship between the payroll register and the employee earnings record.
9. Explain the purpose and use of the Year-to-Date Earnings column of the employee earnings record.
10. Explain how long payroll records must be retained within a company.

The payroll register is useful because it provides a convenient summary of the earnings, deductions, and net pay of each employee for a specific payroll period. However, a business also needs detailed payroll information about individual employees from time to time throughout the year, including totals of earnings, deductions, and net pay. This information is kept in another type of payroll record called an *employee earnings record*. Here, on one record sheet, is the payroll history of each employee for the year.

The personal information at the top of this record comes from the job application form, Form W-4 (Employee's Withholding Allowance Certificate), and the special forms that the employee signs authorizing the withholding of pay for voluntary deductions. The earnings, deductions, and net pay for each payroll period come from the payroll register.

The payroll register and the employee earnings record serve different but equally important functions. In Unit 6, you became familiar with the payroll register. In this unit, you will learn how employee earnings records are prepared and used. Turn back to Figure 6.5 on pages 132 and 133 of Unit 6. Look at the entry for Rose Moraga on line 10. Notice the columns of the payroll register are arranged in the same order as in the columns of the employee earnings record. This facilitates the copying of dollar amounts from the payroll register to the employee earnings record. Compare the payroll register entry for Rose Moraga with the entry on line 3 of the employee earnings record shown in Figure 7.1 on page 156.

FIGURE 7.1   **Employee Earnings Record**

EMPLOYEE EARNINGS RECORD FOR YEAR 20 _05_

Name _Moraga, Rose M._
Address _2278 City Center—Apt. 406_
San Jose, CA 95161
Social Security No. _816-49-6600_
Job Title _Installer's Helper_
Date Employed _February 20, 1997_
Date Terminated _____

Ingram Heating and Cooling
4466 Maritime Way • San Jose, CA 95001

Marital Status   M ☑   S ☐
No. of Withholding Allowances _2 3 (as of 12/20)_
Regular Rate _$16.45 per hour_

Voluntary Deductions:
IRA _____
U.S. Savings Bonds _____

| PAYROLL PERIOD | | HOURS | | EARNINGS | | | DEDUCTIONS | | | | | | | | NET PAY | YEAR-TO-DATE EARNINGS |
Week	Ending Date	Reg.	O.T.	Regular	Overtime or Commission	Total Earnings	Federal Income Tax	Social Security Tax	Medicare Tax	State Income Tax	SDI Tax	IRA	Savings Bonds	Total Deductions	NET PAY	YEAR-TO-DATE EARNINGS
1st Quarter																
1	Jan. 3	40	1	658 00	24 68	682 68	48 00	42 33	9 90	6 54	8 06			114 83	567 85	682 68
2	Jan. 10	40		658 00		658 00	44 00	40 80	9 54	5 18	7 76			107 28	550 72	1,340 68
3	Jan. 17	40	1	658 00	24 68	682 68	48 00	42 33	9 90	6 54	8 06			114 83	567 85	2,023 36
13	Mar. 28	40		658 00		658 00	44 00	40 80	9 54	5 18	7 76			107 28	550 72	8,578 68
14																
1st Quarter Totals				8,529 32	49 36	8,578 68	573 00	531 93	124 38	67 53	101 23			1,398 07	7,180 61	8,578 68
2nd Quarter																
1	Apr. 4	40	2	658 00	49 36	707 36	51 00	43 86	10 26	7 34	8 35			120 81	586 55	9,286 04
13	June 27	40	1	658 00	24 68	682 68	48 00	42 33	9 90	6 54	8 06			114 83	567 85	17,231 40
14																
2nd Quarter Totals				8,554 00	98 72	8,652 72	578 00	536 52	125 46	68 12	102 10			1,410 20	7,242 52	17,231 40
4th Quarter																
1	Oct. 3	40		658 00		658 00	44 00	40 80	9 54	5 18	7 76			107 28	550 72	26,443 40
13	Dec. 26	40	2	658 00	49 36	707 36	42 00	43 86	10 26	5 76	8 35			110 23	597 13	34,388 76
14																
4th Quarter Totals				8,554 00	49 36	8,603 36	511 00	533 46	124 74	67 72	101 52			1,338 44	7,264 92	34,388 76
Totals for year				34,216 00	172 76	34,388 76	2,643 00	2,132 31	498 60	270 71	405 79			5,350 41	29,038 35	34,388 76

THE FORMAT OF THE EMPLOYEE EARNINGS RECORD

Employee earnings records are kept on a year-by-year basis. At the beginning of each calendar year, a new individual record is set up for every employee. Also, when a new employee is hired, an employee earnings record is immediately started for this person. Entries are made in this record for each employee at the end of each payroll period during the year.

The format of the employee earnings record varies somewhat according to the needs of each business. However, the earnings record used by Ingram Heating and Cooling is typical of that in use in many firms.

The heading of the employee earnings record shows the current year as well as the date when the person began employment with the firm. The heading also contains basic information such as the employee's address, social security number, marital status, pay rate, number

Internet Connection

If your company employs contract labor in lieu of full-time or part-time workers, what difference does it make to the IRS and to state employment depart-ments? You can learn about how this practice impacts payroll at http://www.payroll-taxes.com.

of withholding allowances, and amounts of voluntary deductions. If the person leaves the firm, the date of termination is entered in the heading of the employee earnings record.

All of this information is needed to prepare the payroll and to satisfy the requirements of various government regulations. Even the address is important so the W-2 can be mailed at the end of the year.

As changes in employee information occur, the new facts are entered in the heading of the employee earnings record. These changes may involve a job title, marital status, number of withholding allowances, a pay rate, or the amount of a voluntary deduction.

In large businesses, changes in a job title or a pay rate require written authorization from a manager or supervisor. In businesses of any size, changes in marital status or number of withholding allowances should only be made after the employee involved prepares a new Form W-4, Employee's Withholding Allowance Certificate. Similarly, changes in voluntary deductions should be backed by a new authorization form signed by the employee.

All documents that relate to such changes should be kept on file in case there is ever a question about a change. The same is true when a new employee joins a firm. Written authorization should be provided management to add this employee to the payroll records, and the authorization should be placed in the payroll files. See Figure 7.2.

Rose Moraga is a widow and has been claiming two withholding allowances—one for herself and one for her 16-year-old son. In December, Mrs. Moraga's mother, who has limited income, came to live with Rose. Because she will now be providing most of her mother's living expenses, Mrs. Moraga completed a new Form W-4, Employee's Withholding Allowance Certificate, showing an increase from two allowances to three. Notice how this change has been made on her earnings record in Figure 7.1. The notation "as of 12/20" means that the change in withholding allowances will go into effect for the weekly payroll

FIGURE 7.2 **Interoffice Memorandum**

Interoffice Memorandum

Ingram Heating and Cooling
4466 Maritime Way • San Jose, CA 95001

To _____ Mina Hook _____ From _ William Ingram _

Subject _ New Employee _ Date _ October 17, 2005 _

Mary Jameson has joined the firm as a clerk-typist at $11.00 an hour. Her official starting date was October 16. Please set up an earnings record for this new employee. Her Form W-4 and deductions form are attached.

Attachments

Many Americans seem to have a love affair with small business. There are a good many reasons why people start a small business. And there are also a good many reasons why people do not want to work in a small-business environment. Look at these comparisons.

	Firm Size (No. of Employees)				
	25	26–99	100–499	500–999	1,000 or more
Average wage per hour	$9.39	$11.02	$11.92	$11.78	$13.50
Workers covered by retirement plan	13.2%	33.6%	52.9%	52.3%	68.7%
Workers covered by insurance	29.9%	58.3%	72.2%	75%	78.4%
Tenure in current job (in years)	4.4	5.5	6.3	6.8	8.5

But there is one thing that cannot be measured, and that is the independence and adventure of small-business operation. Perhaps this is why we have millions of small businesses. And we must also remember that most of the "big" businesses once were small.

period starting on December 20. The change in withholding allowances will reduce the amount of both state and federal income tax withheld from her weekly paycheck.

Just below the heading of the employee earnings record, the form is divided into six vertical sections. These sections provide space for entering the ending date of the payroll period, hours worked, earnings, deductions, net pay, and year-to-date earnings during the four quarters of the year. A single horizontal line is used to record information for each employee for a payroll period.

The employee earnings record also has space for entering total amounts for each quarter and for the year as a whole. These quarterly and yearly figures are needed for various tax reports that the firm must send to government agencies.

In a manual payroll system, employee earnings records are usually kept on individual sheets in a payroll file or are placed in a binder. For convenience, the sheets are normally arranged in alphabetic order by employee name to match the order in which the employees are listed in the payroll register.

The employee earnings records are set up at the beginning of each year. Of course, an employee earnings record must be set up immediately for each new employee who is hired during the year. The U.S. Department of Labor requires employers to retain employee payroll records for at least three years.

MAKING ENTRIES IN THE EMPLOYEE EARNINGS RECORDS

The payroll register provides the information that is entered in the employee earnings records at the end of each payroll period. The hours worked, earnings, deductions, and net pay are simply *posted* (transferred) from the payroll register to the individual earnings records. The only new item that must be computed for each employee is the amount of the year-to-date earnings.

The year-to-date earnings column is a very important column of the employee earnings record. Before each payroll is prepared, the figures in this column are examined by the payroll clerk to determine whether any employees are *about* to reach the yearly earnings limits for social security tax, state disability insurance tax, state unemployment tax, or any other tax that has a maximum wage base. The amount of the year-to-date earnings is determined by adding the total (gross) earnings for the current period to the previous year-to-date figure.

Point of Interest

Is bigger better? To many, a small town is a wonderful place, and in many regards, these people are right. The U.S. Census Bureau and the federal Office of Management and Budget list 362 metropolitan statistical areas in our country. Just think:

- These 362 metro areas occupy one-sixth of our land.
- They contain 80 percent of our population.
- They provide 84 percent of our jobs.
- They produce 83 percent of our gross national product.
- The wage-benefit package for metro-area workers is almost 50 percent higher than for their small-town or rural counterparts.

NEARING MAXIMUM TAXES

As you have learned, there are some taxes that are paid only on a maximum amount of earnings during a calendar year. For instance, social security taxes (in 2004) are paid only on the first $87,900. After an employee earns more than that amount in a calendar year, social security tax is no longer withheld from the gross earnings or matched by the employer.

There are also state taxes that have maximum amounts of taxable earnings. An example is the California state disability insurance (SDI) tax. In 2004, the maximum earnings subject to this tax was $68,829. Once a worker earns more than that amount, the SDI tax is no longer deducted from gross earnings.

A final illustration of the importance of tracking the year-to-date earnings for each employee is the unemployment tax. Only the first $7,000 of each employee's earnings each year is subject to the federal unemployment tax. Once an employee passes $7,000 in a year, no further federal unemployment tax is due for that employee that year. States set their own maximum amount of earnings subject to the state unemployment tax. Again, once an employee earns more than the maximum amount subject to tax, no further unemployment tax is paid on that employee during that calendar year. Many states use the same $7,000 maximum that the federal government uses.

It is very important for the payroll department to be alert as employees approach the maximum amounts of earnings subject to the various taxes. This is especially true in a manual payroll system. When a business uses a computerized payroll system, it receives an annual software update that contains the current maximum amounts subject to the various taxes. The only change the firm may need to make is to insert the maximum amounts and rates set by its state if those differ from the federal amounts.

CARE IN MAKING ENTRIES

Although the process of making entries in the employee earnings record is not difficult, it must be done carefully and accurately. Otherwise, errors can easily occur. Examples are writing an amount in the wrong column, transposing figures, and placing information in the wrong earnings record. These kinds of errors are easy to make and hard to locate. They can cause serious problems because they will eventually be reflected in the quarterly and yearly totals.

Learning Through Practice

Do Exercise 7.1 on page 167 of this text-workbook.

TOTALING THE EMPLOYEE EARNINGS RECORDS

At the end of each quarter and at the end of the calendar year, it is necessary to total the amounts in the employee earnings records. The quarterly totals are determined by adding the figures for all the payroll periods within the quarter. This work is usually done on a

Internet Connection

You may have questions about how the earned-income credit works, and what your company needs to do regarding this credit. At the Web site http://www. payroll-taxes.com, you can find out how to confidently address your company's responsibilities by doing a search for "earned income credit."

calculator when payroll records are kept by hand. However, in a computerized payroll system, the totals are produced automatically, which saves a great deal of time and effort.

Study the totals for the first quarter in the employee earnings record for Rose Moraga shown in Figure 7.1 on page 156. Notice that all columns in the Earnings, Deductions, and Net Pay sections have been totaled. However, the total that appears in the Year-to-Date Earnings column is the same as the amount computed at the end of the last payroll period in the quarter. This figure was simply brought down to the line for the quarterly totals. The Year-to-Date Earnings column contains a running total of the employee's gross earnings, week by week, throughout the year.

The yearly totals shown at the bottom of the earnings record for Rose Moraga were found by adding together all the quarterly totals. Again, the only exception is the Year-to-Date Earnings column. The fourth quarter year-to-date earnings at the end of the fourth quarter and the end of the year are the same.

Because accuracy is so important, it is a good practice to check the quarterly and yearly totals in each employee earnings record right after they are computed. This can be done by using the same cross-footing process that is used to prove the payroll register. For example, the first-quarter totals for Rose Moraga were verified as shown in the proof statement in Figure 7.3.

FIGURE 7.3
Proof of First Quarter Totals

Proof of First Quarter Totals
Employee Earnings Record for Rose Moraga
March 28, 2005

Earnings		
Regular	$8,529.32	
Overtime	49.36	
Total		$8,578.68
Deductions		
Federal income tax	$ 573.00	
Social security tax	531.93	
Medicare tax	124.38	
State income tax	67.53	
SDI tax	101.23	
Total		$1,398.07
Net Pay		$7,180.61

Costs and salaries seem to keep pace with each other. It is not uncommon to hear some older person talk about having bought a new car in the 1930s that cost "around $600 or $700." That's very low by today's standards. But wages were very low too. Here is another example. There is a town of 30,000 people in northern California that covers several thousand acres. Back in 1880 a man bought the ranch where the town now stands. He paid $850 for the entire ranch. Average-sized building lots there today cost about $80,000.

And what do you think about these prices? There is a large, old hotel in Chicago that is still in operation. In 1885 its menu listed these dinners: roast beef, $.50; lake trout, $.30; beef tongue, $.25, or a fresh lobster dinner for $.40. How much do you suppose salaries were in Chicago in those days?

USING EMPLOYEE EARNINGS RECORDS

Employee earnings records serve the following important purposes:

- They provide the information needed for payroll reports and tax returns that must be sent to federal, state, and local agencies.
- They provide the information needed for a yearly report of earnings, income tax withholdings, and social security and Medicare withholdings that must be sent to each employee.
- They provide the information needed for payroll reports that go to management.
- They provide the information needed to determine when employees reach the yearly earnings limits for certain taxes, such as social security tax and the unemployment taxes.
- They provide the information needed to settle questions that employees may have about their earnings, deductions, and net pay.
- They serve as a handy reference to verify information such as the employee's home address, job title, date employed, and so on.

INTERNAL CONTROL OF PAYROLL RECORDS

It is very important that a business establish a set of internal controls for its payroll records. These controls are designed to ensure accuracy, honesty, efficiency, and confidentiality. Obviously, a large business will have more elaborate controls than a small business. However, even a small firm must take measures to protect the integrity of its payroll system. Following are some common internal controls for payroll:

- Limit access to payroll records to authorized personnel. In a manual system, all payroll records should be kept in locked files. In a computerized system, payroll records should be password protected.
- Set up and enforce strict rules of confidentiality in regard to payroll information.
- Do not allow new employees to be added to the payroll records without written authorization from the appropriate manager.
- Do not allow any changes in job titles or rate of pay without written approval from the appropriate manager.
- Any changes in marital status, withholding allowances, or voluntary deductions are not made without proper written authorization by the employee.
- Payroll records should be checked periodically by someone outside the payroll department (preferably the owner in a small business or a certified public accountant in larger businesses). Large employers typically have an internal auditor who would perform this function.
- The payroll checking account should not be reconciled by the same person who writes the payroll checks.

RETENTION OF PAYROLL RECORDS

The payroll register and the employee earnings records must be kept for a period of three years in order to meet various federal and state requirements. Even if employees leave the firm, their payroll records must remain on file for the specified period of time.

Learning Through Practice

Do Exercise 7.2 on page 167 of this text-workbook.

UNIT 7   REVIEW

Summary

Upon completion of this unit, you should now be able to:

- Prepare the top portion of an employee earnings record.
- Make authorized adjustments or changes in an employee earnings record.
- Post payroll information from the payroll register to the individual employee's earnings record.
- Compute the year-to-date totals for each employee earnings record.
- Understand that the federal and state governments set the rates and amounts of earnings subject to payroll taxes each year.
- Total and prove an employee's earnings record at the end of the quarter and end of the year.
- Explain the policy for payroll records retention that a business should follow.

Study Questions

1. A business prepares an employee earnings record for each employee. When is this record prepared?
2. List five items of information commonly recorded in the heading of an employee earnings record.
3. When would a firm total and prove the amounts that have been entered in the employee earnings record?
4. Why do employee earnings records contain a Year-to-Date Earnings column?
5. What payroll form provides the data about earnings, deductions, and net pay that is entered in the employee earnings records?
6. Which columns of an employee earnings record are totaled at the end of each calendar quarter? What procedures are used to verify the accuracy of the quarterly totals?
7. At the end of the calendar year, the total earnings, deductions, and net pay for the year are entered in each employee earnings record. What amounts are used to compute these totals?
8. List at least three uses of the information recorded in the employee earnings records.
9. Changes in payroll records are not made without proper written authorization. What are some changes that may need to be made? Who authorizes these changes?
10. According to payroll regulations, how long must a business retain the payroll register and employee earnings records?

Discussion Questions

1. What is the basic purpose of the employee earnings record?
2. What specific information is essential in the heading of an employee earnings record?
3. Why must a written and signed authorization notice be in the hands of the payroll department before changes are made in the personal or job information about an employee in the employee earnings record?

4. How long must employee earnings records be kept on file? What value might older records such as this have?

5. Give at least three examples of personal or job information about an employee that is quickly available from the employee earnings record.

REVIEW EXERCISES

In these exercises, use a rate of 6.2 percent on the first $87,900 earned in a calendar year to compute social security tax and a rate of 1.45 percent on all earnings to compute Medicare tax. Use a rate of 1.18 percent on the first $68,829 earned in a calendar year to compute the state disability insurance tax levied on workers in California. Carry amounts to at least three decimal places, and round them to two decimal places.

1. Dennis McCoy is the sales manager of an automobile agency. He is paid monthly. On October 31, his employee earnings record showed year-to-date gross earnings of $85,100. During November, he earned $6,750. Compute the social security tax and the Medicare tax to be deducted from his earnings on November 30.

2. Lisa Chen is a furniture designer. She is paid semimonthly. On November 15, her employee earnings record showed year-to-date gross earnings of $66,250. During the period of November 15 through December 1, she earned $3,150. Compute the social security tax and the Medicare tax to be deducted from her earnings on December 1.

3. Alex Jankowski is an electrician in Oakland, California. He is paid weekly. On July 7, his employee earnings record showed year-to-date gross earnings of $30,840. During the week of July 8 through July 14, he worked 48 hours. His regular hourly rate is $25.50, and he is paid 1 1/2 times this rate for all hours worked beyond 40 in a week.

   a. Compute his regular, overtime, and total earnings for the week.

   b. Compute the state disability insurance tax to be deducted from his earnings on July 14.

4. The following information is taken from the employee earnings records and payroll register of the New Directions Advertising Agency. This firm is located in San Diego, California.

Employee	Year-to-Date Gross Earnings as of Nov. 30	Gross Earnings for Month Ended Dec. 31
John Calder	$31,075	$2,825
Heidi Grant	65,450	5,950
Mark Rosen	54,560	4,960
Dale Simmons	29,150	2,650
Nancy Wyatt	62,920	5,720

   a. Compute the social security tax to be withheld from the earnings of each employee on December 31.

   b. Compute the Medicare tax to be withheld from the earnings of each employee on December 31.

   c. Compute the state disability insurance tax to be withheld from the earnings of each employee on December 31.

   d. Compute the year-to-date gross earnings of each employee on December 31.

5. Robert Melendez is the manager of the All-Star Diner, a restaurant in Los Angeles, California. His employee earnings record shows year-to-date gross earnings of $72,500 as of December 31.

   a. Compute the amount of social security tax that was withheld from his earnings during the year.

   b. Compute the amount of Medicare tax that was withheld from his earnings during the year.

   c. Compute the amount of state disability insurance tax that was withheld from his earnings during the year.

Problems

1. Charles Roth sells medical supplies to hospitals. He is paid semimonthly. On December 31, his employee earnings record showed the following amounts for the last quarter of the year in the Total Earnings, Total Deductions, Net Pay, and Year-to-Date Earnings columns.

Payroll Period Ended	Total Earnings	Total Deductions	Net Pay	Year-to-Date Earnings
				$29,080
10/15	$1,575	$ 332	$1,243	
10/31	1,620	343	1,277	
11/15	1,730	348	1,382	
11/30	1,495	291	1,204	
12/15	1,610	339	1,271	
12/31	1,550	327	1,223	
Quarter Totals	$	$	$	$

   a. Determine the amounts that should appear in the Year-to-Date Earnings column during the fourth quarter.

   b. Determine the fourth quarter totals that should appear in each column.

2. The Clothing Express is a chain of casual clothing stores in Minnesota. Assume that you work in the payroll department at the headquarters of this firm. One of your duties at the end of each year is to audit the totals that appear in the employee earnings records. Refer to Figure 7.4, which is the earnings record for Marianne Osuna, a store manager.

   a. Verify the total earnings, total deductions, net pay, and year-to-date earnings for each payroll period. If you find any errors, cross out the incorrect amounts and indicate the correct amounts.

   b. Verify the total earnings, total deductions, and net pay for each quarter. If you find any errors, cross out the incorrect amounts and indicate the correct amounts.

   c. Verify the total earnings, total deductions, and net pay for the year. If you find any errors, cross out the incorrect amounts and indicate the correct amounts.

3. Prove the quarterly and yearly totals of the employee earnings record that you audited in Problem 2. Using Figure 7.3 as an example, prepare a formal proof for each quarter and for the year.

FIGURE 7.4

EMPLOYEE EARNINGS RECORD FOR YEAR 20 _05_

Name _Osuna, Marianne_

Address _805 West Walnut Street_

St. Paul, MN 55119

Social Security No. _396-44-7912_

Job Title _Manager – Store 7_

Date Employed _May 14, 2005_

Date Terminated _____

Marital Status M ☑ S ☐

No. of Withholding Allowances _1_

Regular Rate _$3,875 per month_

Voluntary Deductions:

IRA _$75 per month_

U.S. Savings Bonds _____

PAYROLL PERIOD		HOURS		EARNINGS			DEDUCTIONS							NET PAY	YEAR-TO-DATE EARNINGS
	Ending Date	Reg.	O.T.	Regular	Overtime or Commission	Total Earnings	Federal Income Tax	Social Security Tax	Medicare Tax	State Income Tax	Health Insurance	Savings Bonds	Total		
1st Quarter															
1	Jan. 31			3,875 00		3,875 00	381 00	240 25	56 19	79 90	27 50	75 00	859 84	3,015 16	3,875 00
2	Feb. 28			3,875 00		3,875 00	381 00	240 25	56 19	79 90	27 50	75 00	859 84	3,015 16	7,750 00
3	Mar. 31			3,875 00		3,875 00	381 00	240 25	56 19	79 90	27 50	75 00	859 84	3,015 16	11,625 00
1st Quarter Totals				11,625 00		11,625 00	1,143 00	720 75	168 57	239 70	82 50	225 00	2,579 52	9,045 48	11,625 00
2nd Quarter															
1	Apr. 30			3,875 00		3,875 00	381 00	240 25	56 19	79 90	27 50	75 00	859 84	3,015 16	15,500 00
2	May 31			3,875 00		3,875 00	381 00	240 25	56 19	79 90	27 50	75 00	859 84	3,015 16	19,375 00
3	June 30			3,875 00		3,875 00	381 00	240 25	56 19	79 90	27 50	75 00	859 84	3,015 16	23,250 00
2nd Quarter Totals				11,625 00		11,625 00	1,143 00	720 75	168 57	239 70	82 50	225 00	2,579 52	9,045 48	23,250 00
3rd Quarter															
1	July 31			3,875 00		3,875 00	381 00	240 25	56 19	79 90	27 50	75 00	859 84	3,015 16	27,125 00
2	Aug. 31			3,875 00		3,875 00	381 00	240 25	56 19	79 90	27 50	75 00	859 84	3,015 16	31,000 00
3	Sept. 30			3,875 00		3,875 00	381 00	240 25	56 19	79 90	27 50	75 00	859 84	3,015 16	34,875 00
3rd Quarter Totals				11,625 00		11,625 00	1,143 00	720 75	168 57	239 70	82 50	225 00	2,579 52	9,045 48	34,875 00
4th Quarter															
1	Oct. 31			3,875 00		3,875 00	381 00	240 25	56 19	79 90	27 50	75 00	859 84	3,015 16	38,750 00
2	Nov. 30			3,875 00		3,875 00	381 00	240 25	56 19	79 90	27 50	75 00	859 84	3,015 16	42,625 00
3	Dec. 31			3,875 00		3,875 00	381 00	240 25	56 19	79 90	27 50	75 00	859 84	3,015 16	46,500 00
4th Quarter Totals				11,625 00		11,625 00	1,143 00	720 75	168 57	239 70	82 50	225 00	2,579 52	9,045 48	46,500 00
Totals for year				46,500 00		46,500 00	4,572 00	2,883 00	674 28	958 80	330 00	900 00	10,316 08	36,181 92	46,500 00

Name _____ Date _____

Unit 7 Exercises

EXERCISE 7.1   The Old World Furniture Restoration Service repairs and refinishes furniture. Its payroll register for the week ended April 7 and its employee earnings records are shown below and on the next page. Transfer the information from the payroll register to the employee earnings records. Be sure to compute the new year-to-date earnings for each employee. (Use the forms below, through page 168.)

EXERCISE 7.2   Bridget Farrell is a medical assistant. Information from her employee earnings record is shown below. Compute her year-to-date earnings for the fourth quarter. Then compute the totals for the fourth quarter and for the year.

Payroll Period Ended	Total Earnings	Total Deductions	Net Pay	Year-to-Date Earnings
Totals for 3 Quarters	$25,380	$5,584	$19,796	$25,380
10/15	$ 1,350	$ 297	$ 1,053	_____
10/31	1,425	313	1,112	_____
11/15	1,350	297	1,053	_____
11/30	1,350	297	1,053	_____
12/15	1,445	318	1,127	_____
12/31	1,350	297	1,053	_____
4th Quarter Totals	$_____	$_____	$_____	_____
Totals for Year	$_____	$_____	$_____	_____

EXERCISE 7.1   **Payroll Register, continued below**

PAYROLL

For the Period Beginning _____ *April 1* , 20 *05* _____ and Ending _____ *April 7* , 20 *05* _____

	EMPLOYEE DATA				HOURS		EARNINGS		
	Name	Marital Status	No.of With. Allow.	Regular Rate	Regular	Overtime	Regular	Overtime	Total Earnings
1	Bell, Roy	M	1				740 00	83 00	823 00
2	Radek, Karl	M	1				770 00	29 00	799 00
3	Rossi, Marie	M	1				708 00	106 00	814 00
4	Scott, John	M	1				720 00	55 00	775 00
							2,938 00	273 00	3,211 00

EXERCISE 7.1   **Payroll Register** *(continued)*

REGISTER

Date Paid _____ , 20 _____

DEDUCTIONS								NET PAY	
Federal Income Tax	Social Security Tax	Medicare Tax	State Income Tax	SDI Tax	IRA	Savings Bonds	Total Deductions	Amount	Check No.
78 00	51 03	11 93	16 08	9 71			166 75	656 25	
73 00	49 54	11 59	14 48	9 43			158 04	640 96	
76 00	50 47	11 80	15 28	9 61			163 16	650 84	
70 00	48 05	11 24	13 68	9 15			152 12	622 88	
297 00	199 09	46 56	59 52	37 90			640 07	2,570 93	

EXERCISE 7.1   Employee Earnings Record

EMPLOYEE EARNINGS RECORD FOR YEAR 20 *05*

Name *Bell, Roy*

PAYROLL PERIOD		HOURS		EARNINGS			DEDUCTIONS								NET PAY	YEAR-TO-DATE EARNINGS
Week	Ending Date	Reg.	O.T.	Regular	Overtime or Commission	Total Earnings	Federal Income Tax	Social Security Tax	Medicare Tax	State Income Tax	SDI Tax	IRA	Savings Bonds	Total Deductions		
1st Quarter Totals				9,620 00	1,079 00	10,699 00	1,014 00	663 39	155 09	209 04	126 25			2,167 77	8,531 23	10,699 00
1																

EXERCISE 7.1   Employee Earnings Record

EMPLOYEE EARNINGS RECORD FOR YEAR 20 *05*

Name *Radek, Karl*

PAYROLL PERIOD		HOURS		EARNINGS			DEDUCTIONS								NET PAY	YEAR-TO-DATE EARNINGS
Week	Ending Date	Reg.	O.T.	Regular	Overtime or Commission	Total Earnings	Federal Income Tax	Social Security Tax	Medicare Tax	State Income Tax	SDI Tax	IRA	Savings Bonds	Total Deductions		
1st Quarter Totals				10,010 00	377 00	10,387 00	949 00	644 02	150 67	188 24	118 12			2,050 05	8,336 95	10,387 00
1																

EXERCISE 7.1   Employee Earnings Record

EMPLOYEE EARNINGS RECORD FOR YEAR 20 *05*

Name *Rossi, Marie*

PAYROLL PERIOD		HOURS		EARNINGS			DEDUCTIONS								NET PAY	YEAR-TO-DATE EARNINGS
Week	Ending Date	Reg.	O.T.	Regular	Overtime or Commission	Total Earnings	Federal Income Tax	Social Security Tax	Medicare Tax	State Income Tax	SDI Tax	IRA	Savings Bonds	Total Deductions		
1st Quarter Totals				9,204 00	1,378 00	10,582 00	988 00	656 11	153 40	198 64	124 87			2,121 02	8,460 98	10,582 00
1																

EXERCISE 7.1   Employee Earnings Record

EMPLOYEE EARNINGS RECORD FOR YEAR 20 *05*

Name *Scott, John*

PAYROLL PERIOD		HOURS		EARNINGS			DEDUCTIONS								NET PAY	YEAR-TO-DATE EARNINGS
Week	Ending Date	Reg.	O.T.	Regular	Overtime or Commission	Total Earnings	Federal Income Tax	Social Security Tax	Medicare Tax	State Income Tax	SDI Tax	IRA	Savings Bonds	Total Deductions		
1st Quarter Totals				9,360 00	715 00	10,075 00	910 00	624 65	146 12	177 84	118 89			1,977 50	8,097 50	10,075 00
1																

Alternate Learning Through Practice Exercises

Unit 7 Exercises

EXERCISE 7.1A Great Events is a firm that plans weddings and parties. Its payroll register for the week ended April 7 and its employee earnings records are shown below and on the next page. Transfer the information from the payroll register to the employee earnings records. Be sure to compute the new year-to-date earnings for each employee. (Use the forms below through page 170.)

EXERCISE 7.2A Frank Medina is a graphic artist at an advertising agency. Information from his employee earnings record is shown below. Compute his year-to-date earnings for the fourth quarter. Then compute the totals for the fourth quarter and for the year.

Payroll Period Ended	Total Earnings	Total Deductions	Net Pay	Year-to-Date Earnings
Totals for 3 Quarters	$31,240	$6,148	$25,092	$31,240
10/15	$ 1,510	$ 292	$ 1,218	_____
10/31	1,560	305	1,255	_____
11/15	1,585	310	1,275	_____
11/30	1,510	292	1,218	_____
12/15	1,625	319	1,306	_____
12/31	1,510	292	1,218	_____
4th Quarter Totals	$_____	$_____	$_____	_____
Totals for Year	$_____	$_____	$_____	_____

EXERCISE 7.1A Payroll Register, continued below

PAYROLL

For the Period Beginning ___*April 1*__, 20 *05*   and Ending ___*April 7*__, 20 *05*

	EMPLOYEE DATA				HOURS		EARNINGS		
	Name	Marital Status	No. of With. Allow.	Regular Rate	Regular	Overtime	Regular	Overtime	Total Earnings
1	Barnes, Rebecca	M	1	$660/wk.	40	2	660 00	49 50	709 50
2	Kerr, Steven	S	0	$580/wk.	40	4	580 00	87 00	667 00
3	Tomassi, Joseph	M	2	$740/wk.	40		740 00		740 00
4	Walsh, Diane	S	1	$620/wk.	40	1	620 00	23 25	643 25
5							2,600 00	159 75	2,759 75
6									

EXERCISE 7.1A Payroll Register *(continued)*

REGISTER

Date Paid _____, 20 _____

DEDUCTIONS								NET PAY		
Federal Income Tax	Social Security Tax	Medicare Tax	State Income Tax	SDI Tax	IRA	Savings Bonds	Total Deductions	Amount	Check No.	
60 00	43 99	10 29	11 28	8 37			133 93	575 57		
93 00	41 35	9 67	22 61	7 87			174 50	492 50		
57 00	45 88	10 73	8 94	8 73			131 28	608 72		
73 00	39 88	9 33	18 11	7 59			147 91	495 34		
283 00	171 10	40 02	60 94	32 56			587 62	2,172 13		

EXERCISE 7.1A   **Employee Earnings Record**

EMPLOYEE EARNINGS RECORD FOR YEAR 20 _05_

Name ___Barnes, Rebecca___

PAYROLL PERIOD		HOURS		EARNINGS			DEDUCTIONS								NET PAY	YEAR-TO-DATE EARNINGS
Week	Ending Date	Reg.	O.T.	Regular	Overtime or Commission	Total Earnings	Federal Income Tax	Social Security Tax	Medicare Tax	State Income Tax	SDI Tax	IRA	Savings Bonds	Total Deductions		
Totals for 1st Quarter				8,580 00	960 00	9,540 00	806 00	591 48	138 33	150 73	112 57			1,799 11	7,740 89	9,540 00
1																

EXERCISE 7.1A   **Employee Earnings Record**

EMPLOYEE EARNINGS RECORD FOR YEAR 20 _05_

Name ___Kerr, Steven___

PAYROLL PERIOD		HOURS		EARNINGS			DEDUCTIONS								NET PAY	YEAR-TO-DATE EARNINGS
Week	Ending Date	Reg.	O.T.	Regular	Overtime or Commission	Total Earnings	Federal Income Tax	Social Security Tax	Medicare Tax	State Income Tax	SDI Tax	IRA	Savings Bonds	Total Deductions		
Totals for 1st Quarter				7,540 00	678 60	8,218 60	1,142 00	509 55	119 17	278 61	96 98			2,146 31	6,072 29	8,218 60
1																

EXERCISE 7.1A   **Employee Earnings Record**

EMPLOYEE EARNINGS RECORD FOR YEAR 20 _05_

Name ___Tomassi, Joseph___

PAYROLL PERIOD		HOURS		EARNINGS			DEDUCTIONS								NET PAY	YEAR-TO-DATE EARNINGS
Week	Ending Date	Reg.	O.T.	Regular	Overtime or Commission	Total Earnings	Federal Income Tax	Social Security Tax	Medicare Tax	State Income Tax	SDI Tax	IRA	Savings Bonds	Total Deductions		
Totals for 1st Quarter				9,620 00	577 20	10,197 20	785 18	632 23	147 86	122 37	120 33			1,807 97	8,389 23	10,197 20
1																

EXERCISE 7.1A   **Employee Earnings Record**

EMPLOYEE EARNINGS RECORD FOR YEAR 20 _05_

Name ___Walsh, Diane___

PAYROLL PERIOD		HOURS		EARNINGS			DEDUCTIONS								NET PAY	YEAR-TO-DATE EARNINGS
Week	Ending Date	Reg.	O.T.	Regular	Overtime or Commission	Total Earnings	Federal Income Tax	Social Security Tax	Medicare Tax	State Income Tax	SDI Tax	IRA	Savings Bonds	Total Deductions		
Totals for 1st Quarter				8,060 00	644 80	8,704 80	983 64	539 70	126 22	244 60	102 72			1,996 88	6,707 92	8,704 80
1																

Unit Eight

Paying Employees

Objectives

Upon completion of this unit, you will be able to:

1. Name some of the very few businesses that may pay employees in cash.
2. Explain why it is necessary to require employees paid in cash to sign a receipt for their wages.
3. Discuss briefly how an EFT (electronic funds transfer) payroll system works.
4. Name the benefits to employees and businesses of using the EFT depositing system for payroll.
5. Demonstrate how to void a payroll check and explain when this should be done.
6. Prepare a payroll check by hand or with a typewriter.
7. Explain how a payroll service bureau works with a small business
8. Understand that a computerized payroll system works in basically the same manner as a manual system.
9. Understand the importance of internal control in the payroll check-writing function.

An efficient payroll system contains complete and accurate records that provide management with the information necessary for the proper operation of the business. It also satisfies the requirements of federal, state, and local payroll laws. Another essential feature of the well-operated payroll system is that employees are paid on time and receive the correct amounts of pay.

Most businesses use computer technology to assist with the payroll function today. Some common elements of most payroll systems, whether records are prepared by hand or by computer, will be explored in this unit. In addition, you will learn how a business actually pays its employees.

The manual payroll procedures demonstrated earlier in this text are the same procedures to be followed when the business uses computers and software to process its payroll. The employees' files must accurately reflect marital status, number of withholding allowances claimed, current pay rate, and all other related payroll information for each employee. Maintenance of payroll information is critical to the software accurately calculating each employee's earnings, deductions, and net pay.

One of the great advantages of a computerized payroll system is that it not only makes the necessary calculations, but it also automatically prepares payroll records, checks, reports for management, and tax forms for the federal government. Most companies that produce payroll software provide their users with yearly updates to reflect changes in the rates of federal and state taxes and changes in the various required payroll forms. You will learn about the federal payroll tax forms in Unit 9.

PAYING IN CASH

Many years ago, it was common for businesses to pay their employees in cash. On payday, each employee received a pay envelope filled with the appropriate amount of currency and coins to equal the amount of net pay. Today only a very small number of businesses pay their employees in cash.

Point of Interest

Money used to come in many forms. In ancient Rome, cattle were considered cash. Some of the earliest Roman coins had images of cattle on them. Such coins were more convenient to handle than live cattle. At various times, beads, nails, fish hooks, salt, licorice, and sea shells have been used as money. The earliest form of paper money was printed in China more than a thousand years ago.

Internet Connection

Sam's been a great employee for four years, but he and his wife have decided to move their family back to Chicago, where he grew up. Now that your company is losing him, how long do you have, by law, to give him his final paycheck? Become aware of what to do when people quit, are fired, or are on strike, at http://www.payroll-taxes.com.

Some of the workers who are paid in cash are farm workers and day laborers. For example, a company that sells its products primarily by using door-to-door salespeople may hire a half dozen or more local workers for one day of work as they canvass a neighborhood. At the end of the day these workers are paid in cash. In another case, a company may wish to deliver to each household a new telephone directory or a newly developed product, such as a new type of soap. It may hire local workers for a day and pay them in cash at the end of the day.

Employee Receipts

When employees are paid in cash, it is important for the firm to obtain receipts from them. As the pay is handed out, each employee is asked to count the money in his or her envelope and then sign a receipt to confirm that the correct sum was paid. A payroll receipt is shown in Figure 8.1. The receipts for the period are filed in case there is ever a question about the payments.

FIGURE 8.1   A Signed Payroll Receipt

PAYROLL RECEIPT

For Payroll Period Ending _____July 18_____ , 20 _05_

Employee Name	Net Payroll Amount	Employee Signature
BROWNING, DAVID N.	$279.80	David Browning
FREEMAN, LOUIS T.	$435.85	Louis Freeman

NOTICE: Signature indicates that the named employee has received the payroll amount in cash, as shown.

How small is small business? According to the House of Representatives, small businesses account for 99.7 percent of America's employers and contribute 47 percent of all sales in the country. Industries dominated by small businesses produced approximately 62 percent of the 3.3 million newly created jobs in 1994.

The Risks of Paying in Cash

Paying employees in cash requires a good deal of work and involves considerable risk. At the end of each payroll period, it is necessary to withdraw a large sum of money from the bank and keep this money in the firm's office until the pay envelopes are given out. While the cash is on hand in the business, there is always the possibility of theft. Paying employees by check is safer, easier, and more efficient, and this is why most businesses issue payroll checks to their employees.

PAYING BY CHECK

There are several methods for preparing payroll checks. In a small firm, the checks may be written by hand or typed. However, most companies today use computer equipment to process their payroll and to print the payroll checks. The format of payroll checks can vary from business to business, but many payroll checks are similar to the one shown in Figure 8.2.

Notice that the statement of earnings and deductions is attached at the top of the check. The employee is instructed to tear off this perforated section before cashing the check and to retain the statement for his or her records. A check of this type is often referred to as a *voucher check*.

Rather than being bound into a checkbook, voucher checks are typically printed two to a page on loose forms, or they are printed on sheets of continuous forms. A check register is used to keep a record of all the checks issued, all the deposits made, and the balance of the account.

FIGURE 8.2   **Payroll Check**

Employee's social security number	PERIOD ENDING	HOURS WORKED		EARNINGS			NET PAY	
				Regular	Overtime or Comm.	Total		
345-90-1611	May 8, 2005	Reg. 40 O.T. 2		728 00	54 60	782 60	614	88

DEDUCTIONS													
Federal Inc. Tax	Social Security Tax		Medicare Tax		State Inc. Tax		SDI Tax		I.R.A		Savings Bonds	Other	Total
76 00	48	52	11	35	12	62	9	23	10	-			167 72

Statement of Earnings and Deductions   Detach and retain for your records.   ZEPHER CULINARY, INC.

ZEPHER CULINARY, INC.
1855 SEVENTH STREET
SAN JOSE, CA 95101

PAYROLL CHECK   No. **1263**   90-306 / 1222

Date _May 11,_ _____ 20 _05_

Pay to
the order of __Evelyn C. Billings__ _____ $ 614.88

Six hundred fourteen and 88/100 _____ Dollars

San Jose Regional Bank
270 College Avenue
San Jose, California, 95105

James T. Nelson

⑆1222⑈0306⑆ 01018⑈057223⑈

For control purposes, payroll checks are always prenumbered. If any checks are voided because of mistakes, they are kept on file so that all check numbers can be accounted for. (When the canceled checks are returned to the business by the bank, the voided checks are merged with them, and all the checks are then filed in numeric order.)

Assume that Zepher Culinary, Inc., pays its employees by check and uses the type of voucher check shown in Figure 8.2 on page 174. The first step in a manual payroll system in preparing one of these checks is to complete the statement of earnings and deductions, using information from the payroll register. The next step is to enter the date, the employee's name, the amount of the payment, and the new account balance in the check register. (If a firm uses checks with stubs that are bound into a checkbook, this information is recorded on a check stub.) The final step in the process is to write the check itself. The amount used is the employee's net pay for the period. After the check is written, its number is entered in the Check Number column of the payroll register.

In most businesses, the person who prepares the payroll checks is not the one who signs them. Thus, the signature line is left blank until all checks have been completed and verified, at which time the checks are submitted to the proper person for signature. In small companies, this person is usually the owner.

Some firms use a payroll check on which is printed the words "Requires two signatures if for more than $2,000" or some similar restriction. A limit such as this requires that *two* executives review the check before it is issued. Two lines are provided on the check to make two signatures possible. Other restrictions may be printed on payroll checks. A common one is a statement such as "Void if not cashed within 60 days."

One of the advantages of paying employees by check is that the firm does not need to obtain receipts from the employees to verify that they were given the correct amount of pay. The canceled checks serve as receipts for the money that was paid. Some banks no longer return canceled checks. Instead, the banks make digital images, front and back, of all checks.

A Case for Decision 8-1

Each July, the Ohio Grain Storage Company has its books audited by an independent accounting firm. All aspects of its records are reviewed. Last year, the auditors found a problem in the payroll records kept by a recently hired payroll clerk. There seemed to be a payroll check missing from almost every payroll period. The payroll clerk admitted that he had made mistakes on the checks and had torn such checks in two and discarded them.

The auditor said that these checks *might* have been written and cashed and then, when the canceled checks were returned to the company, they could have been taken and destroyed. Missing payroll checks could indicate someone is stealing money from the business.

The auditor made a complete review of the entire payroll payment system, determined that such was not the case. The missing checks had *not* been written and cashed. The payroll clerk was greatly relieved and had learned a valuable lesson in the process.

Discussion of the Case

The new clerk was not familiar with the procedure of *voiding and saving* payroll checks on which a mistake has been made. It is essential that the records show that *every* payroll check is accounted for. This means that ruined checks must be marked "VOID" and included in the check file.

Credit card companies are *glad* when you pay only the minimum required on your credit card debt: consider this. You have a $1,000 credit card debt and charge nothing more. You pay that debt off with the minimum required monthly payment. It will take you 20 *years* to pay back the $1,000! And, you will have paid about $2,000 in interest!

The Use of a Special Payroll Account

A very small business with only a few employees will usually issue payroll checks from its regular checking account. However, firms that have a larger staff normally find it more efficient to use a separate checking account for payroll. This procedure makes it easier to reconcile the regular checking account each month and also provides better control over payroll transactions.

In a large company, a separate *payroll checking account* may be set up with a balance that is intended to cover checks for *each* payroll period. After payroll is computed, a check for the total amount is written on the company's regular bank account and deposited in the special payroll checking account. Once this check is taken to the bank and deposited, the individual payroll checks can be issued to the employees.

PREPARING PAYROLL CHECKS

Certain techniques are widely used to ensure that payroll checks are prepared with efficiency, safety, and accuracy.

Writing Checks by Hand

Handwritten checks must be prepared in ink, and no erasures are permitted. Thus, if there is a mistake on a check, it must be voided and a new check written. All words and figures must be entered carefully so that they are accurate and clear and easy to read. In addition, the following procedures should be used for safety. Refer to the check in Figure 8.2 on page 174 to see exactly how these procedures are carried out.

- The employee is identified as fully as possible. Thus it is preferable to use "Evelyn C. Billings" on the check rather than a shorter version of the name such as "E. Billings."
- The name is written in such a way that it would be difficult to alter it if the check fell into the hands of an unauthorized person. Thus the name is placed immediately after the words "Pay to the order of," and a wavy line is used to fill in the remaining space behind the name. This prevents anyone from making a change. For example, someone might alter the name to "E. Billings" to "Evelyn B. Billings" or "Evelyn Billings, Inc."
- The amount in figures is written close to the dollar sign. This makes it impossible to raise the amount by adding another figure in front of those already recorded.
- The amount in words is also written in such a way as to prevent changes. The words start exactly at the beginning of the area provided, and a wavy line is used to fill the remaining space before the word "Dollars."

Typing Checks

In some firms, payroll checks are typewritten. The same basic techniques used in preparing handwritten checks should be applied to typewritten checks. Only a few modifications are necessary. For example, a line of hyphens replaces the wavy line used to fill space on a handwritten check.

Voiding Checks

Whether a payroll check is handwritten or typewritten, it must be voided if there is a mistake. The correct procedure for voiding a payroll check is as follows. First, the word "VOID" is written in large letters across the face of the check and the signature line is torn or cut

Internet Connection

Over half of the private U.S. workforce has direct deposit of paychecks and other payments such as dividends, pensions, annuities, and reimbursements. Almost all government workers are paid that way, saving more than $100 million annually. The National Automated Clearing House Association (http://www.nacha.org) answers questions about this process at http://www.nacha.org.

off. Next, a notation is made in the check register or on the check stub to show that the check was voided. Then the voided check is filed so that it can be accounted for.

Verifying the Accuracy of Checks

After all the payroll checks are prepared, they should be examined carefully and compared with the payroll register to make sure that the names and amounts are correct. Many experienced payroll clerks make a final verification of the figures by adding the amounts of all the checks on a calculator and comparing the total with the total of the Net Pay column in the payroll register. The two sums should be the same. Another useful verification procedure is to compare the checks with the entries in the check register or checkbook to make sure that there is a listing for every check and to verify that all amounts were recorded correctly.

Learning Through Practice   Do Exercise 8.1 on page 187 of this text-workbook.

PAYING BY DIRECT DEPOSIT IN EMPLOYEE CHECKING ACCOUNTS

An increasingly popular method for paying employees is to electronically deposit their earnings into their checking accounts. This system is referred to as direct deposit or electronic funds transfer (EFT). The firm's bank, with instructions from the firm, will make the transfers with bank equipment. The total of the electronic transfers will be deducted from the firm's account. This method is convenient for the firms that use it and favored by many employees. The firms do not have to issue payroll checks, and the employees have money available immediately without the bother of cashing or depositing their checks.

Employee Pay Statements

When the direct-deposit plan is used, each employee is given a statement of earnings and deductions on payday. This verifies that the deposit has been made and also serves as the employee's payroll record. The pay statement for Grace T. Evans, issued by South Town Auto in Newport, Delaware, is shown in Figure 8.3 on page 178. This report provides her with a complete record of her earnings and deductions for the week and proof that her net pay was deposited in her checking account. Direct deposit is the easiest and most efficient method for paying employees, and it is growing rapidly in popularity both with businesses and employees. Most payroll software programs support this method of paying employees.

Learning Through Practice   Do Exercise 8.2 on page 188 of this text-workbook.

PAYROLL PROCESSING BY SERVICE BUREAUS

Many companies choose to outsource their payroll processing to firms called *payroll service bureaus*. These companies find that handling payroll is simply too complex, demands too much time, and drains staff resources. An added advantage to using a payroll service bureau is that such companies keep current on all payroll laws and regulations. Frequent changes in laws,

The federal government is the largest user of *electronic funds transfer* (EFT) and has been for the past 15 years. Instead of being sent by check through the mail, funds are automatically deposited in the bank account of the person or firm that receives payment. The government makes about 2 *billion* of these EFT payments each year. To save time and money involved in preparing checks, the government's goal is to reduce even further the number of payments it makes by check and to increase the number of EFT payments. Not only is EFT convenient (and safer), but by using it the government expects to save $18 million per year in operating costs when the EFT program is fully operational.

FIGURE 8.3   **Employee Pay Statement**

EMPLOYEE PAY STATEMENT

SOUTH TOWN
A U T O
3276 Auto Row
Newport, DE 19804

NAME: _Grace T. Evans_

The amount shown under Net Pay below has been deposited to your account No. _099331_ . This amount is for the pay period beginning _Aug. 10_ , 20 _05_ and ending _Aug. 14_ , 20 _05_ . The money was deposited on _Aug. 17_ , 20 _05_ .

Employee's social security number	PERIOD ENDING	HOURS WORKED		EARNINGS				NET PAY	
		Reg. _40_		Regular	Overtime or Comm.		Total		
816-99-4836	August 14, 2005	O.T. _____							
				1,410	40		1,410	40	996	83

DEDUCTIONS									
Federal Inc. Tax	Social Security Tax	Medicare Tax	State Inc. Tax	IRA	Other	Other	Other	Total	
230 44	87 44	20 45	65 24	10 00				413 57	

regulations, and tax forms require continual in-service for payroll personnel. In addition, many taxing agencies require that reports be filed electronically. For these and many other reasons, companies increasingly realize that it makes financial sense to outsource payroll functions.

The largest payroll service bureau is ADP (Automated Data Processing, Inc.). While ADP is best known for its work in payroll, it has a vast and comprehensive data processing system that has many business applications. The company has more than 30,000 employees located throughout the world and has 60 computer centers across the United States. Although its primary service area is the United States, ADP has many clients in Canada, in Europe, and in Latin America.

ADP does payroll for nearly 65 percent of the medium-sized businesses in the United States that have chosen to outsource their payroll operations. The company focuses on three major markets: national accounts (companies with 1,000 or more employees), major accounts (companies with 100 to 999 employees), and emerging businesses. In the last group, ADP processes payroll for an amazing 325,000 clients.

Since the company serves clients in widely scattered locations, it is necessary that they have knowledge of the payroll tax laws of many foreign countries, U.S. federal regulations, all state payroll tax laws, and all city and county payroll tax regulations. You can imagine how complex a task it must be to keep track of all these laws and the frequent changes in them. The ADP Tax and Financial Services Center interfaces with 2,000 different tax agencies.

A Service Bureau Client

Homeway Living, a chain of retail furniture stores, uses National Data Systems (NDS), to process its payroll. Each Friday evening, the payroll department at Homeway sends the weekly payroll input data to NDS electronically.

NDS runs the input data (employee names, hours worked, etc.) on its computer system. Since NDS has done the payroll for Homeway for some time, it has a data file that contains all the payroll information from the first of the year to the present. The details of this week's payroll are added to the existing data in the year-to-date file.

The computer system at NDS then electronically calculates the earnings, deductions, and net pay of each employee, prints a payroll register, prints payroll checks, and updates the employee earnings records. The system also produces a comprehensive payroll report for the management of Homeway. This report shows payroll costs on a store-by-store basis. While all of these records cannot be illustrated here, Figure 8.4 on page 180 shows the payroll register and a paycheck created by ADP for a sample company. You can see how closely the payroll register compares to the manual payroll registers you have prepared in the exercises in this text.

In addition to processing its weekly payroll, NDS does many other payroll tasks for Homeway.

1. Compute federal, state, and local tax liabilities for each payroll period; prepare the necessary deposit forms; and submit the deposits to the proper agencies.
2. Compute any federal, state, and local taxes that may be due at the end of each quarter and prepare the deposits. Prepare Form 941, Employer's Quarterly Federal Tax Return; the quarterly state unemployment tax report; and the periodic state and local income tax withholding report.
3. Prepare all year-end reports, including Form 940, Employer's Annual Federal Unemployment (FUTA) Tax; Form W-2 for each employee; Form W-3, Transmittal of Wage and Tax Statements; and the required annual state and local reports.

COMPUTERIZED PAYROLL PROCEDURES

The basic procedures used in a computerized payroll system are quite similar whether the work is performed by a business that is handling its own payroll activities or by a service bureau. The following is a description of how a computerized payroll system typically operates.

A payroll master file is created. This file contains the same kinds of data as the employee earnings records in a manual system: basic payroll information for each employee as well as year-to-date figures on earnings, deductions, and net pay. The basic information includes the employee's name, social security number, pay rate, marital status, number of withholding allowances, and types of voluntary deductions. This information is needed by the computer to calculate payroll amounts for the employee and to track tax liabilities.

Each payroll period, the master file is updated to reflect changes such as additions and terminations of employees, changes in marital status, number of withholding allowances, or pay rates. The master file is then ready for use in processing the payroll for the current period.

Based on time cards or other source documents, the input data for the current period is entered. The computer then calculates the earnings, deductions, and net pay for each employee for the current period and enters the information in the master file. It also calculates and records the new year-to-date totals for each employee. The payroll register and paychecks are printed.

A COMPUTERIZED PAYROLL SYSTEM IN A SMALL BUSINESS

The Burger Express is a busy fast-food restaurant in a large midwestern city. Starting with a very limited menu five years ago, it has expanded steadily and now features barbecued ribs, fried chicken, pizza, roast beef sandwiches, fish sandwiches, and chili as well as a wide selection of hamburgers. The restaurant is open from 7 a.m. to midnight seven days a week and has 45 to 55 full-time and part-time employees.

FIGURE 8.4 Payroll Register

Employee Information	Earnings	Rate	Hours	Amount	Federal Taxes		State/Local Taxes		Deductions		Net Pay		Check Cleared?
01 - ADMINISTRATIVE													
ANDERSON, JIM #0007 Single/00	Gross REGULAR	5.2500	40.00	210.00 210.00	SS/Med Fed Wt	16.07 22.67	NJ State	3.02	HOSP 401K	5.00 8.40	Net Pay	**154.84** Direct Deposit	☑
DAVIS, CONNIE #0012 Single/01	Gross REGULAR	5.2500	40.00	210.00 210.00	SS/Med Fed Wt	16.07 15.00	NJ State	2.70	HOSP 401K	5.00 10.50	Net Pay	**160.73** Direct Deposit	
JOHNSON, MATT #0005 Married/00	Gross REGULAR	5.2500	40.00	210.00 210.00	SS/Med Fed Wt	16.07 12.97	NJ State	3.15	HOSP	5.00	Net Pay	**172.81** Direct Deposit	
MORGAN, CHRISTINE #0011 Married/02	Gross REGLAR O/TIME	9.2500 13.8750	40.00 10.00	508.75 370.00 138.75	SS/Med Fed Wt	38.92 41.54	NJ State	7.28	HOSP 401K	5.00 10.18	Net Pay	**405.83** ☐ Check #0000036	
THOMAS, JAMES #0015 Single/01	Gross REGULAR	4.2500	40.00	170.00 170.00	SS/Med Fed Wt	13.01	NJ State		HOSP	5.00 ?.40	Net Pay	**131.32** Direct Deposit	
01 - ADMINISTRATIVE Totals	Gross									5.00 ?.40	**5 Pays**	**1,025.53**	00 48
02 - S...													
COLE...											0 Net Pay	**411.04** Direct Deposit	
RODGE...											Net Pay	**527.83** Direct Deposit	
TOREN, ...											Net Pay	**347.33** ☐ Check #0000037	
VANDERS...											Net Pay	**581.65** Direct Deposit	
YOUNG, GE...											Net Pay	**370.15** Direct Deposit	
02 - SALES Totals				2,030.00 935.00	SS/Med Fed Wt	226.83 423.74	NJ State IL State	39.75 11.68	HOSP	25.00	**5 Pays**	**2,238.00**	

YOUR COMPANY NAME
475 KNAPP AVENUE
ANYTOWN, DE 10101

Pay To The Order Of

CHRISTINE MORGAN
3 MARC DRIVE
HOMETOWN, NJ 12345

Your Bank
Bank Street
Anytown, DE (800) 1-0000

* FOUR HUNDRED FIVE DOLLARS * * * * AND * * * * * 83 CENTS *

Check Date: 9/13/05

36
1-9999 111
9999

$405.83

Pay This Amount

SAMPLE CHECK
NON-NEGOTIABLE
VOID VOID VOID

THIS IS NOT A CHECK

⑈0036⑈ ⑆999999999 2⑆ ⑈ 123456789 ⑈

EASYPAY℠

Client: ZYX
YOUR COMPANY NAME

Payroll Register

Period Covered: **09/02/05 - 09/08/05**
Check Date: **09/13/05**

Run: 32
Week: 37
Qtr: 3
Page: 1

Although this business is considered small, its payroll work is complicated and time-consuming. The hours vary a great deal from week to week for many employees, and there is a large turnover in the part-time staff. Thus, employees are constantly being added to and deleted from the payroll records. Until last year, all payroll procedures for the restaurant were carried out manually by an employee who did bookkeeping activities in the mornings and worked as a cashier in the afternoons. Because payroll was taking up so much time, it became impossible for this employee to handle payroll and all the other financial record-keeping procedures assigned to her. The owner considered two plans to deal with the situation.

One possibility was to outsource the payroll responsibilities. All the bookkeeper would have to do would be to deliver the time cards to the service bureau each week and then pick up the completed payroll register and checks two days later. The service bureau would also produce the end-of-quarter and end-of-year tax reports that the business has to submit to government agencies. This arrangement was convenient, and the cost was reasonable for the amount of work that would be performed.

The alternative plan involved buying a computer so that the business could automate its payroll system. Although this course of action required an investment of several thousand dollars for equipment and programs, the owner preferred it because she knew that the computer would also be available to help her manage the restaurant more effectively as it continued to grow.

The owner wanted to automate all accounting records so that she would be able to receive financial statements more quickly at the end of each month. Such statements would show her the financial condition of the business and the results of its operations. This information would enable her to make timely, informed decisions.

When purchasing the computer, the owner had to select programs that would suit the requirements of the business. For example, to handle its payroll activities, she chose a program that involved as little data entry work for each pay period as possible. She was looking for a program that would be easy to operate and yet would do the required work.

After the computer was installed, the bookkeeper attended several days of software training sponsored by the computer company. In addition, the bookkeeper had to work overtime for a few weekends in order to convert the data in the employee earnings records to a payroll master file. Once this process was completed, the firm's payroll activities became quite simple. Every Monday morning, the bookkeeper added any new employees, totaled the time cards for the previous week, and made other necessary changes that affected the basic payroll information in the master file.

After updating the master file, the bookkeeper used the time cards to enter the regular and overtime hours. The payroll register, showing gross earnings and all deductions, was printed and verified. Voucher payroll checks were printed.

The bookkeeper backed up the payroll master file and stored the disk in a locked, fireproof cabinet.

Finally, the bookkeeper gave the checks to the owner, who signed and distributed them to the employees. The owner also examined the printed payroll register to see what the weekly totals were and then returned the payroll register to the bookkeeper to be filed.

In addition to handling the regular pay period work, the payroll software program prepares all end-of-quarter and end-of-year state and federal tax reports. This further reduces the amount of time the bookkeeper has to spend doing payroll work.

COMPUTERIZED PAYROLL ACCOUNTING

An advantage of computerized payroll processing is the availability of software programs that can be purchased at relatively low cost. It is not necessary to have programs custom-designed. The type and size of a business and the degree to which other accounting functions have been computerized will be key considerations in determining which payroll software to purchase.

A common spreadsheet application used in the business world is Microsoft Excel. Used as a tool for organizing and analyzing data, the spreadsheet can be easily adapted to automate many payroll calculations. A spreadsheet is made up of rows and columns. Letters identify the columns and numbers identify the rows. As you create a spreadsheet, you enter numbers, labels, and formulas into cells. The formulas allow the program to make calculations. Rather than manually entering payroll information into a payroll register, a template file, created on the spreadsheet, can be used each time payroll is to be calculated.

Peachtree Accounting for Windows and QuickBooks are commercial accounting software packages that include payroll processing within the accounting program. Marketed primarily to small and medium-sized businesses, both of these software programs integrate the functions of the general ledger, accounts payable, accounts receivable, payroll, and inventory systems.

The screens in Peachtree and QuickBooks look like paper invoices, checks, purchase orders, and other common business forms that you are already familiar with. Both programs offer online help and tutorials, so that little training is necessary to begin entering accounting data. After the initial payroll setup, when basic employee information is entered and saved, the numbers of hours worked is the only information to be entered. Checks and reports can be printed with just a point-and-click of the mouse.

The following features are commonly found in the payroll component of any integrated accounting program or in stand-alone payroll programs.

- Calculate earnings and deductions for hourly, salaried, commissioned, and tipped employees.
- Calculate federal, state, and local income taxes.
- Calculate social security and Medicare taxes for employees and employers.
- Process 401(k) and pension contributions.
- Track vacation and sick time.
- Print payroll checks singly or in batches.
- Calculate unemployment and workers' compensation obligations.
- Print W-2, 940, 941, and workers' compensation reports.
- Create payroll reports.

INTERNAL CONTROL

Employee wages represent a substantial cost for many businesses. In Unit 7, you learned about the need to establish internal control of payroll records to ensure accuracy, honesty, efficiency, and confidentiality. Here are some internal controls that apply to the payment of the firm's payroll.

- A signed receipt should be obtained for any employee who is paid in cash. This receipt must be kept as part of your proof of payment.
- The establishment of a separate checking account that is used only for payroll makes it easier to keep track of all payroll transactions.
- Use only prenumbered checks for payroll.
- Make sure that access to the payroll checks is limited.
- Have the payroll checking account reconciled every month by someone who did not prepare or sign any of the checks. Keep the reconciliation and canceled checks in a secure location.
- Have a company policy on where and how long voided checks are kept.
- Separate the duties of authorizing payroll, writing the payroll checks, and distributing the payroll checks.
- The firm's payroll records should be periodically audited by an independent accountant outside the company.

UNIT 8   REVIEW

Summary

After studying this unit, you should be able to:

- Comprehend that a manual payroll system works the same way as a computerized payroll system.
- Name some of the few businesses that may pay employees in cash.
- Explain why it is important to obtain a signed receipt from an employee when the employee is paid in cash.
- Know what the initials EFT stand for, and how an EFT payroll transfer works.
- Give some reasons why employees might prefer to have their payroll checks deposited through EFT rather than receiving a check.
- Void a payroll check and know the procedure for retaining the voided check.
- Correctly complete a payroll check.
- Discuss the advantages of using a payroll service bureau.
- Discuss the internal control issues that impact the payroll check-writing function.

Study Questions

1. What are the three methods used to pay employees?
2. When employees are paid in cash, why is it necessary to obtain a signed receipt from them?
3. What are the disadvantages of using cash to pay employee wages and salaries?
4. List the advantages of using a payroll software package?
5. Explain why internal controls are so critical in a payroll system.
6. Payroll checks are not issued when the direct-deposit plan is used. How do employees receive their pay under this plan?
7. Why would the phrase "void after 90 days" be printed on all payroll checks?
8. Describe the procedures for completing a handwritten payroll check.
9. How should payroll checks that contain mistakes be handled?
10. Why would a business have a special checking account for the funds used to pay the payroll?
11. What advantages does a payroll service bureau offer to a small business?
12. Give three examples of internal controls that relate to the function of paying the payroll.

Discussion Questions

1. Best Value Auto Repair has converted from paying its employees in cash to paying them by check. You have been asked to suggest techniques that would ensure accuracy and safety when preparing checks. What procedures would you suggest?
2. Discuss the importance of verifying payroll records and information.
3. Why might employees prefer the direct-deposit plan (EFT) to being paid by check?
4. When employees are paid by EFT, how are they advised of their earnings, deductions, and net pay for the period?
5. When should a business consider changing from a manual payroll system to a computerized payroll system?

REVIEW EXERCISES

In these exercises, use the tax tables in the Appendix to determine federal and state income tax. Use a rate of 6.2 percent to compute social security tax and a rate of 1.45 percent to compute Medicare tax. Use a rate of 1.18 percent to compute the state disability insurance tax levied by California. In your calculations, carry amounts to at least three decimal places and round them to two decimal places.

1. Patrick McManus sells advertising for WKRP, a radio station. He receives a weekly salary of $782. He is single and claims one withholding allowance. Assume that he has required deductions for federal income tax, state income tax, social security tax, Medicare tax, and state disability insurance tax. Also assume that he has a voluntary deduction of $30 a week for an IRA. What amount will appear on his payroll check for the week ended January 16?

2. Leslie Golden sells office furniture to businesses. She receives a weekly salary of $575 and a commission of 2 percent on her sales. During the week ended March 21, her sales totaled $18,650. She is married and claims two withholding allowances. Assume that she has required deductions for federal income tax, state income tax, social security tax, Medicare tax, and state disability insurance tax. Also assume that she has a voluntary deduction of $50 a week for savings bonds. What amount will appear on her payroll check for the week ended March 21?

3. Brett Nielson is a baker at the Parisian Cafe. He is paid $16.85 an hour. During the week ended April 12, he worked 38 hours. He is married and claims one withholding allowance. Assume that he has required deductions for federal income tax, state income tax, social security tax, Medicare tax, and state disability insurance tax. What is his net pay for the week?

4. Naomi Ross is a sewing machine operator at Flair Fashions, a small clothing manufacturer. She receives a regular rate of $12.50 an hour and an overtime rate of 1 1/2 times her regular rate for all hours worked beyond 40 in a week. During the week ended January 7, she worked 45 hours. She is married and claims two withholding allowances. Assume that she has required deductions for federal income tax, state income tax, social security tax, Medicare tax, and state disability insurance tax. What is the amount of net pay that will appear on her payroll check?

5. The following four employees work in the administrative department of Douglas Medical Center. Their regular workweek is 40 hours, and they receive 1 1/2 times their regular hourly rate for any hours worked beyond 40 in a week. Assume that these employees have required deductions for federal income tax, state income tax, social security tax, Medicare tax, and state disability insurance tax. During the week ended March 18, these employees worked the hours shown below.

Employee	Marital Status	Withholding Allowances	Weekly Salary	Hours Worked
Marie Alfonso	M	3	$795	40
Peter DeGraff	S	1	654	36
Joanne Moore	S	0	620	43
Gary Owens	M	1	692	42

These employees are paid by check. What amount will appear on the payroll check of each employee?

6. Read each of the following statements. In the answer column, place a *T* if the statement is true or an *F* if it is false.

   a. The information in the payroll master file of a computerized system is similar to the information in the employee earnings records of a manual system.   1. _____

   b. In a computerized payroll system, it is necessary to prepare the paychecks by hand.   2. _____

   c. As a safety measure in a computerized system, it is a common practice to make backup (duplicate) copies of the payroll master file.   3. _____

d. A large business with thousands of employees and complex payroll operations would surely use a computer to handle its payroll work.

4. _____

e. A computer can produce an updated payroll master file on disk and also print a payroll register.

5. _____

f. The use of different programs for payroll, word processing, billing, and other business applications makes a personal computer a very versatile tool for a small firm.

6. _____

g. The results of payroll calculations made by a mainframe computer are more accurate than those made by a personal computer.

7. _____

Problems

1. Using the check form provided, prepare the payroll check for Ryan C. Curtis (known as RC to everyone) for the week ended November 30. His earnings and deductions are shown below. He worked 40 hours with no overtime. His social security number is 411-12-2004. Use December 2 as the date of the payroll check.

Gross earnings	$1,000.00
Federal income tax withheld	105.00
State income tax withheld	60.00
Social security tax withheld	62.00
Medicare tax withheld	14.50
Health insurance premium withheld	112.00

Employee's social security number	PERIOD ENDING	HOURS WORKED	EARNINGS			NET PAY
		Reg. _____ O.T. _____	Regular	Overtime or Comm.	Total	

DEDUCTIONS									
Federal Inc. Tax	Social Security Tax	Medicare Tax	State Inc. Tax	SDI Tax	I.R.A	Savings Bonds	Other	Total	

Statement of Earnings and Deductions   Detach and retain for your records.   *Zepher Culinary, Inc.*

Zepher Culinary, Inc.
ZCI 1855 Seventh Street
SAN JOSE, CA 95101

PAYROLL CHECK   No. **1263**

90-306
1222

Date _____ 20 ___

Pay to
the order of _____ $ _____

_____ Dollars

San Jose Regional Bank
270 College Avenue
San Jose, California, 95105

⑆1222⑈0306⑆ 01018⑈057223⑈

2. After completing the payroll check for Curtis in Problem 1, but before giving it to him, you discover an error in his gross pay—it should have been $1,200.00 instead of $1,000.00. Show how to void the check, and describe what should be done with the voided check.

   _____

   _____

   _____

   _____

   _____

   _____

3. Jean Smith is the accountant for Houston Office Products. She is currently investigating the possibility of turning the firm's payroll work over to a payroll service bureau. Up to this point, Houston has been using a personal computer to process its payroll. However, the firm has been growing rapidly and its present computerized system does not meet all of its payroll needs well. In part, this is because the firm pays its employees according to four different plans: the salary plan, the hourly rate plan, the commission plan, and the salary-commission plan. Another shortcoming of the present payroll system is that it does not produce state payroll tax returns. It produces only the federal tax returns. Also, the present system can handle only a limited number of deductions. On the other hand, the firm would have to pay a fee to the service bureau for processing its payroll, whereas it owns the equipment and software that it currently uses to handle payroll work. The owner of Houston Office Products is also concerned about the privacy of the firm's payroll records if an outside company processes its payroll.

   If you were Jean Smith, what recommendation would you make about the transfer of payroll work to the outside service bureau? What reasons would you give for your recommendation?

Learning Through Practice

Unit 8 Exercises

EXERCISE 8.1

Sun Communications is a retail business that sells pagers and cellular phones in Fresno, California. For the week ended January 14, two of its employees had the gross earnings, withholding allowances, and voluntary deductions shown below. Both employees are married.

Employee	Gross Earnings	Withholding Allowances	IRA
Awad, Victor	$784.00	2	$50.00
Clark, Susan	826.00	3	25.00

1. Compute the required deductions, total deductions, and net pay for each of these employees. Use the federal and state income tax tables in the Appendix. Use 6.2 percent as the rate for social security tax, 1.45 percent as the rate for Medicare tax, and 1.18 percent as the rate for state disability insurance tax.
2. Prepare a payroll check for each employee. Use the forms provided below and on the next page. The social security numbers are 328-11-8422 for Awad and 743-14-6007 for Clark. Both employees worked 40 hours and had no overtime or commissions. Date the checks January 16.

EXERCISE 8.1 Payroll Checks

Employee's social security number	PERIOD ENDING	HOURS WORKED	EARNINGS			NET PAY
		Reg. _____ O.T. _____	Regular	Overtime or Comm.	Total	

DEDUCTIONS								
Federal Inc. Tax	Social Security Tax	Medicare Tax	State Inc. Tax	SDI Tax	I.R.A	Savings Bonds	Other	Total

Statement of Earnings and Deductions   Detach and retain for your records.

SUN COMMunications

SUN COMMunications
22 River Road
Fresno, CA 93707

PAYROLL CHECK   No. **1264**   90-306 / 1222

Date _____ 20 _____

Pay to the order of _____ $ _____

_____ Dollars

Valley Commercial Bank
1080 Palm Drive
Fresno, CA 93776

⑈1222⑈0306⑈ 01018⑈057223⑈

EXERCISE 8.1 *(continued)*

Employee's social security number	PERIOD ENDING	HOURS WORKED		EARNINGS			NET PAY
		Reg. _____ O.T. _____		Regular	Overtime or Comm.	Total	

DEDUCTIONS								
Federal Inc. Tax	Social Security Tax	Medicare Tax	State Inc. Tax	SDI Tax	I.R.A	Savings Bonds	Other	Total

Statement of Earnings and Deductions   Detach and retain for your records.   *SUN COMMunications*

SUN COMMunications
22 *River Road*
Fresno, CA 93707

PAYROLL CHECK   No. **1263**   90-306 / 1222

Date _____ 20 _____

Pay to
the order of _____ $ _____

_____ Dollars

Valley Commercial Bank
1080 Palm Drive
Fresno, CA 93776

⑈1222⑈0306⑈ 01018⑈057223⑈

EXERCISE 8.2

Assume that Sun Communications has changed to a direct-deposit system for paying its employees. For the week ended April 7, two of its employees had the gross earnings, withholding allowances, and voluntary deductions shown below. Both employees are single.

Employee	Gross Earnings	Withholding Allowances	IRA
Connors, Bridget	$808.00	1	$50.00
Gruzinski, Mark	740.00	1	75.00

1. Compute the required deductions, total deductions, and net pay for each of these employees. Use the federal and state income tax tables in the Appendix. Use 6.2 percent as the rate for social security tax, 1.45 percent as the rate for Medicare tax, and 1.18 percent as the rate for state disability insurance tax.

2. Prepare an employee pay statement for each employee. Use the forms provided on the next page. The social security numbers are 217-10-7311 for Connors and 854-25-7118 for Gruzinski. Both employees worked 40 hours and had no overtime or commissions. The date of the payroll period is April 1 through April 7. The money was deposited on April 9.

EXERCISE 8.2 **Employee Pay Statements**

EMPLOYEE PAY STATEMENT

SUN COMMunications
22 River Road
Fresno, CA 93707

NAME: _____

The amount shown under Net Pay below has been deposited to your account. This amount is for the pay

period beginning _____ , 20 _____ and ending _____ , 20 _____ . The money was deposited

on _____ , 20 _____ .

Employee's social security number	PERIOD ENDING	HOURS WORKED	EARNINGS			NET PAY	
		Reg. _____ O.T. _____	Regular	Overtime or Comm.	Total		

DEDUCTIONS								
Federal Inc. Tax	Social Security Tax	Medicare Tax	State Inc. Tax	SDI Tax	I.R.A	Savings Bonds	Other	Total

EMPLOYEE PAY STATEMENT

SUN COMMunications
22 River Road
Fresno, CA 93707

NAME: _____

The amount shown under Net Pay below has been deposited to your account. This amount is for the pay

period beginning _____ , 20 _____ and ending _____ , 20 _____ . The money was deposited

on _____ , 20 _____ .

Employee's social security number	PERIOD ENDING	HOURS WORKED	EARNINGS			NET PAY	
		Reg. _____ O.T. _____	Regular	Overtime or Comm.	Total		

DEDUCTIONS								
Federal Inc. Tax	Social Security Tax	Medicare Tax	State Inc. Tax	SDI Tax	I.R.A	Savings Bonds	Other	Total

Name _____ Date _____

Unit 8 Exercises

EXERCISE 8.1A

The Plaza Fitness Club provides its members with exercise equipment and classes, a swimming pool, and a spa. The club is located in Fresno, California. For the week ended March 14, two of its employees had the gross earnings, withholding allowances, and voluntary deductions shown below. Both employees are single.

Employee	Gross Earnings	Withholding Allowances	Savings Bonds
Liu, Sarah	$712.00	1	$50.00
Smith, Marshall	698.00	0	25.00

1. Compute the required deductions, total deductions, and net pay for each of these employees. Use the federal and state income tax tables in the Appendix. Use 6.2 percent as the rate for social security tax, 1.45 percent as the rate for Medicare tax, and 1.18 percent as the rate for state disability insurance tax.

2. Prepare a payroll check for each employee. Use the forms provided below and on the next page. The social security numbers are 540-33-0644 for Liu and 965-36-8119 for Smith. Both employees worked 40 hours and had no overtime or commissions. The checks should be dated March 17.

EXERCISE 8.1A **Payroll Checks**

Employee's social security number	PERIOD ENDING	HOURS WORKED	EARNINGS			NET PAY
		Reg. _____ O.T. _____	Regular	Overtime or Comm.	Total	

	DEDUCTIONS								
Federal Inc. Tax	Social Security Tax	Medicare Tax	State Inc. Tax	SDI Tax	I.R.A	Savings Bonds	Other	Total	

Statement of Earnings and Deductions   Detach and retain for your records.   *PLAZA FITNESS CLUB*

PLAZA FITNESS CLUB
10 Commerce Plaza
Fresno, CA 93707

PAYROLL CHECK   No. **1263**   90-306 / 1222

Date _____ 20 ____

Pay to
the order of _____ $ _____

_____ Dollars

SPECIMEN CHECK ONLY

Valley Commercial Bank
1080 Palm Drive
Fresno, CA 93776

⑆1222⑈0306⑆ 01018⑈057223⑈

EXERCISE 8.1A *(continued)*

Employee's social security number	PERIOD ENDING	HOURS WORKED		EARNINGS				NET PAY	
		Reg. _____ O.T. _____		Regular	Overtime or Comm.	Total			

DEDUCTIONS									
Federal Inc. Tax	Social Security Tax	Medicare Tax	State Inc. Tax	SDI Tax	I.R.A	Savings Bonds	Other	Total	

Statement of Earnings and Deductions   Detach and retain for your records.   *PLAZA FITNESS CLUB*

PLAZA FITNESS CLUB
   10 Commerce Plaza
   Fresno, CA 93707

PAYROLL CHECK   No. **1264**

$\frac{90\text{-}306}{1222}$

Date _____ 20 _____

Pay to
the order of _____ $ _____

_____ Dollars

SPECIMEN CHECK ONLY

Valley Commercial Bank
1080 Palm Drive
Fresno, CA 93776

⑆1222⑆0306⑈ 01018⑈057223⑆

EXERCISE 8.2A

Assume that the Plaza Fitness Club has changed to a direct-deposit system for paying its employees. For the week ended May 7, two of its employees had the gross earnings, withholding allowances, and voluntary deductions shown below. Both employees are married.

Employee	Gross Earnings	Withholding Allowances	Savings Bonds
Torres, Frank	$672.00	1	$25.00
Zell, Marianne	728.00	2	25.00

1. Compute the required deductions, total deductions, and net pay for each of these employees. Use the federal and state income tax tables in the Appendix. Use 6.2 percent as the rate for social security tax, 1.45 percent as the rate for Medicare tax, and 1.18 percent as the rate for state disability insurance tax.

2. Prepare an employee pay statement for each employee. Use the forms provided on the next page. The social security numbers are 439-32-9522 for Torres and 076-47-9330 for Zell. Both employees worked 40 hours and had no overtime or commissions. The date of the payroll period is May 1 through May 7. The money was deposited on May 9.

EXERCISE 8.2A   Employee Pay Statements

EMPLOYEE PAY STATEMENT

PLAZA FITNESS CLUB
10 Commerce Plaza
Fresno, CA 93707

NAME: _____

The amount shown under Net Pay below has been deposited to your account. This amount is for the pay

period beginning _____ , 20 _____ and ending _____ , 20 _____ . The money was deposited

on _____ , 20 _____ .

Employee's social security number	PERIOD ENDING	HOURS WORKED	EARNINGS			NET PAY
		Reg. _____ O.T. _____	Regular	Overtime or Comm.	Total	

DEDUCTIONS									
Federal Inc. Tax	Social Security Tax	Medicare Tax	State Inc. Tax	SDI Tax	I.R.A	Savings Bonds	Other	Total	

EMPLOYEE PAY STATEMENT

PLAZA FITNESS CLUB
10 Commerce Plaza
Fresno, CA 93707

NAME: _____

The amount shown under Net Pay below has been deposited to your account. This amount is for the pay

period beginning _____ , 20 _____ and ending _____ , 20 _____ . The money was deposited

on _____ , 20 _____ .

Employee's social security number	PERIOD ENDING	HOURS WORKED	EARNINGS			NET PAY
		Reg. _____ O.T. _____	Regular	Overtime or Comm.	Total	

DEDUCTIONS									
Federal Inc. Tax	Social Security Tax	Medicare Tax	State Inc. Tax	SDI Tax	I.R.A	Savings Bonds	Other	Total	

Federal Payroll Taxes and Tax Returns

Upon completion of this unit, you should be able to:

1. Explain how the employer's share of social security tax and Medicare tax is computed.
2. Describe the lookback table and how it is used.
3. Explain which businesses must use a monthly deposit schedule and which businesses must use a semiweekly deposit schedule.
4. Explain which businesses must use the Electronic Federal Tax Payment System to make deposits of taxes.
5. Explain why use of IRS Publication 509, an annual calendar for federal tax payments, is essential to the payroll department.
6. Describe how to prepare Schedule B of Form 941, Employer's Record of Federal Tax Liability.
7. Explain how Form 8109, Federal Tax Deposit Coupon, is used in paying federal tax obligations.
8. Demonstrate how to complete Form 941, Employer's Quarterly Federal Tax Return.
9. Explain which businesses can use Form 941-V, Payment Voucher, to pay federal income tax withheld and social security and Medicare taxes.
10. Explain how each of the six copies of Form W-2 is used.
11. Demonstrate how to complete a Form W-2, Wage and Tax Statement.
12. Explain how Form W-3, Transmittal of Wage and Tax Statements, is used.
13. Explain how federal unemployment compensation (FUTA) tax is computed and deposited.
14. Explain how Form 940-EZ, Employer's Annual Federal Unemployment (FUTA) Tax Return, is used.
15. Locate and understand the information entered on the common federal payroll tax forms and reports.

Businesses must deduct certain federal, state, and local taxes from employee earnings, send the amounts withheld to the correct agencies, and complete government forms to report information about these taxes. When money is withheld from employee earnings, it immediately becomes, in essence, property of the various government agencies. These monies, while in the possession of the business, do not belong to the business to use as it pleases. These tax withholdings are liabilities of the firm.

Besides withholding taxes, businesses themselves are subject to various payroll taxes, such as the employer's share of social security tax and Medicare tax, federal unemployment compensation tax, and state unemployment compensation tax. These taxes must be paid at specified times and must be reported periodically on government forms. Thus every firm

Internet Connection

If you have questions about federal or state payroll taxes, there's a searchable database at http://www.payroll-taxes.com, which includes an e-mail newsletter about payroll. At http://www.americanpayroll.org get forms and a daily calendar of compliance dates.

is responsible for handling both its own payroll taxes and the taxes owed by its employees. These heavy responsibilities must be carried out as prescribed by law.

In Unit 5, you learned how to determine employee tax deductions. In this unit, you will see how the federal taxes withheld are paid to the government and how they are reported on tax forms. You will also learn about the procedures for computing, paying, and reporting the federal payroll taxes owed by the employer. The handling of state taxes is discussed in Unit 10.

THE EMPLOYER'S SHARE OF SOCIAL SECURITY AND MEDICARE TAXES

The Federal Insurance Contributions Act (FICA) requires that most employees and employers pay taxes to support the federal social security system. In recent years, the amounts withheld from employee earnings for these taxes have increased dramatically. Employers must pay matching amounts. As of this writing, the employee's share of the social security tax is 6.2 percent of the first $87,900 earned in a calendar year. The employee's share of the Medicare tax is 1.45 percent of *all* earnings in a calendar year. Both the social security tax and the Medicare tax withheld from employee wages must be matched by an equal contribution from the employer. Thus, social security and Medicare taxes are now a large obligation for employees and employers. Examine the following example to see the impact of social security and Medicare taxes on a typical salary.

Social Security and Medicare Taxes on a $50,000 Annual Salary	
Employee's contribution to social security	$3,100
Employer's matching contribution to social security	3,100
Employee's contribution to Medicare	725
Employer's matching contribution to Medicare	725
Total taxes	$7,650

The employee share of each of these taxes is deducted from employee earnings by the employer at the end of each payroll period during the calendar year. In the case of social security tax, deductions are made until the maximum amount of taxable earnings for the year is reached (if it is reached). As noted already, all earnings during a calendar year are subject to Medicare tax. Both the social security and Medicare tax rates and the maximum amount of taxable earnings for social security (called the *taxable wage base*) are set by Congress and changed from time to time. Under legislation passed in 1983, the wage base for social security tax will be adjusted each year according to changes in average earnings throughout the United States.

Computing the Tax

The employee's social security and Medicare tax deductions are computed for each payroll period. The amount of taxable earnings for each employee for the period is multiplied by the current social security and Medicare rates. For example, suppose that Helen Johnson, an executive, had taxable earnings of $5,205.18 for the month of March. Using a rate of

6.2 percent for social security tax and a rate of 1.45 percent for Medicare tax, we compute her deductions for these taxes as follows.

Social Security Tax

$5,205.18 taxable earnings

$$\times \ .062$$

$322.72116 = $322.72

Medicare Tax

$5,205.18 taxable earnings

$$\times \ .0145$$

$75.47511 = $75.48

Helen Johnson's employer will withhold these two amounts, $322.72 and $75.48, from her salary for social security and Medicare taxes. The employer will pay matching amounts for each of these taxes. Thus, on her March earnings alone, the employee and employer contributions for social security and Medicare taxes total $796.40.

Social Security and Medicare Taxes on Tips

For employees who receive tips, the employer owes social security and Medicare taxes on their salaries plus any part of their tips that was credited toward the minimum wage. (See Unit 4 for a discussion of tips and the minimum wage.) The employer is not liable for social security and Medicare taxes on tips that were *not* used in computing the minimum wage.

DEPOSITING SOCIAL SECURITY AND MEDICARE TAXES AND FEDERAL INCOME TAXES

The social security tax, Medicare tax, and federal income tax withheld from employee earnings must be sent to the federal government periodically along with the employer's share of social security and Medicare taxes. Some businesses remit or send these taxes by making deposits in an authorized bank or other financial institution. They mail or deliver a check or money order to an authorized financial institution or Federal Reserve bank. However, other taxpayers are required to make their deposits by electronic funds transfer (EFT).

When to Deposit

Employers must pay their tax liabilities according to a *deposit period*. The term *deposit period* refers to the period during which tax liabilities are accumulated for each required deposit due date. There are two deposit schedules, *monthly* and *semiweekly*. Prior to the beginning of each calendar year, businesses must determine which of the two deposit schedules they are required to use. The deposit schedule is based on the total tax liability reported on Form 941 during a four-quarter *lookback period*.

FIGURE 9.1
A Lookback Table

A Lookback Table			
2004 Lookback Period		**2005 Lookback Period**	
3rd Quarter, 2002	$12,000	3rd Quarter, 2003	$13,000
4th Quarter, 2002	$12,350	4th Quarter, 2003	$13,200
1st Quarter, 2003	$11,125	1st Quarter, 2004	$12,500
2nd Quarter, 2003	$11,755	2nd Quarter, 2004	$13,700
Total	$47,230	Total	$52,400

The Lookback Period

A lookback period begins on July 1 and ends on June 30. It is a period of time *before* the present time. In other words, the four *previous* quarters. Lookback payments are determined by the total federal income tax withheld and social security and Medicare taxes reported on Form 941 in the previous four-quarter period.

If the business reported *$50,000 or less* of taxes during the lookback period, the business is a *monthly schedule depositor*. If it reported *more than $50,000* of taxes for the lookback period, the business is a *semiweekly schedule depositor*. Study the chart in Figure 9.1. Notice that the firm's tax payments were *under* $50,000 for the 2004 lookback period, so it was a monthly schedule depositor. However, the next year, total tax payments were *higher* than $50,000, and the firm became a semiweekly schedule depositor.

A monthly schedule depositor must pay its tax liability by the 15th day of the following month. A semiweekly schedule depositor must pay its tax liability within three business days after the payment date of the payroll. The term "semiweekly" is somewhat confusing because it sounds like the taxes must be deposited twice each week. This is not the case. Study the chart in Figure 9.2 on page 198. Notice that the chart refers to "payment days." An employer's tax liability and the timing of the tax deposit begin on the day employees are actually paid.

MONTHLY DEPOSIT EXAMPLE

Suppose that Very Fine Videos, Inc., has been notified by the IRS that it is a monthly depositor. Its employees are paid on the 15th and 30th of each month. The total payroll taxes withheld for each pay period during July are shown in the chart below.

	Federal Income Tax Withheld	**Social Security Tax Withheld**	**Medicare Tax Withheld**
July 15	$750.00	$310.00	$72.50
July 30	750.00	310.00	72.50
July total withholdings	$ 1,500.00	$ 620.00	$145.00
Employer matching taxes		620.00	145.00
July payroll tax liability	$ 1,500.00	$ 1,240.00	$290.00

Very Fine Videos' total tax liability for the July payroll is $3,030.00 ($1,500.00 + $1,240.00 + $290.00). Because the business is a monthly depositor and the last payroll was paid on July 30, the deposit is due by August 15, which is the 15th day of the following month.

SEMIWEEKLY DEPOSIT EXAMPLES

For various reasons, businesses pay their employees on different days, sometimes even on Sundays. Refer again to the chart in Figure 9.2, and consider these examples:

FIGURE 9.2
**Semiweekly Deposit
Schedule**

Semiweekly Deposit Schedule	
Day Employees Are Paid	**Deposit Taxes By**
Wednesday, Thursday, and/or Friday	Following Wednesday
Saturday, Sunday, Monday, and/or Tuesday	Following Friday

1. Denman and Company pays wages once a month, on the last day of the month. Because the business owed more than $50,000 of federal income tax withheld and social security and Medicare taxes during the last lookback period, it must follow a semiweekly deposit schedule. If the last day of the month, payday, falls on Tuesday, the tax deposit must be made by Friday of the same week. If the last day of the month, payday, falls on a Thursday, the tax deposit must be made by the following Wednesday.

2. The Castle Hotel must follow a semiweekly deposit schedule. It pays its employees biweekly, on Monday of every other week. As you can see from Figure 9.2, the business must make its tax deposit by Friday of that week. In fact, because it has two paydays a month, it must make tax deposits twice each month.

3. Ingram Heating and Cooling must follow a semiweekly deposit schedule. This business has a weekly payroll period that starts on Sunday and ends on Saturday. It pays its employees on the following Wednesday. Figure 9.2 shows that the business must make its tax deposit by the following Wednesday (one week later). In fact, since the business pays employees once a week, on Wednesday, it will make a tax deposit every week throughout the year by the Wednesday that follows payday.

Penalties for failure to make deposits of federal taxes on time are severe. It is essential that payroll personnel see to it that these deposits are made according to the schedule specified by the Internal Revenue Service (IRS).

The IRS issues an annual publication, 509, called Tax Calendars. This publication lists the specific dates during the year when each standard IRS tax payment is due as well as the penalties for late payment. This 15-page bulletin is an essential reference for payroll departments. A section of one page from Publication 509 is shown in Figure 9.3.

DEPOSITS MADE BY ELECTRONIC FUNDS TRANSFER AND BY CHECK

Ingram Heating and Cooling has calculated the federal taxes owed during its last lookback period and found that its tax liability was more than $50,000 during that period (the previous four quarters). Therefore, it must remit taxes once each week. After the first weekly payroll of the current year, the business owed a total of $4,474.16 for federal income tax withheld and social security and Medicare taxes (employee and employer shares). This deposit was due by the Wednesday following payday.

After 1997, the Internal Revenue Service made it necessary for certain businesses to use electronic funds transfer for their deposits of federal employment taxes. Firms that are semiweekly depositors of federal income tax withheld and social security and Medicare taxes must make their deposits by means of the *Electronic Federal Tax Payment System (EFTPS)*. (Remember that semiweekly depositors are those businesses that owed more than $50,000 of federal employment taxes during the previous lookback period.) Monthly depositors are not required to use the EFTPS, but they can voluntarily participate in the system if they wish to do so.

Because Ingram Heating and Cooling is a semiweekly depositor, it must use the EFTPS for its deposits of federal income tax withheld and social security and Medicare taxes. Thus, when the firm must deposit a total of $4,474.16 for the taxes owed on its first weekly payroll in January, it communicates the amount to its bank, which electronically transfers the

FIGURE 9.3   **Due Dates for Deposit of Taxes for 2005**

Due Dates for Deposit of Taxes for 2005 Under Semiweekly Rule

First Quarter:		Second Quarter:		Third Quarter:		Fourth Quarter:	
Payroll Date	**Due Date**	**Payroll Date**	**Due Date**	**Payroll Date**	**Due Date**	**Payroll Date**	**Due Date**
Jan 1–4	Jan 7	Apr 1	Apr 6	Jul 1	Jul 7	Oct 1–4	Oct 7
Jan 5–7	Jan 12	Apr 2–5	Apr 8	Jul 2–5	Jul 8	Oct 5–7	Oct 13
Jan 8–11	Jan 14	Apr 6–8	Apr 13	Jul 6–8	Jul 13	Oct 8–11	Oct 14
Jan 12–14	Jan 21	Apr 9–12	Apr 15	Jul 9–12	Jul 15	Oct 12–14	Oct 19
	Jan 24		Apr 20	Jul 13–15	Jul 20	Oct 15–18	Oct 21
Mar 23–25	Mar 30	Jun 18–21	Jun 24	Sep 17–20	Sep 23	Dec 21–23	Dec 29
Mar 26–29	Apr 1	Jun 22–24	Jun 29	Sep 21–23	Sep 28	Dec 24–27	Dec 30
Mar 30–31	Apr 6	Jun 25–28	Jul 1	Sep 24–27	Sep 30	Dec 28–30	Jan 5
		Jun 29–30	Jul 7	Sep 28–30	Oct 5	Dec 31	Jan 6

NOTE: This calendar reflects all federal holidays. A state legal holiday delays a due date only if the IRS office where you are required to file is located in that state.

funds from Ingram's account to an account belonging to the IRS. Businesses that use the EFTPS for their deposits do not issue a check and do not prepare Form 8109, Federal Tax Deposit Coupon, because the tax deposit is deducted directly from the firm's checking account.

In contrast, the Allen Painting Service is a monthly depositor that does not participate in the EFTPS. Therefore, when it must deposit the total taxes of $3,125.77 that it owes for the month of January, it issues a check for this amount and prepares the Form 8109 shown in Figure 9.4. The business submits the check and Form 8109 to its bank, which

FIGURE 9.4   **Form 8109**

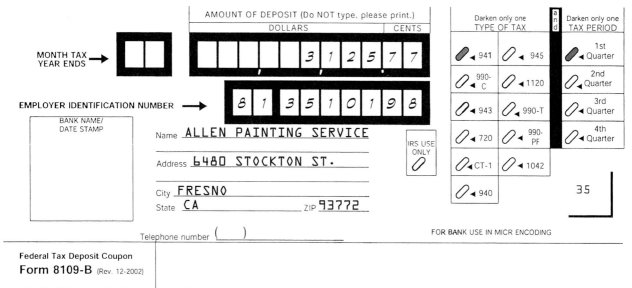

is an authorized financial institution (an institution that is authorized by the IRS to receive deposits of federal taxes).

IRS RULING REDUCES NUMBER OF DEPOSITS BY SMALL BUSINESSES

A recent ruling by the Internal Revenue Service simplifies deposit procedures for some 500,000 small businesses that report employment tax liabilities (liabilities for federal income tax withheld and social security and Medicare taxes). Under this ruling, businesses with less than $2,500 of such liabilities for a quarterly tax return period will not be required to make monthly deposits of employment taxes any longer. Businesses that fall into this category can pay their tax liabilities when they file Form 941 at the end of the quarter.

Learning Through Practice

Do Exercises 9.1 and 9.2 on page 219 of this text-workbook.

REPORTING SOCIAL SECURITY, MEDICARE, AND FEDERAL INCOME TAXES

The federal government requires that employers file several types of detailed reports giving information about the social security tax, Medicare tax, and federal income tax withheld from employee earnings as well as the employer's share of social security and Medicare taxes. Among these reports are Form 941, Employer's Quarterly Federal Tax Return; Schedule B of Form 941, Employer's Record of Federal Tax Liability; Form 8109, Federal Tax Deposit Coupon (for monthly depositors); Form W-2, Wage and Tax Statement; and Form W-3, Transmittal of Wage and Tax Statements.

Schedule B of Form 941, Employer's Record of Federal Tax Liability

Businesses that are on a semiweekly deposit schedule are required to complete Schedule B of Form 941, Employer's Record of Federal Tax Liability. This schedule must be attached to Form 941 when it is filed quarterly. Figure 9.5 on page 201 shows a portion of this form that was completed by Ingram Heating and Cooling. As discussed previously, Ingram has a weekly payroll period that starts on Sunday and ends on Saturday. The employees are paid on the following Wednesday. When Form 941 is filed, Schedule B is used to report the tax liability resulting from each payroll, the total tax liability for each month of the quarter, and the total tax liability for the quarter. The liability for each payroll includes the federal income tax withheld and the employee and employer shares of the social security and Medicare taxes. The date of the liability for each payroll is the date that the payroll is paid, not the date that the payroll period starts or ends.

Form 941, Employer's Quarterly Federal Tax Return

At the end of each quarter, businesses with one or more employees must prepare a payroll report called Form 941, Employer's Quarterly Federal Tax Return. This form should be sent to the IRS on or before the following due dates:

Quarter Ending	Form 941 Filing Due Date
March 31	April 30
June 30	July 31
September 30	October 31
December 31	January 31

FIGURE 9.5   Schedule B (Form 941)

SCHEDULE B (FORM 941) (Rev. January 2002) Department of the Treasury Internal Revenue Service	**Employer's Record of Federal Tax Liability** ▶ See Circular E for more information about employment tax returns. ▶ Attach to Form 941 or 941-SS.	OMB No. 1545-0029

5151

Name as shown on Form 941 (or Form 941-SS) Ingram Heating and Cooling	Employer identification number 77 : 4621093	Date quarter ended 3/31/05

You must complete this schedule if you are required to deposit on a semiweekly schedule, or if your tax liability on any day is $100,000 or more. Show tax liability here, **not** deposits. (The IRS gets deposit data from FTD coupons or EFTPS.)

A. Daily Tax Liability—First Month of Quarter

1		8		15		22		29	
2		9		16		23		30	
3		10		17		24		31	
4		11		18		25			
5		12		19		26			
6	4,474 16	13	4,287 97	20	4,322 83	27	4,596 41		
7		14		21		28			

A Total tax liability for first month of quarter . . . . ▶ | **A** | 17,681 37 |

B. Daily Tax Liability—Second Month of Quarter

1		8		15		22		29	
7		14		21		28			

B Total tax liability for second month of quarter . . . . ▶ | **B** | 19,601 27 |

C. Daily Tax Liability—Third Month of Quarter

1		8		15		22		29	
2		9		16		23		30	
3	4,596 41	10	4,659 37	17	4,392 16	24	4,533 66	31	4,473 94
4		11		18		25			
5		12		19		26			
6		13		20		27			
7		14		21		28			

C Total tax liability for third month of quarter . . . . ▶ | **C** | 22,655 54 |

D Total for quarter (add lines **A**, **B**, and **C**). This should equal line 13 of Form 941 (or line 10 of Form 941-SS) ▶ | **D** | 59,938 18 |

For Paperwork Reduction Act Notice, see page 2.   Cat. No. 11967Q   Schedule B (Form 941) (Rev. 1-2002)

However, if all taxes owed for the quarter have been deposited on time, the employer can delay the filing of Form 941 until May 10, August 10, November 10, and February 10. Refer to the copy of Form 941 in Figure 9.6 on page 203, which shows the federal income tax withheld and social security and Medicare taxes owed by Ingram Heating and Cooling for the first quarter (January, February, and March).

Here are the various steps required to complete Form 941.

- The top portion of the form includes the firm's name and address, its employer's federal identification number, and the ending date for the quarter. This information is usually preprinted on the form.
- Line 1 shows the number of employees that the firm had in the payroll period that includes March 12.
- Line 2 shows the total wages, tips, and other compensation paid to the employees during the quarter that were subject to the withholding of federal income tax.
- Line 3 shows the total federal income tax withheld from wages, tips, and sick pay during the quarter.
- Line 4 is used to record any adjustment in the federal income tax withheld for previous quarters of the year. In this case, there is no adjustment, so the line is left blank.
- Line 5 shows the adjusted total of federal income tax withheld during the quarter. Because there was no adjustment, the figure on this line is the same as the figure on Line 3.
- Line 6a shows the total wages paid during the quarter that were subject to social security tax. This amount is multiplied by 12.4 percent (.124), which is the total of the employee and employer shares of social security tax. The resulting figure appears on Line 6b. Line 6c is used to record the amount of tips received by employees during the quarter that were subject to social security tax. This amount is multiplied by 12.4 percent (.124), and the result appears on Line 6d. Because the employees of Ingram Heating and Cooling receive no tips, Lines 6c and 6d are left blank.
- Line 7a shows the total of the wages and tips paid during the quarter that were subject to Medicare tax. This amount is multiplied by 2.9 percent (.029), which is the total of the employee and employer shares of Medicare tax. The resulting figure appears on Line 7b.
- Line 8 shows the total of the social security and Medicare taxes owed for the quarter. This amount is found by adding the figures on Lines 6b, 6d, and 7b.
- Line 9 is used to record any adjustment of social security and Medicare taxes. In the case of Ingram Heating and Cooling, no adjustment was required.
- Line 10 shows the adjusted total of social security and Medicare taxes for the quarter. Because there was no adjustment on Line 9, the figure on Line 10 is the same as the figure on Line 8.
- Line 11 shows the total of the federal income tax withheld and the social security and Medicare taxes owed for the quarter. This amount is found by adding the figures on Lines 5 and 10.
- Line 12 is used to show any earned income credit (EIC) payments made to employees. Since Ingram Heating and Cooling did not make such payments, Line 12 was left blank.
- Line 13 shows the net taxes owed for the quarter. This amount is found by subtracting the figure on Line 12 from the figure on Line 11.
- Line 14 shows the total deposits made during the quarter.
- Line 15 shows any balance due on the taxes owed for the quarter. This amount is calculated by subtracting the figure on Line 14 from the figure on Line 13. Because Ingram Heating and Cooling deposited all federal income tax withheld and social security and Medicare taxes owed for the quarter, there is no balance due on Line 15.
- Line 16 is used to show any overpayment of taxes for the quarter. In this case, there was no overpayment. (An overpayment occurs when the deposits listed on Line 14 are greater than the net taxes owed, as shown on Line 13.)

FIGURE 9.6 **Form 941**

Form **941**
(Rev. January 2004)
Department of the Treasury
Internal Revenue Service (99)

Employer's Quarterly Federal Tax Return

▶ See separate instructions revised January 2004 for information on completing this return.

Please type or print.

OMB No. 1545-0029

Enter state code for state in which deposits were made **only** if different from state in address to the right ▶ ⬚ (see page 2 of separate instructions).

Name (as distinguished from trade name)

Trade name, if any
INGRAM HEATING AND COOLING

Address (number and street)
4466 MARITIME WAY

Date quarter ended
03/31/2005

Employer identification number
77-4621093

City, state, and ZIP code
SAN JOSE, CA 95001

T	
FF	
FD	
FP	
I	
T	

If address is different from prior return, check here ▶ ⬚

IRS Use

1 1 1 1 1 1 1 1 1 1   2   3 3 3 3 3 3 3   4 4 4   5 5 5
6   7   8 8 8 8 8 8 8   9 9 9 9   10 10 10 10 10 10 10 10 10 10

A If you **do not have to file** returns in the future, check here ▶ ⬚ and enter date final wages paid ▶

B If you are a seasonal employer, see **Seasonal employers** on page 1 of the instructions and check here ▶ ⬚

1	Number of employees in the pay period that includes March 12th . ▶	**1**	14			
2	Total wages and tips, plus other compensation (see separate instructions)			**2**	195,748	48
3	Total income tax withheld from wages, tips, and sick pay			**3**	29,988	66
4	Adjustment of withheld income tax for preceding quarters of **this calendar year**			**4**		
5	Adjusted total of income tax withheld (line 3 as adjusted by line 4)			**5**	29,988	66

6	Taxable social security wages	**6a**	195,748	48	× 12.4% (.124) =	**6b**	24,272	81
	Taxable social security tips	**6c**			× 12.4% (.124) =	**6d**		
7	Taxable Medicare wages and tips . . .	**7a**	195,748	48	× 2.9% (.029) =	**7b**	5,676	71

8	Total social security and Medicare taxes (add lines 6b, 6d, and 7b). **Check here if wages are not subject to social security and/or Medicare tax** . . . . ▶ ⬚	**8**	29,949	52
9	Adjustment of social security and Medicare taxes (see instructions for required explanation) Sick Pay $_____ ± Fractions of Cents $_____ ± Other $_____ =	**9**		
10	Adjusted total of social security and Medicare taxes (line 8 as adjusted by line 9)	**10**	29,949	52
11	**Total taxes** (add lines 5 and 10)	**11**	59,938	18
12	Advance earned income credit (EIC) payments made to employees (see instructions) . . .	**12**		
13	Net taxes (subtract line 12 from line 11). **If $2,500 or more, this must equal line 17, column (d) below (or line D of Schedule B (Form 941))**	**13**	59,938	18
14	Total deposits for quarter, including overpayment applied from a prior quarter	**14**	59,938	18
15	**Balance due** (subtract line 14 from line 13). See instructions	**15**		

16 **Overpayment.** If line 14 is more than line 13, enter excess here ▶ $ _____
and check if to be: ⬚ Applied to next return **or** ⬚ Refunded.

- **All filers:** If line 13 is less than $2,500, **do not** complete line 17 or Schedule B (Form 941).
- **Semiweekly schedule depositors:** Complete Schedule B (Form 941) and check here . . . . ▶ ☑
- **Monthly schedule depositors:** Complete line 17, columns (a) through (d), and check here. . . . . ▶ ⬚

17	Monthly Summary of Federal Tax Liability. (Complete **Schedule B (Form 941)** instead, if you were a semiweekly schedule depositor.)			
	(a) First month liability	**(b)** Second month liability	**(c)** Third month liability	**(d)** Total liability for quarter

Third Party Designee

Do you want to allow another person to discuss this return with the IRS (see separate instructions)? ⬚ **Yes.** Complete the following. ⬚ **No**

Designee's name ▶ | Phone no. ▶ ( ) | Personal identification number (PIN) ▶ ⬚⬚⬚⬚⬚

Sign Here

Under penalties of perjury, I declare that I have examined this return, including accompanying schedules and statements, and to the best of my knowledge and belief, it is true, correct, and complete.

Signature ▶ *William J. Ingram*
Print Your Name and Title ▶ William J. Ingram, President
Date ▶ 4/6/2005

For Privacy Act and Paperwork Reduction Act Notice, see back of Payment Voucher.   Cat. No. 17001Z   Form **941** (Rev. 1-2004)

Following Line 16, semiweekly schedule depositors are instructed to complete Schedule B, which they must attach to Form 941. Monthly schedule depositors are instructed to complete Line 17. Each type of depositor must place a check mark in the box that shows which schedule it uses.

Following Line 17 is a section titled Third Party Designee. The business may choose to allow another person, usually the accountant who prepared the Form 941, to discuss this return directly with the IRS without having to submit a power of attorney to the IRS. The designee must provide a phone number and a personal identification number. The Yes box should be checked if the business wants to utilize this feature.

Form 941 is signed and dated by the appropriate business official. Notice that this person is subject to penalties of perjury if he or she has knowingly supplied any false information on Form 941.

In 1998, the Internal Revenue Service started a new system called *941 TeleFile*. Under this system, many employers can file Form 941 by telephone. There is no charge for the telephone call. The IRS provides step-by-step instructions during the call, repeats all entries so that the caller can check their accuracy, and does all calculations for the caller. The IRS determines the caller's tax liability for the quarter and any overpayment or balance due during the call. Use of 941 TeleFile is optional for those businesses that are eligible for it. Businesses that are not eligible must continue to file the paper version of Form 941.

Form 941-V, Payment Voucher

As noted previously, businesses that owe less than $2,500 in federal employment taxes during a quarter need not deposit the taxes. Instead, they can pay these taxes when they file Form 941 after the end of the quarter. To accompany the check for the amount owed, such businesses must submit Form 941-V, Payment Voucher. An example of this form is shown in Figure 9.7. It was prepared by Frank's Pizza Express, which owed a total of $763.92 for federal income tax withheld and social security and Medicare taxes (employee and employer shares) at the end of the first quarter. This firm is operated by Frank Marino and his son, who are partners. They employ only a few part-time workers to make deliveries.

Form 941-V is simple to prepare. The employer identification number (EIN) for the business is entered in Box 1. The total deposit being made is entered in Box 2. The tax period covered by the deposit is shown in Box 3 by darkening in the appropriate quarter (1st, 2nd, 3rd, or 4th). The name and address of the business are entered in Box 4. The check that accompanies Form 941-V should be made payable to the United States Treasury.

Form 8109, Federal Tax Deposit Coupon

You have already become acquainted with the use of Form 8109 by monthly depositors of federal income tax withheld and social security and Medicare taxes (Figure 9.4 on page 199).

FIGURE 9.7 **Form 941-V**

While it looks like a very simple form, it is one that is critically important and it must be completed accurately and submitted on time.

Form 8109 is supplied to businesses by the Internal Revenue Service in a coupon booklet containing a supply of the forms. The IRS keeps track of the number of these forms a business uses and automatically sends additional forms when a business needs them. Form 8109 is preprinted with the employer's name, address, and identification number. When submitting a deposit, the employer enters the amount in the space provided and darkens the areas that show the type of tax being deposited and the tax period to which the deposit applies. After a deposit is made, Form 8109 is forwarded by the bank to an IRS service center and the amount is recorded in the employer's account.

Completing Form 8109

The IRS gives very specific directions about the entry of certain types of information on Form 8109. Because the IRS uses optical-scanning equipment to process this form, the amount of the deposit should be printed by hand, not typed. A soft lead pencil should be used; and no dollar signs, commas, or decimal points should be entered. The numbers in the amount should be large and easy to read. A soft lead pencil should also be used to darken the areas that identify the type of tax being deposited and the tax period to which the deposit applies. In the case of Figure 9.4, the type of tax is 941 and the tax period is the first quarter. Because the deposit consists of federal income tax withheld and social security and Medicare taxes, and these taxes are reported on Form 941 at the end of each quarter, 941 is used to identify the type of tax. The firm's telephone number must also be entered on Form 8109.

A photocopy of Form 8109 should never be submitted. Only the original form is acceptable. However, a business will generally make and keep a photocopy of the completed form for its own records.

Notice that a firm's employer identification number, name, and address are preprinted on Form 8109. This type of printing is machine-readable, which is why a firm must use the Form 8109 supplied to it by the IRS. Any organization with one or more employees must have an employer identification number (EIN). New businesses may obtain an employer identification number by filing an application (Form SS-4) with the IRS. This form is available from all offices of the IRS and from some offices of the Social Security Administration. Additional options for obtaining an EIN are applying online through www.irs.gov or by telephoning the IRS. See the IRS Web site for instructions.

DEPOSIT EXCEPTIONS

There is an exception to the IRS deposit rules that we discussed previously. Businesses that accumulate $100,000 or more of federal income tax withheld and social security and Medicare taxes owed during *any* deposit period must make a deposit on the next banking day after reaching the $100,000 level. This situation affects larger businesses that are semiweekly depositors.

Deposits on Banking Days

If a deposit schedule calls for a deposit on a day that is not a banking day, the deposit is considered on time if it is made by the close of the next banking day. In addition to federal and state bank holidays, Saturdays and Sundays are treated as nonbanking days. Semiweekly schedule depositors have at least three banking days to make a deposit. Thus, if any of the three weekdays after the end of a semiweekly period is a bank holiday, these depositors have one additional banking day to make their deposits.

AUTHORIZED DEPOSITARIES

Most commercial banks are authorized by the IRS to receive deposits of federal income tax withheld and social security and Medicare taxes owed. Some trust companies, savings and loan associations, and credit unions are also permitted to handle such deposits. If a firm

The Internet is growing! According to a recent study by the U.S. Commerce Department, traffic on the Internet is doubling every 100 days. Business use is still the fastest growing segment, but as many as 100 million Americans now participate in this worldwide network. It is now possible to obtain tax information and forms from the Internal Revenue Service at a site that it maintains on the Internet. The address of this site is www.irs.gov.

does not have access to an authorized depositary institution, the taxes must be sent directly to the Federal Reserve Bank serving its area.

Learning Through Practice

Do Exercise 9.3 on page 220 of this text-workbook.

FORMS W-2 AND W-3

Form W-2, Wage and Tax Statement

At the end of each calendar year, employers must report the wages earned by each employee and the federal income tax, social security tax, and Medicare tax withheld from those wages during the year. This information is provided to both the employee and the federal government on Form W-2, Wage and Tax Statement. Employers also report state and local income taxes withheld on Form W-2. For example, the Form W-2 shown in Figure 9.8 includes California income tax. This Form W-2 serves the needs of the state tax agency as well as the needs of the federal government.

FIGURE 9.8 **Form W-2**

a Control number				
	22222	Void ☐	For Official Use Only ▶ OMB No. 1545-0008	

b Employer identification number 77-4621093	1 Wages, tips, other compensation 45344.00	2 Federal income tax withheld 8112.00
c Employer's name, address, and ZIP code Ingram Heating and Cooling 4466 Maritime Way San Jose, CA 95001	3 Social security wages 45344.00	4 Social security tax withheld 2811.33
	5 Medicare wages and tips 45344.00	6 Medicare tax withheld 657.49
	7 Social security tips	8 Allocated tips

d Employee's social security number 427-88-1172	9 Advance EIC payment	10 Dependent care benefits

e Employee's first name and initial Pamela J. Cook	Last name	11 Nonqualified plans	12a See instructions for box 12

238 Agular Street
San Jose, CA 95150

13 Statutory employee ☐ Retirement plan ☐ Third-party sick pay ☐	12b

14 Other 535.06 CASDI	12c
	12d

f Employee's address and ZIP code

15 State CA	Employer's state ID number 315-3792-6	16 State wages, tips, etc. 45344.00	17 State income tax 2334.80	18 Local wages, tips, etc.	19 Local income tax	20 Locality name

Form **W-2** Wage and Tax Statement

2005

Department of the Treasury—Internal Revenue Service

For Privacy Act and Paperwork Reduction Act Notice, see back of Copy D.

Copy A For Social Security Administration — Send this entire page with Form W-3 to the Social Security Administration; photocopies are **not** acceptable.

Cat. No. 10134D

Do Not Cut, Fold, or Staple Forms on This Page — Do Not Cut, Fold, or Staple Forms on This Page

While Form W-2, Wage and Tax Statement, appears complicated, it is not difficult for most businesses to prepare. Much of the requested information is simply transferred from the employee earnings records that were kept during the year. There are typically six copies of Form W-2:

Copy A, For the Social Security Administration

Copy 1, For the state, city, or local tax agency

Copy B, For the employee, to be filed with his or her federal income tax return

Copy C, For the employee's records

Copy 2, For the employee, to be filed with his or her state, city, or local income tax return

Copy D, For the employer's records

The back of Copy B of Form W-2 provides information for the employee. This information is somewhat complex, but is nonetheless important for the employee to be familiar with. Copy B is the one that the employee attaches to his or her federal income tax return.

A number of the boxes on Form W-2 request information that deals with relatively rare and somewhat complicated situations and applies to a limited number of employees. These boxes are not discussed here. The IRS provides detailed written instructions for completing these boxes and other boxes on Form W-2. The IRS also provides assistance over the telephone when employers have questions about items on Form W-2.

- Box a can be used to record a control number that identifies the Form W-2 issued to each employee. Small businesses such as Ingram Heating and Cooling normally do not assign such numbers and therefore leave this box blank. (The number 22222 that appears to the right of Box a is preprinted on the form for use by the Social Security Administration.)

- Box b shows the employer's federal identification number. This number must be on all IRS documents that the employer files.

- Box c shows the employer's name, address, and ZIP code.

- Box d shows the employee's social security number.

- Box e shows the employee's name (first name, middle initial, and last name).

- Box f shows the employee's address and ZIP code.

- Box 1 lists the wages, tips, and other compensation paid to the employee during the calendar year.

- Box 2 lists the federal income tax withheld from the employee's earnings during the year.

- Box 3 lists the wages paid to the employee during the year that were subject to social security tax.

- Box 4 lists the social security tax withheld from the earnings of the employee during the year.

- Box 5 lists the wages and tips paid to the employee during the year that were subject to Medicare tax.

- Box 6 lists the Medicare tax withheld from the earnings of the employee during the year.

- Box 12 is used to report pretax items related to the payroll, such as 401-k contributions and SIMPLE IRA contributions. Another commonly reported item in Box 12 is Sec. 125 Cafeteria Plan contributions.

- Box 14 is used by Ingram Heating and Cooling to show the state disability insurance (SDI) tax withheld from the employee's earnings during the year. This amount is identified with the letters CASDI. (CA stands for California and indicates that the tax was levied by the state of California.) Most states do not have this type of tax, and employers in those states may not need to use Box 14. However, they may have some other type of withholding to list in Box 14.

- Box 15 gives the two-letter identification for the state where the employer is located and also lists the employer's state identification number.

- Box 16 lists the wages, tips, and other compensation paid to the employee during the year on which state income tax was due.
- Box 17 lists the state income tax withheld from the earnings of the employee during the year.

The other boxes on Form W-2 do not apply to the employees of Ingram Heating and Cooling. Note that the information in Boxes d, e, f, 1, 2, 3, 4, 5, 6, 12, 14, 16, and 17 of the Form W-2 shown in Figure 9.8 is taken directly from the employee earnings record.

Employers must prepare a Form W-2 for each employee who worked for the business during the calendar year or had federal income tax, social security tax, or Medicare tax withheld during the year. The form must be given to the employee by January 31 of the following year. People who leave the firm before the end of the calendar year should also receive Form W-2 by January 31. However, if an employee who is leaving asks to have Form W-2 sooner, the employer must provide it within 30 days after the request or 30 days after the last wage payment, whichever is later.

Form W-2 can be obtained from the IRS or can be purchased from an office supply store. Commercially printed versions of this form are acceptable as long as they meet certain government standards. Photocopies should never be used for Form W-2. They are not acceptable.

Because the government now uses *optical-scanning equipment* to read the information on Form W-2, these forms should be typewritten or printed, not handwritten. No dollar signs should be used with amounts, and no commas should be used in the amounts. Errors on Copy A of these forms should not be corrected by erasing the information, striking it over, or covering it with correction fluid. Instead, a new form should be prepared. There is a Void box at the top of the Form W-2 that should be checked if you make an error on the form and must prepare another form.

Since 1988, the IRS has required that employers who file 250 or more Forms W-2 provide the information on magnetic tape or disk.

Learning Through Practice

Do Exercise 9.4 on page 222 of this text-workbook.

Form W-3, Transmittal of Wage and Tax Statements

Employers must file Copy A of the Form W-2 for each employee with the Social Security Administration on or before February 28. These documents must be accompanied by Form W-3, Transmittal of Wage and Tax Statements.

Form W-3 is used to report the *total* wages paid to all employees during the last calendar year and the *total* federal income tax, social security tax, and Medicare tax withheld from the wages of all employees during the year. Form W-3 also reports the number of Forms W-2 being sent to the government. The totals that appear on Form W-3 must be consistent with the individual figures listed on the Forms W-2 that the business submits. The totals on Form W-3 must also agree with the quarterly totals shown on the Forms 941 filed during the year. The Form W-3 shown in Figure 9.9 was prepared at Ingram Heating and Cooling.

Notice how the Form W-3 in Figure 9.9 was prepared.

- Box a is for a control number. Ingram Heating and Cooling has left this box blank because it does not use a control number.
- In Box b, an *X* is entered to indicate that this Form W-3 is filed by a payer of Form 941 taxes (federal income tax withheld and social security and Medicare taxes).
- Box c indicates the number of Forms W-2 that are being submitted with Form W-3.
- Box e lists the employer's federal identification number.
- Box f shows the employer's name.
- Box g shows the employer's address.
- Box 15 shows the state where the employer is located and the employer's state identification number.

FIGURE 9.9   **Form W-3**

DO NOT STAPLE OR FOLD

a Control number	33333	For Official Use Only ▶ OMB No. 1545-0008		

b Kind of Payer ▶	941 [X] Military [ ] 943 [ ] Hshld. emp. [ ] Medicare govt. emp. [ ] CT-1 [ ] Third-party sick pay [ ]	1 Wages, tips, other compensation $ 760046.04	2 Federal income tax withheld $ 116474.80

3 Social security wages $ 657886.04 | 4 Social security tax withheld $ 40788.93

c Total number of Forms W-2   16 | d Establishment number | 5 Medicare wages and tips $ 760046.04 | 6 Medicare tax withheld $ 11020.67

e Employer identification number   77-4621093 | 7 Social security tips $ | 8 Allocated tips $

f Employer's name

Ingram Heating and Cooling
4466 Maritime Way
San Jose, CA 95001

9 Advance EIC payments $ | 10 Dependent care benefits $

11 Nonqualified plans $ | 12 Deferred compensation $

13 For third-party sick pay use only

14 Income tax withheld by payer of third-party sick pay $

g Employer's address and ZIP code

h Other EIN used this year

15 State Employer's state ID number CA	315-3792-6	16 State wages, tips, etc. $	17 State income tax $

18 Local wages, tips, etc. $ | 19 Local income tax $

Contact person
W. J. Ingram | Telephone number (408) 222-3190 | For Official Use Only

E-mail address | Fax number (408) 222-4655

Under penalties of perjury, I declare that I have examined this return and accompanying documents, and, to the best of my knowledge and belief, they are true, correct, and complete.

Signature ▶ *William J. Ingram*   Title ▶ *President*   Date ▶ *1/10/05*

Form **W-3** Transmittal of Wage and Tax Statements   **2005**   Department of the Treasury Internal Revenue Service

Send this entire page with the entire Copy A page of Form(s) W-2 to the Social Security Administration. Photocopies are not acceptable.

Do not send any payment (cash, checks, money orders, etc.) with Forms W-2 and W-3.

- Box 1 lists the total wages, tips, and other compensation paid to employees during the year.
- Box 2 indicates the total federal income tax withheld from the earnings of the employees during the year.
- Box 3 shows the total wages paid to employees during the year that were subject to social security tax.
- Box 4 indicates the total social security tax withheld from the earnings of the employees during the year.
- Box 5 shows the total wages paid to employees during the year that were subject to Medicare tax.
- Box 6 shows the total Medicare tax withheld from the earnings of the employees during the year.
- Boxes 16, 17, 18, and 19 provide wage and income tax information for state and local income tax returns.

Across the bottom of the form is a line that is used to indicate the contact person within the firm, the telephone number of the firm, its fax number, and its e-mail address. In a large firm, the contact person might be the payroll manager. In a small firm like Ingram Heating and Cooling, the contact person would probably be an officer or the owner (if the business is a sole proprietorship). Form W-3 is signed by an officer, owner, or manager, and the date of completion is entered.

The first page of the completed Form W-3, along with Copy A of the W-2 forms for all employees, must be sent directly to the Social Security Administration.

The IRS sends Form W-3 to employers during the fourth quarter of each year. Like the Forms W-2, Form W-3 should be typewritten or printed by a computer. No dollar signs or commas should be used with the dollar amounts.

Learning Through Practice

Do Exercise 9.5 on page 223 of this text-workbook.

FEDERAL UNEMPLOYMENT COMPENSATION TAX

In addition to old-age, survivors, and disability insurance, the Social Security Act of 1935 established a program of unemployment insurance. This program is designed to help workers who are temporarily jobless by giving them weekly *unemployment compensation benefits* that replace part of their lost wages. The Federal Unemployment Tax Act requires most employers to pay a tax to support the federal unemployment insurance program.

The Unemployment Insurance System

After the passage of the Social Security Act, every state set up its own unemployment insurance program. These programs operate in partnership with the federal program and actually pay out the necessary benefits to jobless workers. The states impose a payroll tax on employers in order to finance their unemployment insurance programs. Thus, covered employers are subject to both federal and state unemployment compensation taxes.

A worker who loses his or her job must apply for unemployment benefits at a local office of the state unemployment insurance department. If the person is eligible to receive the benefits and does not find a new job within a short waiting period (usually a week), the unemployment office will begin issuing weekly compensation checks. The amount paid is normally some percentage of the person's previous weekly earnings up to a certain maximum figure. Each state sets its own maximum amounts payable to unemployed workers.

A jobless worker receives unemployment compensation benefits for a limited period of time, usually about 26 weeks. However, the person must actively look for employment during this period and must take any suitable position in his or her field that becomes available.

Eligibility standards, benefit levels, and payment periods vary from state to state. The federal government may, in difficult economic times, extend the period during which payments are made.

Computing the FUTA Tax

Only employers are required to pay the federal unemployment tax; employees do not contribute to the FUTA tax. As of this writing, the rate for the FUTA tax is 6.2 percent of the first $7,000 paid to each employee during a calendar year. This rate has been stable for the past several years. Congress sets the FUTA rate and may make changes from time to time. Congress also establishes the rules that determine which employers and employees are covered by FUTA.

Although the rate for the FUTA tax is set at 6.2 percent, employers are allowed to take a credit for the state unemployment insurance (SUTA) tax they pay. The credit can be as high as 5.4 percent, and thus may reduce the actual FUTA contribution to 0.8 percent. States grant lower unemployment tax rates to businesses that have few employees who apply for unemployment benefits. Because Ingram Heating and Cooling has a good employment record, it is allowed the full credit of 5.4 percent. This reduces its FUTA tax rate to 0.8 percent.

The amount of FUTA tax that a business owes is usually computed at the end of each quarter. The person who does payroll work for the firm multiplies the total of the taxable earnings for the quarter by the applicable tax rate. For example, Ingram Heating and Cooling had taxable wage payments of $91,000 during the first quarter of one year. The firm's total wage payments were $190,011.51. However, as noted previously, only the first $7,000 paid to each employee in a calendar year is subject to FUTA tax. Because Ingram has an applicable FUTA rate of 0.8 percent (.008), the amount of FUTA tax that it owes for the first quarter is computed as follows.

$91,000	total taxable earnings of employees
$\times$ .008	applicable FUTA tax rate
$ 728	amount of the FUTA tax for the quarter

Depositing the FUTA Tax

After the FUTA tax is computed at the end of each quarter, it is necessary to determine whether the firm must deposit the amount owed. The rules for making such deposits are fairly simple. If the FUTA tax due at the end of any quarter is more than $100, the amount must be deposited on or before the last day of the following month, as shown here.

If the FUTA tax due at the end of the first, second, or third quarter is $100 or less, no deposit is necessary. The undeposited amount is simply carried over to the next quarter and added to the sum owed for that quarter. This procedure continues until the total undeposited tax exceeds $100.

When to Deposit Futa Taxes	
Quarter Ending	**Due Date for Deposit**
March 31	April 30
June 30	July 31
September 30	October 31
December 31	January 31

For example, suppose a firm owes FUTA tax of $76 for the first quarter and $52 for the second quarter. No deposit is made at the end of the first quarter, but a deposit of $128 must be made after the second quarter ($76+$52=$128). If the amount owed is $100 or less at the end of the fourth quarter, the firm can either deposit it or pay it directly to the IRS when filing Form 940 or Form 940-EZ, Employer's Annual Federal Unemployment (FUTA) Tax Return. This tax report must be sent to the government on or before January 31 of the next year if any tax is still due.

Deposits of FUTA tax can be made by electronic funds transfer using the government's Electronic Federal Tax Payment System (EFTPS) or by submitting a check and a completed Form 8109, Federal Tax Deposit Coupon, to an authorized financial institution. The procedure for preparing Form 8109 for a deposit of FUTA taxes is almost the same as the procedure discussed previously for a deposit of federal income tax withheld and social security and Medicare taxes (page 196). The only difference is in the completion of the Type of Tax section of Form 8109. For a deposit of FUTA tax, it is necessary to darken the area labeled 940 in the Type of Tax section. The number 940 stands for Form 940, the tax return used to report the employer's FUTA liability and payments to the federal government at the end of the year.

Learning Through Practice

Do Exercises 9.6 and 9.7 on page 224 of this text-workbook.

Reporting the FUTA Tax

At the end of the calendar year, every employer who is subject to FUTA must prepare a report showing the taxable wages paid during the year, the amount of tax owed, the deposits made, and the tax due (if any). This report, which is called Form 940 or 940-EZ, Employer's Annual Federal Unemployment (FUTA) Tax Return, must be filed with the IRS by January 31.

However, if all deposits were made on time and no tax is due, the filing of Form 940 can be delayed until February 10.

If a firm owes FUTA tax of $100 or less at the end of the year and plans to pay it when filing Form 940-EZ rather than depositing it beforehand, the firm prepares Form 940-EZ(V), Payment Voucher. This form appears at the bottom of Form 940-EZ. To pay the amount owed, the firm detaches the payment voucher and submits it with a check payable to the United States Treasury.

A copy of Form 940-EZ that was prepared by Ingram Heating and Cooling appears in Figure 9.10 on page 213. This business is able to use the simpler Form 940-EZ rather than Form 940 because it could answer "yes" to the three questions asked on the reverse side of the form:

1. Did you pay unemployment contributions to only one state?
2. Did you pay all state unemployment contributions by January 31?
3. Were all wages that were taxable for FUTA also taxable for your state's unemployment tax?

A Case for Decision 9-1

Even on the slowest days George Dodd's desk and file cabinets were covered by stacks of papers. You can imagine how they looked in January of this year when he was preparing quarterly and annual tax forms. Of course, as the only payroll clerk at Arrow Trucking, which has 88 employees, George Dodd had many different tasks to perform and a lot of paperwork to complete. For this reason, Gail Rogers, the office manager, often urged him to make a list of vital activities at the beginning of each week and then check off the items as he finished them during the week. However, George always felt that he was too busy to bother with such a list.

In the middle of February, George had some quiet days, and Miss Rogers suggested that he clean up his desk and file cabinets. Under a big stack of paper, he found a copy of Form 940, the Employer's Annual Federal Unemployment (FUTA) Tax Return, which he had started to work on but never completed. Because the firm owed some FUTA tax, Form 940 should have been mailed by January 31 with a check for the amount due. Naturally, George was upset. He knew that the firm would be required to pay a penalty for lateness.

When George spoke to Miss Rogers about the situation, she asked him to consider a transfer to a simpler job.

Discussion of the Case

Payroll work involves a great deal of responsibility. The people who do this work must operate in an orderly manner and use efficient procedures. George Dodd's disorganized and over-crowded desk and office invited trouble. Payroll activities cannot be carried out properly under such conditions. George also made a mistake by not planning his weekly tasks and keeping track of all tax forms and tax payments. It is essential to set up and follow a schedule for preparing tax forms and reports and for making payments on time.

Completing Form 940-EZ, Employer's Annual Federal Unemployment (FUTA) Tax Return

Most of the information reported on Form 940-EZ is taken from the payroll and tax records that a business keeps during the year.

- The top portion of the form shows the firm's name and address and employer's federal identification number as well as the calendar year. (This information is preprinted on the form before the IRS sends it to the firm.)

FIGURE 9.10 Form 940-EZ and EZ Payment Voucher

Form **940-EZ**

Department of the Treasury
Internal Revenue Service

Employer's Annual Federal Unemployment (FUTA) Tax Return

▶ See the separate Instructions for Form 940-EZ for information on completing this form.

OMB No. 1545-1110

20**04**

	T		
	FF		
	FD		
	FP		
	I		
	T		

You must complete this section. ▶

Name (as distinguished from trade name)

Trade name, if any
INGRAM HEATING AND COOLING

Address (number and street)
4466 MARITIME WAY

Calendar year
2004

Employer identification number (EIN)
77-4621090

City, state, and ZIP code
SAN JOSE, CA 95001

Answer the questions under **Who May Use Form 940-EZ** *on page 2. If you cannot use Form 940-EZ, you must use Form 940.*

A Enter the amount of contributions paid to your state unemployment fund (see the separate instructions) . . ▶ $ .... 2,075 | 06

B (1) Enter the name of the state where you have to pay contributions . . . . ▶ California
.......(2) Enter your state reporting number as shown on your state unemployment tax return ▶ 315-3792-6

If you will not have to file returns in the future, check here (see **Who Must File** in separate instructions) and complete and sign the return. ▶ ☐
If this is an Amended Return, check here (see **Amended Returns** in the separate instructions) . . . . ▶ ☐

Part I	**Taxable Wages and FUTA Tax**			
1	Total payments (including payments shown on lines 2 and 3) during the calendar year for services of employees	1	760,046	04
2	Exempt payments. (Explain all exempt payments, attaching additional sheets if necessary.) ▶	2		
3	Payments of more than $7,000 for services. Enter only amounts over the first $7,000 paid to each employee **(see the separate instructions)**	3	661,233	54
4	Add lines 2 and 3	4	661,233	54
5	**Total taxable wages** (subtract line 4 from line 1) . . . . ▶	5	98,812	50
6	**FUTA tax.** Multiply the wages on line 5 by .008 and enter here. **(If the result is over $100, also complete Part II.)**	6	790	50
7	Total FUTA tax deposited for the year, including any overpayment applied from a prior year	7	771	20
8	**Balance due** (subtract line 7 from line 6). Pay to the "United States Treasury." . . . . . . ▶	8	19	30
	If you owe more than $100, see **Depositing FUTA tax** in the separate instructions.			
9	**Overpayment** (subtract line 6 from line 7). Check if it is to be: ☐ **Applied to next return** or ☐ **Refunded** ▶	9		

Part II	**Record of Quarterly Federal Unemployment Tax Liability** (Do not include state liability.) **Complete only if line 6 is over $100.**				
Quarter	First (Jan. 1 – Mar. 31)	Second (Apr. 1 – June 30)	Third (July 1 – Sept. 30)	Fourth (Oct. 1 – Dec. 31)	Total for year
Liability for quarter	630.50	82.40	58.30	19.30	790.50

Third–Party Designee

Do you want to allow another person to discuss this return with the IRS (see the separate instructions)? ☐ **Yes.** Complete the following. ☐ **No**

Designee's name ▶   Phone no. ▶ ( )   Personal identification number (PIN) ▶ ☐☐☐☐☐

Under penalties of perjury, I declare that I have examined this return, including accompanying schedules and statements, and, to the best of my knowledge and belief, it is true, correct, and complete, and that no part of any payment made to a state unemployment fund claimed as a credit was, or is to be, deducted from the payments to employees.

Signature ▶ *William J. Ingram*   Title (Owner, etc.) ▶ *President*   Date ▶ 1/10/05

For Privacy Act and Paperwork Reduction Act Notice, see the separate instructions. ▼ **DETACH HERE** ▼   Cat. No. 10983G   Form **940-EZ** (2004)

Form **940-V(EZ)**

Department of the Treasury
Internal Revenue Service

Payment Voucher

Use this voucher only when making a payment with your return.

OMB No. 1545-1110

20**04**

Complete boxes 1, 2, and 3. Do not send cash, and do not staple your payment to this voucher. Make your check or money order payable to the "United States Treasury." Be sure to enter your employer identification number (EIN), "Form 940-EZ," and "2004" on your payment.

1 Enter your employer identification number (EIN).	2 **Enter the amount of your payment.** ▶	Dollars	Cents
77 : 4621090		19	30
	3 Enter your business name (individual name for sole proprietors).		
	Ingram Heating and Cooling		
	Enter your address.		
	4466 Maritime Way		
	Enter your city, state, and ZIP code.		
	San Jose, CA 95001		

Internet Connection

Federal tax information for business can be located at www.irs.gov. Topics include items of interest such as filing deadlines, changes in rulings and procedures, forms, and contact numbers. The IRS will e-mail a newsletter to you upon subscription.

- Item A asks for the amount of contributions that the firm paid its state unemployment fund during the calendar year.
- Item B-1 asks for the name of the state where contributions were paid.
- Item B-2 asks for the firm's state reporting number.

Part I
- This part of Form 940-EZ shows the calculation of taxable wages and the amount of FUTA tax owed for the year.
- Line 1 asks for the amount of the total payments made to the employees for their services during the calendar year.
- Line 2 asks for the amount of payments made during the year that were exempt from FUTA tax. In the case of Ingram Heating and Cooling, no exempt payments were made.
- Line 3 asks for the amount of payments of more than $7,000 made to the employees for their services during the year. (Remember that only the first $7,000 paid to each employee during a calendar year is subject to FUTA tax.)
- Line 4 asks for the total of the exempt payments. This amount is found by adding the figures on Lines 2 and 3.
- Line 5 asks for the total of the taxable wages. This amount is determined by subtracting the figure on Line 4 from the figure on Line 1.
- Line 6 asks for the amount of FUTA tax owed for the year. This amount is calculated by multiplying the total taxable wages shown on Line 5 by the FUTA rate of 0.8 percent (.008).
- Line 7 asks for the total FUTA tax that the firm deposited during the year.
- Line 8 asks for the balance of FUTA tax that is due. This amount is found by subtracting the figure on Line 7 from the figure on Line 6. If no balance is due Line 8 is left blank. However, Ingram Heating and Cooling owes a balance of $19.30, which it will submit with Form 940-EZ(V), Payment Voucher.
- Line 9 asks for the amount of any overpayment. (An overpayment occurs when the deposits listed on Line 7 are greater than the FUTA tax owed for the year, as shown on Line 6.)

Part II
- This part of Form 940-EZ shows the firm's quarter-by-quarter liability for FUTA tax during the year. Note that this section reports the tax owed for each quarter, not the tax deposited.
- The quarterly amounts are added, and the total is recorded in the last box of Part II. This amount must match the amount of FUTA tax reported on Line 6 of Part I.

Form 940-EZ is signed by an officer, owner, or manager; and the date of completion is entered.

Learning Through Practice

Do Exercise 9.8 on page 225 of this text-workbook.

UNIT 9   REVIEW

Summary

This unit provided information about the collection and deposit of federal payroll taxes. Some of these taxes were withheld from employee earnings and other taxes were paid by the employer. Many federal tax forms were introduced in this unit. Specifically, you should now be able to:

- Compute the amount of social security and Medicare taxes the employer is required to match each payroll period.
- Know how a business is classified as a monthly or semiweekly depositor and when deposits are due.
- Understand how the Electronic Federal Tax Payment System works and which employers must use this system to make payroll tax deposits.
- Complete a Form 941 and its related Schedule B, if applicable.
- Complete a Form 941-V, Payment Voucher, to make a tax deposit, and understand when employers can use this form for making a deposit that is due.
- Understand what information appears on Form W-2 and when Form W-2 should be given to employees.
- Know how to complete Form W-3 and when it is due.
- Complete Form 940-EZ.
- Compute the amount of federal unemployment tax and understand the due dates for depositing the tax.

Study Questions

1. Explain the procedures for calculating the employer's share of the social security and Medicare taxes.
2. For what purpose is Form 8109 used?
3. What is the Electronic Federal Tax Payment System (EFTPS)? Which depositors must use this system?
4. What type of information is reported on Form 940-EZ?
5. When must employers issue Form W-2 to their employees? If an employee leaves a firm and requests Form W-2, how long does the firm have to meet this request?
6. Employers must prepare a quarterly tax return showing the wages paid to employees, the federal income tax withheld, and the social security and Medicare taxes owed (employee and employer shares).
   a. What form is used to report this information?
   b. What are the dates for filing the tax return?
   c. Which firms can use the payment voucher that comes with this tax return?
7. What is the purpose of the Form W-2 issued to each employee?
8. What is the purpose of Form W-3? When must employers file this form?
9. What is the taxable wage base for FUTA tax? When is FUTA tax computed by the employer? When is FUTA tax deposited by the employer?
10. What is the purpose of Schedule B of Form 941? What firms must prepare Schedule B?
11. During its last lookback period, ABC Inc. owed $87,240 of federal employment taxes. What type of depositor will this firm be? How about XYZ Inc., which owed $36,592 of federal employment taxes during its last lookback period?
12. Who pays the FUTA tax—the employee or the employer? Who pays social security and Medicare taxes?
13. What is 941 TeleFile?

1. How much did each of the following businesses owe in federal income tax withheld, social security tax, and Medicare tax during its last lookback period? Will the business be a monthly or semiweekly depositor in the next calendar year?

   a. During its last lookback period, Sam's Old-Time Barbeque Restaurant had the following tax liabilities.

   Third quarter of 20X3, $14,248   First quarter of 20X4, $12,287
   Fourth quarter of 20X3, $11,375   Second quarter of 20X4, $13,620

   b. During its last lookback period, Precision Auto Service had the following tax liabilities.

   Third quarter of 20X3, $10,322   First quarter of 20X4, $12,840
   Fourth quarter of 20X3, $12,496   Second quarter of 20X4, $11,752

2. The following information will be used to prepare Form 941, Employer's Quarterly Federal Tax Return, for the fourth quarter at Morgan Computer Graphics, a design firm.

   Total wages, $74,625.00
   Total federal income tax withheld, $9,119.00
   Taxable social security wages, $69,540.00
   Taxable Medicare wages, $74,625.00
   Total deposits for quarter, $19,906.09

   a. What amount of social security tax is owed for the quarter? Use 12.4 percent of the taxable wages to compute the required amount.
   b. What amount of Medicare tax is owed for the quarter? Use 2.9 percent of the taxable wages to compute the required amount.
   c. What is the total of all the federal taxes owed for the quarter?
   d. Is there any balance due at the end of the quarter? If so, how much?

3. The following information will be used to prepare Form 940-EZ, Employer's Annual Federal Unemployment (FUTA) Tax Return, at the end of the current year at Morgan Computer Graphics.

   Total payments (wages), $353,500
   Total exempt payments (wages), $283,500
   First quarter deposit, $378.00
   Second quarter deposit, $102.00
   Third quarter deposit, 0
   Undeposited FUTA tax for the third quarter, $60.00

   a. What is the total amount of taxable wages for FUTA?
   b. What amount of FUTA tax does the firm owe for the year? Use 0.8 percent as the FUTA rate.
   c. What is the total amount of FUTA tax deposited during the year?
   d. What amount of FUTA tax does the firm owe for the fourth quarter?
   e. What balance of FUTA tax must the firm pay at the end of the year?

4. The table that follows contains payroll data for the employees of the Broadway Talent Agency. This data is for the week ended March 7.

Employee	Marital Status	Withholding Allowances	Gross Earnings
Jennifer Dorn	M	2	$1,220
Sharon Li	S	0	785
Kyle Mason	S	1	540
Frank Ortega	M	3	975
Sarah Wells	M	1	630
Martin Ziegler	M	4	1,350

   a. Determine the amount of federal income tax to be withheld from the earnings of each employee. Use the tax tables in the Appendix.
   b. Compute the amount of social security tax (6.2 percent) and Medicare tax (1.45 percent) to be withheld from each employee's earnings. Assume that all earnings are taxable.
   c. Compute the total gross earnings for the period.
   d. Compute the employer's share of social security tax and the employer's share of Medicare tax.

e. Compute the agency's total tax liability for the period. Include the federal income tax withheld, the employer and employee shares of social security tax, and the employer and employee shares of Medicare tax.

5. The Sky High Ski Lodge pays its employees on a weekly basis. Their gross earnings and federal income tax withheld during January are listed below.

Payroll Period Ended	Gross Earnings	Federal Income Tax Withheld
January 7	$17,690	$1,945
14	18,240	2,006
21	17,830	1,961
28	18,580	2,044

a. Compute the total of the employer and employee shares of the social security tax for each payroll. Use 12.4 percent to find this amount.
b. Compute the total of the employer and employee shares of the Medicare tax for each payroll. Use 2.9 percent to find this amount.
c. What is the amount of the deposit of federal taxes that the firm must make for each payroll?

6. Sun-N-Surf Fashions paid wages and salaries of $290,000 last year. Of this amount, $264,000 was subject to social security tax and $67,200 was subject to FUTA tax. All wages and salaries were subject to Medicare tax.

a. Compute the employer's share of social security tax that the firm owed last year. Use 6.2 percent as the rate.
b. Compute the employer's share of Medicare tax that the firm owed last year. Use 1.45 percent as the rate.
c. Compute the FUTA tax that the firm owed last year. Use 0.8 percent as the rate.

7. The Alpha Copy Center paid the following wages to its full-time and part-time employees last year.

Employee	Yearly Wages
Abdul Ahmed	$34,200
Michael Chase	22,140
Denise DeFalco	6,800
Ruth Foster	28,000
Shawn Sellers	7,050
Mary Warren	15,850
Jordan Whitfield	6,950

a. Compute the total amount of wages subject to FUTA tax last year.
b. Compute the total amount of FUTA tax owed for the year. Use 0.8 percent as the rate.

Problems

1. During the past year, Digitek Consulting paid the following salaries to its employees.

Employee	Yearly Salary
Steven Schiff, president	$128,000
Donna Lopez, vice president	95,000
Reed McPherson, consultant	66,000
Joan Selby, executive assistant	37,000

a. Compute the amount of social security tax that was withheld from the earnings of each employee during the year. Use a wage base of $87,900 and a rate of 6.2 percent.
b. Compute the amount of Medicare tax that was withheld from the earnings of each employee during the year. Use a rate of 1.45 percent.

c. Compute the amount of social security tax that the firm owed on the salaries of its employees during the year.

d. Compute the amount of Medicare tax that the firm owed on the salaries of its employees during the year.

2. At the end of the fourth quarter of the current year, the Clark Insurance Agency used the following information to prepare Form 941, Employer's Quarterly Federal Tax Return.

Total wages, $149,250.00
Total federal income tax withheld, $18,402.00
Taxable social security wages, $139,250.00
Taxable Medicare wages, $149,250.00
Total deposits for quarter, $39,997.25

a. What amount of social security tax is owed for the quarter? Use 12.4 percent of the taxable wages to compute the required amount.

b. What amount of Medicare tax is owed for the quarter? Use 2.9 percent of the taxable wages to compute the required amount.

c. What is the total of all the federal taxes owed for the quarter?

d. Is there any balance due at the end of the quarter? If so, how much?

3. Voyager Inc. is a travel agency that specializes in luxury vacations. Last year, the firm paid the following salaries to its employees.

Employee	Yearly Salary
Lisa Gordon	$89,500
Patrick Hurley	34,670
Keith Sloan	51,250
Laura Tarantino	87,000
Ann Waslewski	42,310

a. Compute the total amount of taxable wages for social security tax. The yearly wage base for each employee is $87,900.

b. Compute the employer's share of the social security tax for the year. Use 6.2 percent as the rate.

c. Compute the total amount of taxable wages for Medicare tax.

d. Compute the employer's share of the Medicare tax for the year. Use 1.45 percent as the rate.

e. Compute the total amount of taxable wages for FUTA tax. The yearly wage base for each employee is $7,000.

f. Compute the amount of FUTA tax that the employer owes for the year. Use 0.8 percent as the rate.

4. At the end of the current year, the Spotless Car Wash used the following information to prepare Form 940-EZ, Employer's Annual Federal Unemployment (FUTA) Tax Return.

Total payments (wages), $151,225
Total exempt payments (wages), $79,125
First quarter deposit, $341.20
Second quarter deposit, $182.30
Third quarter deposit, 0
Undeposited FUTA tax for the third quarter, $30.20

a. What is the total amount of taxable wages for FUTA?

b. What amount of FUTA tax does the firm owe for the year? Use 0.8 percent as the FUTA rate.

c. What is the total amount of FUTA tax deposited during the year?

d. What amount of FUTA tax does the firm owe for the fourth quarter?

e. What balance of FUTA tax must the firm pay at the end of the year?

Learning Through Practice

Unit 9 Exercises

EXERCISE 9.1

The Sunnyside Garden Center pays its employees on a weekly basis. Its payroll register for the week ended March 21 shows the following totals: gross earnings of $8,465.00, federal income tax withheld of $1,121.00, social security tax withheld of $524.83, and Medicare tax withheld of $122.74.

a. Compute the total federal taxes owed for the period.

Federal income tax withheld	$ _____
Employee share of social security tax	_____
Employer share of social security tax	_____
Employee share of Medicare tax	_____
Employer share of Medicare tax	_____
Total federal taxes owed	$ _____

b. During its last lookback period, the firm had a total liability of $86,754.00 for federal taxes. Is the firm a monthly or semiweekly depositor in the current year?

EXERCISE 9.2

The Spick-and-Span Laundry pays its employees on a monthly basis. The payroll register that it prepared on April 30 shows the following totals: gross earnings of $10,160.00, federal income tax withheld of $1,118.00, social security tax withheld of $629.92, and Medicare tax withheld of $147.32.

a. Compute the total federal taxes owed for the period.

Federal income tax withheld	$ _____
Employee share of social security tax	_____
Employer share of social security tax	_____
Employee share of Medicare tax	_____
Employer share of Medicare tax	_____
Total federal taxes owed	$ _____

b. During its last lookback period, the firm had a total liability of $32,563.00 for federal taxes. Is the firm a monthly or semiweekly depositor in the current year?

c. Assume that the firm does not have to use electronic funds transfer for deposits. Instead, it submits Form 8109 and a check to its bank. Complete Form 8109, Federal Tax Deposit Coupon, found on page 220, in order to deposit the federal taxes owed for the April 30 payroll. Enter the amount of the deposit, and darken the areas for the correct type of tax and the correct tax period. The firm's telephone number is 515-555-2789.

EXERCISE 9.2 (d) **Form 8109**

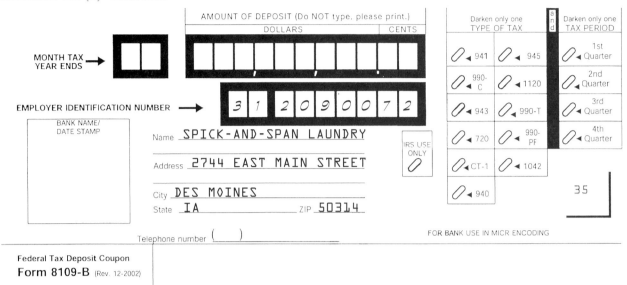

EXERCISE 9.3   Prepare Form 941, Employer's Quarterly Federal Tax Return, for Vanguard Media, an advertising agency. Use the form on page 221. The period covered is the quarter ending March 31 of the current year. This firm has five employees and pays them twice a month. The table below shows the totals for gross earnings, federal income tax withheld, social security tax withheld, and Medicare tax withheld for each payroll period during the quarter. All earnings were subject to social security tax and Medicare tax.

Date Salaries Paid	Gross Earnings	Federal Income Tax	Social Security Tax	Medicare Tax
January 15	$6,815.00	$749.00	$422.53	$98.82
January 31	6,422.00	706.00	398.16	93.12
February 15	7,135.00	784.00	442.37	103.46
February 28	6,590.00	723.00	408.58	95.56
March 15	7,048.00	775.00	436.98	102.20
March 31	6,720.00	739.00	416.64	97.44

The following deposits were made on a monthly basis for the quarter.

Month Ended	Date of Deposit	Amount of Deposit
January 31	February 6	$3,480.26
February 28	March 5	3,606.93
March 31	April 7	3,620.50

Use April 23 of the current year as the date of the tax return. Leave the signature line blank because the form will be signed by Carl Van Dusen, the president. Note that some lines of the form contain zeros. These lines are for adjustments and other items that do not apply to the firm at this time.

EXERCISE 9.3 **Form 941**

Form 941
(Rev. January 2004)
Department of the Treasury
Internal Revenue Service (99)

Employer's Quarterly Federal Tax Return

▶ See separate instructions revised January 2004 for information on completing this return.

Please type or print.

Enter state code for state in which deposits were made **only** if different from state in address to the right ▶ (see page 2 of separate instructions).

Name (as distinguished from trade name)	Date quarter ended	OMB No. 1545-0029
	03/31/05	T
Trade name, if any	Employer identification number	FF
VANGUARD MEDIA	77-3462800	FD
Address (number and street)	City, state, and ZIP code	FP
3793 MONUMENT STREET	DOWNEY, CA 90241	I
		T

If address is different from prior return, check here ▶

IRS Use

1 1 1 1 1 1 1 1 1 1 1   2   3 3 3 3 3 3 3 3   4 4 4   5 5 5
6   7   8 8 8 8 8 8 8   9 9 9 9 9   10 10 10 10 10 10 10 10 10 10

A If you **do not have to file** returns in the future, check here ▶ ☐ and enter date final wages paid ▶
B If you are a seasonal employer, see **Seasonal employers** on page 1 of the instructions and check here ▶ ☐

1	Number of employees in the pay period that includes March 12th . ▶	1
2	Total wages and tips, plus other compensation (see separate instructions)	2
3	Total income tax withheld from wages, tips, and sick pay	3
4	Adjustment of withheld income tax for preceding quarters of **this calendar year**	4
5	Adjusted total of income tax withheld (line 3 as adjusted by line 4)	5

6	Taxable social security wages	6a		$\times$ 12.4% (.124) =	6b
	Taxable social security tips	6c		$\times$ 12.4% (.124) =	6d
7	Taxable Medicare wages and tips . . .	7a		$\times$ 2.9% (.029) =	7b

8	Total social security and Medicare taxes (add lines 6b, 6d, and 7b). **Check here if wages are not subject to social security and/or Medicare tax** . . . . ▶ ☐	8
9	Adjustment of social security and Medicare taxes (see instructions for required explanation) Sick Pay $ _____ ± Fractions of Cents $ _____ ± Other $ _____ =	9
10	Adjusted total of social security and Medicare taxes (line 8 as adjusted by line 9)	10
11	**Total taxes** (add lines 5 and 10)	11
12	Advance earned income credit (EIC) payments made to employees (see instructions) . . .	12
13	Net taxes (subtract line 12 from line 11). **If $2,500 or more, this must equal line 17, column (d) below (or line D of Schedule B (Form 941))**	13
14	Total deposits for quarter, including overpayment applied from a prior quarter	14
15	**Balance due** (subtract line 14 from line 13). See instructions . . .	15
16	**Overpayment.** If line 14 is more than line 13, enter excess here ▶ $ _____

and check if to be: ☐ Applied to next return   **or**   ☐ Refunded.

- **All filers:** If line 13 is less than $2,500, **do not** complete line 17 **or** Schedule B (Form 941).
- **Semiweekly schedule depositors:** Complete Schedule B (Form 941) and check here . . . . ▶ ☐
- **Monthly schedule depositors:** Complete line 17, columns (a) through (d), and check here . . . . ▶ ☐

17	**Monthly Summary of Federal Tax Liability.** (Complete **Schedule B (Form 941)** instead, if you were a semiweekly schedule depositor.)			
	(a) First month liability	**(b)** Second month liability	**(c)** Third month liability	**(d)** Total liability for quarter

Third Party Designee

Do you want to allow another person to discuss this return with the IRS (see separate instructions)?   ☐ **Yes.** Complete the following.   ☐ **No**

Designee's name ▶   Phone no. ▶ (   )   Personal identification number (PIN) ▶

Sign Here

Under penalties of perjury, I declare that I have examined this return, including accompanying schedules and statements, and to the best of my knowledge and belief, it is true, correct, and complete.

Signature ▶   Print Your Name and Title ▶   Date ▶

For Privacy Act and Paperwork Reduction Act Notice, see back of Payment Voucher.   Cat. No. 17001Z   Form **941** (Rev. 1-2004)

EXERCISE 9.4   Prepare a copy of Form W-2, Wage and Tax Statement, for Susan Silver, an employee of Alliance Communications, a provider of Internet service. Use the form below. The business is located at 922 Vernon Street, Hayward, CA 94545. The firm's federal identification number is 52-2645983, and its state identification number is 317-8642-7.

Obtain the necessary information about the employee from her earnings record, which is shown below. Use Box 14 of Form W-2 to report the amount withheld for the state disability insurance (SDI) tax levied by California. Identify this amount with the letters *CASDI.*

EXERCISE 9.4   **Employee Earnings Record**

EMPLOYEE EARNINGS RECORD FOR YEAR 2005

Name: Susan A. Silver
Address: 6169 Rosemont Avenue
Hayward, CA 94545
Social Security No. 073-48-9961
Job Title: Technical Operations Supervisor
Date Employed: July 15, 2002
Date Terminated:

Marital Status: M ☒ S ☐
No. of Withholding Allowances: 1
Regular Rate: $3,520 per month

Voluntary Deductions:
IRA: $150 per month
U.S. Savings Bonds:

PAYROLL PERIOD		HOURS		EARNINGS			DEDUCTIONS								NET PAY	YEAR-TO-DATE EARNINGS
Week	Ending Date	Reg.	O.T.	Regular	Overtime or Commission	Total Earnings	Federal Income Tax	Social Security Tax	Medicare Tax	State Income Tax	SDI Tax	IRA	Savings Bonds	Total Deductions		
Totals for year				42,240 00		42,240 00	3,996 00	2,618 88	612 48	814 80	498 43	1,800 00		10,340 59	31,899 41	42,240 00

EXERCISE 9.4   **Form W-2**

a Control number	22222	Void ☐	For Official Use Only ▶ OMB No. 1545-0008		
b Employer identification number				1 Wages, tips, other compensation	2 Federal income tax withheld
c Employer's name, address, and ZIP code				3 Social security wages	4 Social security tax withheld
				5 Medicare wages and tips	6 Medicare tax withheld
				7 Social security tips	8 Allocated tips
d Employee's social security number				9 Advance EIC payment	10 Dependent care benefits
e Employee's first name and initial	Last name			11 Nonqualified plans	12a See instructions for box 12
				13 Statutory employee ☐ Retirement plan ☐ Third-party sick pay ☐	12b
				14 Other	12c
					12d
f Employee's address and ZIP code					
15 State Employer's state ID number	16 State wages, tips, etc.	17 State income tax	18 Local wages, tips, etc.	19 Local income tax	20 Locality name

Form **W-2** Wage and Tax Statement   **2005**   Department of the Treasury—Internal Revenue Service

Copy A For Social Security Administration — Send this entire page with Form W-3 to the Social Security Administration; photocopies are **not** acceptable.   Cat. No. 10134D

For Privacy Act and Paperwork Reduction Act Notice, see back of Copy D.

Do Not Cut, Fold, or Staple Forms on This Page — Do Not Cut, Fold, or Staple Forms on This Page

EXERCISE 9.5

Prepare Form W-3, Transmittal of Wage and Tax Statements, for the Fontana Real Estate Company. Use the form that appears below. This business is located at 5258 Silk Road, Paterson, NJ 07503.

The firm's federal identification number is 76-1328564, and its state identification number is 42-4797238. Assume that with Form W-3, Marie Fontana is submitting Forms W-2 for 12 employees. The firm's classification for Kind of Payer is 941. The payroll totals for the year are shown below.

Wages paid, $549,620.00

Federal income tax withheld, $61,458.00

Social security wages, $523,110.00

Medicare wages, $549,620.00

State income tax withheld, $10,922.00

Compute and enter the social security tax withheld (6.2 percent of taxable wages) and the Medicare tax withheld (1.45 percent of taxable wages). Use February 21 of the current year as the date of the form. Leave the signature line blank because the form will be signed by Marie Fontana, the president of the firm. The telephone number is 201-555-8655.

EXERCISE 9.5   Form W-3

DO NOT STAPLE OR FOLD

a Control number	33333	For Official Use Only ▶ OMB No. 1545-0008		
b **Kind of Payer** ▶ 941 ☐ CT-1 ☐ Military ☐ Hshld. emp. ☐ 943 ☐ Medicare govt. emp. ☐ Third-party sick pay ☐		1 Wages, tips, other compensation $	2 Federal income tax withheld $	
		3 Social security wages $	4 Social security tax withheld $	
c Total number of Forms W-2	d Establishment number	5 Medicare wages and tips $	6 Medicare tax withheld $	
e Employer identification number		7 Social security tips $	8 Allocated tips $	
f Employer's name		9 Advance EIC payments $	10 Dependent care benefits $	
		11 Nonqualified plans $	12 Deferred compensation $	
		13 For third-party sick pay use only		
g Employer's address and ZIP code		14 Income tax withheld by payer of third-party sick pay $		
h Other EIN used this year				
15 State Employer's state ID number		16 State wages, tips, etc. $	17 State income tax $	
		18 Local wages, tips, etc. $	19 Local income tax $	
Contact person		Telephone number ( )	For Official Use Only	
E-mail address		Fax number ( )		

Under penalties of perjury, I declare that I have examined this return and accompanying documents, and, to the best of my knowledge and belief, they are true, correct, and complete.

Signature ▶   Title ▶   Date ▶

Form **W-3** **Transmittal of Wage and Tax Statements**   **2005**   Department of the Treasury Internal Revenue Service

Send this entire page with the entire Copy A page of Form(s) W-2 to the Social Security Administration. Photocopies are not acceptable.

Do not send any payment (cash, checks, money orders, etc.) with Forms W-2 and W-3.

EXERCISE 9.6   Do the following work for Wang Audio Products, a firm that manufactures high-quality stereo speakers.

1. Compute the FUTA tax owed for each quarter of the year, using 0.8 percent as the FUTA rate. The taxable wages were $52,510 for the quarter ending March 31; $31,380 for the quarter ending June 30; $12,152 for the quarter ending September 30; and $7,245 for the quarter ending December 31.

FUTA tax owed for first quarter $ _____

FUTA tax owed for second quarter   _____

FUTA tax owed for third quarter   _____

FUTA tax owed for fourth quarter   _____

2. Answer the following questions about deposits of FUTA tax by Wang Audio Products.

a. Is it necessary for the firm to make a deposit at the end of the first quarter?   _____

b. If a deposit is necessary after the first quarter, what is the due date?   _____

c. Is it necessary for the firm to make a deposit at the end of the second quarter?   _____

d. If a deposit is necessary after the second quarter, what is the due date?   _____

e. Is it necessary for the firm to make a deposit at the end of the third quarter?   _____

f. If a deposit is necessary after the third quarter, what is the due date?   _____

g. Is it necessary for the firm to make a deposit at the end of the fourth quarter?   _____

h. If a deposit is necessary after the fourth quarter, what is the due date?   _____

EXERCISE 9.7   During the first quarter of the current year, Susie's Primary School paid wages of $36,215.00 that were subject to FUTA tax. Use a rate of 0.8 percent to compute the amount of FUTA tax that the firm owes for the first quarter. Then prepare Form 8109, Federal Tax Deposit Coupon, below. Enter the amount of the deposit, and darken the areas for the correct type of tax and the correct tax period. The firm's telephone number is 214-555-7621.

EXERCISE 9.7   **Form 8109**

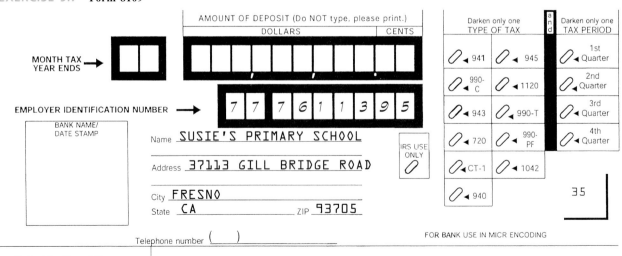

Federal Tax Deposit Coupon
Form 8109-B (Rev. 12-2002)

EXERCISE 9.8

Prepare Form 940-EZ, Employer's Annual Federal Unemployment (FUTA) Tax Return, for the Majestic Movie Theater. Use the form on page 226.

The business made unemployment insurance contributions of $3,098.52 to the state of Virginia. Its state reporting number is 62-8846-7. The firm's wage payments for the year totaled $335,620. Of this amount, $172,540 was exempt from FUTA tax (above the $7,000 taxable wage base for each employee for the year). The following table shows the FUTA tax that the firm owed at the end of each quarter and the deposits that it made.

Quarter	FUTA Tax Owed	Date of Deposit	Amount of Deposit
First	$685.44	April 27	$685.44
Second	474.57	July 29	474.57
Third	91.37		0
Fourth	53.26	January 24	144.63

Use January 26 of the current year as the date of this tax return. Leave the signature line blank. Kirby Wilson, the president of the firm, will sign the form.

EXERCISE 9.8   Form 940-EZ

Form **940-EZ**	**Employer's Annual Federal Unemployment (FUTA) Tax Return**	OMB No. 1545-1110
Department of the Treasury Internal Revenue Service	▶ See the separate Instructions for Form 940-EZ for information on completing this form.	2004

			T	
	Name (as distinguished from trade name)	Calendar year 2004	FF	
			FD	
You must complete this section. ▶	Trade name, if any MAJESTIC MOVIE THEATER	Employer identification number (EIN) 37-6061227	FP	
			I	
	Address (number and street) 22 OAK AVENUE	City, state, and ZIP code SPRINGFIELD, VA 22153	T	

Answer the questions under **Who May Use Form 940-EZ** on page 2. *If you cannot use Form 940-EZ, you must use Form 940.*

A   Enter the amount of contributions paid to your state unemployment fund (see the separate instructions) . . ▶ $ ....

B   (1) Enter the name of the state where you have to pay contributions . . . . ▶ ....

(2) Enter your state reporting number as shown on your state unemployment tax return ▶

If you will not have to file returns in the future, check here (see **Who Must File** in separate instructions) and complete and sign the return. ▶ ☐

If this is an Amended Return, check here (see **Amended Returns** in the separate instructions) . . . . ▶ ☐

Part I   Taxable Wages and FUTA Tax

1	Total payments (including payments shown on lines 2 and 3) during the calendar year for services of employees	**1**	
2	Exempt payments. (Explain all exempt payments, attaching additional sheets if necessary.) ▶	**2**	
3	Payments of more than $7,000 for services. Enter only amounts over the first $7,000 paid to each employee **(see the separate instructions)**	**3**	
4	Add lines 2 and 3	**4**	
5	**Total taxable wages** (subtract line 4 from line 1) . . . . ▶	**5**	
6	**FUTA tax.** Multiply the wages on line 5 by .008 and enter here. **(If the result is over $100, also complete Part II.)**	**6**	
7	Total FUTA tax deposited for the year, including any overpayment applied from a prior year	**7**	
8	**Balance due** (subtract line 7 from line 6). Pay to the "United States Treasury." . . . . ▶	**8**	
	If you owe more than $100, see **Depositing FUTA tax** in the separate instructions.		
9	**Overpayment** (subtract line 6 from line 7). Check if it is to be: ☐ **Applied to next return** or ☐ **Refunded** ▶	**9**	

Part II   Record of Quarterly Federal Unemployment Tax Liability (Do not include state liability.) **Complete only if line 6 is over $100.**

Quarter	First (Jan. 1 – Mar. 31)	Second (Apr. 1 – June 30)	Third (July 1 – Sept. 30)	Fourth (Oct. 1 – Dec. 31)	Total for year
Liability for quarter					

Third-Party Designee   Do you want to allow another person to discuss this return with the IRS (see the separate instructions)? ☐ **Yes.** Complete the following.   ☐ **No**

Designee's name ▶ _____   Phone no. ▶ ( )   Personal identification number (PIN) ▶

Under penalties of perjury, I declare that I have examined this return, including accompanying schedules and statements, and, to the best of my knowledge and belief, it is true, correct, and complete, and that no part of any payment made to a state unemployment fund claimed as a credit was, or is to be, deducted from the payments to employees.

Signature ▶ _____   Title (Owner, etc.) ▶ _____   Date ▶ _____

For Privacy Act and Paperwork Reduction Act Notice, see the separate instructions.   ▼ **DETACH HERE** ▼   Cat. No. 10983G   Form **940-EZ** (2004)

Alternate Learning Through Practice Exercises

Unit 9 Exercises

EXERCISE 9.1A

Roadway Auto Repair pays its employees on a weekly basis. Its payroll register for the week ended January 31 shows the following totals: gross earnings of $3,628.00, federal income tax withheld of $442.62, social security tax withheld of $224.96, and Medicare tax withheld of $52.61.

a. Compute the total federal taxes owed for the period.

Federal income tax withheld	$ _____
Employee share of social security tax	_____
Employer share of social security tax	_____
Employee share of Medicare tax	_____
Employer share of Medicare tax	_____
Total federal taxes owed	$ _____

b. During its last lookback period, the firm had a total liability of $49,324.52 for federal taxes. Is the firm a monthly or semiweekly depositor in the current year?

EXERCISE 9.2A

Deluxe Bridal Creations pays its employees on a monthly basis. The payroll register that it prepared on March 31 shows the following totals: gross earnings of $22,540.00, federal income tax withheld of $2,749.00, social security tax withheld of $1,397.48, and Medicare tax withheld of $326.83.

a. Compute the total federal taxes owed for the period.

Federal income tax withheld	$ _____
Employee share of social security tax	_____
Employer share of social security tax	_____
Employee share of Medicare tax	_____
Employer share of Medicare tax	_____
Total federal taxes owed	$ _____

b. During its last lookback period, the firm had a total liability of $74,451.28 for federal taxes. Is the firm a monthly or semiweekly depositor in the current year?

c. Assume that the firm does not have to use electronic funds transfer for deposits. Instead, it submits Form 8109 and a check to its bank. Complete Form 8109, Federal Tax Deposit Coupon, found on page 228, in order to deposit the federal taxes owed for the March 31 payroll. Enter the amount of the deposit, and darken the areas for the correct type of tax and the correct tax period. The firm's telephone number is 515-728-9134.

EXERCISE 9.2A (d) **Form 8109**

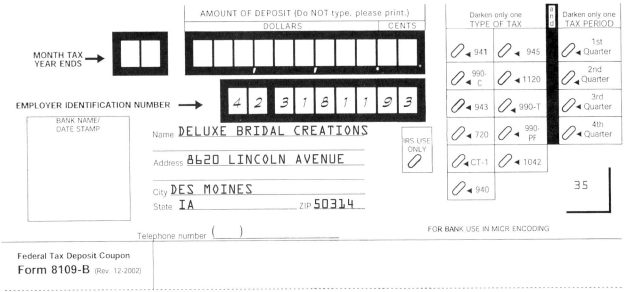

EXERCISE 9.3A

Prepare Form 941, Employer's Quarterly Federal Tax Return, for Sports Watch, a Web site. Use the form on page 229. The period covered is the quarter ending March 31 of the current year. This firm has four employees and pays them twice a month. The table below shows the totals for gross earnings, federal income tax withheld, social security tax withheld, and Medicare tax withheld for each payroll period during the quarter. All earnings were subject to social security tax and Medicare tax.

Date Salaries Paid	Gross Earnings	Federal Income Tax	Social Security Tax	Medicare Tax
January 15	$5,452.00	$599.00	$338.02	$79.05
January 31	5,138.00	564.00	318.56	74.50
February 15	5,708.00	627.00	353.90	82.77
February 28	6,240.00	685.00	386.88	90.48
March 15	5,362.00	589.00	332.44	77.75
March 31	6,176.00	668.00	382.91	89.55

The following deposits were made on a monthly basis for the quarter.

Month Ended	Date of Deposit	Amount of Deposit
January 31	February 4	$2,783.26
February 28	March 6	3,140.06
March 31	April 5	3,022.30

Use April 21 of the current year as the date of the tax return. Leave the signature line blank because the form will be signed by Daniel Metz, the president. Note that some lines of the form contain zeros. These lines are for adjustments and other items that do not apply to the firm at this time.

EXERCISE 9.3A **Form 941**

Form **941**
(Rev. January 2004)
Department of the Treasury
Internal Revenue Service (99)

Employer's Quarterly Federal Tax Return

▶ **See separate instructions revised January 2004 for information on completing this return.**
Please type or print.

OMB No. 1545-0029

Enter state code for state in which deposits were made **only** if different from state in address to the right ▶ [:] (see page 2 of separate instructions).

Name (as distinguished from trade name)

Trade name, if any
SPORTS WATCH

Address (number and street)
9801 DELTA DRIVE

Date quarter ended
03/31/05

Employer identification number
81-4573912

City, state, and ZIP code
DOWNEY, CA 90241

T	
FF	
FD	
FP	
I	
T	

If address is different from prior return, check here ▶ [ ]

IRS Use

1 1 1 1 1 1 1 1 1 1   2   3 3 3 3 3 3 3 3   4 4 4   5 5 5

6   7   8 8 8 8 8 8 8   9 9 9 9 9   10 10 10 10 10 10 10 10 10 10

A   If you **do not have to file** returns in the future, check here ▶ [ ] and enter date final wages paid ▶

B   If you are a seasonal employer, see **Seasonal employers** on page 1 of the instructions and check here ▶ [ ]

1	Number of employees in the pay period that includes March 12th . ▶	1	
2	Total wages and tips, plus other compensation (see separate instructions)	2	
3	Total income tax withheld from wages, tips, and sick pay	3	
4	Adjustment of withheld income tax for preceding quarters of **this calendar year**	4	
5	Adjusted total of income tax withheld (line 3 as adjusted by line 4)	5	
6	Taxable social security wages	6a	× 12.4% (.124) =	6b
	Taxable social security tips	6c	× 12.4% (.124) =	6d
7	Taxable Medicare wages and tips . . .	7a	× 2.9% (.029) =	7b
8	Total social security and Medicare taxes (add lines 6b, 6d, and 7b). **Check here if wages are not subject to social security and/or Medicare tax** . . . . ▶ [ ]	8	
9	Adjustment of social security and Medicare taxes (see instructions for required explanation) Sick Pay $ _____ ± Fractions of Cents $ _____ ± Other $ _____ =	9	
10	Adjusted total of social security and Medicare taxes (line 8 as adjusted by line 9)	10	
11	**Total taxes** (add lines 5 and 10)	11	
12	Advance earned income credit (EIC) payments made to employees (see instructions) . . .	12	
13	Net taxes (subtract line 12 from line 11). **If $2,500 or more, this must equal line 17, column (d) below (or line D of Schedule B (Form 941))**	13	
14	Total deposits for quarter, including overpayment applied from a prior quarter	14	
15	**Balance due** (subtract line 14 from line 13). See instructions	15	
16	**Overpayment.** If line 14 is more than line 13, enter excess here ▶ $ _____		

and check if to be: [ ] Applied to next return   **or**   [ ] Refunded.

- **All filers:** If line 13 is less than $2,500, **do not** complete line 17 or Schedule B (Form 941).
- **Semiweekly schedule depositors:** Complete Schedule B (Form 941) and check here . . . . ▶ [ ]
- **Monthly schedule depositors:** Complete line 17, columns (a) through (d), and check here. . . . . . . ▶ [ ]

17	Monthly Summary of Federal Tax Liability. (Complete **Schedule B (Form 941)** instead, if you were a semiweekly schedule depositor.)			
	(a) First month liability	**(b)** Second month liability	**(c)** Third month liability	**(d)** Total liability for quarter

Third Party Designee

Do you want to allow another person to discuss this return with the IRS (see separate instructions)?   [ ] **Yes.** Complete the following.   [ ] **No**

Designee's name ▶

Phone no. ▶ (   )

Personal identification number (PIN) ▶ [ ][ ][ ][ ][ ]

Sign Here

Under penalties of perjury, I declare that I have examined this return, including accompanying schedules and statements, and to the best of my knowledge and belief, it is true, correct, and complete.

Signature ▶

Print Your Name and Title ▶

Date ▶

For Privacy Act and Paperwork Reduction Act Notice, see back of Payment Voucher.   Cat. No. 17001Z   Form **941** (Rev. 1-2004)

EXERCISE 9.4A Prepare a copy of Form W-2, Wage and Tax Statement, for Kristen Palmer, an employee of Ross Biotech Research. Use the form below. The business is located at 1241 Fremont Avenue, Hayward, CA 94545. The firm's federal identification number is 63-3756094, and its state identification number is 428-9753-8.

Obtain the necessary information about the employee from her earnings record, which is shown below. Use Box 14 of Form W-2 to report the amount withheld for the state disability insurance (SDI) tax levied by California. Identify this amount with the letters *CASDI*.

EXERCISE 9.4A **Employee Earnings Record**

EMPLOYEE EARNINGS RECORD FOR YEAR 2005

Name: Kristen M. Palmer
Address: 219 Harlan Street
Hayward, CA 94545
Social Security No. 184-59-1272
Job Title: Laboratory Technician
Date Employed: March 21, 2002
Date Terminated: _____

Marital Status: M ☒ S ☐
No. of Withholding Allowances: 1
Regular Rate: $3,750 per month

Voluntary Deductions:
IRA: $150 per month
U.S. Savings Bonds: _____

PAYROLL PERIOD		HOURS		EARNINGS			DEDUCTIONS								NET PAY	YEAR-TO-DATE EARNINGS
Week	Ending Date	Reg.	O.T.	Regular	Overtime or Commission	Total Earnings	Federal Income Tax	Social Security Tax	Medicare Tax	State Income Tax	SDI Tax	IRA	Savings Bonds	Total Deductions		
	Totals for year			45,000 00		45,000 00	4,356 00	2,790 00	652 50	910 80	531 00	1,800 00		11,040 30	33,959 70	45,000 00

EXERCISE 9.4A **Form W-2**

a Control number 22222 Void ☐	For Official Use Only ▶ OMB No. 1545-0008	
b Employer identification number	**1** Wages, tips, other compensation	**2** Federal income tax withheld
c Employer's name, address, and ZIP code	**3** Social security wages	**4** Social security tax withheld
	5 Medicare wages and tips	**6** Medicare tax withheld
	7 Social security tips	**8** Allocated tips
d Employee's social security number	**9** Advance EIC payment	**10** Dependent care benefits
e Employee's first name and initial Last name	**11** Nonqualified plans	**12a** See instructions for box 12
	13 Statutory employee ☐ Retirement plan ☐ Third-party sick pay ☐	**12b**
	14 Other	**12c**
		12d
f Employee's address and ZIP code		
15 State Employer's state ID number	**16** State wages, tips, etc. **17** State income tax	**18** Local wages, tips, etc. **19** Local income tax **20** Locality name

Form **W-2** **Wage and Tax Statement**   **2005**   Department of the Treasury—Internal Revenue Service

Copy A For Social Security Administration — Send this entire page with Form W-3 to the Social Security Administration; photocopies are **not** acceptable.

For Privacy Act and Paperwork Reduction Act Notice, see back of Copy D.

Cat. No. 10134D

Do Not Cut, Fold, or Staple Forms on This Page — Do Not Cut, Fold, or Staple Forms on This Page

EXERCISE 9.5A

Prepare Form W-3, Transmittal of Wage and Tax Statements, for DeSouza Home Health Care. Use the form that appears below. This business is located at 672 Davis Avenue, Paterson, NJ 07503.

The firm's federal identification number is 65-0217453, and its state identification number is 31-3686127. Assume that with Form W-3, Rosemary DeSouza is submitting Forms W-2 for 15 employees. The firm's classification for Kind of Payer is 941. The payroll totals for the year are shown below.

Wages paid, $697,580.00
Federal income tax withheld, $76,664.00
Social security wages, $692,130.00
Medicare wages, $697,580.00
State income tax withheld, $21,927.00

Compute and enter the social security tax withheld (6.2 percent of taxable wages) and the Medicare tax withheld (1.45 percent of taxable wages). Use February 19 of the current year as the date of the form. Leave the signature line blank because the form will be signed by Rosemary DeSouza, the president of the firm. The telephone number is 201-426-7543.

EXERCISE 9.5A   Form W-3

DO NOT STAPLE OR FOLD

a Control number	33333	For Official Use Only ▶ OMB No. 1545-0008		
b **Kind of Payer** ▶ 941 ☐ CT-1 ☐ Military ☐ Hshld. emp. ☐ 943 ☐ Medicare govt. emp. ☐ Third-party sick pay ☐		1 Wages, tips, other compensation $		2 Federal income tax withheld $
		3 Social security wages $		4 Social security tax withheld $
c Total number of Forms W-2	d Establishment number	5 Medicare wages and tips $		6 Medicare tax withheld $
e Employer identification number		7 Social security tips $		8 Allocated tips $
f Employer's name		9 Advance EIC payments $		10 Dependent care benefits $
		11 Nonqualified plans $		12 Deferred compensation $
		13 For third-party sick pay use only		
		14 Income tax withheld by payer of third-party sick pay $		
g Employer's address and ZIP code				
h Other EIN used this year				
15 State Employer's state ID number		16 State wages, tips, etc. $		17 State income tax $
		18 Local wages, tips, etc. $		19 Local income tax $
Contact person		Telephone number ( )		For Official Use Only
E-mail address		Fax number ( )		

Under penalties of perjury, I declare that I have examined this return and accompanying documents, and, to the best of my knowledge and belief, they are true, correct, and complete.

Signature ▶ _____   Title ▶ _____   Date ▶ _____

Form **W-3** Transmittal of Wage and Tax Statements   **2005**   Department of the Treasury Internal Revenue Service

Send this entire page with the entire Copy A page of Form(s) W-2 to the Social Security Administration. Photocopies are not acceptable.

Do not send any payment (cash, checks, money orders, etc.) with Forms W-2 and W-3.

EXERCISE 9.6A   Do the following work for Spectrum Wireless, a manufacturer of wireless routers, adapters, and network cards.

1. Compute the FUTA tax owed for each quarter of the year, using 0.8 percent as the FUTA rate. The taxable wages were $96,430.00 for the quarter ending March 31; $43,385.00 for the quarter ending June 30; $21,250.00 for the quarter ending September 30; and $8,672.00 for the quarter ending December 31.

FUTA tax owed for first quarter $ _____

FUTA tax owed for second quarter   _____

FUTA tax owed for third quarter   _____

FUTA tax owed for fourth quarter   _____

2. Answer the following questions about deposits of FUTA tax by Spectrum Wireless.

a. Is it necessary for the firm to make a deposit at the end of the first quarter?   _____

b. If a deposit is necessary after the first quarter, what is the due date?   _____

c. Is it necessary for the firm to make a deposit at the end of the second quarter?   _____

d. If a deposit is necessary after the second quarter, what is the due date?   _____

e. Is it necessary for the firm to make a deposit at the end of the third quarter?   _____

f. If a deposit is necessary after the third quarter, what is the due date?   _____

g. Is it necessary for the firm to make a deposit at the end of the fourth quarter?   _____

h. If a deposit is necessary after the fourth quarter, what is the due date?   _____

EXERCISE 9.7A   During the first quarter of the current year, Park West Dental Associates paid wages of $57,452.00 that were subject to FUTA tax. Use a rate of 0.8 percent to compute the amount of FUTA tax that the firm owes for the first quarter. Then prepare Form 8109, Federal Tax Deposit Coupon, below. Enter the amount of the deposit, and darken the areas for the correct type of tax and the correct tax period. The firm's telephone number is 214-316-5407.

EXERCISE 9.7A   Form 8109

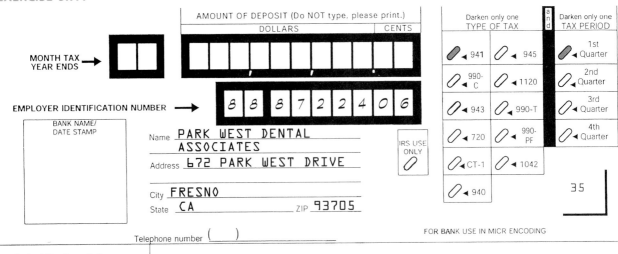

Federal Tax Deposit Coupon
Form 8109-B (Rev. 12-2002)

EXERCISE 9.8A   Prepare Form 940–EZ, Employer's Annual Federal Unemployment (FUTA) Tax Return, for the Royal Motel. Use the form below.

The business made unemployment insurance contributions of $2,497.74 to the state of Virginia. Its state reporting number is 51-7735-6. The firm's wage payments for the year totaled $252,780. Of this amount, $121,370.00 was exempt from FUTA tax (above the $7,000 wage base for each employee for the year). The following table shows the FUTA tax that the firm owed at the end of each quarter and the deposits that it made.

Quarter	FUTA Tax Owed	Date of Deposit	Amount of Deposit
First	$505.56	April 25	$505.56
Second	363.81	July 26	363.81
Third	132.95	Sept. 25	132.95
Fourth	48.96	Jan. 24	48.96

Use January 27 of the current year as the date of this tax return. Leave the signature line blank. Howard Engel, the president of the firm, will sign the form.

EXERCISE 9.8A   **Form 940-EZ**

Form **940-EZ**	**Employer's Annual Federal Unemployment (FUTA) Tax Return**	OMB No. 1545-1110
Department of the Treasury Internal Revenue Service	► See the separate Instructions for Form 940-EZ for information on completing this form.	20**04**

You must complete this section. ▶

Name (as distinguished from trade name)		Calendar year **2004**	T
			FF
Trade name, if any **ROYAL MOTEL**		Employer identification number (EIN) **48-7172338**	FD
			FP
Address (number and street) **18 ELM AVENUE**		City, state, and ZIP code **SPRINGFIELD, VA 22153**	I
			T

Answer the questions under **Who May Use Form 940-EZ** on page 2. *If you cannot use Form 940-EZ, you must use Form 940.*

A   Enter the amount of contributions paid to your state unemployment fund (see the separate instructions)   . ▶ $ ....

B   (1) Enter the name of the state where you have to pay contributions   . . . . ▶ ....

(2) Enter your state reporting number as shown on your state unemployment tax return ▶

If you will not have to file returns in the future, check here (see **Who Must File** in separate instructions) **and complete and sign the return.** ▶ ☐

If this is an Amended Return, check here (see **Amended Returns** in the separate instructions)   . . . . ▶ ☐

Part I   **Taxable Wages and FUTA Tax**

1	Total payments (including payments shown on lines 2 and 3) during the calendar year for services of employees	1	
2	Exempt payments. (Explain all exempt payments, attaching additional sheets if necessary.) ▶	2	
3	Payments of more than $7,000 for services. Enter only amounts over the first $7,000 paid to each employee **(see the separate instructions)**	3	
4	Add lines 2 and 3	4	
5	**Total taxable wages** (subtract line 4 from line 1) . . . . ▶	5	
6	**FUTA tax.** Multiply the wages on line 5 by .008 and enter here. **(If the result is over $100, also complete Part II.)**	6	
7	Total FUTA tax deposited for the year, including any overpayment applied from a prior year	7	
8	Balance due (subtract line 7 from line 6). Pay to the "United States Treasury." . . . . ▶ If you owe more than $100, see **Depositing FUTA tax** in the separate instructions.	8	
9	**Overpayment** (subtract line 6 from line 7). Check if it is to be: ☐ **Applied to next return** or ☐ **Refunded** ▶	9	

Part II   **Record of Quarterly Federal Unemployment Tax Liability** (Do not include state liability.) **Complete only if line 6 is over $100.**

Quarter	First (Jan. 1 – Mar. 31)	Second (Apr. 1 – June 30)	Third (July 1 – Sept. 30)	Fourth (Oct. 1 – Dec. 31)	Total for year
Liability for quarter					

Third–Party Designee   Do you want to allow another person to discuss this return with the IRS (see the separate instructions)?   ☐ **Yes.** Complete the following.   ☐ **No**

Designee's name ▶	Phone no. ▶ ( )	Personal identification number (PIN) ▶	

Under penalties of perjury, I declare that I have examined this return, including accompanying schedules and statements, and, to the best of my knowledge and belief, it is true, correct, and complete, and that no part of any payment made to a state unemployment fund claimed as a credit was, or is to be, deducted from the payments to employees.

Signature ▶   Title (Owner, etc.) ▶   Date ▶

For Privacy Act and Paperwork Reduction Act Notice, see the separate instructions.   ▼ **DETACH HERE** ▼   Cat. No. 10983G   Form **940-EZ** (2004)

State Payroll Taxes and Tax Reports

Upon completion of this unit, you should be able to:

1. Explain how state unemployment compensation systems function.
2. Compute the SUTA tax owed by a firm.
3. Explain how SUTA tax is deposited.
4. Explain how state disability insurance programs function.
5. Compute state disability insurance tax.
6. Explain the purpose of workers' compensation insurance.
7. Compute the estimated and actual premiums for workers' compensation insurance.
8. Explain how state income tax is withheld and deposited.
9. Complete a quarterly state tax return that reports wages paid and income tax withheld.
10. Complete an annual state report of wages paid and taxes owed.
11. Describe the purpose and value of a payroll calendar.

The handling of federal withholding and payroll taxes is only one phase of the tax work that businesses must perform. You have already learned that most states require businesses to deduct state income tax from employee earnings and that some states require the withholding of other taxes. Each state has an unemployment insurance tax and some have a disability insurance tax.

In this unit, you will learn about the procedures for handling state withholding and payroll taxes. You will also see examples of forms that are used to accompany deposits of state taxes and to report information about these taxes. As you study the material presented here, keep in mind that taxes differ from state to state. Thus, people who do payroll work must be thoroughly familiar with the tax regulations and forms in their own states. And they must keep up to date.

REPORTING NEWLY HIRED EMPLOYEES

In recent years, businesses and individuals have experienced more and more requests for personal information from various government agencies. While some people feel that many of these requests for personal information are an invasion of their privacy, upon reflection, we can usually understand that there are good reasons why the government is asking for such data. A case in point is a federal regulation that went into effect in 1998. This regulation makes it necessary for all employers to report information about new employees to a state agency within two weeks of hiring them. The reason for this regulation is to provide the state with information needed to track parents who are delinquent in their child support obligations. Figure 10.1 shows a section of California Form DE 34, Report of New Employee(s).

Internet Connection

How do income tax withholdings vary by state? Find out at http://www.payroll-taxes.com. You can also locate payroll tax information Web sites, both state and federal, at http://www.payroll-taxes.com.

FIGURE 10.1   **Report of New Employees**

STATE UNEMPLOYMENT COMPENSATION TAX

After the passage of the Social Security Act of 1935, which established the federal unemployment insurance system, all the states set up their own unemployment insurance programs. As you learned in Unit 9, the state programs operate in partnership with the federal system. The states maintain local unemployment insurance offices that handle the claims from jobless workers, check those claims, and pay benefits.

Each state sets its own rules with regard to eligibility, amount of benefits, and length of the payment period. However, these rules must meet standards determined by the federal government.

Computing the SUTA Tax

Remember that the Federal Unemployment Tax Act (FUTA) imposes a tax on most employers to support the federal unemployment insurance system. As of this writing, the FUTA tax is 6.2 percent of the first $7,000 in wages earned by each employee during the calendar year. However, the federal government allows a credit of up to 5.4 percent for the state unemployment insurance (SUTA) tax that the employer pays. Thus, the amount of FUTA tax actually owed may be as low as 0.8 percent (6.2 percent − 5.4 percent = 0.8 percent).

The tax rates imposed by state unemployment compensation laws vary. For example, as of this writing, California had rates of 0.9 percent to 5.4 percent. Texas had rates of

Tax audit? Not to worry. The Internal Revenue Service concentrates most of its auditing efforts on high-income taxpayers (those who earn $100,000 or more a year) and large businesses (those with assets of at least $250 million). In fiscal year 2004, the IRS audited 195,200 high-income taxpayers and more than 4,400 large businesses.

Audit rates for lower-income taxpayers and small businesses have dropped in recent years. For example, fewer than 7,300 small businesses (those with assets of less than $10 million) were audited by the IRS in fiscal year 2004. This represented a decrease of 46 percent from the 13,600 small businesses audited in fiscal year 2003.

0.67 percent to 8.47 percent, and New York had rates of 1.5 percent to 9.9 percent. In each state, employers who provide steady work for their employees pay the lower unemployment tax rates. Firms with less favorable employment records are subject to the higher rates.

The wage base for SUTA tax also differs in many states, but some states use the same wage base that is used for FUTA tax. For example, as of this writing, California is among the states where employers are required to pay SUTA tax on the first $7,000 earned by each employee in the calendar year. However, in comparison, Minnesota had a base of $22,000 for SUTA tax, New Jersey had a base of $23,900, Texas had a base of $9,000, and New York had a base of $8,500.

In almost every state, the SUTA tax is paid only by employers; employees are not subject to this tax. However, there are a few states that require contributions from both employees and employers.

All states have an *experience-rating* (or *merit-rating*) plan that affects the amount of SUTA tax employers pay. There is usually a range of rates, and employers who offer the steadiest work are subject to the lowest rate. On the other hand, the poorer a firm's employment record, the higher its SUTA tax rate. The formula used to determine experience ratings varies from state to state, and some states allow employers to make voluntary contributions in order to obtain better ratings. Every firm should be familiar with the plan used in its own state, because a favorable experience rating can mean substantial savings in the payment of SUTA tax.

The SUTA tax is normally computed and paid on a quarterly basis. To find the amount owed, the person who does payroll work for the firm multiplies the total of the taxable earnings of employees for the quarter by the applicable tax rate. For example, suppose that the total taxable earnings are $49,084 and the applicable SUTA rate is 2.1 percent. Here is how the SUTA tax would be computed:

```
$   49,084   total taxable earnings of employees
  × .021     applicable SUTA tax rate
  _____
    49084
    98168
  _____
$1,030.764 = $1,030.76 amount owed for SUTA tax
```

In California, the maximum amount of SUTA tax that an employer pays for each employee during a year, as of this writing, is $378 ($7,000 × .054). At first glance, this may not seem to be a large amount. Yet a business with 1,000 employees that is subject to the maximum SUTA rate of 5.4 percent would pay $378,000 in SUTA tax during a year, whereas a business with 1,000 employees that has a SUTA rate of 2.1 percent would pay $147,000 ($7,000 × .021 = $147 × 1,000 = $147,000). Obviously, a lower SUTA tax rate is very advantageous to a business. Those lower rates are granted to businesses that provide steady employment and avoid high employee turnover.

Learning Through Practice

Do Exercises 10.1 and 10.2 on page 251 of this text-workbook.

Point of Interest

Compound interest—the saver's friend. Even modest savings can grow steadily through the power of compound interest. For example, consider what would happen to a $1,000 investment at interest rates of 3 percent and 6 percent over various time periods. (The interest is compounded annually in this example.)

Interest Rate	Growth of an Investment of $1,000 in:				
	5 Years	10 Years	15 Years	20 Years	25 Years
3%	$1,160	$1,340	$1,560	$1,800	$2,090
6%	1,340	1,790	2,400	3,210	4,290

Responding to Unemployment Benefit Claims

The handling of claims for unemployment insurance benefits varies from state to state. However, the procedure used in California is typical. Immediately after a jobless person applies for unemployment insurance benefits, the state sends a notice of the claim to that person's last employer. Applications for unemployment insurance are made at one of the state's many employment development offices. The employer is asked to check the information that the claimant has provided, correct any errors or untrue statements, and give additional information if necessary.

A state unemployment counselor interviews the person filing a claim for unemployment benefits. Some of the questions asked by the counselor deal with personal history and employment background. However, the focus of the interview is to determine the reason why the claimant lost his or her job. Only claimants who are unemployed through no fault of their own are entitled to benefits. Claimants who have been discharged for misconduct or voluntarily quit do not receive unemployment benefits. As discussed already, when a jobless person applies for unemployment benefits, the state sends a notice to the person's last employer. This form allows the former employer to check the information given by the claimant and correct any inaccuracies. After a claim is approved, the state sends a second notice to the former employer showing the amount of benefits awarded to the jobless person.

Minimum and maximum weekly unemployment benefits differ from state to state. As of this writing, Hawaii provides benefits that range from a low of $5 per week to a high of $395 per week, while the range of weekly benefits in Illinois runs from $51 to $315. California pays a minimum of $40 per week and a maximum of $410 per week. (The maximum in California is scheduled to increase to $450 per week in 2005 and $490 per week in 2006.)

Employers must keep records that show each employee's starting and ending dates with the firm, the reason why an employee leaves a job, and other facts that may be needed by state authorities to determine eligibility for unemployment insurance benefits. Not only are employers required by law to keep this information, but it is in their best interests to do so in order to prevent the payment of unjustified claims and thereby develop a poor (and expensive) experience rating.

State Disability Insurance Tax

In some states, an employee who is unable to work because of an illness, injury, or accident that is not job related may be eligible to receive benefits from *state disability insurance (SDI)*. In Unit 5, you learned about the deduction for state disability insurance tax that is made in California. As of this writing, California, Hawaii, New Jersey, New York, and Rhode Island have laws that require disability insurance. Since the details of such laws vary, employers who are affected must become familiar with the rules regarding tax rates, payment schedules, and reporting procedures in their own state.

In some states, both employers and employees pay disability insurance tax. In other states, this tax is imposed entirely on employees; employers do not contribute. California is an example of a state where only the employees pay for disability insurance through a withholding tax. As of this writing, the rate for SDI tax in California is 1.18 percent (.0118) of the first $68,829 earned by each employee during a calendar year. Thus, the maximum withholding for this tax during a year would be $812.18. The employer must deduct SDI tax at the end of every payroll period until the employee reaches the maximum amount for the year. Periodically, the employer must remit the SDI tax collected to the state. In California, this is done by electronic funds transfer or by submitting a check and a completed payroll tax deposit coupon.

Each state has its own schedule of disability insurance benefits and its own rules for establishing eligibility for such benefits. There are many specific regulations that determine the amount of disability pay, the length of time for which payments will be made, and the disabilities covered. As of this writing, the maximum weekly disability insurance benefit in California is $728.

WORKERS' COMPENSATION INSURANCE

Sometimes a worker is injured on the job or develops an illness that is job related. *Workers' compensation insurance* was developed to protect employees and their families against the loss of income that results from job-related injuries, illnesses, or even death. Most states have laws requiring employers to provide workers' compensation insurance for their employees.

Many businesses obtain workers' compensation insurance by purchasing it from a private insurance company or by making payments to a state-operated insurance fund. However, some large companies have set up their own workers' compensation insurance plan with state approval.

Employers pay the full cost of workers' compensation insurance except in Oregon, Washington, and New Mexico, where employees must also contribute. The rates for this kind of insurance vary according to the types of jobs that employees hold. The more dangerous the work, the higher the rate. Thus, a manufacturing company would pay a higher rate for its factory employees than for its office employees.

There are different arrangements for handling the premiums on workers' compensation insurance, but one common practice is for employers to pay the insurance company an estimated premium at the beginning of each year. The estimated premium is based on the rate for each type of employee and the estimated amount of their wages for the year.

At the end of the year, the premium is adjusted according to the actual payroll for the year. If the estimated premium was too low, the firm pays an additional sum. If the estimated premium was too high, the firm receives a credit from the insurance company toward the next year's premium. Study the following example, which illustrates the calculation of the estimated and actual premiums for workers' compensation insurance at one firm.

An Example of Workers' Compensation Insurance

The Globe Manufacturing Company buys workers' compensation insurance from a private insurance company and pays a premium of $1.57 per $100 of wages for its office employees and $3.35 per $100 of wages for its factory employees. At the beginning of last year, the firm estimated its total premium for workers' compensation insurance as shown here:

Job Classification	Premium Rate	Estimated Total Wages	Estimated Premium
Office work	$1.57 per $100	$132,000	$ 2,072.40
Factory work	$3.35 per $100	985,000	32,997.50
Total estimated premium			$35,069.90

At the end of the year, the firm's payroll clerk determined the actual premium owed for workers' compensation insurance as shown below. Because the actual premium owed is greater than the estimated premium paid, a balance is due the insurance company. The firm therefore sends a check for this amount to the insurance company.

Job Classification	Premium Rate	Actual Total Wages	Actual Premium
Office work	$1.57 per $100	$138,000	$ 2,166.60
Factory work	$3.35 per $100	996,500	33,382.75
Total actual premium owed			$35,549.35
Less total estimated premium paid			35,069.90
Balance due insurance company			$ 479.45

Generally, firms whose employees have few job-related accidents or illnesses are able to obtain reduced rates for workers' compensation insurance. This arrangement is similar to the experience-rating system used to determine the rates for SUTA tax.

Learning Through Practice   Do Exercises 10.3 and 10.4 on pages 251 and 252 of this text-workbook.

SPECIAL STATE PAYROLL TAXES

Some states have special kinds of taxes that employers are required to pay, based on the amount of their payroll. For example, California imposes an Employment Training Tax (ETT), which is paid by employers on a quarterly basis. This tax is used by the state to finance training for both employed and unemployed workers. The rate of the ETT is 0.1 percent (.001) of the first $7,000 earned by each employee during a calendar year. Thus, the maximum ETT paid for each employee during a year is $7 ($7,000 × .001). This may seem like a minor amount, but the ETT can be significant for a large business. For example, one California bank has 50,000 employees. Its ETT for a year will therefore amount to $350,000 (50,000 × $7).

STATE INCOME TAX

State income taxes have become increasingly common. As of this writing, forty states, the District of Columbia, and Puerto Rico have laws requiring that individuals pay income tax on their wages and salaries and requiring that employers withhold this tax. The states without personal income tax withholding from employee earnings are Alaska, Connecticut, Florida, Nevada, New Hampshire, South Dakota, Tennessee, Texas, Washington, and Wyoming.

In Unit 5, you learned about the procedures for deducting state income tax from employee earnings. Of course, the rates used, the schedule for making deposits of the amounts withheld, and the tax forms to be filed vary from state to state. Thus, it is essential for payroll personnel to be aware of the income tax regulations in their own states.

Obtaining Information About State Income Tax

Most states publish a tax guide for employers. In states that require the withholding of income tax from employee earnings, these guides include tax tables and extensive information about income tax regulations. Increasingly, states also provide income tax information and forms over the Internet through Web sites that they maintain. Examples of questions about state income tax that are covered by the tax guide published by California are as follows:

- Should state income tax be withheld from the payment to a consultant who spends one week in a business in order to solve a particular problem?

- Are the payments made to an employee who is on sick leave because of an illness or injury subject to state income tax withholding?

- Is the cost of employer-financed group life insurance part of an employee's taxable income?
- Should state income tax be withheld from bonuses and profit-sharing payments made to employees?
- If a California employee earns one-third of her income in Nevada and the rest in California, must she pay California income tax on the entire earnings?

These situations illustrate just a few of the problems that a person who does payroll work might face. Solutions to such problems can generally be found in the employer's tax guide published by the state where the business is located. Most states also provide assistance over the telephone when payroll personnel have questions.

Tax regulations, even seemingly insignificant ones, change from time to time. Tax forms also change. For this reason, many states revise their tax guides for employers each year. It is essential that a payroll department always have available the current version of the employer's tax guide for its state.

California has a publication called *Sample Forms Guide,* which it issues each year. While this publication does not include all of the tax forms used by the state, it does show the most common forms with sample entries, which are very helpful to payroll employees.

Depositing and Reporting State Withholding and Payroll Taxes

The forms and procedures used to deposit and report the various withholding and payroll taxes differ from state to state. However, the deposit and reporting requirements in California are fairly typical. The payroll-related taxes that are remitted by businesses in California are:

- Unemployment Insurance (SUTA, which is called UI in California)
- Employment Training Tax (ETT)
- State Disability Insurance Tax (SDI)
- California Personal Income Tax (PIT)

In California, employers must deposit the SDI and PIT taxes withheld from employee earnings on a schedule that is determined by the schedule they follow for depositing federal employment taxes (federal income tax withheld, social security tax, and Medicare tax). For example, Ingram Heating and Cooling is a semiweekly depositor of federal employment taxes and is therefore a semiweekly depositor of California withholding taxes—SDI and PIT. Other firms must make deposits on the next banking day, monthly, or quarterly, depending on their federal deposit status. Employers must deposit UI and ETT taxes on a quarterly basis but may deposit these payroll taxes more often if they wish.

Some employers must make their deposits of SDI and PIT taxes by means of electronic funds transfer (EFT). As of this writing, employers who owed more than $20,000 of SDI and PIT taxes in the last lookback period (July 1 to June 30) are required to use EFT. Ingram Heating and Cooling falls into this category. Such employers are not required to make deposits of UI and ETT taxes by electronic funds transfer but are allowed to do so if they wish. Employers who are not obligated to make EFT deposits of SDI and PIT taxes may participate in the EFT system on a voluntary basis.

A special bulletin is available explaining how the EFT system in California works and what employers must do to join the system. The most basic requirement is to complete a form called the Electronic Funds Transfer Authorization Agreement. This form identifies the bank that will transfer deposits electronically from the employer's account to a state account. Both the employer and a bank official must sign the form.

Employers who are not required to use the EFT system or do not choose to do so voluntarily must make their deposits by issuing a check for the taxes owed and preparing California Form DE 88, Payroll Tax Deposit Coupon. The check and the completed Form DE 88 are sent to the Employment Development Department (EDD) in Sacramento in a

FIGURE 10.2 **Payroll Tax Deposit**

EDD Employment Development Department State of California

PAYROLL TAX DEPOSIT DE 88ALL (TYPE OR PRINT IN BLACK INK ONLY):

1. PAY DATE: MUST BE COMPLETED — 0 3 3 1 0 4 (Last PAY DATE covered by deposit)

2. DEPOSIT SCHEDULE: (MARK ONE BOX ONLY) — NEXT BANKING DAY [ ] SEMI-WEEKLY [ ] MONTHLY [X] QUARTERLY [ ]

STATE OF CALIFORNIA
EMPLOYMENT DEVELOPMENT DEPARTMENT
P O BOX 826276
SACRAMENTO, CA 94230-6276

Employer Name: GARY DRAKE
Employer DBA: T/A DRAKE TV REPAIR

Indicate your Account Number here; Please enter on your check: 621 7584 2

3. QUARTER COVERED: 0 4 1

EMPLOYMENT DEVELOPMENT DEPARTMENT

01880698

4. DEPOSIT AMOUNTS:

	Rate	Tax	Amount
A)	1.8%	UI	403.20
B)	0.1%	ETT	22.40
C)	1.18%	SDI	88.50
D)		California PIT	507.40
E)		Penalty	
F)		Interest	
G)		TOTAL PAID $	1021.50

PAY THIS AMOUNT
TOTAL LINES A THROUGH F.
DO NOT FOLD OR STAPLE.
Make check payable to EDD.

PREPARER'S SIGNATURE x *Gary Drake* TELEPHONE NO. (408) 523-7462

DEPARTMENT USE ONLY DE 88ALL Rev. 16 (1-04) (INTERNET)

CUT ALONG DASHED LINES

preprinted DE 88 envelope supplied by the state. The Form DE 88 shown above (Figure 10.2) was prepared by Drake TV Repair, a small firm that is a monthly depositor of SDI and PIT taxes. This deposit includes the UI and ETT taxes owed for the first quarter (Lines A and B) and the SDI and PIT taxes owed for the month of March (Lines C and D). Lines E and F were left blank because Drake does not owe any penalty or interest. Line G shows the total of the deposit.

California provides employers with preprinted copies of Form DE 88 in coupon books. It also provides preprinted mailing envelopes. Only employers who do not participate in the electronic funds transfer system use Form DE 88.

Due Dates for Depositing State Withholding and Payroll Taxes

As noted previously, employers in California are classified as next banking day, semiweekly, monthly, or quarterly depositors of state withholding taxes (SDI and PIT taxes) according to their status as depositors of federal employment taxes (federal income tax withheld, social security tax, and Medicare tax). If a next banking day, semiweekly, or monthly depositor of federal employment taxes owes *more than $500 in PIT taxes* when a federal deposit is due, the firm must deposit its SDI and PIT taxes with the state of California. If the employer owes $500 or less in PIT taxes, the undeposited amount is carried over to the next payroll period and added to the amount of PIT taxes owed on the next payday. As soon as the undeposited amount of PIT exceeds $500, a deposit of SDI and PIT taxes is made. For quarterly depositors of federal employment taxes, the SDI and PIT taxes owed at the end of a quarter must be sent to the state by the 15th of the following month if the PIT taxes total *$350 or more.* If the PIT taxes due are less than $350, the quarterly depositor must pay the SDI and PIT taxes by the end of the month following the close of the quarter (April 30, July 31, October 31, and January 31).

Turn back to Figure 9.2 on page 198 and Figure 9.3 on page 199 if you wish to review the semiweekly deposit schedule for federal employment taxes. The monthly deposit schedule is explained on page 196 in Unit 9.

The two payroll taxes that employers in California must pay—UI and ETT—are due on a quarterly basis. They must be deposited in the month following the close of the quarter. They are due on April 1, July 1, October 1, and January 1 and delinquent if not paid by

April 30, July 31, October 31, and January 31. As noted previously, employers are permitted to deposit UI and ETT taxes more often if they wish to do so. For example, a semi-weekly or monthly depositor may prefer to remit the UI and ETT taxes that it owes along with the state withholding taxes—SDI and PIT.

QUARTERLY WAGE AND WITHHOLDING REPORT

At the end of each quarter, California requires that employers prepare Form DE 6, Quarterly Wage and Withholding Report. The purpose of Form DE 6 is to provide information about the wages paid to each employee during the quarter and the California personal income tax (PIT) withheld from those wages. A portion of the Form DE 6 prepared by Ingram Heating and Cooling for the quarter ended March 31 is shown in Figure 10.3 on page 243. Notice that this form lists the name and social security number of each employee, the total wages paid to the employee, the wages subject to PIT, and the amount of PIT withheld. The due dates for filing Form DE 6 are April 1, July 1, October 1, and January 1. However, employers have some additional time to prepare this form. It is not considered delinquent if filed by the last day of the month following the close of each quarter—April 30, July 31, October 31, and January 31.

Form DE 6 *must be submitted* even if no wages were paid to employees during the quarter. Seven employees can be listed on one page of this form. Therefore, a business with more than seven employees must use multiple pages. It should be noted that all employees who worked at a firm during the quarter must be listed, even if they left the firm before the end of the quarter. Form DE 6 is easy to complete because the required information can be taken directly from the employee earnings records.

Firms that have a large number of employees—250 or more employees—must supply Form DE 6 on magnetic media, either magnetic disks or tape. Firms with fewer than 250 employees are permitted to file Form DE 6 on magnetic media if they wish and are now urged by California to do so.

ANNUAL RECONCILIATION STATEMENT

California requires that employers file Form DE 7, Annual Reconciliation Statement, at the end of the calendar year. This report is due on January 1 of each year and delinquent on January 31. The purpose of Form DE 7 is to reconcile the various state payroll and withholding taxes owed for the year with the amounts deposited during the year. Figure 10.4 on page 244 shows the Form DE 7 prepared by Ingram Heating and Cooling. Notice that it reports the total subject wages paid during the year, the amounts owed by the employer for state unemployment tax (UI) and employment training tax (ETT), the amounts withheld by the employer for state disability insurance tax (SDI) and California personal income tax (PIT), the total contributions (deposits) made during the year, and the amount of taxes due or overpaid at the end of the year.

WAGE AND TAX STATEMENTS

For many years, California required that employers submit a copy of a federal form—Form W-2, Wage and Tax Statement—for each employee at the end of the calendar year to report the state income tax withheld from the employee's earnings during the year. It is no longer necessary for employers to submit a copy of Form W-2 to California, but employers must continue to list state income tax on Form W-2. They must also list the California disability insurance tax withheld (CASDI). Refer to Figure 9.8 on page 206 in Unit 9 to see an example of a Form W-2 that includes California income tax and SDI tax.

Learning Through Practice   Do Exercises 10.5, 10.6, and 10.7 on pages 252–256 of this text-workbook.

FIGURE 10.3 **Quarterly Wage and Withholding Report**

LOCAL INCOME TAX

Some cities and counties impose an income tax of their own on residents and on people who work within their boundaries. The rules for deducting this tax, remitting the amounts withheld to the proper agency, and reporting information about the total wages and deductions for each employee vary from area to area. However, the general procedures are usually very similar to those used for state income tax.

FIGURE 10.4   **Annual Reconciliation Statement**

EDD Employment Development Department
State of California

ANNUAL RECONCILIATION STATEMENT

PLEASE TYPE THIS FORM - DO NOT ALTER PREPRINTED INFORMATION

00070104

YEAR ENDED DEC. 31, 2004 DUE JAN. 1, 2005   DELINQUENT IF NOT POSTMARKED OR RECEIVED BY   JAN. 31, 2005

YEAR 2004

EMPLOYER ACCOUNT NO.
315-3792-6

INGRAM HEATING AND COOLING
4466 MARITIME WAY
SAN JOSE, CA 95001

DEPT. USE ONLY

DO NOT ALTER THIS AREA

P1 P2 C P U S A

T

EFFECTIVE DATE   Mo.   Day   Yr.

FEIN   77-4621093

CHECK BOX IF:

A. NO WAGES PAID THIS YEAR ☐

B. OUT OF BUSINESS _____ ☐
Date

ADDITIONAL FEINS

C. TOTAL SUBJECT WAGES PAID THIS CALENDAR YEAR ➤ 814,527 63

D. UNEMPLOYMENT INSURANCE (UI) (Total Employee Wages up to $7,000 per employee per calendar year)

(D1) UI %		(D2) UI TAXABLE WAGES		(D3) UI CONTRIBUTIONS
2.1	TIMES	91,000 00	=	1,911 00

E EMPLOYMENT TRAINING TAX (ETT)

(E1) ETT %			(E2) ETT CONTRIBUTIONS
0.1	TIMES	UI Taxable Wages (D2) .... =	91 00

F. STATE DISABILITY INSURANCE (SDI) (Total Employee Wages up to $68,829 per employee per calendar year)

(F1) SDI %		(F2) SDI TAXABLE WAGES		(F3) SDI EMPLOYEE CONTRIBUTIONS WITHHELD
1.18	TIMES	386,144 00	=	4,556 50

PIT WITHHELD PER FORMS W-2 AND/OR 1099R

G. CALIFORNIA PERSONAL INCOME TAX (PIT) WITHHELD ➤ 29,963 96

H. **SUBTOTAL** (Add Items D3, E2, F3, and G) ➤ 36,522 46

I. LESS: CONTRIBUTIONS AND WITHHOLDINGS PAID FOR THE YEAR (**DO NOT** INCLUDE PENALTY AND INTEREST PAYMENTS) ➤ 36,522 46

J. TOTAL TAXES DUE OR OVERPAID (Item H minus Item I) ➤ 0

If amount due, prepare a Payroll Tax Deposit, DE 88, and mail to P.O. Box 826276, Sacramento, CA 94230-6276. Mailing payments with DE 7 delays payment processing and may result in an erroneous penalty and interest charges. **Mandatory EFT filers must remit all SDI/PIT deposits by EFT to avoid Non-Compliance Penalty.**

K. Be sure to sign this declaration: *I declare that the information herein is true and correct to the best of my knowledge and belief.*

Signature *William J. Ingram*   Title **President**   Phone (408) 222-4655   Date 1/12/05
(Owner, Accountant, Preparer, etc.)

SIGN AND MAIL TO: State of California / Employment Development Department / P.O. Box 826286 / Sacramento CA 94230-6286

DE 7 Rev. 4 (1-04) **(INTERNET)**   Page 1 of 2   CU

Internet Connection

You may wish to join in on a cyberspace chat about payroll taxes. To subscribe to this listserv, look up http://www.payroll-taxes.com.

Like state governments, many local governments that levy withholding or payroll taxes publish tax guides for employers. These guides provide detailed information about regulations, forms, and payment deadlines.

SETTING UP A PAYROLL CALENDAR

A calendar of payroll activities is an important tool for anyone who does payroll work. This is particularly true for a business that is on a semiweekly schedule for making deposits of federal and state taxes. Most businesses are responsible for completing a wide variety of payroll tasks, not the least of which are the preparation of numerous tax deposits and reports during the year. Even highly experienced payroll clerks may have difficulty remembering all of the dates for required tasks. In any case, tax deposits and reports are too important to trust to someone's memory, especially since government agencies charge a penalty for late payments and late filing of reports.

The surest way to avoid missing the correct date for making a tax deposit or filing a tax report is to set up and use a payroll calendar. It is helpful if this calendar also includes the dates when the payroll must be computed and checks must be issued. Consulting the payroll calendar on a daily basis helps personnel in the payroll department to manage their time well so that all tasks are taken care of on schedule. The calendar also allows payroll personnel to anticipate and plan for periods when the workload will be especially heavy.

A portion of the payroll calendar used by Ingram Heating and Cooling is shown in Figure 10.5 on page 246. Notice that the tasks involving federal tax deposits and reports are typed in capital letters, whereas the tasks involving state tax deposits and reports are underlined. A payroll calendar can be formatted in many different ways. The objective is to create a guide that provides the most help to members of the payroll department.

Also notice that the payroll calendar for Ingram Heating and Cooling contains separate dates for preparing and filing major tax returns, such as Form 941, Employer's Quarterly Federal Tax Return, and California Form DE 6, Quarterly Wage and Withholding Report. This procedure allows time to deal with any problems that may arise when preparing the tax returns and time to carefully check the completed tax returns and submit them to Mr. Ingram for his signature. A realistic payroll calendar provides time for checking the accuracy of payroll tax returns before they are filed.

FIGURE 10.5   **Payroll Calendar**

INGRAM HEATING AND COOLING
Payroll Calendar for 2005

Date	Task
Monday, January 9	Collect and total the time sheets for the week of January 1-7.
Tuesday, January 10	Compute and record the payroll for the week of January 1-7.
Wednesday, January 11	Issue and distribute the paychecks for the week of January 1-7.
Monday, January 16	MAKE AN ELECTRONIC FUNDS TRANSFER DEPOSIT OF FEDERAL INCOME TAX WITHHELD, SOCIAL SECURITY TAX, AND MEDICARE TAX FOR THE PAYROLL OF JANUARY 1-7.
Monday, January 16	Make an electronic funds transfer deposit of California disability insurance tax withheld and personal income tax withheld for the payroll of January 1-7.
Monday, April 1	Total the employee earnings records for the quarter ended March 31.
Tuesday, April 2	PREPARE FORM 941, EMPLOYER'S QUARTERLY FEDERAL TAX RETURN, AND SCHEDULE B, EMPLOYER'S RECORD OF FEDERAL TAX LIABILITY.
Wednesday, April 3	Prepare California Form DE 6, Quarterly Wage and Withholding Report.
Wednesday, April 10	FILE FORM 941 AND SCHEDULE B, WHICH ARE DUE BY APRIL 30.
Wednesday, April 10	File California Form DE 6, which is due by April 30.

UNIT 10 REVIEW

Summary

This unit provided you with a fundamental understanding of the procedures for computing state payroll taxes, depositing state payroll and withholding taxes, and preparing state payroll tax reports. After studying this unit, you should be able to:

- Explain how state unemployment compensation systems work.
- Calculate SUTA tax and other state payroll taxes.
- Explain the deposit procedures for state payroll and withholding taxes.
- Prepare a deposit form for state payroll and withholding taxes.
- Understand workers' compensation insurance and know how to calculate the estimated and actual premiums.
- Prepare quarterly and annual forms reporting state payroll and withholding taxes.
- Explain the use of a payroll calendar.

Study Questions

1. What is the purpose of the SUTA tax?
2. What is the purpose of the disability insurance tax imposed by some states?
3. What is the purpose of the workers' compensation insurance that employers purchase?
4. What must a worker who loses his or her job do in order to obtain unemployment benefits?
5. Who pays the SUTA tax?
6. The federal unemployment insurance system allows employers to claim a credit for the SUTA tax they pay. This credit reduces the amount of FUTA tax owed. What is the current maximum credit that employers can claim?
7. The California system for handling claims for unemployment insurance benefits is typical of those used in many other states. Explain the procedures used in California.
8. What kinds of information are employers required to keep for SUTA purposes?
9. In many states, employers can obtain workers' compensation insurance by purchasing it from a private insurance company or by making payments to a state-operated insurance fund. Explain how the premium for this type of insurance is computed at the beginning of each year and how it is adjusted at the end of the year.
10. Most states require employers to make periodic deposits of SUTA tax and to report this tax on payroll tax forms. Briefly explain the procedures involved. Use California as an example.

Discussion Questions

1. Check the unemployment insurance law in your state to determine the following:
   a. What are the eligibility requirements for receiving unemployment benefits?
   b. What are the minimum and maximum weekly benefits paid to unemployed workers?
   c. What procedures must an unemployed worker follow to receive benefits?
   d. What actions, if any, can unemployed workers who have been denied benefits take to have their cases reconsidered?
2. Check the employer experience-rating plan used in your state to determine the following:
   a. How is the SUTA tax rate determined by a new employer?
   b. What is the wage base for the SUTA tax?
   c. What is the lowest SUTA tax rate? The highest SUTA tax rate?
   d. What are the employer's responsibilities for paying and reporting SUTA tax?

3. If your state has an income tax law, investigate this law and then answer the following questions:

   a. Must employers withhold the state income tax?

   b. Are all wage payments subject to the withholding of state income tax?

   c. What are the requirements for depositing state income tax?

   d. What kinds of information about state income tax must employers keep in their records?

REVIEW EXERCISES

1. During the past year, $572,050 of the payroll at the North Star Publishing Company was subject to unemployment tax. Compute the FUTA and SUTA taxes that the firm owes. The SUTA rate for the year is 2.2 percent, and the FUTA rate is 0.8 percent.

2. The Atlas Office Cleaning Service had a total payroll of $377,400 last year. Of this amount, $248,200 was exempt from both federal and state unemployment taxes. Compute the FUTA and SUTA taxes owed for the year. Use 2.6 percent as the SUTA rate and 0.8 as the FUTA rate.

3. During the past year, Eileen Monahan earned $37,500 as a marketing representative for the Hudson Medical Supply Company. This firm has a SUTA rate of 2.5 percent on the first $9,000 paid to each employee and a FUTA rate of 0.8 percent on the first $7,000 paid to each employee.

   a. Compute the FUTA and SUTA taxes that the firm owes on the salary of Eileen Monahan.

   b. Assume that the Hudson Medical Supply Company now has a SUTA rate of 3.2 percent because of a less favorable experience rating. Compute the SUTA tax that the firm owes for Eileen Monahan at this higher rate.

4. Vista Electronics paid the following wages to four production employees during the first quarter of the current year: Peter Colby, $7,240; Ellen D'Angelo, $8,165; Gail Grant, $6,920; and John Ortiz, $6,880. The state in which the firm is located has a yearly SUTA wage base of $7,000, which is the same as the yearly FUTA wage base. The firm's favorable experience rating resulted in a SUTA rate of 1.7 percent for the current year. The FUTA rate is 0.8 percent.

   a. Of the total wages paid during the first quarter, what amount is subject to FUTA and SUTA taxes?

   b. How much does the firm owe for FUTA tax? for SUTA tax?

5. Every January, Concord Steel Products must make a payment to the workers' compensation insurance fund operated by its state. The payment is based on the estimated wages of its employees for the year. The rates are $0.15 per $100 of wages for office employees and $1.20 per $100 of wages for factory employees. For the current year, the firm estimates that the wages of its office employees will total $160,000 and the wages of its factory employees will total $970,000. Compute the total amount of the estimated premium that the firm must pay for workers' compensation insurance in January.

6. The payroll records of Concord Steel Products at the end of the year show that the firm actually paid $156,000 to its office employees and $975,000 to its factory employees.

   a. Use the rates given in Review Exercise 5 to determine the amount of the actual premium for workers' compensation insurance that the firm owes at the end of the year.

   b. What is the difference between the estimated premium that was paid and the actual premium owed? Is this amount a balance due the insurance fund or a balance due the firm?

7. Glen Ridge Executive Travel is a firm that makes travel arrangements for corporate managers. It buys workers' compensation insurance for its staff from the Midland Insurance Company. It pays $0.22 per $100 of salaries for all employees. Last year, Glen Ridge estimated that its employees would earn $425,000 in the current year. Compute the estimated premium for workers' compensation insurance.

8. At the end of the current year, payroll records show that the actual earnings of the employees of Glen Ridge Executive Travel totaled $419,000. Use the rate for workers' compensation insurance given in Review Exercise 7 to compute the actual premium owed for the year and the credit that is due the firm from its insurance company.

9. For the coming year, Glen Ridge Executive Travel expects that its employees will earn $450,000. Using the rate given in Review Exercise 7, compute the estimated premium for the year. Then, apply the credit found in Review Exercise 8 to the estimated premium in order to determine the amount of the check that the firm must send to its insurance company.

10. Ray's Donut Shop has two full-time employees and two part-time employees who are paid on a weekly basis. The state where the business is located requires it to withhold both a state income tax and a state disability insurance tax from employee earnings. The rate of the income tax is 2 percent, and the rate of the disability insurance tax is 0.5 percent. During the week ended December 14, the shop's employees had the earnings shown below. Compute the amounts to be deducted from each employee's earnings for state income tax and state disability insurance tax.

Employee	Weekly Earnings
Kerry Jones	$385
Julie O'Donnell	167
Nina Ravinski	442
Scott Sanders	136

Problems

1. Bayshore Restaurant Design is located in the San Francisco Bay Area of California. During the past year, the firm paid the following salaries and withheld the following amounts of state income tax.

Employee	Yearly Salary	State Income Tax Withheld
Karen Morita, president	$102,320	$3,912.34
David Shaw, architect	78,500	2,314.92
Lynn Katz, interior designer	63,270	1,359.84
Paul McNair, project coordinator	37,800	524.64
Tracy Nelson, secretary	32,750	351.84
Garth Adams, design trainee	25,680	322.62

a. Compute the amount of state disability insurance (SDI) tax withheld from each employee's earnings during the year. Use a rate of 1.18 percent. The yearly wage base is $68,829 for each employee.

b. Compute the amount of SUTA tax that the firm owed for the year. Use a rate of 2.1 percent. The yearly wage base is $7,000 for each employee.

c. At the end of each year, the firm must file a tax return that reports the SUTA tax owed, the state income tax withheld, and the SDI tax withheld during the year. This tax return also reconciles the amounts owed with the tax deposits that the firm made throughout the year. Compute the total of the SUTA tax owed, state income tax withheld, and SDI tax withheld during the year.

d. The firm's deposits of SUTA tax, state income tax, and SDI tax during the year totaled $13,174.66. Does the firm owe any tax at the end of the year? If so, how much?

2. The following table shows the gross earnings of the full-time and part-time employees of the Delta Drugstore during the past year.

Employee	Gross Earnings
Cheryl Cook	$38,250
Roger Devane	41,700
Bonnie Kemp	6,240
Joyce Kessler	25,310
Darren Long	5,800
Joseph Vecchio	6,900

a. The business is located in a state that levies an income tax of 2 percent on employee earnings. How much did the business withhold from the earnings of each employee last year for state income tax?

b. The city where the business is located levies an income tax of 1.2 percent on employee earnings. How much did the business withhold from the earnings of each employee last year for city income tax?

c. The business must pay SUTA tax of 2.7 percent on the first $7,000 earned by each employee during the calendar year. How much SUTA tax did the business owe last year?

d. Compute the total wages paid, the total state income tax withheld, and the total city income tax withheld. The business must report each of these amounts on an end-of-year state tax return.

e. The business deposits the SUTA tax owed, the state income tax withheld, and the city income tax withheld with a state agency. (This agency sends the city income tax to a city agency periodically.) During the past year, the business made deposits totaling $5,052.78. Compute the total of the SUTA tax owed, the state income tax withheld, and the city income tax withheld. Does the business owe any balance to the state at the end of the year? If so, how much?

Unit 10 Exercises

EXERCISE 10.1

During the second quarter of the current year, the Hilltop Hotel paid wages of $229,570. Of this sum, $98,220 was subject to FUTA tax and $112,760 was subject to SUTA tax. (The state where Hilltop is located has a higher wage base for unemployment tax than the federal government does.) Compute the amounts that the business owes for FUTA tax and SUTA tax at the end of the quarter. Use 0.8 percent as the FUTA rate and 3.1 percent as the SUTA rate.

FUTA tax owed $_____

SUTA tax owed $_____

EXERCISE 10.2

The Green Thumb Lawn Care Service paid the following wages to its full-time and part-time employees during the first quarter of the current year.

Employee	Wages for Quarter	Employee	Wages for Quarter
John Alioto	$7,250	Eric Lindahl	$4,320
Brian Casey	3,890	Sally Werner	7,460
Ann Douglas	5,600	Roy Yamaguchi	7,500

The state where the firm is located has a yearly wage base of $7,000 for SUTA tax, which is the same as the yearly wage base for FUTA tax. Determine the total amount of wages for the quarter that was subject to unemployment taxes. Then compute the amounts that the firm owes for FUTA tax and SUTA tax at the end of the quarter. Use 0.8 percent as the FUTA rate and 1.9 percent as the SUTA rate.

Total taxable wages $_____

FUTA tax owed $_____

SUTA tax owed $_____

EXERCISE 10.3

Dairy Rich Products, a maker of ice cream and frozen yogurt, buys workers' compensation insurance from the Reliable Insurance Company. It pays a premium of $0.17 per $100 of wages for its office employees and $1.30 per $100 of wages for its factory employees. The firm estimates that the total wages of its office employees in the upcoming year will be $150,000 and the total wages of its factory employees will be $840,000. Compute the estimated premium due for workers' compensation insurance in the upcoming year.

Estimated premium for office employees $_____

Estimated premium for factory employees   _____

Total estimated premium $_____

EXERCISE 10.4

At the end of the year, the payroll records of Dairy Rich Products showed that the firm actually paid total wages of $162,500 to its office employees and total wages of $837,400 to its factory employees. Use the rates given in Exercise 10.3 to compute the actual premium owed for workers' compensation insurance for the year.

Actual premium for office employees $_____

Actual premium for factory employees   _____

Total actual premium $_____

Compare the total actual premium found in Exercise 10.4 with the total estimated premium found in Exercise 10.3. Determine the difference. Is this difference a payment owed to the insurance company or a credit owed to the firm? Use a check mark to indicate your answer.

Estimated premium paid	$ _____
Actual premium owed	_____
Difference	$ _____
Payment owed to insurance company	_____
Credit owed to firm	_____

EXERCISE 10.5

Market Advisers, a market research firm, is located in San Diego, California. It has six employees and pays them on a monthly basis. The following table shows their gross earnings and deductions for state taxes during the first two months of the current year. The firm made a deposit of the taxes withheld in January and must now deposit the taxes withheld in February. Prepare California Form DE 88, Payroll Tax Deposit Coupon, to accompany the deposit. This form appears below. Enter the payroll date of 02/28 and the last two digits of the current year. Use an *X* to indicate the payment type (Monthly). In the box for payment quarter, enter the last two digits of the year followed by the number 1 for the first quarter. Enter the amount of SDI tax withheld on line C and the amount of state income tax withheld on line D (California PIT). Enter the total of the deposit on line G. Enter the firm's telephone number, which is 619-555-2767. Leave the signature line blank. Martin DeSantis, the president, will sign the form.

Employee No.	January Gross Earnings	January SDI Tax	January State Income Tax	February Gross Earnings	February SDI Tax	February State Income Tax
1	$3,160	$37.29	$ 51.05	$3,160	$37.29	$ 51.05
2	2,240	26.43	16.30	2,370	27.97	18.70
3	5,120	60.42	168.91	5,120	60.42	168.91
4	3,800	44.84	83.32	3,800	44.84	83.32
5	3,350	39.53	58.25	3,350	39.53	58.25
6	2,470	29.15	22.25	2,540	29.97	24.65

EXERCISE 10.5 **Payroll Tax Deposit**

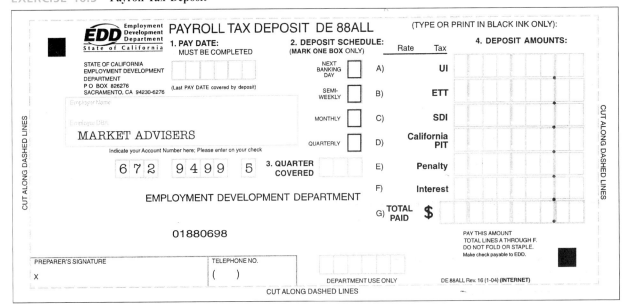

EXERCISE 10.6

During March of the current year, the employees of Market Advisers had the gross earnings and deductions for state taxes that are shown below. Use this information and the information for January and February given in Exercise 10.5 to prepare California Form DE 6, Quarterly Wage and Withholding Report. This form appears on page 254.

- In Section A, enter 6 as the number of employees for the first, second, and third months.
- Enter the social security number and name of each employee. Omit dashes in the social security numbers, and write the names in capital letters. Enter the total wages paid to each employee during the quarter in the boxes for Total Subject Wages and PIT Wages. (PIT is an abbreviation for "personal income tax.") Do not use commas in the amounts. Enter the total state income tax withheld from the earnings of each employee.
- At the bottom of the form, enter the total of all wages paid during the quarter in the boxes for Total Subject Wages This Page and Total PIT Wages This Page (Boxes J and K). Enter the total state income tax withheld from all employees during the quarter in Box L. Enter the same three amounts in the boxes for the grand totals (Boxes M, N, and O). Do not use commas in the amounts.
- The form will be signed by Martin DeSantis, the president. The date of the form is April 20 of the current year. The firm's telephone number is 619-555-2767.

Employee No.	Name	Social Security No.	March Gross Earnings	March SDI Tax	March State Income Tax
1	Drew T. Ames	068-58-9943	$3,280	$38.70	$ 55.85
2	Lisa J. Bailey	327-41-6275	2,330	27.49	18.70
3	Martin H. DeSantis	189-33-8692	5,120	60.42	168.91
4	Ruth P. Niles	259-06-5777	3,800	44.84	83.32
5	Paul A. Shimura	082-79-3401	3,350	39.53	58.25
6	Joan R. Zelesko	274-23-1668	2,520	29.74	24.65

Market Advisers does not have to report information about state unemployment tax on Form DE 6, but it must deposit any SUTA tax owed for the quarter after the end of March. The first $7,000 of wages paid to each employee during a calendar year are subject to SUTA tax. The firm has a SUTA rate of 1.5 percent for the current year. Determine the total amount of taxable wages for the quarter and the amount of SUTA tax owed.

Total taxable wages for SUTA $ _____

SUTA tax owed for quarter $ _____

EXERCISE 10.7

At the end of each year, Market Advisers must prepare California Form DE 7, Annual Reconciliation Statement, to report the SUTA (UI) tax owed, the employment training tax (ETT) owed, the state disability insurance (SDI) tax withheld, and the state income tax (PIT) withheld during the year (see page 255). This form also reports the total of all deposits made during the year and any taxes due or taxes overpaid as of the end of the year. The firm's payroll records show the following information. Compute the total wages paid in the first quarter from the amounts given in Exercises 10.5 and 10.6.

SUTA and ETT taxable wages for year, $42,000   SUTA rate, 1.5 percent
SDI taxable wages for year, $244,000   ETT rate, 0.1 percent
Total wages paid in second quarter, $60,760   SDI rate, 1.18 percent
Total wages paid in third quarter, $61,220   SUTA wage base, $7,000
Total wages paid in fourth quarter, $61,140   SDI wage base, $68,829
Total state income tax withheld, $5,158.56
Total deposits of state taxes, $8,709.76

Exercise continues on page 256.

EXERCISE 10.6 **Quarterly Wage and Withholding Report**

EDD Employment Development Department
State of California

QUARTERLY WAGE AND WITHHOLDING REPORT

PLEASE TYPE THIS FORM PER INSTRUCTIONS ON REVERSE
You must FILE this report even if you had no payroll. If you had no payroll, complete Items C or D and P.

Page number __1__ of __1__

00060198

YR	QTR
0 4	1

QUARTER ENDED March 31, 2004 DUE April 1, 2004

DELINQUENT IF NOT POSTMARKED OR RECEIVED BY April 30, 2004

EMPLOYER ACCOUNT NO.
6 7 2 9 4 9 9 5

MARKET ADVISERS
557 MISSION DRIVE
SAN DIEGO, CA 92108

DO NOT ALTER THIS AREA

P1 ☐   C ☐   T ☐   S ☐   W ☐   A ☐

EFFECTIVE DATE
Mo.   Day   Yr.   WIC

A. **EMPLOYEES** full time and part time who worked during or received pay subject to UI for payroll period **which includes the 12th** of the month.

1st Mo.   2nd Mo.   3rd Mo.

B. ☐ Check this box if you are reporting ONLY Voluntary Plan DI wages on this page. Report PIT Wages and PIT Withheld, if appropriate. (See instructions for Item B.)

C. ☐ NO PAYROLL   D. ☐ OUT OF BUSINESS / FINAL REPORT

Date _____

E. SOCIAL SECURITY NUMBER   F. EMPLOYEE NAME (FIRST NAME)   (M.I.) (LAST NAME)
G. TOTAL SUBJECT WAGES   H. PIT WAGES   I. PIT WITHHELD

E. SOCIAL SECURITY NUMBER   F. EMPLOYEE NAME (FIRST NAME)   (M.I.) (LAST NAME)
G. TOTAL SUBJECT WAGES   H. PIT WAGES   I. PIT WITHHELD

E. SOCIAL SECURITY NUMBER   F. EMPLOYEE NAME (FIRST NAME)   (M.I.) (LAST NAME)
G. TOTAL SUBJECT WAGES   H. PIT WAGES   I. PIT WITHHELD

E. SOCIAL SECURITY NUMBER   F. EMPLOYEE NAME (FIRST NAME)   (M.I.) (LAST NAME)
G. TOTAL SUBJECT WAGES   H. PIT WAGES   I. PIT WITHHELD

E. SOCIAL SECURITY NUMBER   F. EMPLOYEE NAME (FIRST NAME)   (M.I.) (LAST NAME)
G. TOTAL SUBJECT WAGES   H. PIT WAGES   I. PIT WITHHELD

E. SOCIAL SECURITY NUMBER   F. EMPLOYEE NAME (FIRST NAME)   (M.I.) (LAST NAME)
G. TOTAL SUBJECT WAGES   H. PIT WAGES   I. PIT WITHHELD

E. SOCIAL SECURITY NUMBER   F. EMPLOYEE NAME (FIRST NAME)   (M.I.) (LAST NAME)
G. TOTAL SUBJECT WAGES   H. PIT WAGES   I. PIT WITHHELD

J. TOTAL SUBJECT WAGES THIS PAGE   K. TOTAL PIT WAGES THIS PAGE   L. TOTAL PIT WITHHELD THIS PAGE

M. GRAND TOTAL SUBJECT WAGES   N. GRAND TOTAL PIT WAGES   O. GRAND TOTAL PIT WITHHELD

P. *I declare that the information herein is true and correct to the best of my knowledge and belief.*

Preparer's Signature _____ Title _____ Phone ( ) _____ Date _____
(Owner, Accountant, Preparer, etc.)

DE 6   Rev. 4 (2-04)   MAIL TO: State of California / Employment Development Department / P.O. Box 826288 / Sacramento, CA 94230-6288

EXERCISE 10.7   **Annual Reconciliation Statement**

EDD Employment Development Department
State of California

ANNUAL RECONCILIATION STATEMENT

PLEASE TYPE THIS FORM - DO NOT ALTER PREPRINTED INFORMATION

00070104

YEAR ENDED December 31, 2004   DUE January 1, 2005   DELINQUENT IF NOT POSTMARKED OR RECEIVED BY January 31, 2005

YEAR
2004

EMPLOYER ACCOUNT NO.
672-9499-5

MARKET ADVISERS
557 MISSION DRIVE
SAN DIEGO, CA 92108

DEPT. USE ONLY

DO NOT ALTER THIS AREA

P1	P2	C	P	U	S	A

T

EFFECTIVE DATE   Mo.   Day   Yr.

FEIN   **48-3584121**

ADDITIONAL FEINS

CHECK BOX IF:

A. NO WAGES PAID THIS YEAR ☐

B. OUT OF BUSINESS _____ ☐
Date

C. TOTAL SUBJECT WAGES PAID THIS CALENDAR YEAR ⟶

D. UNEMPLOYMENT INSURANCE (UI)   (Total Employee Wages up to   per employee per calendar year)

(D1) UI %   TIMES   (D2) UI TAXABLE WAGES   = (D3) UI CONTRIBUTIONS

E EMPLOYMENT TRAINING TAX (ETT)

(E1) ETT %   TIMES   UI Taxable Wages (D2) ....   = (E2) ETT CONTRIBUTIONS

F. STATE DISABILITY INSURANCE (SDI)   (Total Employee Wages up to $ per employee per calendar year)

(F1) SDI %   TIMES   (F2) SDI TAXABLE WAGES   = (F3) SDI EMPLOYEE CONTRIBUTIONS WITHHELD

G. CALIFORNIA PERSONAL INCOME TAX (PIT) WITHHELD ⟶   PIT WITHHELD PER FORMS W-2 AND/OR 1099R

H. **SUBTOTAL** (Add Items D3, E2, F3, and G) ⟶

I. LESS: CONTRIBUTIONS AND WITHHOLDINGS PAID FOR THE YEAR (**DO NOT** INCLUDE PENALTY AND INTEREST PAYMENTS) ⟶

J. TOTAL TAXES DUE OR OVERPAID (Item H minus Item I) ⟶

If amount due, prepare a Payroll Tax Deposit, DE 88, and mail to P.O. Box 826276, Sacramento, CA 94230-6276. Mailing payments with DE 7 delays payment processing and may result in an erroneous penalty and interest charges. **Mandatory EFT filers must remit all SDI/PIT deposits by EFT to avoid Non-Compliance Penalty.**

K. Be sure to sign this declaration: *I declare that the information herein is true and correct to the best of my knowledge and belief.*

Signature _____   Title _____   Phone (___) _____   Date _____
(Owner, Accountant, Preparer, etc.)

SIGN AND MAIL TO: State of California / Employment Development Department / P.O. Box 826286 / Sacramento CA 94230-6286

DE 7 Rev. 4 (1-04) **(INTERNET)**   Page 1 of 2   CU

(Continued from Exercise 10.7 on page 253.)

Use the following procedures to complete Form DE 7.

- On Line C, enter the total wages for the year.
- On Line D, enter $7,000 next to "Total Employee Wages up to." Enter the SUTA (UI) rate and SUTA (UI) taxable wages. Compute and enter the amount of SUTA tax owed for the year.
- On Line E, enter the ETT rate. Compute and enter the amount of ETT tax owed for the year.
- On Line F, enter $68,829 next to "Total Employee Wages up to." Enter the SDI rate and the SDI taxable wages. Compute and enter the amount of SDI tax owed for the year.
- On Line G, enter the total state income tax withheld for the year.
- Add the amounts in Boxes D3, E2, and F3 and on Line G. Enter the total of the four amounts on Line H.
- Enter the total of the deposits for the year on Line I.
- Subtract the total of the deposits on Line I from the total of the state taxes owed on Line H. If the two amounts are equal, enter a zero on Line J. If there is a difference, enter the amount on Line J.
- Leave the signature line blank. Martin DeSantis, the president, will sign the form. The firm's telephone number is 619/538-2767. The date of the form is January 20 of the current year.

Alternate Learning Through Practice Exercises

Unit 10 Exercises

EXERCISE 10.1A

During the second quarter of the current year, the Playland Amusement Park paid wages of $464,230. Of this sum, $195,610 was subject to FUTA tax and $226,470 was subject to SUTA tax. (The state where Playland is located has a higher wage base for unemployment tax than the federal government does.) Compute the amounts that the business owes for FUTA tax and SUTA tax at the end of the quarter. Use 0.8 percent as the FUTA rate and 3.2 percent as the SUTA rate.

FUTA tax owed $_____

SUTA tax owed $_____

EXERCISE 10.2A

The Crossroads Convenience Store paid the following wages to its full-time and part-time employees during the first quarter of the current year.

Employee	Wages for Quarter	Employee	Wages for Quarter
Peter Arnez	$8,160	Joyce Lee	$7,610
Scott Carlson	4,570	David Rybak	4,200
Maria DePaulo	7,250	Corey Thomas	5,340

The state where the firm is located has a yearly wage base of $7,000 for SUTA tax, which is the same as the yearly wage base for FUTA tax. Determine the total amount of wages for the quarter that was subject to unemployment taxes. Then compute the amounts that the firm owes for FUTA tax and SUTA tax at the end of the quarter. Use 0.8 percent as the FUTA rate and 1.5 percent as the SUTA rate.

Total taxable wages $_____

FUTA tax owed $_____

SUTA tax owed $_____

EXERCISE 10.3A

Evergreen Office Products, a maker of pads, file folders, and stationery, buys workers' compensation insurance from the Allied Insurance Company. It pays a premium of $0.20 per $100 of wages for its office employees and $1.40 per $100 of wages for the employees who work in its paper mills. The firm estimates that the total wages of its office employees in the upcoming year will be $425,000 and the total wages of its mill employees will be $3,600,000. Compute the estimated premium due for workers' compensation insurance in the upcoming year.

Estimated premium for office employees $_____

Estimated premium for mill employees   _____

Total estimated premium $_____

Exercise 10.4A

At the end of the year, the payroll records of Evergreen Office Products showed that the firm actually paid total wages of $418,000 to its office employees and total wages of $3,605,000 to its mill employees. Use the rates given in Exercise 10.3A to compute the actual premium owed for workers' compensation insurance for the year.

Actual premium for office employees $_____

Actual premium for mill employees   _____

Total actual premium $_____

Compare the total actual premium found in Exercise 10.4A with the total estimated premium found in Exercise 10.3A. Determine the difference. Is this difference a payment owed to the insurance company or a credit owed to the firm? Use a check mark to indicate your answer.

Estimated premium paid $_____

Actual premium owed   _____

Difference $_____

Payment owed to insurance company   _____

Credit owed to firm   _____

EXERCISE 10.5A

Lawton Associates, a public relations firm, is located in San Diego, California. It has six employees and pays them on a monthly basis. The following table shows their gross earnings and deductions for state taxes during the first two months of the current year. The firm made a deposit of the taxes withheld in January and must now deposit the taxes withheld in February. Prepare California Form DE 88, Payroll Tax Deposit, to accompany the deposit. This form appears below. Enter the payroll date of 02/28 and the last two digits of the current year. Use an *X* to indicate the payment type (monthly). In the box for payment quarter, enter the last two digits of the year followed by the number 1 for the first quarter. Enter the amount of SDI tax withheld on line C and the amount of state income tax withheld on line D (California PIT). Enter the total of the deposit on line G. Enter the firm's telephone number, which is 619–434–1656. Leave the signature line blank. Alice Lawton, the president, will sign the firm.

Employee No.	January Gross Earnings	January SDI Tax	January State Income Tax	February Gross Earnings	February SDI Tax	February State Income Tax
1	$3,520	$41.54	$ 67.90	$3,520	$41.54	$ 67.90
2	2,740	32.33	77.14	2,830	33.39	83.42
3	6,150	72.57	230.14	6,150	72.57	230.14
4	3,600	42.48	70.30	3,600	42.48	70.30
5	4,220	49.80	101.46	4,220	49.80	101.46
6	2,910	34.34	91.42	2,970	35.05	91.42

EXERCISE 10.5A   **Payroll Tax Deposit**

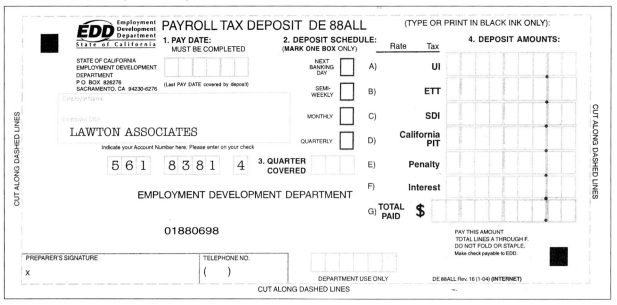

EXERCISE 10.6A

During March of the current year, the employees of Lawton Associates had the gross earnings and deductions for state taxes that are shown below. Use this information and the information for January and February given in Exercise 10.5A to prepare California Form DE 6, Quarterly Wage and Withholding Report. This form appears on page 260.

- In Section A, enter 6 as the number of employees for the first, second, and third months.
- Enter the social security number and name of each employee. Omit dashes in the social security numbers, and write the names in capital letters. Enter the total wages paid to each employee during the quarter in the boxes for Total Subject Wages and PIT Wages. (PIT is an abbreviation for "personal income tax.") Do not use commas in the amounts. Enter the total state income tax withheld from the earnings of each employee.
- At the bottom of the form, enter the total of all wages paid during the quarter in the boxes for Total Subject Wages This Page and Total PIT Wages This Page (Boxes J and K). Enter the total state income tax withheld from all employees during the quarter in Box L. Enter the same three amounts in the boxes for the grand totals (Boxes M, N, and O). Do not use commas in the amounts.
- The form will be signed by Alice Lawton, the president. The date of the form is April 22 of the current year. The firm's telephone number is 619–434–1656.

Employee No.	Name	Social Security No.	March Gross Earnings	March SDI Tax	March State Income Tax
1	Doris M. Bauer	057–46–8832	$3,520	$41.54	$ 67.90
2	Jeffrey A. Bernal	216–30–5164	2,790	32.92	77.14
3	Alice T. Lawton	078–22–7581	6,150	72.57	230.14
4	Ryan S. Tucker	148–15–4626	3,710	43.78	75.90
5	James R. Walsh	193–81–4512	4,220	49.80	101.46
6	Dana C. Zerin	385–34–2779	2,940	34.69	91.42

Lawton Associates does not have to report information about state unemployment tax on Form DE 6, but it must deposit any SUTA tax owed for the quarter after the end of March. The first $7,000 of wages paid to each employee during a calendar year are subject to SUTA tax. The firm has a SUTA rate of 1.3 percent for the current year. Determine the total amount of taxable wages for the quarter and the amount of SUTA tax owed.

Total taxable wages for SUTA $_____

SUTA tax owed for quarter $_____

EXERCISE 10.7A

At the end of each year, Lawton Associates must prepare California Form DE 7, Annual Reconciliation Statement, to report the SUTA (UI) tax owed, the employment training tax (ETT) owed, the state disability insurance (SDI) tax withheld, and the state income tax (PIT) withheld during the year (see page 261). This form also reports the total of all deposits made during the year and any taxes due or taxes overpaid as of the end of the year. The firm's payroll records show the following information. Compute the total wages paid in the first quarter from the amounts given in Exercises 10.5A and 10.6A.

SUTA and ETT taxable wages for the year, $42,000
SDI taxable wages for the year, $278,539
Total wages paid in the second quarter, $71,540
Total wages paid in the third quarter, $70,990
Total wages paid in the fourth quarter, $71,220
Total state income tax withheld, $7,824.88
Total deposits of state taxes, $11,699.64

SUTA rate, 1.3 percent
ETT rate, 0.1 percent
SDI rate, 1.18 percent
SUTA wage base, $7,000
SDI wage base, $68,829

Exercise continues on page 262.

EXERCISE 10.6A   **Quarterly Wage and Withholding Report**

EDD Employment Development Department
State of California

QUARTERLY WAGE AND WITHHOLDING REPORT

PLEASE TYPE THIS FORM PER INSTRUCTIONS ON REVERSE
You must FILE this report even if you had no payroll. If you had no payroll, complete Items C or D and P.

Page number __1__ of __1__

00060198

YR	QTR
0 4	1

QUARTER ENDED March 31, 2004 DUE April 1, 2004   DELINQUENT IF NOT POSTMARKED OR RECEIVED BY April 30, 2004

EMPLOYER ACCOUNT NO.
5 6 1 8 3 8 1 4

LAWTON ASSOCIATES
752 GATEWAY PLAZA
SAN DIEGO, CA 92108

DO NOT ALTER THIS AREA
Pt ☐ C ☐ T ☐ S ☐ W ☐ A ☐
EFFECTIVE DATE
Mo.   Day   Yr.   WIC

A. **EMPLOYEES** full time and part time who worked during or received pay subject to UI for payroll period **which includes the 12th** of the month.
1st Mo.   2nd Mo.   3rd Mo.

B. ☐ Check this box if you are reporting ONLY Voluntary Plan DI wages on this page. Report PIT Wages and PIT Withheld, if appropriate. (See instructions for Item B.)

C. ☐ NO PAYROLL   D. ☐ OUT OF BUSINESS / FINAL REPORT
Date _____

E. SOCIAL SECURITY NUMBER   F. EMPLOYEE NAME (FIRST NAME)   (M.I.) (LAST NAME)
G. TOTAL SUBJECT WAGES   H. PIT WAGES   I. PIT WITHHELD

E. SOCIAL SECURITY NUMBER   F. EMPLOYEE NAME (FIRST NAME)   (M.I.) (LAST NAME)
G. TOTAL SUBJECT WAGES   H. PIT WAGES   I. PIT WITHHELD

E. SOCIAL SECURITY NUMBER   F. EMPLOYEE NAME (FIRST NAME)   (M.I.) (LAST NAME)
G. TOTAL SUBJECT WAGES   H. PIT WAGES   I. PIT WITHHELD

E. SOCIAL SECURITY NUMBER   F. EMPLOYEE NAME (FIRST NAME)   (M.I.) (LAST NAME)
G. TOTAL SUBJECT WAGES   H. PIT WAGES   I. PIT WITHHELD

E. SOCIAL SECURITY NUMBER   F. EMPLOYEE NAME (FIRST NAME)   (M.I.) (LAST NAME)
G. TOTAL SUBJECT WAGES   H. PIT WAGES   I. PIT WITHHELD

E. SOCIAL SECURITY NUMBER   F. EMPLOYEE NAME (FIRST NAME)   (M.I.) (LAST NAME)
G. TOTAL SUBJECT WAGES   H. PIT WAGES   I. PIT WITHHELD

E. SOCIAL SECURITY NUMBER   F. EMPLOYEE NAME (FIRST NAME)   (M.I.) (LAST NAME)
G. TOTAL SUBJECT WAGES   H. PIT WAGES   I. PIT WITHHELD

J. TOTAL SUBJECT WAGES THIS PAGE   K. TOTAL PIT WAGES THIS PAGE   L. TOTAL PIT WITHHELD THIS PAGE

M. GRAND TOTAL SUBJECT WAGES   N. GRAND TOTAL PIT WAGES   O. GRAND TOTAL PIT WITHHELD

P. I declare that the information herein is true and correct to the best of my knowledge and belief.

Preparer's Signature _____ Title _____ Phone (___) _____ Date _____
(Owner, Accountant, Preparer, etc.)

DE 6   Rev. 4 (2-04)   MAIL TO: State of California / Employment Development Department / P.O. Box 826288 / Sacramento, CA 94230-6288

EXERCISE 10.7A Annual Reconciliation Statement

EDD Employment Development Department
State of California

ANNUAL RECONCILIATION STATEMENT

00070104

PLEASE TYPE THIS FORM - DO NOT ALTER PREPRINTED INFORMATION

YEAR ENDED December 31, 2004   DUE January 1, 2005   DELINQUENT IF NOT POSTMARKED OR RECEIVED BY January 31, 2005

YEAR 2004

EMPLOYER ACCOUNT NO.
561-8381-4

LAWTON ASSOCIATES
752 GATEWAY PLAZA
SAN DIEGO, CA 92108

DEPT. USE ONLY

DO NOT ALTER THIS AREA

P1 P2 C P U S A
T

EFFECTIVE DATE   Mo.   Day   Yr.

FEIN 37-2473010

ADDITIONAL FEINS

CHECK BOX IF:

A. NO WAGES PAID THIS YEAR ☐

B. OUT OF BUSINESS _____ ☐
Date

C. TOTAL SUBJECT WAGES PAID THIS CALENDAR YEAR ....➤

D. UNEMPLOYMENT INSURANCE (UI)   (Total Employee Wages up to ____ per employee per calendar year)

(D1) UI %   TIMES   (D2) UI TAXABLE WAGES   =   (D3) UI CONTRIBUTIONS

E EMPLOYMENT TRAINING TAX (ETT)

(E1) ETT %   TIMES   UI Taxable Wages (D2) ....   =   (E2) ETT CONTRIBUTIONS

F. STATE DISABILITY INSURANCE (SDI)   (Total Employee Wages up to $ ____ per employee per calendar year)

(F1) SDI %   TIMES   (F2) SDI TAXABLE WAGES   =   (F3) SDI EMPLOYEE CONTRIBUTIONS WITHHELD

PIT WITHHELD PER FORMS W-2 AND/OR 1099R

G. CALIFORNIA PERSONAL INCOME TAX (PIT) WITHHELD ....➤

H. **SUBTOTAL** (Add Items D3, E2, F3, and G) ....➤

I. LESS: CONTRIBUTIONS AND WITHHOLDINGS PAID FOR THE YEAR (**DO NOT** INCLUDE PENALTY AND INTEREST PAYMENTS) ....➤

J. TOTAL TAXES DUE OR OVERPAID (Item H minus Item I) ....➤

If amount due, prepare a Payroll Tax Deposit, DE 88, and mail to P.O. Box 826276, Sacramento, CA 94230-6276. Mailing payments with DE 7 delays payment processing and may result in an erroneous penalty and interest charges. **Mandatory EFT filers must remit all SDI/PIT deposits by EFT to avoid Non-Compliance Penalty.**

K. Be sure to sign this declaration: *I declare that the information herein is true and correct to the best of my knowledge and belief.*

Signature _____   Title _____   Phone (___) _____   Date _____
(Owner, Accountant, Preparer, etc.)

SIGN AND MAIL TO: State of California / Employment Development Department / P.O. Box 826286 / Sacramento CA 94230-6286

DE 7 Rev. 4 (1-04) **(INTERNET)**   Page 1 of 2   CU

(Continued from Exercise 10.7A on page 259.)

Use the following procedures to complete Form DE 7.

- On Line C, enter the total wages for the year.
- On Line D, enter $7,000 next to "Total Employee Wages up to." Enter the SUTA rate and the SUTA taxable wages. Compute and enter the amount of SUTA tax owed for the year.
- On Line E, enter the ETT rate. Compute and enter the amount of ETT tax owed for the year.
- On Line F, enter $68,829 next to "Total Employee Wages up to." Enter the SDI rate and the SDI taxable wages. Compute and enter the amount of SDI tax owed for the year.
- On Line G, enter the total state income tax withheld for the year.
- Add the amounts in Boxes D3, E2, and F3 and on Line G. Enter the total of the four amounts on Line H.
- Enter the total of the deposits for the year on Line I.
- Subtract the total of the deposits on Line I from the total of the state taxes owed on Line H. If the two amounts are equal, enter a zero on Line J. If there is a difference, enter the amount on Line J.
- Leave the signature line blank. Alice Lawton, the president, will sign the form. The firm's telephone number is 619–434–1656. The date of the form is January 23 of the current year.

Accounting for Payroll

Objectives

Upon completion of this unit, you should be able to:

1. Explain why it is necessary to summarize payroll transactions in the general ledger of a firm.
2. Define basic accounting terms such as *journal, ledger, post,* and *account balance.*
3. Describe the chart of accounts and its use.
4. Identify the ledger accounts dealing with payroll as being asset, liability, or expense accounts.
5. Indicate how to increase or decrease the ledger accounts that deal with payroll.
6. Explain why payroll records are often set up as a subsidiary module within an accounting system.
7. Journalize payroll transactions.
8. Understand how payroll transactions are posted from the journal to the ledger.
9. Explain the accounting treatment of employee salaries, wages, and bonuses.
10. Explain the accounting treatment of the taxes withheld from employee earnings and the employer's payroll taxes.
11. Explain the accounting treatment of voluntary deductions such as deductions for IRAs and savings bonds.

Can you imagine the human labor required to hand process the payroll and prepare payroll checks for a large company before computers? It was very labor-intensive work prone to many errors. Thanks largely to the introduction of integrated accounting software programs, payroll tasks are handled more easily, quickly, and accurately in today's business environment. The use of accounting software makes the recording of all business transactions more efficient. Throughout this text you have learned about the many payroll functions that a business must perform. At regular intervals, payroll information must be entered in the company's accounting records.

THE SUBSIDIARY PAYROLL MODULE WITHIN THE ACCOUNTING SYSTEM

The payroll register, the employee earnings records, and other related records are used to satisfy legal requirements imposed by federal, state, and local governments and to meet a business's need for detailed payroll information. However, these records are not part of the firm's general accounting system. Payroll records form a subsidiary module that integrates into the accounting system.

At the end of each payroll period and at other points during the year, payroll transactions are brought into the accounting system by journalizing and posting appropriate entries.

Internet Connection

These entries *summarize* payroll amounts. For example, the subsidiary payroll records at a large company might show earnings and deductions for each of 4,500 employees at the end of a payroll period. Yet in the firm's accounting system, a single entry summarizes the expense and liabilities for these earnings and deductions.

If you wanted to find out what the net pay was for a particular employee for a certain week, you would *not* look in the general accounting system of the company. Rather, you would look in the *subsidiary payroll module.* There you would find all the details regarding the employee's pay for every week of the year: hours worked, earnings, deductions, and net pay amounts. You would even find the number of each payroll check issued to the employee. Payroll transactions are *summarized* in the company's general accounting records. Details are contained in the subsidiary payroll records.

ACCOUNTING RECORDS FOR PAYROLL

An accounting system provides a business with an organized method to keep track of its financial affairs. The information gathered by the accounting system makes it possible to determine the financial condition of the firm and the results of its operations.

Most accounting systems are built around two basic types of records: journals and ledgers. A *journal* is a chronological (day-by-day) listing of transactions. Each financial transaction is entered in the journal, regardless of its type. Journals may be handwritten or computerized.

A *ledger* is a group of accounts. Each account provides a record of a particular financial item over a period of time. There are ledger accounts for land, buildings, sales, purchases, merchandise on hand, salaries, payroll taxes, and many other financial items. Each account shows the balance of the item at the start of the period, any increases or decreases during the period, and the balance at the end of the period.

Transactions are recorded in a journal (*journalized*), and then the amounts are *posted* (transferred) to the proper ledger accounts. In a manual accounting system, these records are often kept in bound books or in binders or folders that contain lined forms with appropriate columns. In a computerized accounting system, the journals and ledger accounts consist of forms that appear on the computer screen. Of course, the forms can be printed.

Many different types of journals and ledgers are used in business. Each firm selects the types that are best suited to its operations.

While some very small businesses may still prepare the payroll by hand, the wide availability of accounting software with a payroll module included has made it possible for most firms to use the computer in performing all payroll functions today. Many of these software programs are very inexpensive and easy to learn.

DOUBLE-ENTRY ACCOUNTING

In a double-entry accounting system, at least two accounts are affected by each transaction. In other words, each transaction requires a *double entry.*

Point of Interest

It seems that everyone wants an automobile. But that has been true for a long time. Note the declining amount of work required to own one of the popular automobiles listed here.

Year	Manufacturer	Number Produced	Price of Car	Months of Work Required to Buy a Car
1900	Oldsmobile	fewer than 20	$ 1,500	47
1925	Model T Ford	1,650,000	600	7
1950	Chevrolet	1,425,000	1,450	6
1975	Chevrolet Impala	421,684	4,631	5
1998	Toyota Camry	397,000	20,218	6

Example

The Perez Travel Agency pays $350 cash for a new office desk. The account Office Furniture is increased by $350, and the account Cash is decreased by the same amount. One account is debited for $350 (entry on the left side) and one is credited for $350 (entry on the right side).

Prior to the purchase of the desk, there was a balance of $6,360 in the Cash account and a balance of $3,800 in the Office Furniture account. Notice how the transaction looks when it is recorded in the ledger accounts that are affected by the purchase of the new desk. This information is shown below in T accounts.

Office Furniture			Cash		
Old Bal.	3,800		Old Bal.	6,360	Desk 350
Desk	350				
New Bal.	4,150		New Bal.	6,010	

There is now less cash, but more office furniture. One thing of value—cash—was exchanged for another thing of value, the desk. There are equal and opposite entries in these two accounts. Notice how the balance of Office Furniture increased by $350 and the balance of Cash decreased by $350.

Sometimes, more than two accounts are involved in an accounting entry. This is called a *compound entry.*

Example

Suppose that in the previous example the desk is purchased partially on credit. A down payment of $50 cash is required, but the remaining $300 is on credit.

1. The Cash account is decreased by $50.
2. The business now owes a debt of $300 to the firm from which it purchased the desk. Therefore, it is necessary to increase an account called Accounts Payable by $300.
3. The Office Furniture account is increased by $350, the cost of the desk.

This transaction is recorded by debiting Office Furniture for $350, crediting Cash for $50, and crediting Accounts Payable for $300. Notice that the debit to Office Furniture of $350 is balanced by the two credits, one for $50 and one for $300. Although there are two credits, they equal the one debit in dollar amount. Thus there are "equal and opposite entries." These entries show that the company now has a new desk that cost $350, it made a $50 cash down payment, and it has a debt (or account payable) of $300. Regardless of the number of accounts affected by a transaction, the total debits must equal the total credits.

Office Furniture		
Old Bal.	3,800	
Desk	350	
New Bal.	4,150	

Cash				
Old Bal.	6,360	Desk		50
New Bal.	6,310			

Accounts Payable		
	Old Bal.	—
	Desk	300
	New Bal.	300

CHART OF ACCOUNTS

A *chart of accounts* is a listing of all the general ledger accounts used by a business. The *general ledger* is the main ledger of a business. It contains the accounts that appear on the firm's financial statements. The chart of accounts serves as a guide for the recording of transactions.

Examine the partial chart of accounts given here. It shows the general ledger accounts that are used to make the necessary payroll entries at Ingram Heating and Cooling. Of course, there are other accounts used in this business—Rent Expense, Utilities Expense, Insurance Expense, and so on. Although payroll account titles may vary somewhat from business to business, these accounts are typical of the ones that many firms use for recording payroll-related transactions.

The payroll-related accounts shown in the partial chart of accounts represent assets, liabilities, and expense items. *Assets* are things of value owned by a business: cash, bank accounts, office furniture, buildings, delivery vans, furniture, merchandise on hand, and so on. *Liabilities* are amounts that are owed, for bank loans, goods purchased on credit, unpaid taxes, and other debts. *Expenses* are the costs of operating the business: telephone service, electricity, employee salaries, rent, taxes, and so on. The account numbers appear before the account titles. (The system used to number accounts may vary somewhat from business to business.)

Ingram Heating and Cooling
Partial Chart of Accounts

Assets

101   Cash
       (Plus other assets)

Liabilities

221   Employee Federal Income Taxes Payable
222   Social Security Taxes Payable
224   Medicare Taxes Payable
230   Savings Bonds Payable
231   IRA Contributions Payable
232   Employee State Income Taxes Payable
233   Employee State Disability Insurance Taxes Payable
234   Federal Unemployment Taxes Payable
235   State Unemployment Taxes Payable
240   State Employment Training Taxes Payable
241   Salaries and Wages Payable
       (Plus other liabilities)

Expenses

518   Salaries and Wages Expense
519   Payroll Taxes Expense (Plus other expenses)

Learning Through Practice   Do Exercise 11.1 on page 287 of this text-workbook.

UNDERSTANDING THE LEDGER ACCOUNTS

It is important to know what effects the various types of payroll transactions have on the ledger accounts and how these effects are recorded. Careful analysis of payroll transactions before making accounting entries helps ensure accuracy. Look at the blank general ledger account shown in Figure 11.1.

Notice that, starting from the left, the ledger account has a date column, a description column, a posting reference column, and four money columns. At the top of the account, there is space for showing the account title and number.

The first two money columns are used to record the debit or credit amount involved in each entry. The last two money columns are used to show the current debit or credit balance of the account as a result of each entry. The posting reference (Post. Ref.) column identifies the source of each entry in the account—the journal where the transaction was originally recorded and the page in that journal.

When analyzing transactions, accountants often jot entries in penciled *T accounts*. (See Figure 11.1.) This helps them visualize complex transactions that are to be journalized. T accounts are used in this unit to represent general ledger accounts.

FIGURE 11.1   **Ledger Account and T Account**

GENERAL LEDGER ACCOUNT

ACCOUNT _____   ACCOUNT NO. _____

DATE	DESCRIPTION	POST. REF.	DEBIT	CREDIT	BALANCE	
					DEBIT	CREDIT

T ACCOUNT

Salaries and Wages

You are aware that transactions cause increases and decreases in account balances. The double-entry system specifies exactly how such changes must be recorded in the different kinds of accounts. For example, the debit (left) side of an asset account or an expense account is used to enter increases, while the credit (right) side of these two types of accounts is used to record decreases. The opposite is true for liability accounts. The debit (left) side shows decreases, and the credit (right) side shows increases. (Only the types of accounts that are used for payroll transactions are illustrated here.)

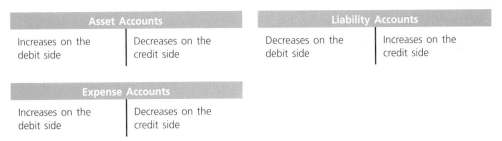

Asset Accounts		Liability Accounts	
Increases on the debit side	Decreases on the credit side	Decreases on the debit side	Increases on the credit side

Expense Accounts	
Increases on the debit side	Decreases on the credit side

Consider the effect of employee earnings. Payroll causes an increase in the operating expenses of a business. Thus, at the end of each payroll period, the Salaries and Wages Expense account must be debited for the total gross earnings of the employees.

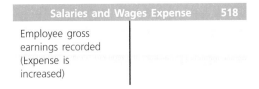

Salaries and Wages Expense	518
Employee gross earnings recorded (Expense is increased)	

The required credit would be to the Salaries and Wages Payable account. This account reflects the net amount of the salaries and wages that are due to be paid. Here is how that account would appear.

Salaries and Wages Payable	241
	Employee net pay recorded (Liability is increased)

The entry to Salaries and Wages Expense (a debit) must be matched by credit entries of equal value. Since the salaries and wages are *payable,* they are a *liability* of the company. Thus a liability account must be increased. Salaries and Wages Payable is increased by the amount of the *net* pay earned by the employees.

Amounts Withheld from Salaries and Wages

Notice that the debit to Salaries and Wages Expense in the preceding example is for *gross* earnings. The credit to Salaries and Wages Payable is for *net* pay. The difference between the two amounts is the various deductions made from employee earnings. These deductions are liabilities of the company until they are paid.

A business is responsible for all amounts withheld from employee earnings *until they are paid* to the proper authorities. Thus at the end of each payroll period, the appropriate liability accounts must be credited for *all* of the required and voluntary deductions. Later, as the money is paid out, these accounts are debited to show the decrease in liabilities. The

Times change, and so do values. In the early days of oil drilling in eastern Texas, oil sold for $.03 per barrel. On the other hand, at that time water sold for $6 per barrel.

The area had lots of oil with only a minimal market, but there was a shortage of water.

Cash account is credited as the obligations are paid, because cash payments cause a decrease in the asset Cash.

By viewing the effects of the payroll transactions as they will appear in the various accounts, you can get a general idea of how this system works. Of course, before transactions are entered in the ledger accounts, they must first be recorded in a journal. Remember that a journal is a day-by-day, running record of financial transactions. The ledger shows the effects of the transactions on the individual accounts.

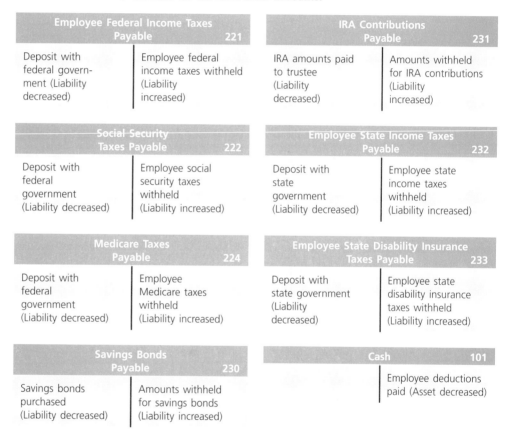

Employee Federal Income Taxes Payable 221	
Deposit with federal government (Liability decreased)	Employee federal income taxes withheld (Liability increased)

IRA Contributions Payable 231	
IRA amounts paid to trustee (Liability decreased)	Amounts withheld for IRA contributions (Liability increased)

Social Security Taxes Payable 222	
Deposit with federal government (Liability decreased)	Employee social security taxes withheld (Liability increased)

Employee State Income Taxes Payable 232	
Deposit with state government (Liability decreased)	Employee state income taxes withheld (Liability increased)

Medicare Taxes Payable 224	
Deposit with federal government (Liability decreased)	Employee Medicare taxes withheld (Liability increased)

Employee State Disability Insurance Taxes Payable 233	
Deposit with state government (Liability decreased)	Employee state disability insurance taxes withheld (Liability increased)

Savings Bonds Payable 230	
Savings bonds purchased (Liability decreased)	Amounts withheld for savings bonds (Liability increased)

Cash 101	
	Employee deductions paid (Asset decreased)

As noted previously, the net pay of the employees for a payroll period represents a liability and is recorded by crediting the Salaries and Wages Payable account. When paychecks are issued to the employees, the Salaries and Wages Payable account is debited to record the decrease in liabilities and the Cash account is credited to record the corresponding decrease in assets.

Salaries and Wages Payable 241	
Paychecks issued to employees (Liability decreased)	Net pay recorded before paychecks are issued (Liability increased)

Cash 101	
	Paychecks issued for net pay of employees (Asset decreased)

Point of Interest

Many businesses now hire temporary employees to work on special assignments or take the place of their own employees who are ill or on a leave of absence. There were about 185,000 temporary employees in 1970 compared to an estimated 2.3 million in 1996. This number continues to grow.

The Employer's Payroll Taxes

In addition to entering employee earnings, deductions, and net pay at the end of each payroll period, a business must record its *own* payroll taxes. These taxes include the employer's matching social security and Medicare contributions and its federal and state unemployment taxes. Such items cause an increase in operating expenses and an increase in liabilities until the sums are remitted to the correct government agencies. Some of these expenses will not be paid immediately, but at the end of the quarter. However, as the liabilities occur, they must be recorded.

When the taxes are deposited (paid), the appropriate liability accounts are debited to show the decrease in the firm's liabilities and the Cash account is credited to show the decrease in assets caused by the payments.

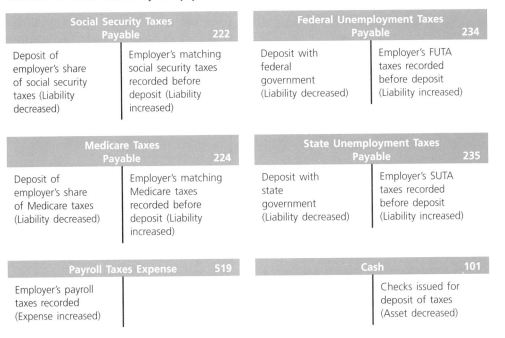

The illustrations in this section provide a summary of how the effects of payroll transactions are reflected in the ledger accounts. Refer to these illustrations whenever necessary as you study the procedures for journalizing and posting actual payroll entries in this unit.

Learning Through Practice

Do Exercises 11.2 and 11.3 on pages 287 through 288 of this text-workbook.

JOURNALIZING AND POSTING ENTRIES FOR PAYROLL

Before payroll amounts are recorded in the ledger accounts, they must be entered in a journal. So that you can see these transactions more clearly, each payroll transaction that you will study is journalized separately. To ensure that the accounting records are kept up to date, the journal entries and the postings to the ledger are done as soon as possible after the transactions occur.

Recording Employee Earnings and Deductions

The totals of the payroll register provide the information needed to make an accounting entry for employee earnings, deductions, and net pay at the end of each payroll period. Once the payroll register is completed and checked for accuracy, the appropriate figures are journalized and then posted (transferred) to the proper accounts.

Part of the payroll register prepared at Ingram Heating and Cooling for the weekly payroll period ended January 17 is shown in Figure 11.2 on pages 272 and 273.

Notice how the column totals from the payroll register are used to make the journal entry shown in Figure 11.3 on page 272. Also notice the brief explanation below the entry. An explanation is required for any journal entry. The numbers in the Post. Ref. column indicate the specific account to which each amount has been posted (transferred). Also notice that the single debit of $14,608.87 is balanced by eight credits that equal the *total* debit amount, $14,608.87.

Once the journal entry has been completed, the amounts are posted to the various accounts. For the sake of simplicity, T accounts are shown on page 273 rather than the actual ledger accounts.

The total of the gross earnings for the period ($14,608.87) is debited to the Salaries and Wages Expense account. This figure is matched by credits to seven liability accounts for the totals of the various types of deductions plus a credit to another liability account—Salaries and Wages Payable—for the total net pay ($10,718.30). Notice that the total of the debits equals the total of the credits. The purpose of this entry is to establish the firm's expense and liabilities for the January 17 payroll in the general accounting records. It does not take the place of the data in the payroll register and the employee earnings records. These records supply detailed payroll information that the business is required to keep.

Once the payroll is journalized, the transaction can be posted to the proper ledger accounts. Figure 11.4, page 273, shows the T accounts with the amounts correctly posted. Remember that the T accounts only *represent* actual general ledger accounts. But they do show you how the accounts are affected.

Computing the Employer's Payroll Taxes

It is common practice to make an accounting entry for the employer's payroll taxes at the end of each payroll period even though there may be no need to deposit these taxes (to pay them) until later, perhaps not until the end of the quarter. By following this practice, a business can be sure that its accounting records always reflect its total expense and liabilities for the payroll taxes. The firm is also in a better position to make timely deposits of these taxes and thereby avoid penalties for late payment. The employer's payroll taxes normally consist of social security tax, Medicare tax, federal unemployment (FUTA) tax, and state unemployment (SUTA) tax.

Social Security and Medicare Taxes

The social security tax and Medicare tax represent the employer's contribution to the social security and Medicare systems. Remember that both the employee and the employer make tax payments to support these two federal programs. As stated in earlier units, the employee's rate of tax for social security is 6.2 percent of the first $87,900 of earnings. The employee's rate of tax for Medicare is 1.45 percent of all earned wages. Employers, then, are taxed at the same rate for the matching portion of this payroll tax liability.

Because of rounding of the amounts of Medicare and social security taxes to be withheld, most employers simply match the amounts withheld from employee pay instead of making a second calculation for the employer's contribution to these two funds. This factor often enters into the completion of the Form 941 at the end of each quarter because the taxes are computed using the combined rates of tax (12.2 percent for social security and 2.9 percent for Medicare). Recall that Form 941 (see page 203) has an adjustment for social security and Medicare taxes due to rounding on line 9 that allows a reconciliation of the amounts calculated on the form to the actual amounts withheld for each tax times 2. Multiplying by 2 achieves the matching of the amounts for the employer.

FIGURE 11.2   **Payroll Register**

PAYROLL

For the Period Beginning __January 11__, __2005__   and Ending __January 17__, __2005__

		EMPLOYEE DATA				HOURS		EARNINGS		
	Name	Marital Status	No. of With. Allow.	Regular Rate	Regular	Overtime	Regular	Overtime	Total Earnings	
1	Biddle, Henry	M	2	$32.80 per hr.	40	2	1,312 00	98 40	1,410 40	
2	Cook, Pamela	S	1	$872 per wk.	40		872 00		872 00	
12	Potter, Robert	M	3	$29.60 per hr.	40	1½	1,184 00	66 60	1,250 60	
13	Zanka, Donald	M	3	$18.20 per hr.	40	2	728 00	54 60	782 60	
14	Totals						13,662 80	946 07	14,608 87	
15										
16										
17										

Care should be taken in tracking the year-to-date amounts of earnings subject to the social security tax in each pay period because this tax has a maximum limit of earnings that is subject to the tax. The employer, therefore, is also only subject to matching the social security tax withheld on earnings up to the current maximum earnings ($87,900 in this text).

Ingram will owe $905.75 to match the social security taxes withheld from employees and $211.81 to match the Medicare taxes withheld from employees.

Federal and State Unemployment Taxes

The amounts of federal unemployment (FUTA) tax and state unemployment (SUTA) tax that the employer owes are, as was true with social security and Medicare taxes, also determined by multiplying the total taxable earnings by the applicable tax rate. As of this writing, the FUTA tax rate is 6.2 percent on the first $7,000 of each employee's annual earnings. However, the FUTA rate is often decreased based upon the rate

FIGURE 11.3   **General Journal**

GENERAL JOURNAL

PAGE __2__

DATE		DESCRIPTION OF ENTRY	POST. REF.	DEBIT	CREDIT
2005 Jan.	17	Salaries and Wages Expense	518	14608 87	
		Employee Federal Income Taxes Payable	221		1806 97
		Social Security Taxes Payable	222		905 75
		Medicare Taxes Payable	224		211 81
		Employee State Income Taxes Payable	232		488 66
		Employee State Disability Insurance Taxes Payable	233		172 38
		IRA Contributions Payable	231		215 00
		Savings Bonds Payable	230		90 00
		Salaries and Wages Payable	241		10718 30
		Payroll for week ending January 17, 2005.			

FIGURE 11.2 *(continued)*

REGISTER

Date Paid _____ , 20 _____

				DEDUCTIONS										NET PAY		
Federal Income Tax		Social Security Tax		Medicare Tax		State Income Tax		SDI Tax		IRA		Savings Bonds		Total Deductions		Amount	Check No.
249	14	87	44	20	45	46	85	16	64	10	00			430	52	979	88	
130	00	54	06	12	64	37	91	10	29	15	00	10	00	269	90	602	10	
125	00	77	54	18	13	33	44	14	76	20	00	10	00	298	87	951	73	
54	00	48	52	11	35	8	96	9	23	10	00			142	06	640	54	
1,806	97	905	75	211	81	488	66	172	38	215	00	90	00	3,890	57	10,718	30	

assigned by the state for SUTA tax. Ingram Heating and Cooling has an assigned rate of 0.8 percent for FUTA tax and 3.4 percent for SUTA tax. In California, where Ingram is located, SUTA tax, like FUTA tax, is paid on the first $7,000 that an employee earns in a year.

The employee earnings records kept by Ingram showed that as of January 17, no employee had exceeded the annual wage base of $7,000 for FUTA and SUTA taxes. Thus the taxable earnings for FUTA for the January 17 payroll period were $14,608.87. The FUTA tax owed was $116.87 ($14,608.87 × .008 = $116.87). The SUTA tax owed was $496.70 ($14,608.87 × .034 = $496.70).

FIGURE 11.4   **T Accounts**

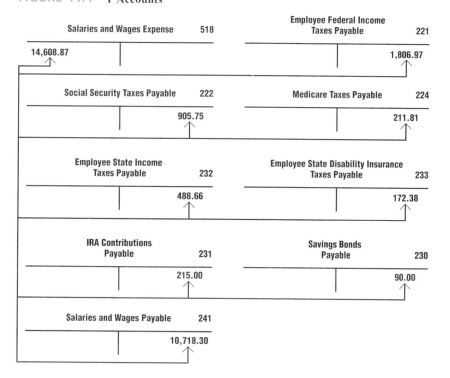

FIGURE 11.5 **General Journal**

GENERAL JOURNAL					PAGE 2	

DATE		DESCRIPTION OF ENTRY	POST. REF.	DEBIT	CREDIT
2005 Jan.	17	Payroll Taxes Expense	519	1 7 4 5 74	
		Social Security Taxes Payable	222		9 0 5 75
		Medicare Taxes Payable	224		2 1 1 81
		Federal Unemployment Taxes Payable	234		1 1 6 87
		State Unemployment Taxes Payable	235		4 9 6 70
		State Employment Training Taxes Payable	240		1 4 61
		Employer's payroll taxes for January 17 payroll.			

Other Employer Taxes

California has another state payroll tax for business that is identified as the employment training tax (ETT). This tax is paid quarterly and is set at 0.1 percent of the first $7,000 of yearly earnings for each employee. The ETT tax provides funding to businesses to upgrade the job skills of their employees. For the January 17 payroll, Ingram owed $14.61 of ETT tax ($14,608.87 × .001 = $14.61).

Recording the Employer's Payroll Taxes

Generally, a single journal entry is made to record all the payroll taxes that the employer owes. For Ingram Heating and Cooling, these taxes include social security, Medicare, FUTA, SUTA, and ETT. The necessary general journal entry is shown in Figure 11.5. Notice that there is a single debit to Payroll Taxes Expense with balancing credits to the five liability accounts.

The Payroll Taxes Expense account is debited for the total of these taxes ($1,745.74), and the appropriate liability accounts are credited for the individual tax amounts ($905.75 for social security, $211.81 for Medicare, $116.87 for FUTA, $496.70 for SUTA, and $14.61 for ETT). These amounts must be submitted to the appropriate federal and state agencies when due.

The posting of this journal entry to the ledger accounts is shown by means of T accounts in Figure 11.6.

FIGURE 11.6 **T Accounts**

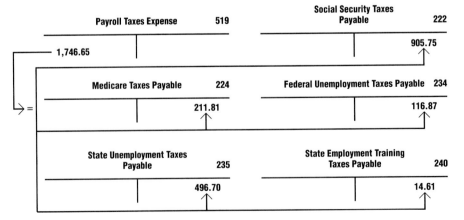

Point of Interest

The major sectors of our economy at different time periods are shown in the following tables. Notice how the share of each sector has changed. For example, in 1900 approximately 20 percent of our economy was based on agriculture. This sector of the economy, owing to new technology, has decreased continually since that time until today it is less than 2 percent. Yet we are producing far more agricultural products—enough to supply all of our needs and that of many other countries around the world as well.

1900	
Manufacturing	37.9%
Services	33.0
Agriculture	20.0
Government	8.6

1925	
Manufacturing	36.5%
Services	39.0
Agriculture	13.4
Government	11.1

1950	
Manufacturing	28.5%
Services	53.7
Agriculture	7.0
Government	10.8

1975	
Manufacturing	21.8%
Services	59.5
Agriculture	3.4
Government	15.3

2000	
Manufacturing	17.4%
Services	67.9
Agriculture	1.7
Government	13.0

JOURNALIZING AND POSTING PAYMENT OF THE PAYROLL

In many businesses, some time elapses between the computation of earnings, deductions, and net pay at the end of a payroll period and the actual payment of employees. Meanwhile, the Salaries and Wages Payable account reflects the amount owed to the employees. Remember that this liability is recorded when the payroll is journalized and posted. Once the employees are paid, another entry must be made debiting Salaries and Wages Payable and crediting Cash. The journal entry shown in Figure 11.7 below was made at Ingram Heating and Cooling to record payment of the January 17 payroll on January 21. The figure used ($10,718.30) is the total net pay for the period.

After the data from the journal entry is posted, the firm's liability for salaries and wages is reduced from $10,718.30 to zero. You can see this in the T accounts shown in Figure 11.8.

FIGURE 11.7   General Journal

	GENERAL JOURNAL				PAGE 3
DATE	DESCRIPTION OF ENTRY	POST. REF.	DEBIT	CREDIT
2005 Jan. 21	Salaries and Wages Payable	241	10 71 8 30	
	Cash	101		10 71 8 30
	Payment of January 17 payroll.			

FIGURE 11.8   T Accounts

Salaries and Wages Payable	241		Cash	101
10,718.30	Bal. 10,718.30			10,718.30

JOURNALIZING AND POSTING DEPOSITS OF PAYROLL TAXES

Employers are responsible for making periodic deposits of the amounts withheld from employee earnings for federal and state taxes. These liabilities were entered into the general accounting records earlier for the payroll of January 17. Look again at the journal entry in Figure 11.3 on page 272 and the accounts that were affected in Figure 11.4 on page 273.

The liabilities for the employer's payroll taxes produced by the January 17 payroll were journalized as shown in Figure 11.5 on page 274. This entry was posted to the accounts in Figure 11.6 on page 274. Look again at those two illustrations. The payroll taxes recorded there must also be deposited at regular intervals.

Frequency of Tax Deposits

The frequency of making tax deposits is determined by the amounts that are owed to federal and state agencies. Some large businesses must make a deposit of federal withholding taxes one banking day after payment of their payroll because their tax liability is $100,000 or more. Most other businesses must follow a semiweekly or monthly schedule for making deposits of federal withholding taxes. Ingram Heating and Cooling is a semiweekly depositor. Businesses that owe very small amounts of federal withholding taxes are permitted to pay them quarterly when they file Form 941.

When businesses deposit federal withholding taxes (the federal income tax, social security tax, and Medicare tax deducted from employee earnings), they must also deposit the employer's matching share of social security tax and Medicare tax. A check or electronic payment for the total of these tax amounts is submitted.

The schedule for depositing state withholding taxes varies from state to state. In California, where Ingram Heating and Cooling is located, deposits of state withholding taxes (the state income tax and state disability insurance tax deducted from employee earnings) are made either on the next banking day after payment of the payroll, semiweekly, monthly, or quarterly. The deposit schedule depends on the amount of taxes owed. Ingram is a semiweekly depositor of state withholding taxes.

Businesses must deposit federal unemployment tax (FUTA) on a quarterly basis when the amount owed is at least $100. In California, businesses are also required to make quarterly deposits of state unemployment tax (SUTA) and employment training tax (ETT). Generally, these quarterly deposits (federal and state) are due no later than the last day of the month that follows the end of a quarter. The first quarter unemployment taxes would be due no later than April 30.

Remitting Federal Withholding Taxes

On January 21, Ingram Heating and Cooling paid the payroll for the week ended January 17. At that time, the firm had the following liabilities for federal withholding taxes and the employer's matching share of social security and Medicare taxes.

Employee federal income taxes withheld	$1,806.97
Employee social security taxes withheld	905.75
Employer social security taxes	905.75
Employee Medicare taxes withheld	211.81
Employer Medicare taxes	211.81
Total owed	$4,042.09

Because Ingram is a semiweekly depositor and because the payment date for the January 17 payroll fell on Wednesday, January 21, its deposit was due by the next Wednesday. Therefore, on Tuesday, January 27, the firm made an electronic deposit of $4,042.09. This deposit included both the federal withholding taxes from the January 17 payroll and the employer's matching share of social security and Medicare taxes.

FIGURE 11.9   **General Journal**

		GENERAL JOURNAL				PAGE _3_

DATE		DESCRIPTION OF ENTRY	POST. REF.	DEBIT	CREDIT
2005 Jan.	27	Employee Federal Income Taxes Payable	221	1 806 97	
		Social Security Taxes Payable	222	1 811 50	
		Medicare Taxes Payable	224	423 62	
		Cash	101		4 042 09
		Deposit of federal taxes for January 17 payroll.			

Figure 11.9 shows how this deposit was recorded in the firm's general journal. Figure 11.10 illustrates the effects of the deposit on the ledger accounts. Notice that the balances of the liability accounts are reduced to zero.

Remitting State Withholding Taxes

On January 21, after paying the January 17 payroll, Ingram Heating and Cooling had the following liabilities for state withholding taxes.

Employee state income taxes withheld	$488.66
Employee state disability insurance taxes withheld	172.38
Total owed	$661.04

Because Ingram is a semiweekly depositor of state withholding taxes, it made an electronic deposit of $661.04 on January 27. This deposit was recorded in the general journal by debiting Employee State Income Taxes Payable for $488.66, debiting Employee state Disability Insurance Taxes Payable for $172.38, and crediting Cash for $661.04. The entry was posted to the appropriate ledger accounts.

Remitting Federal Unemployment Tax

If a business owes more than $100 of federal unemployment tax at the end of a quarter, it must deposit the amount. This is done by making an electronic payment or by issuing a

FIGURE 11.10   **T Accounts**

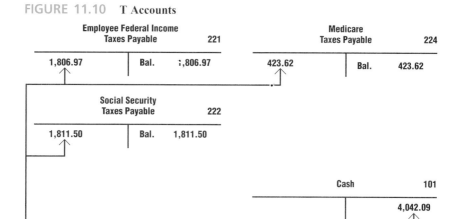

FIGURE 11.11   **General Journal**

GENERAL JOURNAL   PAGE __9__

DATE		DESCRIPTION OF ENTRY	POST. REF.	DEBIT	CREDIT
2005 Mar.	31	Federal Unemployment Taxes Payable	234	7 37 60	
		Cash	101		7 37 60
		Deposit of FUTA tax for first quarter.			

FIGURE 11.12   **T Accounts**

Federal Unemployment Taxes Payable 234		Cash 101
737.60	Bal. 737.60	737.60

check and submitting it with a completed Form 8109, Federal Tax Deposit Coupon, to an authorized financial institution. If a business owes $100 or less of FUTA tax, it can carry over the amount to the next quarter.

On March 31, the Federal Unemployment Taxes Payable account at Ingram Heating and Cooling had a balance of $737.60. This balance represents the total of the FUTA tax recorded by the firm during the first quarter. Ingram made the necessary deposit and then journalized and posted the transaction, as shown in Figures 11.11 and 11.12.

Remitting State Unemployment Tax and ETT Tax

Generally, states require that businesses make quarterly deposits of state unemployment tax. In California, where Ingram Heating and Cooling is located, it is also necessary to deposit another tax—the Employment Training Tax (ETT)—on a quarterly basis. The two tax amounts are deposited at the same time by means of electronic payment or by sending a check to the appropriate state agency along with a completed Form DE 88, Payroll Tax Deposit.

On March 31, the State Unemployment Taxes Payable account at Ingram Heating and Cooling had a balance of $3,134.80. The State Employment Training Taxes Payable account had a balance of $92.20. These balances are the result of entries made throughout the first quarter to record the firm's liability for SUTA and ETT.

Ingram remitted a total of $3,227 on March 31 to deposit the SUTA and ETT taxes owed for the first quarter. The journal entry for this transaction is shown in Figure 11.13. The posting of the entry to the appropriate accounts appears in Figure 11.14.

FIGURE 11.13   **General Journal**

GENERAL JOURNAL   PAGE __9__

DATE		DESCRIPTION OF ENTRY	POST. REF.	DEBIT	CREDIT
2005 Mar.	31	State Unemployment Taxes Payable	235	3 1 34 80	
		State Employment Training Taxes Payable	240	92 20	
		Cash	101		3 2 27 00
		Deposit of SUTA and ETT taxes for first quarter.			

FIGURE 11.14   **T Accounts**

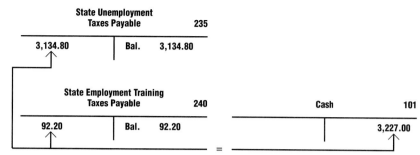

JOURNALIZING AND POSTING PAYMENT OF AMOUNTS WITHHELD FOR VOLUNTARY DEDUCTIONS

Many businesses allow employees to have voluntary deductions made from their earnings. These deductions cover items such as health insurance, life insurance, a pension plan, an IRA account, savings bonds, a stock purchase plan, union dues, and charitable contributions. Large firms often provide a broad range of voluntary deductions, whereas small firms usually offer just a few such deductions.

As you have already seen, Ingram Heating and Cooling makes available voluntary deductions for government savings bonds and for IRA contributions. The specified amounts are withheld from employee earnings at the end of each payroll period and then paid out at intervals.

At the end of each month, Ingram buys savings bonds for any employees who have accumulated enough funds. The remaining amounts are retained until the employees involved have contributed the funds needed for a purchase.

On January 31, the Savings Bonds Payable account at Ingram had a balance of $450. Ingram was able to buy $300 of savings bonds for employees and give them to the employees. This transaction was recorded as shown in Figures 11.15 and 11.16.

A local bank acts as trustee for the IRA accounts of the employees of Ingram Heating and Cooling who belong to its IRA plan. At the end of each month, Ingram transfers the IRA contributions of these employees to the bank, which places the appropriate sums in their IRA accounts.

FIGURE 11.15   **General Journal**

GENERAL JOURNAL   PAGE _3_____

DATE		DESCRIPTION OF ENTRY	POST. REF.	DEBIT	CREDIT
2005 Jan.	31	Savings Bonds Payable	230	300 00	
		Cash	101		300 00
		Purchase of savings bonds for employees.			

FIGURE 11.16   **T Accounts**

Savings Bonds Payable		230		Cash		101
300.00	Old Bal.	450.00			300.00	
	New Bal.	150.00				

FIGURE 11.17   **General Journal**

		GENERAL JOURNAL				PAGE 3	
DATE		**DESCRIPTION OF ENTRY**	**POST. REF.**	**DEBIT**		**CREDIT**	
2005 Jan.	31	IRA Contributions Payable	231	1,075 00			
		Cash	101			1,075 00	
		Transfer of IRA contributions of employees to trustee.					

FIGURE 11.18   **T Accounts**

IRA Contributions Payable		231		Cash		101
1,075	Bal.	1,075			1,075	

On January 31, the IRA Contributions Payable account at Ingram had a balance of $1,075. The firm issued a check for this amount to the bank and provided a record of the funds contributed by each employee during the month. The general journal entry made at Ingram to record the transfer of IRA funds appears in Figure 11.17. The postings to the ledger are illustrated in Figure 11.18.

In its role as trustee, the bank sends the employees quarterly statements showing the status of their IRA accounts. These statements list the opening balance for the period, the contributions made, the interest earned, and the ending balance.

ACCOUNTING FOR EMPLOYEE BONUS PAYMENTS

Some companies have a bonus policy that provides for special payments to employees. Very often these bonus payments are given at the end of the year or during the holiday season. In some cases, the company sets a profit goal and, if the goal is met or exceeded, provides a bonus to all employees at the end of the year. In other cases, companies simply give bonuses to selected employees who have made notable contributions to the success of the business. In all cases, bonus payments are taxable because wages and bonuses are subject to all federal and state payroll taxes.

Learning Through Practice   Do Exercises 11.4 through 11.8 on pages 288 through 289 of this text-workbook.

UNIT 11   REVIEW

Summary   This unit provided you with a fundamental understanding of how a payroll module integrates into the general accounting system of a business. You learned about some of the basic accounting rules, records, and general journal entries related to payroll. After studying this unit, you should be able to:

- Record the payroll summary entry in a general journal.
- Post the payroll entries to the individual ledger accounts.
- Understand the meaning of a subsidiary payroll module and how it relates to the firm's accounting information system.
- Record and post the entries for the employer's unemployment taxes and other business taxes.
- Record the payment (deposit) and posting of all federal and state payroll taxes.
- Understand the meaning of asset, liability, and expense accounts used in payroll-related accounting records.

Study Questions

1. What payroll record provides the data needed to make an accounting entry for employee earnings, deductions, and net pay?

2. What is the purpose of making accounting entries at the end of each payroll period?

3. Why are deductions from employee earnings treated as liabilities in a business's accounting records?

4. Why are separate liability accounts used to record the social security, Medicare, FUTA, and SUTA taxes?

5. Name the types of accounts that would be used to record each of the following payroll transactions, and indicate whether debit or credit entries would be made in these accounts. (Consider asset, liability, and expense accounts as the possible types.)

   a. Recorded employee earnings, deductions, and net pay.

   b. Recorded the employer's social security taxes, Medicare taxes, FUTA taxes, and SUTA taxes for a payroll period.

   c. Issued a check to deposit employee federal income taxes, social security taxes, and Medicare taxes, as well as the employer's share of social security taxes and Medicare taxes.

   d. Made a quarterly payment to the insurance company for health insurance premiums that were deducted from employee earnings.

   e. Issued paychecks to the employees.

6. What journal entry is made when a business purchases savings bonds for its employees?

7. What accounts are debited and credited when a deposit is made for employee federal income taxes and the employee and employer shares of social security taxes and Medicare taxes.

8. What amount from the payroll register is debited to the Salaries and Wages Expense account?

9. What amount from the payroll register is credited to the Salaries and Wages Payable account?

10. Why is a journal entry necessary when employees are paid?

REVIEW EXERCISES

If journal paper is available, use it to complete Review Exercises 1 through 5. Otherwise, use regular lined paper. Omit all explanations from the journal entries. When it is necessary to compute tax amounts, use a rate of 6.2 percent for social security tax, a rate of 1.45 percent for Medicare tax, and a rate of 0.8 percent for FUTA tax. Assume that the transactions took place during the current year.

1. E-Tech Sports operates a Web site for sports fans. It pays its employees on a monthly basis. In January, gross earnings totaled $8,400 and federal income tax withheld totaled $1,075.

   a. As of January 31, prepare a journal entry to record employee earnings and the deductions for federal income tax, social security tax, and Medicare tax.

   b. As of January 31, prepare a journal entry to record the employer's payroll taxes. All earnings for January are subject to social security tax, Medicare tax, FUTA tax, and SUTA tax. The firm's SUTA rate is 1.7 percent.

   c. As of February 3, prepare a journal entry to record payment of the payroll.

2. The Golden Door Health and Fitness Club has six employees. Their gross earnings for the weekly payroll period ended July 7 were $2,720. Their deductions included $348 for federal income tax and $150 for health insurance premiums.

   a. As of July 7, prepare a journal entry to record employee earnings and the deductions for federal income tax, social security tax, Medicare tax, and health insurance.

b. As of July 7, prepare a journal entry to record the employer's payroll taxes. All earnings for the week ended July 7 are subject to social security tax and Medicare tax. However, only $835 is subject to FUTA tax and SUTA tax. The firm's SUTA rate is 2.2 percent.

c. As of July 10, prepare a journal entry to record payment of the payroll.

3. During the month ended May 31, Quickie Auto Repair paid wages of $10,600 and withheld federal income tax totaling $1,557. On June 12, the firm made a deposit of the federal income tax withheld, the employee and employer shares of the social security tax, and the employee and employer shares of the Medicare tax. A check was issued for the total amount owed. Prepare the journal entry to record the deposit.

4. Sailor Dan's Seafood Restaurant is required to withhold union dues from the wages of its employees. The amounts deducted are sent to the treasurer of the union five days after the end of each month. During April, the restaurant withheld a total of $400 for union dues. Prepare a journal entry to record payment of this sum on May 5.

5. During the quarter ended June 30, E-Toy City, a toy store located in Oakland, California, withheld state income tax of $691.24 and state disability insurance tax of $204.68 from the salaries of its employees. The firm issued a check to deposit the total. Prepare a journal entry to record this deposit on July 3.

Problems

1. Comedy Productions pays its employees semimonthly. It uses the following accounts to record its payroll transactions.

Comedy Productions
Chart of Accounts (Partial)

Assets

101   Cash

Liabilities

221   Employee Federal Income Taxes Payable
222   Social Security Taxes Payable
223   Medicare Taxes Payable
224   Employee State Income Taxes Payable
225   Federal Unemployment Taxes Payable
226   State Unemployment Taxes Payable
227   United Way Contributions Payable
228   Salaries and Wages Payable

Expenses

551   Payroll Taxes Expense
552   Salaries and Wages Expense

The totals shown in Figure 11.19 were taken from the payroll registers prepared on June 15 and June 30.

FIGURE 11.19   **Payroll Register**

PAYROLL REGISTER

| Pay Period | Total Earnings | DEDUCTIONS | | | | | Total Deductions | NET PAY |
		Fed. Income Tax	Soc. Sec. Tax	Medicare Tax	State Income Tax	United Way		
June 15	6,730 00	861 00	417 26	97 59	148 06	97 00	1,620 91	5,109 09
June 30	6,875 00	880 00	426 25	99 69	151 25	97 00	1,654 19	5,220 81

Instructions:

a. Analyze the following transactions, and prepare journal entries for them. Use the journal paper given on the next two pages. Omit all explanations. Assume that the transactions took place during the current year.

b. When computing the employer's payroll taxes, use 0.8 percent for FUTA tax and 1.3 percent for SUTA tax.

Transactions:

June 1   Sent a check for $186 to the United Way for contributions withheld from employee earnings during May.

3   Issued paychecks totaling $5,083.28 for the May 31 payroll.

10   Issued a check for $297.93 to deposit the state income tax withheld from employee earnings during May.

11   Completed Form 8109 and issued a check for $3,631.76 to deposit federal income tax withheld ($1,654), the employee share ($801.46) and employer share ($801.46) of social security tax, and the employee share ($187.42) and employer share ($187.42) of Medicare tax for the May 15 and May 31 payrolls.

15   Recorded the semimonthly payroll.

15   Recorded the employer's payroll taxes. All earnings are subject to social security, Medicare, FUTA, and SUTA taxes.

18   Issued paychecks to the employees for the June 15 payroll.

30   Recorded the semimonthly payroll.

30   Recorded the employer's payroll taxes. All earnings are subject to social security and Medicare taxes. However, only $4,600 is taxable for FUTA and SUTA.

July 1   Sent a check for $194 to the United Way for contributions withheld from employee earnings during June.

2   Completed Form 8109 and issued a check for $310.19 to deposit the FUTA tax owed for the second quarter.

3   Issued paychecks to the employees for the June 30 payroll.

5   Filed the quarterly state unemployment tax return and sent a check for $504.07 to pay the SUTA tax owed for the second quarter.

9   Completed Form 8109 and issued a check for $3,822.58 to deposit federal income tax withheld ($1,741), the employee share ($843.51) and employer share ($843.51) of social security tax, and the employee share ($197.28) and employer share ($197.28) of Medicare tax for the June 15 and June 30 payrolls.

10   Issued a check for $299.31 to deposit the state income tax withheld from employee earnings during June.

GENERAL JOURNAL

PAGE _____

DATE	DESCRIPTION OF ENTRY	POST. REF.	DEBIT	CREDIT

GENERAL JOURNAL

PAGE _____

DATE	DESCRIPTION OF ENTRY	POST. REF.	DEBIT	CREDIT

Learning Through Practice

Unit 11 Exercises

EXERCISE 11.1

People who do payroll work are sometimes required to make accounting entries for payroll transactions. A knowledge of accounting records is therefore valuable for anyone who may become involved in payroll activities. Complete each of the following statements about accounting records. Write your answers in the answer column.

Answer

1. A(n) _____ _____ _____ is a list of the general ledger accounts used in a business.

   1. _____

2. _____ and _____ are two types of accounting records used to enter payroll transactions.

   2. _____

3. A(n) _____ is a chronological (day-by-day) listing of transactions.

   3. _____

4. Amounts are entered first in the _____ and are then posted to the _____.

   4. _____

5. Three types of accounts a business uses for recording payroll transactions are _____, _____, and _____ accounts.

   5. _____

6. Accounts are identified by an account _____ and an account _____.

   6. _____

7. A(n) _____ is a group of accounts.

   7. _____

8. A debit entry totaling $1,000 must be matched by a(n) _____ entry totaling $1,000.

   8. _____

9. Payroll records are sometimes referred to as a(n) _____ module within the accounting system.

   9. _____

10. Transferring a journal entry to the ledger is referred to as _____.

   10. _____

EXERCISE 11.2

Each of the following items represents an asset, a liability, or an expense for a business. Indicate the correct classification for each item by using *A, L,* or *E.* Write your answers in the answer column.

Answer

1. The total gross earnings of the firm's employees

   1. _____

2. The federal income tax deducted from employee earnings

   2. _____

3. Union dues that have been withheld from employee earnings and not yet sent to the union

   3. _____

4. The employer's payroll taxes

   4. _____

5. The net pay owed to employees at the end of a payroll period

   5. _____

6. The social security tax withheld from employee earnings

   6. _____

7. Undeposited SUTA tax

   7. _____

8. Cash

   8. _____

9. Savings bond deductions that have not yet been used to buy bonds for the employees

   9. _____

10. The state income tax withheld from employee earnings

   10. _____

EXERCISE 11.3

Before any payroll transaction is entered in a journal, it should be analyzed to determine what accounts are affected, whether each account is increased or decreased, and whether the increase or decrease is recorded as a debit or credit. Following is a list of increases and decreases in accounts as a result of transactions. Indicate whether each increase or decrease would be recorded by debiting or crediting the account involved. Place a check mark in the correct column. Refer to the account classifications in this partial chart of accounts.

**Texas Kitchens
Chart of Accounts (Partial)**

Assets

101   Cash

Liabilities

221   Employee Federal Income Taxes Payable
222   Social Security Taxes Payable
223   Medicare Taxes Payable
224   Employee State Income Taxes Payable
225   Federal Unemployment Taxes Payable
226   State Unemployment Taxes Payable
227   Savings Bonds Payable
228   Salaries and Wages Payable

Expenses

551   Payroll Taxes Expense
552   Salaries and Wages Expense

	Debit	Credit
1. Increase Medicare Taxes Payable to record the amount withheld from employee earnings.	1. _____	_____
2. Decrease Cash to record payment of the payroll.	2. _____	_____
3. Increase Salaries and Wages Payable to record the amounts owed to employees.	3. _____	_____
4. Decrease Federal Unemployment Taxes Payable to record the deposit of FUTA tax.	4. _____	_____
5. Increase Payroll Taxes Expense to record the payroll taxes owed by the employer.	5. _____	_____
6. Decrease Medicare Taxes Payable to record the deposit of these taxes.	6. _____	_____
7. Increase Salaries and Wages Expense to record the payroll.	7. _____	_____
8. Decrease Savings Bonds Payable to record the purchase of savings bonds for the employees.	8. _____	_____
9. Increase State Unemployment Taxes Payable to record the SUTA tax owed by the employer.	9. _____	_____
10. Decrease Salaries and Wages Payable to record payment of the payroll.	10. _____	_____

EXERCISE 11.4   The information shown here is from the payroll register of Texas Kitchens, a retail store that sells kitchen cabinets and appliances. The amounts are for the week ended March 28 of the current year. Prepare the journal entry needed to record the payroll. Use the general journal given on page 290. A partial chart of accounts for Texas Kitchens appears in Exercise 11.3.

Total gross earnings	$2,640.00
Total employee federal income tax withheld	337.00
Total employee social security tax withheld	163.68
Total employee Medicare tax withheld	38.28
Total employee state income tax withheld	57.26
Total savings bonds deductions	125.00
Total net pay	1,918.78

Note: Save the general journal for use in Exercises 11.5 and 11.6.

EXERCISE 11.5

Prepare the journal entry to record the employer's payroll taxes for the March 28 payroll at Texas Kitchens. To compute these taxes, use the following rates: 0.8 percent for FUTA tax and 2 percent for SUTA tax. The entire amount of gross earnings listed in Exercise 11.4 is subject to these taxes. (Use the general journal from Exercise 11.4 for your entry.)

EXERCISE 11.6

On March 31 of the current year, Texas Kitchens issued paychecks to its employees. These paychecks are for the weekly payroll period ended March 28. (See Exercise 11.4.) Prepare the journal entry that is needed to record payment of this payroll. (Continue to use the general journal from Exercise 11.4.)

EXERCISE 11.7

After the Erwin Construction Company recorded its payroll and its employer payroll taxes for the week ended June 30 of the current year, its general ledger showed a balance of $3,456 in the Employee Federal Income Taxes Payable account, a balance of $2,618 in the Social Security Taxes Payable account, and a balance of $783 in the Medicare Taxes Payable account. On July 2, the firm prepared Form 8109 and issued a check for the total of the amounts owed. It then deposited these taxes in the Lee National Bank. Prepare a journal entry to record the deposit. Use the general journal on page 291.

EXERCISE 11.8

On July 22 of the current year, Penn's Country Cooking, a restaurant, issued a check for $192 to cover the FUTA tax it owed for the first and second quarters. The firm then submitted this deposit to its bank along with a completed copy of Form 8109. Prepare a journal entry for this deposit. Use the general journal on page 292.

GENERAL JOURNAL

PAGE _____

DATE		DESCRIPTION OF ENTRY	POST. REF.	DEBIT	CREDIT

GENERAL JOURNAL

PAGE _____

DATE	DESCRIPTION OF ENTRY	POST. REF.	DEBIT	CREDIT

GENERAL JOURNAL

PAGE _____

DATE		DESCRIPTION OF ENTRY	POST. REF.	DEBIT	CREDIT

Alternate Learning Through Practice Exercises

Unit 11 Exercises

EXERCISE 11.1A

People who do payroll work are sometimes required to make accounting entries for payroll transactions. A knowledge of accounting records is therefore valuable for anyone who may become involved in payroll activities. Read the definitions given below and then match each of them with the correct accounting term. In the answer column, write the identifying letter of the term.

Accounting Terms

A. Account balance   F. Journal

B. Assets   G. Journalizing

C. Compound entry   H. Ledger

D. Double-entry accounting I. Liabilities

E. Expenses   J. Posting

Definitions   **Answer**

1. A chronological (day-by-day) listing of transactions   1. _____

2. A group of accounts   2. _____

3. A system of accounting in which at least two accounts
   are affected by each transaction   3. _____

4. Things of value owned by a business   4. _____

5. The difference between the total debits and the total
   credits in an account   5. _____

6. The process of recording transactions in a journal   6. _____

7. The amounts that a business owes   7. _____

8. An accounting entry that involves more than two accounts   8. _____

9. The costs of operating a business   9. _____

10. The process of transferring entries from a journal
    to a ledger   10. _____

EXERCISE 11.2A

Each of the following items represents an asset, a liability, or an expense for a business. Indicate the correct classification for each item by using *A, L,* or *E*. Write your answers in the answer column.

                                                                        Answer

1. The state income tax deducted from employee earnings   1. _____

2. The employer's payroll taxes   2. _____

3. The total gross earnings of the firm's employees   3. _____

4. The social security tax withheld from employee earnings   4. _____

5. Undeposited FUTA tax   5. _____

6. Cash   6. _____

7. The federal income tax deducted from employee earnings   7. _____

8. The net pay owed to employees at the end of a payroll period   8. _____

9. IRA contributions withheld from employee earnings but not yet
   transferred to the trustee for the IRA funds   9. _____

10. SUTA tax for the quarter that has not yet been sent to the state 10. _____

EXERCISE 11.3A

Before any payroll transaction is entered in a journal, it should be analyzed to determine what accounts are affected, whether each account is increased or decreased, and whether the increase or decrease is recorded as a debit or credit. Following is a list of increases and decreases in accounts as a result of transactions. Indicate whether each increase or decrease would be recorded by debiting or crediting the account involved. Place a check mark in the correct column. Refer to the account classifications in this partial chart of accounts.

**Sunrise Health Food
Chart of Accounts (Partial)**

Assets

101   Cash

Liabilities

221   Employee Federal Income Taxes Payable
222   Social Security Taxes Payable
223   Medicare Taxes Payable
224   Employee State Income Taxes Payable
225   Federal Unemployment Taxes Payable
226   State Unemployment Taxes Payable
227   Savings Bonds Payable
228   Salaries and Wages Payable

Expenses

551   Salaries and Wages Expense
552   Payroll Taxes Expense

	Debit	Credit
1. Increase Salaries and Wages Expense to record the payroll.	1. _____	_____
2. Increase Social Security Taxes Payable to record the amount withheld from employee earnings.	2. _____	_____
3. Decrease State Unemployment Taxes Payable to record the deposit of SUTA tax.	3. _____	_____
4. Increase Salaries and Wages Payable to record the amounts owed to employees.	4. _____	_____
5. Decrease Cash to record payment of the payroll.	5. _____	_____
6. Decrease Savings Bonds Payable to record the purchase of savings bonds for the employees.	6. _____	_____
7. Decrease Salaries and Wages Payable to record payment of the payroll.	7. _____	_____
8. Increase Payroll Taxes Expense to record the payroll taxes owed by the employer.	8. _____	_____
9. Decrease Social Security Taxes Payable to record the deposit of these taxes.	9. _____	_____
10. Increase Federal Unemployment Taxes Payable to record the FUTA tax owed by the employer.	10. _____	_____

EXERCISE 11.4A   The information shown here is from the payroll register of Sunrise Health Food, a retail store. The amounts are for the week ended January 28 of the current year. Prepare the journal entry needed to record the payroll. Use the general journal given on page 296. A partial chart of accounts for Sunrise Health Food appears in Exercise 11.3A.

Total gross earnings	$3,960.00
Total employee federal income tax withheld	432.00
Total social security tax withheld	245.52
Total Medicare tax withheld	57.42
Total employee state income tax withheld	83.16
Total saving bonds deductions	175.00
Total net pay	2,966.90

Note: Save the general journal for use in Exercises 11.5A and 11.6A.

EXERCISE 11.5A

Prepare the journal entry to record the employer's payroll taxes for the January 28 payroll at Sunrise Health Food. To compute these taxes, use the following rates: 0.8 percent for FUTA tax and 1.5 percent for SUTA tax. The entire amount of gross earnings listed in Exercise 11.4A is subject to these taxes. (Use the general journal from Exercise 11.4A for your entry.)

EXERCISE 11.6A

On January 31 of the current year, Sunrise Health Food issued paychecks to its employees. These paychecks are for the weekly payroll period ended January 28. (See Exercise 11.4A.) Prepare the journal entry that is needed to record payment of this payroll. (Continue to use the general journal from Exercise 11.4A.)

EXERCISE 11.7A

After the South Beach Motel recorded its payroll and its employer payroll taxes for the week ended March 31 of the current year, its general ledger showed a balance of $2,764 in the Employee Federal Income Taxes Payable account, a balance of $2,118 in the Social Security Taxes Payable account, and a balance of $626 in the Medicare Taxes Payable account. On April 2, the firm prepared Form 8109 and issued a check for the total of the amounts owed. It then deposited these amounts in the Lincoln National Bank. Prepare a journal entry to record the deposit. Use the general journal on page 297.

EXERCISE 11.8A

On July 27 of the current year, True-Comfort Shoes, a retail store, issued a check for $136 to cover the FUTA tax it owed for the first and second quarters. The firm then submitted this deposit to its bank with a completed copy of Form 8109. Prepare a journal entry for this deposit. Use the general journal on page 298.

GENERAL JOURNAL

PAGE _____

DATE	DESCRIPTION OF ENTRY	POST. REF.	DEBIT	CREDIT

GENERAL JOURNAL   PAGE _____

DATE	DESCRIPTION OF ENTRY	POST. REF.	DEBIT	CREDIT

GENERAL JOURNAL   PAGE _____

DATE	DESCRIPTION OF ENTRY	POST. REF.	DEBIT	CREDIT

Appendix

Tax Tables

This appendix contains the following tax tables:

SINGLE Persons—WEEKLY Payroll Period

(For Wages Paid Through December 2004)

If the wages are—		And the number of withholding allowances claimed is—										
At least	But less than	0	1	2	3	4	5	6	7	8	9	10
		The amount of income tax to be withheld is—										
$0	$55	$0	$0	$0	$0	$0	$0	$0	$0	$0	$0	$0
55	60	1	0	0	0	0	0	0	0	0	0	0
60	65	1	0	0	0	0	0	0	0	0	0	0
65	70	2	0	0	0	0	0	0	0	0	0	0
70	75	2	0	0	0	0	0	0	0	0	0	0
75	80	3	0	0	0	0	0	0	0	0	0	0
80	85	3	0	0	0	0	0	0	0	0	0	0
85	90	4	0	0	0	0	0	0	0	0	0	0
90	95	4	0	0	0	0	0	0	0	0	0	0
95	100	5	0	0	0	0	0	0	0	0	0	0
100	105	5	0	0	0	0	0	0	0	0	0	0
105	110	6	0	0	0	0	0	0	0	0	0	0
110	115	6	0	0	0	0	0	0	0	0	0	0
115	120	7	1	0	0	0	0	0	0	0	0	0
120	125	7	1	0	0	0	0	0	0	0	0	0
125	130	8	2	0	0	0	0	0	0	0	0	0
130	135	8	2	0	0	0	0	0	0	0	0	0
135	140	9	3	0	0	0	0	0	0	0	0	0
140	145	9	3	0	0	0	0	0	0	0	0	0
145	150	10	4	0	0	0	0	0	0	0	0	0
150	155	10	4	0	0	0	0	0	0	0	0	0
155	160	11	5	0	0	0	0	0	0	0	0	0
160	165	11	5	0	0	0	0	0	0	0	0	0
165	170	12	6	0	0	0	0	0	0	0	0	0
170	175	12	6	0	0	0	0	0	0	0	0	0
175	180	13	7	1	0	0	0	0	0	0	0	0
180	185	13	7	1	0	0	0	0	0	0	0	0
185	190	14	8	2	0	0	0	0	0	0	0	0
190	195	14	8	2	0	0	0	0	0	0	0	0
195	200	15	9	3	0	0	0	0	0	0	0	0
200	210	16	9	3	0	0	0	0	0	0	0	0
210	220	18	10	4	0	0	0	0	0	0	0	0
220	230	19	11	5	0	0	0	0	0	0	0	0
230	240	21	12	6	1	0	0	0	0	0	0	0
240	250	22	13	7	2	0	0	0	0	0	0	0
250	260	24	15	8	3	0	0	0	0	0	0	0
260	270	25	16	9	4	0	0	0	0	0	0	0
270	280	27	18	10	5	0	0	0	0	0	0	0
280	290	28	19	11	6	0	0	0	0	0	0	0
290	300	30	21	12	7	1	0	0	0	0	0	0
300	310	31	22	13	8	2	0	0	0	0	0	0
310	320	33	24	15	9	3	0	0	0	0	0	0
320	330	34	25	16	10	4	0	0	0	0	0	0
330	340	36	27	18	11	5	0	0	0	0	0	0
340	350	37	28	19	12	6	0	0	0	0	0	0
350	360	39	30	21	13	7	1	0	0	0	0	0
360	370	40	31	22	14	8	2	0	0	0	0	0
370	380	42	33	24	15	9	3	0	0	0	0	0
380	390	43	34	25	17	10	4	0	0	0	0	0
390	400	45	36	27	18	11	5	0	0	0	0	0
400	410	46	37	28	20	12	6	0	0	0	0	0
410	420	48	39	30	21	13	7	1	0	0	0	0
420	430	49	40	31	23	14	8	2	0	0	0	0
430	440	51	42	33	24	15	9	3	0	0	0	0
440	450	52	43	34	26	17	10	4	0	0	0	0
450	460	54	45	36	27	18	11	5	0	0	0	0
460	470	55	46	37	29	20	12	6	0	0	0	0
470	480	57	48	39	30	21	13	7	1	0	0	0
480	490	58	49	40	32	23	14	8	2	0	0	0
490	500	60	51	42	33	24	15	9	3	0	0	0
500	510	61	52	43	35	26	17	10	4	0	0	0
510	520	63	54	45	36	27	18	11	5	0	0	0
520	530	64	55	46	38	29	20	12	6	0	0	0
530	540	66	57	48	39	30	21	13	7	1	0	0
540	550	67	58	49	41	32	23	14	8	2	0	0
550	560	69	60	51	42	33	24	15	9	3	0	0
560	570	70	61	52	44	35	26	17	10	4	0	0
570	580	72	63	54	45	36	27	18	11	5	0	0
580	590	73	64	55	47	38	29	20	12	6	0	0
590	600	75	66	57	48	39	30	21	13	7	1	0

SINGLE Persons—WEEKLY Payroll Period
(For Wages Paid Through December 2004)

If the wages are—		And the number of withholding allowances claimed is—										
At least	But less than	0	1	2	3	4	5	6	7	8	9	10
		The amount of income tax to be withheld is—										
$600	$610	$78	$67	$58	$50	$41	$32	$23	$14	$8	$2	$0
610	620	80	69	60	51	42	33	24	15	9	3	0
620	630	83	70	61	53	44	35	26	17	10	4	0
630	640	85	72	63	54	45	36	27	18	11	5	0
640	650	88	73	64	56	47	38	29	20	12	6	0
650	660	90	75	66	57	48	39	30	21	13	7	1
660	670	93	78	67	59	50	41	32	23	14	8	2
670	680	95	80	69	60	51	42	33	24	15	9	3
680	690	98	83	70	62	53	44	35	26	17	10	4
690	700	100	85	72	63	54	45	36	27	18	11	5
700	710	103	88	73	65	56	47	38	29	20	12	6
710	720	105	90	75	66	57	48	39	30	21	13	7
720	730	108	93	78	68	59	50	41	32	23	14	8
730	740	110	95	80	69	60	51	42	33	24	15	9
740	750	113	98	83	71	62	53	44	35	26	17	10
750	760	115	100	85	72	63	54	45	36	27	18	11
760	770	118	103	88	74	65	56	47	38	29	20	12
770	780	120	105	90	75	66	57	48	39	30	21	13
780	790	123	108	93	78	68	59	50	41	32	23	14
790	800	125	110	95	80	69	60	51	42	33	24	15
800	810	128	113	98	83	71	62	53	44	35	26	17
810	820	130	115	100	85	72	63	54	45	36	27	18
820	830	133	118	103	88	74	65	56	47	38	29	20
830	840	135	120	105	90	75	66	57	48	39	30	21
840	850	138	123	108	93	78	68	59	50	41	32	23
850	860	140	125	110	95	80	69	60	51	42	33	24
860	870	143	128	113	98	83	71	62	53	44	35	26
870	880	145	130	115	100	85	72	63	54	45	36	27
880	890	148	133	118	103	88	74	65	56	47	38	29
890	900	150	135	120	105	90	76	66	57	48	39	30
900	910	153	138	123	108	93	78	68	59	50	41	32
910	920	155	140	125	110	95	81	69	60	51	42	33
920	930	158	143	128	113	98	83	71	62	53	44	35
930	940	160	145	130	115	100	86	72	63	54	45	36
940	950	163	148	133	118	103	88	74	65	56	47	38
950	960	165	150	135	120	105	91	76	66	57	48	39
960	970	168	153	138	123	108	93	78	68	59	50	41
970	980	170	155	140	125	110	96	81	69	60	51	42
980	990	173	158	143	128	113	98	83	71	62	53	44
990	1,000	175	160	145	130	115	101	86	72	63	54	45
1,000	1,010	178	163	148	133	118	103	88	74	65	56	47
1,010	1,020	180	165	150	135	120	106	91	76	66	57	48
1,020	1,030	183	168	153	138	123	108	93	78	68	59	50
1,030	1,040	185	170	155	140	125	111	96	81	69	60	51
1,040	1,050	188	173	158	143	128	113	98	83	71	62	53
1,050	1,060	190	175	160	145	130	116	101	86	72	63	54
1,060	1,070	193	178	163	148	133	118	103	88	74	65	56
1,070	1,080	195	180	165	150	135	121	106	91	76	66	57
1,080	1,090	198	183	168	153	138	123	108	93	78	68	59
1,090	1,100	200	185	170	155	140	126	111	96	81	69	60
1,100	1,110	203	188	173	158	143	128	113	98	83	71	62
1,110	1,120	205	190	175	160	145	131	116	101	86	72	63
1,120	1,130	208	193	178	163	148	133	118	103	88	74	65
1,130	1,140	210	195	180	165	150	136	121	106	91	76	66
1,140	1,150	213	198	183	168	153	138	123	108	93	78	68
1,150	1,160	215	200	185	170	155	141	126	111	96	81	69
1,160	1,170	218	203	188	173	158	143	128	113	98	83	71
1,170	1,180	220	205	190	175	160	146	131	116	101	86	72
1,180	1,190	223	208	193	178	163	148	133	118	103	88	74
1,190	1,200	225	210	195	180	165	151	136	121	106	91	76
1,200	1,210	228	213	198	183	168	153	138	123	108	93	79
1,210	1,220	230	215	200	185	170	156	141	126	111	96	81
1,220	1,230	233	218	203	188	173	158	143	128	113	98	84
1,230	1,240	235	220	205	190	175	161	146	131	116	101	86
1,240	1,250	238	223	208	193	178	163	148	133	118	103	89

$1,250 and over   Use Table 1(a) for a **SINGLE person**.

MARRIED Persons—WEEKLY Payroll Period

(For Wages Paid Through December 2004)

If the wages are—		And the number of withholding allowances claimed is—										
At least	But less than	0	1	2	3	4	5	6	7	8	9	10
		The amount of income tax to be withheld is—										
$0	$125	$0	$0	$0	$0	$0	$0	$0	$0	$0	$0	$0
125	130	0	0	0	0	0	0	0	0	0	0	0
130	135	0	0	0	0	0	0	0	0	0	0	0
135	140	0	0	0	0	0	0	0	0	0	0	0
140	145	0	0	0	0	0	0	0	0	0	0	0
145	150	0	0	0	0	0	0	0	0	0	0	0
150	155	0	0	0	0	0	0	0	0	0	0	0
155	160	0	0	0	0	0	0	0	0	0	0	0
160	165	1	0	0	0	0	0	0	0	0	0	0
165	170	1	0	0	0	0	0	0	0	0	0	0
170	175	2	0	0	0	0	0	0	0	0	0	0
175	180	2	0	0	0	0	0	0	0	0	0	0
180	185	3	0	0	0	0	0	0	0	0	0	0
185	190	3	0	0	0	0	0	0	0	0	0	0
190	195	4	0	0	0	0	0	0	0	0	0	0
195	200	4	0	0	0	0	0	0	0	0	0	0
200	210	5	0	0	0	0	0	0	0	0	0	0
210	220	6	0	0	0	0	0	0	0	0	0	0
220	230	7	1	0	0	0	0	0	0	0	0	0
230	240	8	2	0	0	0	0	0	0	0	0	0
240	250	9	3	0	0	0	0	0	0	0	0	0
250	260	10	4	0	0	0	0	0	0	0	0	0
260	270	11	5	0	0	0	0	0	0	0	0	0
270	280	12	6	0	0	0	0	0	0	0	0	0
280	290	13	7	1	0	0	0	0	0	0	0	0
290	300	14	8	2	0	0	0	0	0	0	0	0
300	310	15	9	3	0	0	0	0	0	0	0	0
310	320	16	10	4	0	0	0	0	0	0	0	0
320	330	17	11	5	0	0	0	0	0	0	0	0
330	340	18	12	6	0	0	0	0	0	0	0	0
340	350	19	13	7	1	0	0	0	0	0	0	0
350	360	20	14	8	2	0	0	0	0	0	0	0
360	370	21	15	9	3	0	0	0	0	0	0	0
370	380	22	16	10	4	0	0	0	0	0	0	0
380	390	23	17	11	5	0	0	0	0	0	0	0
390	400	24	18	12	6	0	0	0	0	0	0	0
400	410	25	19	13	7	1	0	0	0	0	0	0
410	420	26	20	14	8	2	0	0	0	0	0	0
420	430	27	21	15	9	3	0	0	0	0	0	0
430	440	28	22	16	10	4	0	0	0	0	0	0
440	450	30	23	17	11	5	0	0	0	0	0	0
450	460	31	24	18	12	6	0	0	0	0	0	0
460	470	33	25	19	13	7	1	0	0	0	0	0
470	480	34	26	20	14	8	2	0	0	0	0	0
480	490	36	27	21	15	9	3	0	0	0	0	0
490	500	37	28	22	16	10	4	0	0	0	0	0
500	510	39	30	23	17	11	5	0	0	0	0	0
510	520	40	31	24	18	12	6	0	0	0	0	0
520	530	42	33	25	19	13	7	1	0	0	0	0
530	540	43	34	26	20	14	8	2	0	0	0	0
540	550	45	36	27	21	15	9	3	0	0	0	0
550	560	46	37	29	22	16	10	4	0	0	0	0
560	570	48	39	30	23	17	11	5	0	0	0	0
570	580	49	40	32	24	18	12	6	0	0	0	0
580	590	51	42	33	25	19	13	7	1	0	0	0
590	600	52	43	35	26	20	14	8	2	0	0	0
600	610	54	45	36	27	21	15	9	3	0	0	0
610	620	55	46	38	29	22	16	10	4	0	0	0
620	630	57	48	39	30	23	17	11	5	0	0	0
630	640	58	49	41	32	24	18	12	6	0	0	0
640	650	60	51	42	33	25	19	13	7	1	0	0
650	660	61	52	44	35	26	20	14	8	2	0	0
660	670	63	54	45	36	27	21	15	9	3	0	0
670	680	64	55	47	38	29	22	16	10	4	0	0
680	690	66	57	48	39	30	23	17	11	5	0	0
690	700	67	58	50	41	32	24	18	12	6	0	0
700	710	69	60	51	42	33	25	19	13	7	1	0
710	720	70	61	53	44	35	26	20	14	8	2	0
720	730	72	63	54	45	36	27	21	15	9	3	0
730	740	73	64	56	47	38	29	22	16	10	4	0

MARRIED Persons—WEEKLY Payroll Period
(For Wages Paid Through December 2004)

If the wages are—		And the number of withholding allowances claimed is—										
At least	But less than	0	1	2	3	4	5	6	7	8	9	10
		The amount of income tax to be withheld is—										
$740	$750	$75	$66	$57	$48	$39	$30	$23	$17	$11	$5	$0
750	760	76	67	59	50	41	32	24	18	12	6	1
760	770	78	69	60	51	42	33	25	19	13	7	2
770	780	79	70	62	53	44	35	26	20	14	8	3
780	790	81	72	63	54	45	36	27	21	15	9	4
790	800	82	73	65	56	47	38	29	22	16	10	5
800	810	84	75	66	57	48	39	30	23	17	11	6
810	820	85	76	68	59	50	41	32	24	18	12	7
820	830	87	78	69	60	51	42	33	25	19	13	8
830	840	88	79	71	62	53	44	35	26	20	14	9
840	850	90	81	72	63	54	45	36	27	21	15	10
850	860	91	82	74	65	56	47	38	29	22	16	11
860	870	93	84	75	66	57	48	39	30	23	17	12
870	880	94	85	77	68	59	50	41	32	24	18	13
880	890	96	87	78	69	60	51	42	33	25	19	14
890	900	97	88	80	71	62	53	44	35	26	20	15
900	910	99	90	81	72	63	54	45	36	27	21	16
910	920	100	91	83	74	65	56	47	38	29	22	17
920	930	102	93	84	75	66	57	48	39	30	23	18
930	940	103	94	86	77	68	59	50	41	32	24	19
940	950	105	96	87	78	69	60	51	42	33	25	20
950	960	106	97	89	80	71	62	53	44	35	26	21
960	970	108	99	90	81	72	63	54	45	36	27	22
970	980	109	100	92	83	74	65	56	47	38	29	23
980	990	111	102	93	84	75	66	57	48	39	30	24
990	1,000	112	103	95	86	77	68	59	50	41	32	25
1,000	1,010	114	105	96	87	78	69	60	51	42	33	26
1,010	1,020	115	106	98	89	80	71	62	53	44	35	27
1,020	1,030	117	108	99	90	81	72	63	54	45	36	28
1,030	1,040	118	109	101	92	83	74	65	56	47	38	29
1,040	1,050	120	111	102	93	84	75	66	57	48	39	31
1,050	1,060	121	112	104	95	86	77	68	59	50	41	32
1,060	1,070	123	114	105	96	87	78	69	60	51	42	34
1,070	1,080	124	115	107	98	89	80	71	62	53	44	35
1,080	1,090	126	117	108	99	90	81	72	63	54	45	37
1,090	1,100	127	118	110	101	92	83	74	65	56	47	38
1,100	1,110	129	120	111	102	93	84	75	66	57	48	40
1,110	1,120	130	121	113	104	95	86	77	68	59	50	41
1,120	1,130	132	123	114	105	96	87	78	69	60	51	43
1,130	1,140	133	124	116	107	98	89	80	71	62	53	44
1,140	1,150	135	126	117	108	99	90	81	72	63	54	46
1,150	1,160	136	127	119	110	101	92	83	74	65	56	47
1,160	1,170	138	129	120	111	102	93	84	75	66	57	49
1,170	1,180	139	130	122	113	104	95	86	77	68	59	50
1,180	1,190	141	132	123	114	105	96	87	78	69	60	52
1,190	1,200	142	133	125	116	107	98	89	80	71	62	53
1,200	1,210	144	135	126	117	108	99	90	81	72	63	55
1,210	1,220	145	136	128	119	110	101	92	83	74	65	56
1,220	1,230	147	138	129	120	111	102	93	84	75	66	58
1,230	1,240	148	139	131	122	113	104	95	86	77	68	59
1,240	1,250	150	141	132	123	114	105	96	87	78	69	61
1,250	1,260	152	142	134	125	116	107	98	89	80	71	62
1,260	1,270	155	144	135	126	117	108	99	90	81	72	64
1,270	1,280	157	145	137	128	119	110	101	92	83	74	65
1,280	1,290	160	147	138	129	120	111	102	93	84	75	67
1,290	1,300	162	148	140	131	122	113	104	95	86	77	68
1,300	1,310	165	150	141	132	123	114	105	96	87	78	70
1,310	1,320	167	153	143	134	125	116	107	98	89	80	71
1,320	1,330	170	155	144	135	126	117	108	99	90	81	73
1,330	1,340	172	158	146	137	128	119	110	101	92	83	74
1,340	1,350	175	160	147	138	129	120	111	102	93	84	76
1,350	1,360	177	163	149	140	131	122	113	104	95	86	77
1,360	1,370	180	165	150	141	132	123	114	105	96	87	79
1,370	1,380	182	168	153	143	134	125	116	107	98	89	80
1,380	1,390	185	170	155	144	135	126	117	108	99	90	82
1,390	1,400	187	173	158	146	137	128	119	110	101	92	83

$1,400 and over   Use Table 1(b) for a **MARRIED person**.

SINGLE PERSONS, DUAL INCOME MARRIED
OR MARRIED WITH MULTIPLE EMPLOYERS----WEEKLY PAYROLL PERIOD

(FOR WAGES PAID IN 2004)

IF WAGES ARE...   AND THE NUMBER OF WITHHOLDING ALLOWANCES CLAIMED IS...

AT LEAST	BUT LESS THAN	0	1	2	3	4	5	6	7	8	9	10 OR MORE
					...THE AMOUNT OF INCOME TAX TO BE WITHHELD SHALL BE...							
$1	$140											
140	150	0.86										
150	160	0.96										
160	170	1.06										
170	180	1.17										
180	190	1.37										
190	200	1.57										
200	210	1.77	0.19									
210	220	1.97	0.39									
220	230	2.17	0.59									
230	240	2.37	0.79									
240	250	2.57	0.99									
250	260	2.77	1.19									
260	270	2.97	1.39									
270	280	3.17	1.59	0.01								
280	290	3.37	1.79	0.21								
290	300	3.57	1.99	0.41								
300	310	3.77	2.19	0.61								
310	320	3.97	2.39	0.81								
320	330	4.17	2.59	1.01								
330	340	4.45	2.87	1.29								
340	350	4.85	3.27	1.60	0.11							
350	360	5.25	3.67	2.09	0.51							
360	370	5.65	4.07	2.49	0.91							
370	380	6.05	4.47	2.89	1.31							
380	390	6.45	4.87	3.29	1.71	0.13						
390	400	6.85	5.27	3.69	2.11	0.53						
400	410	7.25	5.67	4.09	2.51	0.93						
410	420	7.65	6.07	4.49	2.91	1.33						
420	440	8.25	6.67	5.09	3.51	1.93	0.35					
440	460	9.05	7.47	5.89	4.31	2.73	1.15					
460	480	9.85	8.27	6.69	5.11	3.53	1.95	0.37				
480	500	10.69	9.11	7.53	5.95	4.37	2.79	1.21				
500	520	11.89	10.31	8.73	7.15	5.57	3.99	2.41	0.83			
520	540	13.09	11.51	9.93	8.35	6.77	5.19	3.61	2.03	0.45		
540	560	14.29	12.71	11.13	9.55	7.97	6.39	4.81	3.23	1.65	0.07	
560	580	15.49	13.91	12.33	10.75	9.17	7.59	6.01	4.43	2.85	1.27	
580	600	16.69	15.11	13.53	11.95	10.37	8.79	7.21	5.63	4.05	2.47	0.89
600	620	17.89	16.31	14.73	13.15	11.57	9.99	8.41	6.83	5.25	3.67	2.09
620	660	19.69	18.11	16.53	14.95	13.37	11.79	10.21	8.63	7.05	5.47	3.89
660	700	22.61	21.03	19.45	17.87	16.29	14.71	13.13	11.55	9.97	8.39	6.81
700	740	25.81	24.23	22.65	21.07	19.49	17.91	16.33	14.75	13.17	11.59	10.01
740	780	29.01	27.43	25.85	24.27	22.69	21.11	19.53	17.95	16.37	14.79	13.21
780	820	32.21	30.63	29.05	27.47	25.89	24.31	22.73	21.15	19.57	17.99	16.41
820	860	35.77	34.19	32.61	31.03	29.45	27.87	26.29	24.71	23.13	21.55	19.97
860	900	39.49	37.91	36.33	34.75	33.17	31.59	30.01	28.43	26.85	25.27	23.69
900	940	43.21	41.63	40.05	38.47	36.89	35.31	33.73	32.15	30.57	28.99	27.41
940	980	46.93	45.35	43.77	42.19	40.61	39.03	37.45	35.87	34.29	32.71	31.13
980	1020	50.65	49.07	47.49	45.91	44.33	42.75	41.17	39.59	38.01	36.43	34.85
1020	1060	54.37	52.79	51.21	49.63	48.05	46.47	44.89	43.31	41.73	40.15	38.57
1060	1100	58.09	56.51	54.93	53.35	51.77	50.19	48.61	47.03	45.45	43.87	42.29

1100 and over   (Table Amount PLUS 9.3 Percent of the Amount Over 1080)

MARRIED PERSONS----WEEKLY PAYROLL PERIOD

(FOR WAGES PAID IN 2004)

IF WAGES ARE...   AND THE NUMBER OF WITHHOLDING ALLOWANCES CLAIMED IS...

AT LEAST	BUT LESS THAN	0	1	2	3	4	5	6	7	8	9	10 OR MORE
				...THE AMOUNT OF INCOME TAX TO BE WITHHELD SHALL BE...								
$1	$140											
140	150	0.86										
150	160	0.96										
160	170	1.06										
170	180	1.16										
180	190	1.26										
190	200	1.36										
200	210	1.46										
210	220	1.56										
220	230	1.66	0.08									
230	240	1.76	0.18									
240	250	1.86	0.28									
250	260	1.96	0.38									
260	270	2.06	0.48									
270	280	2.16	0.58									
280	290	2.26	0.68									
290	300	2.42	0.84									
300	310	2.62	1.04									
310	320	2.82	1.24									
320	330	3.02	1.44									
330	340	3.22	1.64									
340	350	3.42	1.84									
350	360	3.62	2.04									
360	370	3.82	2.24									
370	380	4.02	2.44									
380	390	4.22	2.64									
390	400	4.42	2.84	0.08								
400	410	4.62	3.04	0.28								
410	420	4.82	3.24	0.48								
420	440	5.12	3.54	0.78								
440	460	5.52	3.94	1.18								
460	480	5.92	4.34	1.58								
480	500	6.32	4.74	1.98	0.40							
500	520	6.72	5.14	2.38	0.80							
520	540	7.12	5.54	2.78	1.20							
540	560	7.52	5.94	3.18	1.60	0.02						
560	580	7.92	6.34	3.58	2.00	0.42						
580	600	8.32	6.74	3.98	2.40	0.82						
600	620	8.86	7.28	4.38	2.80	1.22						
620	640	9.66	8.08	4.78	3.20	1.62	0.04					
640	660	10.46	8.88	5.18	3.60	2.02	0.44					
660	680	11.26	9.68	5.74	4.16	2.58	1.00					
680	700	12.06	10.48	6.54	4.96	3.38	1.80	0.22				
700	720	12.86	11.28	7.34	5.76	4.18	2.60	1.02	0.00			
720	740	13.66	12.08	8.14	6.56	4.98	3.40	1.82	0.24			
740	760	14.46	12.88	8.94	7.36	5.78	4.20	2.62	1.04			
760	780	15.26	13.68	9.74	8.16	6.58	5.00	3.42	1.84	0.26		
780	800	16.06	14.48	10.54	8.96	7.38	5.80	4.22	2.64	1.06		
800	820	16.86	15.28	11.34	9.76	8.18	6.60	5.02	3.44	1.86	0.28	
820	840	17.66	16.08	12.14	10.56	8.98	7.40	5.82	4.24	2.66	1.08	
840	860	18.46	16.88	12.94	11.36	9.78	8.20	6.62	5.04	3.46	1.88	0.30

--- CONTINUED NEXT PAGE ---

MARRIED PERSONS----WEEKLY PAYROLL PERIOD

(FOR WAGES PAID IN 2004)

IF WAGES ARE...		AND THE NUMBER OF WITHHOLDING ALLOWANCES CLAIMED IS...										
AT LEAST	BUT LESS THAN	0	1	2	3	4	5	6	7	8	9	10 OR MORE
		...THE AMOUNT OF INCOME TAX TO BE WITHHELD SHALL BE...										
860	880	19.26	17.68	13.74	12.16	10.58	9.00	7.42	5.84	4.26	2.68	1.10
880	900	20.06	18.48	14.54	12.96	11.38	9.80	8.22	6.64	5.06	3.48	1.90
900	920	20.86	19.28	15.34	13.76	12.18	10.60	9.02	7.44	5.86	4.28	2.70
920	940	21.92	20.34	16.14	14.56	12.98	11.40	9.82	8.24	6.66	5.08	3.50
940	960	23.12	21.54	16.94	15.36	13.78	12.20	10.62	9.04	7.46	5.88	4.30
960	980	24.32	22.74	17.74	16.16	14.58	13.00	11.42	9.84	8.26	6.68	5.10
980	1000	25.52	23.94	18.82	17.24	15.66	14.08	12.50	10.92	9.34	7.76	6.18
1000	1020	26.72	25.14	20.02	18.44	16.86	15.28	13.70	12.12	10.54	8.96	7.38
1020	1040	27.92	26.34	21.22	19.64	18.06	16.48	14.90	13.32	11.74	10.16	8.58
1040	1060	29.12	27.54	22.42	20.84	19.26	17.68	16.10	14.52	12.94	11.36	9.78
1060	1080	30.32	28.74	23.62	22.04	20.46	18.88	17.30	15.72	14.14	12.56	10.98
1080	1100	31.52	29.94	24.82	23.24	21.66	20.08	18.50	16.92	15.34	13.76	12.18
1100	1120	32.72	31.14	26.02	24.44	22.86	21.28	19.70	18.12	16.54	14.96	13.38
1120	1160	34.52	32.94	27.82	26.24	24.66	23.08	21.50	19.92	18.34	16.76	15.18
1160	1200	36.92	35.34	30.22	28.64	27.06	25.48	23.90	22.32	20.74	19.16	17.58
1200	1240	39.32	37.74	32.62	31.04	29.46	27.88	26.30	24.72	23.14	21.56	19.98
1240	1280	41.94	40.36	35.02	33.44	31.86	30.28	28.70	27.12	25.54	23.96	22.38
1280	1320	45.14	43.56	37.42	35.84	34.26	32.68	31.10	29.52	27.94	26.36	24.78
1320	1360	48.34	46.76	40.45	38.87	37.29	35.71	34.13	32.55	30.97	29.39	27.81
1360	1400	51.54	49.96	43.65	42.07	40.49	38.91	37.33	35.75	34.17	32.59	31.01
1400	1440	54.74	53.16	46.85	45.27	43.69	42.11	40.53	38.95	37.37	35.79	34.21
1440	1480	57.94	56.36	50.05	48.47	46.89	45.31	43.73	42.15	40.57	38.99	37.41
1480	1520	61.14	59.56	53.25	51.67	50.09	48.51	46.93	45.35	43.77	42.19	40.61
1520	1560	64.34	62.76	56.45	54.87	53.29	51.71	50.13	48.55	46.97	45.39	43.81
1560	1600	67.73	66.15	59.65	58.07	56.49	54.91	53.33	51.75	50.17	48.59	47.01
1600	1640	71.45	69.87	62.85	61.27	59.69	58.11	56.53	54.95	53.37	51.79	50.21
1640	1680	75.17	73.59	66.52	64.94	63.36	61.78	60.20	58.62	57.04	55.46	53.88
1680	1720	78.89	77.31	70.24	68.66	67.08	65.50	63.92	62.34	60.76	59.18	57.60
1720	1760	82.61	81.03	73.96	72.38	70.80	69.22	67.64	66.06	64.48	62.90	61.32
1760	1800	86.33	84.75	77.68	76.10	74.52	72.94	71.36	69.78	68.20	66.62	65.04
1800	1840	90.05	88.47	81.40	79.82	78.24	76.66	75.08	73.50	71.92	70.34	68.76
1840	1880	93.77	92.19	85.12	83.54	81.96	80.38	78.80	77.22	75.64	74.06	72.48
1880	1920	97.49	95.91	88.84	87.26	85.68	84.10	82.52	80.94	79.36	77.78	76.20
1920	1960	101.21	99.63	92.56	90.98	89.40	87.82	86.24	84.66	83.08	81.50	79.92
1960	2000	104.93	103.35	96.28	94.70	93.12	91.54	89.96	88.38	86.80	85.22	83.64
2000	2040	108.65	107.07	100.00	98.42	96.84	95.26	93.68	92.10	90.52	88.94	87.36
2040	2080	112.37	110.79	103.72	102.14	100.56	98.98	97.40	95.82	94.24	92.66	91.08
2080	2120	116.09	114.51	107.44	105.86	104.28	102.70	101.12	99.54	97.96	96.38	94.80
2120	2160	119.81	118.23	111.16	109.58	108.00	106.42	104.84	103.26	101.68	100.10	98.52
2160	2200	123.53	121.95	114.88	113.30	111.72	110.14	108.56	106.98	105.40	103.82	102.24

| 2200 and over | (Table Amount PLUS 9.3 Percent of the Amount Over 2180) |

CALIFORNIA WITHHOLDING SCHEDULES FOR 2004
METHOD A---WAGE BRACKET TABLE METHOD

TABLE 1 - LOW INCOME EXEMPTION TABLE

| PAYROLL PERIOD | SINGLE, DUAL INCOME MARRIED OR MARRIED WITH MULTIPLE EMPLOYERS | MARRIED | | UNMARRIED HEAD OF HOUSEHOLD |
| | | ALLOWANCES ON DE 4 OR W-4 | | |
		'0' OR '1'	'2' OR MORE	
WEEKLY	$196	$196	$390	$390
BIWEEKLY	$391	$391	$781	$781
SEMI-MONTHLY	$424	$424	$846	$846
MONTHLY	$848	$848	$1,692	$1,692
QUARTERLY	$2,544	$2,544	$5,076	$5,076
SEMI-ANNUAL	$5,089	$5,089	$10,151	$10,151
ANNUAL	$10,177	$10,177	$20,302	$20,302
DAILY/MISCELLANEOUS	$39	$39	$78	$78

TABLE 2 - ESTIMATED DEDUCTION TABLE

ADDITIONAL WITHHOLDING ALLOWANCES *	WEEKLY	BI-WEEKLY	SEMI-MONTHLY	MONTHLY	QUARTERLY	SEMI-ANNUAL	ANNUAL	DAILY/ MISC.
1	$19	$38	$42	$83	$250	$500	$1,000	$4
2	$38	$77	$83	$167	$500	$1,000	$2,000	$8
3	$58	$115	$125	$250	$750	$1,500	$3,000	$12
4	$77	$154	$167	$333	$1,000	$2,000	$4,000	$15
5	$96	$192	$208	$417	$1,250	$2,500	$5,000	$19
6	$115	$231	$250	$500	$1,500	$3,000	$6,000	$23
7	$135	$269	$292	$583	$1,750	$3,500	$7,000	$27
8	$154	$308	$333	$667	$2,000	$4,000	$8,000	$31
9	$173	$346	$375	$750	$2,250	$4,500	$9,000	$35
10**	$192	$385	$417	$833	$2,500	$5,000	$10,000	$38

* Number of Additional Withholding Allowances for Estimated Deductions claimed on form DE-4 or W-4.

** If the number of Additional Withholding Allowances for Estimated Deductions claimed is greater than 10, multiply the amount shown for one Additional Allowance by the number claimed.

Glossary of Payroll Terms

A

Account A separate record of each asset, liability, owner's equity, revenue, and expense item that a business has.

Annualizing method A method of determining an employee's income tax withholding for each payroll period by prorating the estimated yearly amount of tax over all payroll periods.

Assets Items of value that a business owns.

B

Bank transfer form A form used by businesses that pay their employees by the direct-deposit plan. This form shows the name, checking account number, and net pay of each employee. It authorizes the bank to transfer funds from the business's checking account to the accounts of the employees.

Biweekly Every two weeks.

Block flowchart A diagram using boxes and arrows to illustrate each step in a procedure.

Bonus A payment made to an employee as a reward for extra effort on the job.

C

Calendar year A 12-month period starting January 1 and ending December 31.

Chart of accounts A listing of the accounts in a firm's general ledger.

Circular E, Employer's Tax Guide A booklet published by the Internal Revenue Service for use by employers in making deductions for federal income tax and social security tax.

Commission plan A payment plan in which salespeople receive a percentage of their sales.

Computer Network A series of personal computers that share information through a common data base or share software through a server.

Contribution report A quarterly tax return filed with the state by an employer. It shows the wages paid during the period and the tax amounts owed. The types of taxes covered by such a report depend on the state but may include state income tax, state unemployment compensation tax, and state disability insurance tax.

Credit an account Enter an amount on the right side of an account.

Cross-footing The process of verifying the accuracy of column totals by adding and subtracting them.

Current Tax Payment Act A federal law passed in 1943 that requires employers to withhold federal income taxes from the earnings of their employees.

Custom-made payroll form A payroll form that has been specially designed to meet the needs of one business.

D

Debit an account Enter an amount on the left side of an account.

Deductions Amounts withheld by an employer from an employee's earnings.

Direct-deposit plan A method of paying employees by depositing their net pay in their individual checking accounts.

E

Employee earnings record A payroll record that employers keep for each employee throughout a calendar year. This record lists hours worked, earnings, deductions, and net pay by payroll period.

Employee Retirement Income Security Act (ERISA) A federal law passed in 1974 to regulate the operations of pension funds.

Exemption An allowance that reduces the amount of an employee's earnings that is subject to income tax.

Expense A cost of operating a business.

Experience rating A method used by states to adjust an employer's payment of SUTA tax because of a favorable or unfavorable employment record.

F

Fair employment laws Laws that prohibit discrimination in employment practices on the basis of age, race, color, religion, sex, or national origin.

Fair Labor Standards Act (FLSA) A law passed by Congress in 1938 that regulates wages and hours of work. This law established a minimum wage and set standards for overtime pay.

Federal Insurance Contributions Act (FICA) A law that requires the payment of social security tax by employees and employers.

Federal Unemployment Tax Act (FUTA) A law that requires employer payments for the unemployment insurance portion of the social security system.

FICA tax A tax paid by both the employee and employer to support the federal social security system.

File A collection of related records in a computer system.

Flowchart A diagram that shows the various steps in a procedure and the sequence in which the steps occur.

Form I-9 The form that provides employment eligibility verification. Must be on file for all employees.

Form SS-5 The form that must be used to obtain a social security number.

Form 940, Employer's Annual Federal Unemployment Tax Return A tax report filed by an employer at the end of the calendar year to show the firm's liability for federal unemployment tax, the amount of tax deposited during the year, and the balance owed.

Form 941, Employer's Quarterly Federal Tax Return A tax report filed by an employer every three months to show the amount of federal income tax withheld from employee earnings, employer and employee liabilities for FICA tax, the amount of federal income and FICA tax deposited during the quarter, and the balance owed.

Form 8109, Federal Tax Deposit Coupon A form that must accompany each deposit of federal taxes in an authorized financial institution. It is used for deposits of employee federal income tax, FICA tax, and FUTA tax, as well as for deposits of other federal taxes. Form 8109 shows the total amount of tax being deposited.

Form W-2, Wage and Tax Statement A form used by an employer to report the amount of wages paid to an employee during a calendar year and the taxes withheld from those wages.

Form W-3, Transmittal of Income and Tax Statements A form that an employer files with the Social Security Administration each year when submitting copies of Form W-2 for all employees. Form W-3 shows the total taxes withheld from the employees.

Form W-4, Employee's Withholding Allowance Certificate A form that an employee must file with his or her employer to show the number of withholding allowances claimed for federal income tax purposes.

G

Garnishment A court-ordered deduction from an employee's wages to pay overdue debts.

Gross earnings Total regular earnings plus total overtime earnings.

H

Hourly-rate plan A payment plan in which employees receive a fixed amount for each hour worked.

I

Income tax A tax on the gross earnings of individuals that is levied by the federal government and many state and local governments.

Individual retirement account (IRA) A retirement account created and funded by an individual.

Input Data entered into a computer system.

Internal control A series of procedures and actions that are followed to protect a business's assets.

Internal Revenue Service (IRS) A government agency that enforces the federal income tax laws.

J

Job application form A form on which job applicants give detailed information about their education, skills, and work experience.

Journal A chronological record of business transactions, also a book of original entry.

L

Ledger A group of accounts used by a business.

Liabilities Amounts owed to creditors.

M

Magnetic disk A recordlike plastic or metal disk on which data can be stored magnetically. Files in computerized payroll systems are often kept on these disks.

Magnetic tape A mylar tape on which data can be stored magnetically. Files in computerized payroll systems are often kept on this type of tape.

Mainframe computer A powerful, high-speed computer with large internal memory.

Memory The unit of a computer where information is stored.

Minimum wage Minimum hourly rate of pay established by law.

N

Net pay Total gross earnings minus total deductions.

O

Overtime Time worked beyond 40 hours in a week.

Overtime earnings Earnings for all time worked beyond 40 hours in a week. This amount is computed by multiplying the overtime hours by the overtime rate.

P

Payroll checking account A special checking account set up by a business in order to issue employee paychecks.

Payroll register A record that lists the hours worked, earnings, deductions, and net pay of all employees for a payroll period.

Payroll service bureau A company that specializes in preparing payroll records for other businesses. Such companies make extensive use of computers to process payroll data for their clients.

Personnel file A record that contains information about the hiring, appraisal, transfer, promotion, and termination of an employee.

Piece-rate plan A payment plan in which employee earnings are based on the units produced.

Posting Transferring an amount from a journal to an account in the ledger.

Pre-tax deduction A deduction from gross earnings that is subtracted before the income tax deduction is calculated.

Production records Records that show the number of items an employee produces.

Profit-sharing plan A plan in which a business distributes part of its profits to employees in the form of cash or stock.

Q

Quarter Three calendar months.

R

Regular earnings   Earnings for the first 40 hours worked in a week.

Regular hours   The first 40 hours worked in a week.

S

Salary plan   A payment plan in which employees receive a fixed amount for each payroll period.

Salary-plus-commission plan   A payment plan in which the earnings of salespeople are based on a combination of time spent on the job and sales made.

Semimonthly   Twice a month.

Social Security Act   A law passed by Congress in 1935 to provide financial security for workers and their families.

Social security number   A number issued by the Social Security Administration that identifies an employee's social security account.

Standard payroll forms   Forms that can be used by many businesses because they have columns for basic payroll data.

State Disability Insurance (SDI) Tax   A tax levied by some states to provide disability insurance for employees.

State Unemployment Tax Acts (SUTA)   A tax levied by all states to provide income for unemployed workers. Usually, only the employer pays this tax.

T

Tax deposit   The payment of taxes owed to the government by an employer. This payment is made in a bank or other financial institution authorized by the government to receive tax money from employers.

Taxable wage base   Maximum amount of wages paid in a calendar year that is subject to a tax.

Time card   A form that contains a record of the hours worked by an employee. Normally, a time clock is used to enter arrival and departure times on the time card.

Time sheet   A time record that shows each employee's time of arrival and departure. The employee may sign in and out, or a supervisor may make the entries.

U

Unemployment compensation benefits   Payments made to workers who are temporarily unemployed.

V

Voluntary deductions   Optional deductions from an employee's earnings for such items as health insurance and savings bonds.

Voucher checks   Checks that usually have a detachable stub. When a voucher check is used for payroll, the stub contains a statement of earnings and deductions for the employee.

W

Wage-bracket method   A method of determining the amount of income tax to be withheld from an employee's earnings by taking the amount from a tax table.

Withholding allowance   An exemption that an employee claims for income tax purposes. Each exemption reduces the amount of federal income tax owed.

Workers' compensation insurance   Insurance paid for by employers that protects employees and their families against loss of income resulting from job-related accidents, disability, or death.

Index

Pennsylvania, 6
Pension plans, 113
Pension security laws, 9
Personal Income Tax (PIT), 240, 242
Personal Responsibility and Work Opportunity Reconciliation
        Act of 1996, 9, 30
Personnel file, 22
Piece-rate plan, 84–86
PIT. *See* California Personal Income Tax (PIT)
Pretax payroll deductions, 100, 108
Production records, 62, 63
Profit-sharing, 88–89
Publications. *See* Forms and publications
Puerto Rico, 8, 108

Q

Quarter-hour system, 58
Quarterly wage and withholding reports, 242, 243
QuickBooks, 182

R

Rhode Island, 6, 8, 109, 237
Roth Individual Retirement Account, 112

S

Salary plan, 82–84
Salary-plus-commission plan, 87–88
Sales records, 62, 63
Savings plans, 113
SDI. *See* State disability insurance (SDI) tax
Semiweekly schedule depositors, 197–198
Service bureau payroll processing, 177–179
Social security
    Federal Insurance Contribution Act (FICA), 3
    Federal Unemployment Tax Act (FUTA), 3, 4–5
    Medicare, 3
    old-age, survivors, and disability insurance
        (OASDI), 2–3
    payroll deductions and, 106–107
    payroll deposits, 196–197
    sample application form, 23
    social security laws, 2–4
    social security numbers, 22–24
Social Security Act of 1935, 2, 210, 235
Social Security Administration (SSA), 24
South Carolina, 6
South Dakota, 6, 108, 239
Special payroll accounts, 176
SSA. *See* Social Security Administration (SSA)
State disability insurance (SDI) tax, 109–110, 159,
        237–238, 241
State income taxes, 239–242
State payroll taxes and reports. *See also* Payroll
        deductions
    accounting for, 269–270, 277–278
    annual reconciliation statements, 241, 244
    deposits, 240–242, 252
    electronic funds transfers (EFT), 240
    Employment Training Tax (ETT), 239, 240, 241–242

State payroll taxes and reports (*cont.*)
    experience-rating plans, 236
    local income tax, 243
    newly hired employees and, 234
    payroll calendar, 246–247
    quarterly wage and withholding report, 242, 243
    sample forms, 241, 242, 243, 244
    state disability insurance (SDI) tax, 237–238, 240
    state income tax, 239–242
    state unemployment tax (UI), 241–242
    SUTA, 235–238, 240
    unemployment benefit claims, 237
    wage and tax statements, 242–243
    workers compensation insurance, 238–239
State unemployment insurance (SUI), 110
State unemployment tax acts (SUTA)
    accounting for, 272–274, 278–279
    deposits, 240–242
    FUTA calculation and, 210
    overview of, 4–5
    reporting, 235–242
    state disability insurance (SDI) tax, 237–238, 240
State unemployment tax, 241–242
State withholding tax, 108–109
Subsidiary payroll module, 263–264
SUI. *See* State unemployment insurance (SUI)

T

Tardiness, 60–62
Tax Tables, 299–307
Temporary workers, 64
Tennessee, 6, 108, 239
Texas, 6, 108, 236, 239
Time and work records
    computation of time worked, 57–58
    contract workers, 65
    filing time records, 60
    flextime systems, 61–62
    labor distribution, 62, 64
    need for, 55–56
    payroll period, 54–55
    production records, 62, 63
    sales records, 62, 63
    tardiness and, 60–62
    temporary workers, 64
    time sheets, 58–60
    timekeeping devices and systems, 56–57
    work-at-home arrangements, 61
Time cards, 56–57
Time clocks, 56–57
Tips
    federal payroll tax returns and, 202
    federal withholding tax and, 110
    gross earnings and, 89
    W-2 form and, 207

U

UI. *See* State unemployment tax (UI)
Unemployment compensation, 210, 237
Unemployment tax. *See* Federal Unemployment Tax Act (FUTA); State
        unemployment tax acts (SUTA); State unemployment tax (UI)